DIVINE SUBSTANCE

DIVINE SUBSTANCE

BY

CHRISTOPHER STEAD

OXFORD
AT THE CLARENDON PRESS
1977

Oxford University Press, Walton Street, Oxford OX2 6DP

OXFORD LONDON GLASGOW NEW YORK
TORONTO MELBOURNE WELLINGTON CAPE TOWN
IBADAN NAIROBI DAR ES SALAAM LUSAKA ADDIS ABABA
KUALA LUMPUR SINGAPORE JAKARTA HONG KONG TOKYO
DELHI BOMBAY CALCUTTA MADRAS KARACHI

© *Oxford University Press 1977*

British Library Cataloguing in Publication Data
Stead, George Christopher
   Divine substance
   Bibl. – Index
   ISBN 0–19–826630–8
   1. Title
   212
   God
   Substance (philosophy)

*Printed in Great Britain
at the University Press, Oxford
by Vivian Ridler
Printer to the University*

PREFACE

THIS study belongs partly to logic, partly to the history of ancient philosophy, and partly to theology. I intend to review the concept of substance as developed by the ancient Greek philosophers, and especially by Aristotle; and then to consider how, when, and in what degree this concept affected the doctrine of God developed by Christian writers of the first four centuries A.D., and especially the Trinitarian concept of one God in three Persons.

'The concept of substance' is, of course, a piece of technical shorthand; the so-called concept is really a complex of notions embodied in a changing tradition of philosophical thought. In the main I shall be dealing with the notions expressed by the Greek word *ousia* and by some other closely related terms which came to be rendered in Latin by *substantia*. It will soon be made clear that the English word 'substance' is by no means an exact equivalent of *ousia*; there is of course a continuity of philosophical tradition which connects them, but the English term underlines some of the classical implications of *ousia* and obscures others. At times it might seem more appropriate to write of the 'being' of God or natural objects, or to use some colourless term such as 'entity'; or again to adapt one's rendering to the context and speak sometimes of 'existence' or 'reality', sometimes of 'essence' or 'nature', sometimes of 'material' or 'stuff'. But there are disadvantages in breaking up what to the ancients was a single complex of thought; and on balance I prefer the conventional term 'substance' as on the whole the least inadequate to convey the whole range of associations which would influence the writers of the early Christian centuries.

I have not conceived this as a purely historical study; on the contrary I have tried to give serious attention to the logical problems presented by terms like 'being', 'identity', and 'unity'. Further, it has been my ambition not only to clarify such problems but to commend them to the attention of Christian theologians; since it seems that writers on the history of Christian thought are sometimes handicapped by an uncertain grasp both of ancient philosophy and of modern logic. Such a weakness is especially disabling when it comes to considering the fundamental problems of theism. To take an instance; one cannot read far in this field without encountering the opinion that we can know with certainty *that* God is, but we can never discover *what* he is; his existence is certain, his nature must remain an impenetrable mystery: while others have held that in speaking of God the distinction is invalid; His existence is identical with His essence. One cannot begin to examine such views without asking how the distinction between 'existence' and 'nature' is to be conceived, and how it was conceived by the writers in question. One of my objects will be to investigate this conceptual framework and examine the concepts and structure of thought from which it proceeds.

Two main objections have to be faced by any writer in this field. The first is that the task is ludicrously disproportionate to his powers. One might seem to think that the being of God, the mystery at the heart of all reality, could all be disclosed in a book of some hundreds of pages. I hope I have kept in mind the limitations proper to scholarship. I have tried to examine the works of some philosophers, and of some Christian thinkers who used their ideas, with the object of reaching a precise understanding of the conceptual and logical apparatus with which they conducted their thoughts about God. For my part, I believe that the problems with which they were concerned were real problems and that their attempted solutions have a permanent value for Christian thought. But I hope I shall have something to say to historians and philosophers who do not share this belief; and I shall try to base my discussion in the neutral territories of philology and the history of ideas.

If any originality is claimed for this discussion, it will mainly rest on the kind of precision I have tried to achieve; for precise thinking is a double-edged weapon, and if one attempts a precise explanation of the thought of an ancient writer, it is dangerously easy to suggest that some form of words not only is itself precise but also precisely represents what the ancient writer took himself to mean and was taken to mean by his readers. But in many cases these two conditions cannot both be satisfied. I shall therefore take it as a principle of method that a precise descriptive apparatus should not be used to describe imprecise thoughts as

if they were precise. That would be faulty scholarship; the reproduction of a blurred picture ought to be blurred. There is, of
course, a place for an exegetical approach to ancient philosophy
and to patristics; but if one attempts to clarify, develop, and
correct the thought of an ancient writer, it should be remembered
that this interpretation of his work is a modern production; it
cannot, as such, have played any part in the history of ancient
thought.

On the other hand, though the critic must not impose his own
ideas upon the writers he studies, it is important that he be clear-
headed himself; and this is nowhere more necessary than in
discussing the being of God, where our language and concepts
are subjected to the severest strain. I take it, then, that the uses
of precision are these; it should help one towards a more dis-
criminating appraisal of philosophical and theological statements, even if these cannot be translated into modern terms
which are both precise and precisely equivalent; it should help
one to assess the degree of precision with which they were formulated and understood; it should help one to estimate the
influence exerted by one ancient writer upon another, and particularly by philosophers on Christian theologians; and it should
free one from misleading comments and inferences springing
from an over-simplified picture of ancient usage.

A second objection may well arise from the side of theology.
Granted there are real problems, it may be said, it is nevertheless
a mistake to project a massive investigation which ignores the
really pressing concerns of the day in order to deal with niceties
like the elaborations of Christian orthodoxy. The simple answer,
I think, is that one cannot deal with everything at once. Where
I deal with the Christian doctrine of the Trinity, I shall consider
it as a conceptual structure built upon certain common Christian
convictions; it is not my present intention to review those convictions themselves. Whether the New Testament supports us in
thinking of Jesus as a being coequal and coeternal with the God
and Father whom he acknowledged; whether the New Testament itself can be shown to deserve the respect in which it has
traditionally been held; for that matter, whether the traditional
language about God is meaningful at all: these are questions
which no Christian thinker can afford to forget. And readers who
decidedly reject the Christian answers on these points will find

an element of unreality in any discussion which looks towards Trinitarian theology. Yet its historic importance is undeniable; it was attempted by pagan Platonists and others as well as by Christians; it can claim a measure of respect even from the agnostic as an intellectual achievement in its own right. And it presents problems enough to fill a book without apologetic excursions into neighbouring fields.

I may add here a few words on the presentation of my material. The discussion moves from philosophy towards theology by way of a large middle ground, in which I examine the views of ancient philosophers and theologians; and it tends to become rather more detailed as it progresses. The first chapter should be intelligible to any reasonably patient reader who has no previous training in philosophy. The next few call for some elementary acquaintance, but not more, with Plato, Aristotle, and the Stoics. And I have at all stages tried to avoid unnecessary technicalities. But Chapters VIII and IX deal with subjects which have been intensively discussed by professional theologians, and have had to be developed in some detail; though I think the book will still be useful to some who have to leave these chapters unread.

I have therefore given the relevant Greek texts in full to meet the needs of professional scholars; but I have added translations or paraphrases, so that the book can be read without previous knowledge of Greek. For simplicity's sake, I have often given single Greek words in English characters, but not where constructed phrases or sentences are found near by, when Greek letters are used. It may be helpful to set down a short list of commonly used words and phrases, so that equivalents may be recognized.

οὐσία	(ousia)	substance, etc.
(τὸ) εἶναι (infinitive)	(to einai)	to be
(τὸ) ὄν (neuter participle)	(to on)	that which is
(τὰ) ὄντα (its plural)	(ta onta)	(the) things that are
ὁμοούσιος	(homoousios)	of one substance, co-essential, etc.
ἐκ τῆς οὐσίας	(ek tēs ousias)	of (from) the substance
ἐξ ἑτέρας οὐσίας	(ex heteras ousias)	of (from) another substance

Εἶδος and ἰδέα are used more or less interchangeably by Plato to refer to the eternal ideals or prototypes which he postulated to explain our use of universal terms, amongst other reasons; when used in this distinctive sense I reproduce them as Form and Idea, so spelt with capitals. Plato's Ideas are objective realities; he repels the suggestion, which modern usage of the word conveys, that ideas are products of our minds.

'Υπόστασις (hypostasis) is roughly equivalent to 'reality', but in practice often means an individual reality, a thing; but in Trinitarian theology it corresponds to the Latin *persona*, and so is conventionally translated 'person'. *Νοῦς, λόγος*, and *πνεῦμα* can perhaps be recognized as nous, logos, and pneuma, which are more or less naturalized English words; 'mind', 'word', and 'spirit' are the most usual translations.

My debts of gratitude to instructors, colleagues, and friends are so extensive that I can acknowledge them only in general terms; but particular thanks are due to Professor J. L. Ackrill of Oxford and to Professor Charles Kannengiesser of Paris, who not only read considerable parts of the manuscript but also submitted detailed comments and corrections. My wife has been an incomparable strength and support; my children too have helped me more than they realize. For the sake of the family I will ask readers to note the peculiar pronunciation of my name. It rhymes with 'Creed'; at least, that is a rhyme which I would happily pick out. I am strongly committed to the Socratic ideal of respectful but uninhibited inquiry; but the Creed is still central to my way of thinking. In the pages that follow, I have sometimes had to deal roughly with friends, and with beliefs, that I hold in loyalty and affection. But I can trust in the generosity of those friends; and of

> my Friend indeed
> who at my need
> His life did spend.

G. C. S.

Ely, July 1975

CONTENTS

ABBREVIATIONS

CH	*Corpus Hermeticum*, ed. A. D. Nock and A.-J. Festugière
CQ	*Classical Quarterly*
DG	*Doxographi Graeci*, ed. H. Diels
EH	*Entretiens sur l'antiquité classique, Fondation Hardt*
GCS	*Die griechischen christlichen Schriftsteller der ersten Jahrhunderte*
GPT	G. L. Prestige, *God in Patristic Thought*
JHS	*Journal of Hellenic Studies*
JTS	*Journal of Theological Studies*
LGP	*The Cambridge History of Later Greek and Early Medieval Philosophy*, ed. A. H. Armstrong
LSJ	Liddell–Scott–Jones, *A Greek–English Lexicon*, 9th edition
NAG	*Nachrichten von der Akademie der Wissenschaften in Göttingen*
NPNF	*Library of Nicene and Post-Nicene Fathers*
PAS	*Proceedings of the Aristotelian Society*
PG	*Patrologia Graeca*, ed. J. P. Migne
PGL	*Patristic Greek Lexicon*, ed. G. W. H. Lampe
PR	*Philosophical Review*
PTI	W. D. Ross, *Plato's Theory of Ideas*
REG	*Revue des études grecques*
RHR	*Revue de l'histoire des religions*
RHT	A.-J. Festugière, *La Révélation d'Hermès Trismégiste*
SVF	*Stoicorum Veterum Fragmenta*, ed. H. von Arnim
TLZ	*Theologische Literaturzeitung*
Urk	*Urkunden zur Geschichte des arianischen Streites* (Athanasius, *Werke* iii. 1, ed. H.-G. Opitz)
VC	*Vigiliae Christianae*
ZKG	*Zeitschrift für Kirchengeschichte*
ZNW	*Zeitschrift für die neutestamentliche Wissenschaf*

I

A CONCEPTUAL FRAMEWORK

(i) *Abstract Nouns*

THE concept of substance first comes to light in the history of the Greek word *ousia*. But the historical development can hardly be grasped without some preliminary sketch of the logical patterns involved. I shall therefore at once attempt such a sketch.

Part of the complexity of the task results from the fact that *ousia* soon became a philosophers' technical term; it is a term which was used in formulating theories, and it is a term towards which theories were directed. But it seems safe to say that the word was current in common speech before it was adopted by philosophers; and further, that the theories, although they have affected its sense, have not completely obscured the normal pattern of Greek usage. From the standpoint of etymology, *ousia* means 'being'; it is the abstract noun connected with the verb 'to be'.[1] As such, it combines some logical features which are common to abstract nouns with others belonging to the verb 'to be'. We shall consider these in turn.

An abstract noun is usually thought to refer to a quality or a set of characteristics, such as 'whiteness' or 'humanity'. 'Humanity' denotes the set of characteristics which are generally found, or ought to be found, in men. But its sense is commonly extended, as when we speak of 'rendering a service to humanity'; in this context 'humanity' refers not to characteristics but to actual people; it is practically equivalent to 'men' or 'mankind' or 'the human race'. Individual men are *characterized by* humanity in the first sense, but *belong to*, or *are members of*, humanity in the second sense.

It is natural to distinguish these two senses as 'abstract' and

---

[1] Οὐσία is formed from ὤν, the participial form of εἰμί; cf. γερουσία from γέρων. It resembles the feminine form οὖσα; but there is no reason to think that it derives from it specifically.

'concrete' respectively; but this requires a word of caution. Almost every form of naming involves some kind of abstraction; thus even if I use the term 'humanity' in its concrete sense, I refer to a set of individual beings by means of a common quality which they all possess; and in doing so I am necessarily ignoring, or abstracting from, their other qualities. Nevertheless there is a reasonably clear distinction between naming a quality and naming a set of individuals by means of a common quality, and we may properly reserve the term 'abstract' for the former case. In much the same way we can speak of 'the prime minister' in the abstract in a book of constitutional theory, with reference to *any* holder of that office; it is quite another matter when we refer—by means of his office—to a particular individual.

Greek abstract nouns, I believe, behave much like English ones; indeed the use of abstract for concrete and vice versa is commonly noted in grammar books. But there is another variation in usage to be considered, which is much less easy to detect in Greek than in English. We speak of 'virtue', but also of 'a virtue'; of 'difficulty', but also of 'a difficulty', and so on. Sometimes one usage is well established, while the other (for no obvious reason) is relatively rare or non-existent. Thus it is normal to speak of 'a quality', and hardly anyone but a philosopher would speak quite generally of 'quality'. On the other hand 'humanity' is generally used without the article; one does not speak of 'a humanity', though it is completely natural to speak of 'a courtesy' or 'a kindness'.

When we speak of 'an x' we are using a singular expression as contrasted with a possible plural, and so are referring to an example as contrasted with a group. But when do we think of y as an example of x? If x denotes a quality, y may denote a more specific quality; thus we say 'courage is a virtue'; and in this sentence 'courage', though more specific, is abstract in the same way as 'virtue' is abstract. But in another sense virtue, or courage, may be exemplified by a particular person or act; we cannot, it is true, refer to any particular act as 'a virtue', and we do not speak of 'a courage' at all; but we can cite parallel cases; thus 'a courtesy' means 'a courteous act'; 'an oddity' means 'an odd person'. On the other hand, although an abstract-seeming noun is sometimes used to refer to a concrete whole or collection of individuals, this latter can only be exemplified by some part or subgroup, or by a particular individual; a concrete whole cannot be *exemplified* by a characteristic, however broadly or narrowly defined. Thus 'a community' has to indicate some particular subgroup within the totality of mankind; it cannot indicate some characteristic or form of behaviour which several groups might display.

This discussion has necessarily been conducted in terms of English usage; but similar examples could I think be given from other modern languages as well as from Greek and Latin. Greek is of course our special concern. By no means all its abstract nouns admit of these variations, but there is an important minority that can take a specific sense, or a concrete sense, or both. Ἀπορία can mean 'a difficulty'; ἀρετή can mean 'a noble deed'; and though a difficulty might recur, a noble deed could well be unrepeatable. Δύναμις ('power') can signify a powerful being, or an act of power; in suitable contexts it can mean 'a miracle', 'an army' or 'an angel'. And since we have mentioned 'humanity', it may be worth noting that ἀνθρωπότης can be used to mean 'the human race' (Philo, *Quod. Det. Pot.* 76; Clement, *Paed.* i. 83. 3, ii. 95. 2; Hippolytus, *Ref.* x. 33. 12; many other examples in *PGL*, though *LSJ* notes only 'abstract humanity'). The same sort of variety is found in neuter adjectives used with the article; the ambiguity of τὸ καλόν ('beauty', 'excellence') is well known.

I shall try to show that the usage of *ousia* shows the same variations as we have noted in the cases of other abstract nouns; though it is somewhat unusual in combining several different kinds of variation that are not commonly found together. The picture we have drawn so far would suggest that *ousia* can be used in two ways, according as we would translate it 'being', or 'a being'. The first case may be subdivided into the abstract sense, when it denotes some very general property or attribute (possibly reality or actuality, if that is how 'being' should be regarded) corresponding to the Greek τὸ εἶναι; and a concrete sense, denoting something (or everything) that is real or actual, in Greek τὸ ὄν. Used like 'a being', it might denote a particular form of the attribute we are discussing, say a particular manner or mode of existing. More probably it will mean an example of being in the concrete sense, and so either some class or kind of being, or some individual being.

The possibilities are thus fairly numerous; but there are two

further points which have to be made. We have said that
examples may be either subclasses or individuals; and at first
sight it seems that we can be reasonably clear as to when we are
speaking of individuals. There are devices of language which
help to indicate our meaning; thus in English we may speak of
'this *x*' or 'an *x*' or 'the *x*'. Greek, however, lacks the second of
these means, the indefinite article, and the third is somewhat
unreliable in both languages, since Greek habitually uses the
definite article with abstract nouns; and what is worse, both
languages use it with collective expressions. When we say 'the lion
is the king of beasts' we are not referring to any particular lion,
but to lions in general; and both Greek and French, though not
English, adopt a similar usage in the case of men, and speak of
ὁ ἄνθρωπος, 'l'homme'.

In the case of 'the lion', therefore, we can distinguish an 'instantial' and a 'typical' use of the phrase; and our methods of
reference can be tabulated thus:

Species: the lion (typical sense); or, lions.
Individual: a lion; or, the lion (instantial sense); or, this lion.

Thus the distinction between 'a lion' and 'the lion' is not quite
what one might expect. 'A lion' indicates some unspecified
example; 'the lion' indicates *either* some specified example, *or*
the species as a whole. This last variation in usage is fairly familiar;
and Aristotle dealt with it by introducing the expression ὁ τὶς
ἄνθρωπος, 'the man so-and-so', as distinct from ὁ ἄνθρωπος, 'man'.

But the picture becomes more complex when we have to take
account of sub-classifications. Let us consider another species, the
monkey. If we were asked for an example of a monkey, it would
seem natural to reply 'the chimpanzee', rather than to cite a
particular individual, say Sambo. Thus in suitable contexts the
whole class of chimpanzees can be referred to as 'a monkey' or
'this monkey'—or even as 'the monkey' (in question); accordingly
our usage has to be tabulated as follows:

Species: the monkey; monkeys.
Sub-species: a monkey; the monkey; this monkey; these
    monkeys.
Individual: a monkey; the monkey; this monkey.

Now it might seem as if 'the monkey' should properly refer to
a genuine individual specimen, and that in using it to indicate

e.g. the chimpanzee, we are making an artificial adaptation of language; and Aristotle's 'two-level' theory has encouraged this belief. But this type of case shades off into another, in which the example that springs to mind is in fact a class-expression, and it is the genuine individual case that seems artificial. Thus if told to think of a letter, we should probably answer 'A', rather than indicate some particular A which occurs in a document or some particular utterance; and 'a syllable' naturally suggests 'BA' rather than '*this* BA that I am now writing'. These are both actual instances considered by Aristotle; but his account of the matter differs from the one I have suggested here in that he assumed that 'Ba' was an example of 'syllable' in the same way as 'this (individual) lion' is an example of 'the lion'; and this, I believe, has encouraged some very persistent mistakes. I shall presently attempt to show that the examples I have given from nouns denoting concrete realities like lions and monkeys are truly applicable to more abstract expressions such as *ousia*.

In considering such questions of usage, the context of an expression must always be borne in mind. Thus 'this speech' would naturally be taken to mean 'the speech which so-and-so uttered on a particular occasion'; but the same phrase, 'this speech', could be used to refer to the wording which is common to all copies or recitations of the speech. Again 'this letter' might well suggest a particular material object, namely this piece of notepaper together with the writing on it. But suppose the letter be copied, does the copy count as 'another letter'? It will depend upon the context; the author will probably reckon it as another copy of the same letter, the office-boy as another letter to be stamped and posted separately.

My second additional point is designed to correct some imprecisions which have been tolerated so far. I have spoken of 'individual' instances, and my typical examples have been material particulars like 'this lion' or 'this letter'. In doing so I may seem to have endorsed the time-honoured theory which connects generality with form and regards matter as the guarantee of individuality, taking 'individual' to mean 'an ultimate instance of which no instances can be given'. By way of correction, let us consider a very general word which indicates a material. 'Iron' is such a word. Perhaps its most obvious sense is that which we have called the collective; it refers to the totality of a type of metal, however it is distributed about the world.[2] But it can be regarded as a characteristic, or range of characteristics, possessed by objects like hinges or shovels. 'This iron' would denote some example of iron; but, like 'this monkey', it need not necessarily refer to a truly individual example; it might mean this alloy or blend of iron, whether collectively or, perhaps, as an attributive phrase. What then shall we regard as a truly individual example of 'this iron'? The most obvious case will be some iron object possessing a definite form, such as this stove; and this could suggest that words denoting material characteristics are 'individuated by their form', to use the technical jargon, just as it might seem that words denoting formal characteristics were individuated by their material embodiment. In fact, however, a particular instance of iron need not be, in any ordinary sense, an individual *object*; 'this iron' might refer to the iron underlying my paddock, whose nature and distribution, though relatively fixed, are wholly unknown to me, and which has none of the natural boundaries which we normally associate with individual objects.

My second point, then, can be summed up in these two statements:

(a) Generality and particularity involve questions of logical form; but have no unique relation with geometrical or spatio-temporal form, as contrasted with matter.

(b) An example of x need not be a true particular; and a true particular need not be an individual; granted that individuals provide the clearest instances of such particulars.

Accordingly, if *ousia* displays the logical features which we have found in other abstract nouns, we shall encounter the following range of meanings.

1 A Characteristic	2 A Reality so characterized
1 B Sub-forms of 1 A	2 B Sub-classes of 2 A
1 C Completely determinate forms of 1 A	2 C Individual members of 2 A

Where the term is used comprehensively, it can mean either 1 A or 2 A, and only the singular noun can be used. Where the grammar indicates that some selection is being made (in English, by 'this x', 'an x', etc.) the remaining four senses are all possible.

[2] Cf. W. V. Quine, 'Identity, Ostension and Hypostasis', in *From a Logical Point of View.*

It is not very easy to find a word which displays all these features; but we might experiment with 'civilization'. It seems clear that at the top level, used only in the singular, it can indicate certain features of societies, or alternatively the aggregate of societies possessing these features. At the lowest level 'this civilization' could (I think) mean 'the civilized behaviour of *this* society', and could frame at least a mock-humorous comment on some instance of it (1 C); it certainly can mean 'this civilized society'. The intermediate level is a little less easy to detect; but no doubt 'this civilization' can mean 'this type of civilization', and so refer either to 'the typical features of, e.g., bronze-age societies' or to 'the aggregate of bronze-age societies'. We note, then, that a collective singular at level B is interchangeable with a straightforward plural at level C, just as the class of spaniels may be referred to at will as 'this dog' or 'these dogs'; more generally, a collective singular at one level is interchangeable with a plural at a lower level.

This discussion has introduced some fairly familiar points. Readers who are logicians will have recognized the reference to the 'type-token' ambiguity; and those who are not may be consoled by the promise that the points which have been compactly assembled here will be paraded in a more leisurely fashion in the pages that follow. We pass then to discuss the verb 'to be'.

(ii) *The Notion of Being*

Modern logic has been able to break new ground by drawing a sharp distinction between the grammatical form of sentences and their logical force. Two sentences may look very much alike; yet the logician will differentiate them in a manner which to the uninitiated appears disconcerting. This is eminently true of sentences involving the verb 'to be'. Consider, for example, the following:

(1) God is.
(2) Albion is Britain.
(2a) A triangle is a three-sided polygon.
(3) Socrates is a man.
(3a) Socrates is ill.
(3b) Man is an animal.

In its English phrasing, (1) is archaic. One can still talk naturally of 'God's being', but the modern form of the indicative is 'God exists'. In either form, however, this case is distinct in that the verb 'is', or 'exists', occurs without a predicate. Philosophers realized very early that some distinction has to be made between the existential 'is' and other uses of it; the need was apparent to Aristotle, and indeed was glimpsed by Plato, at least in his late dialogue, the *Sophist*. But the nature of the distinction is not easy to grasp and has long been debated.

Idealist philosophers have held that the fundamentally important truth about any x is that which declares what kind of being x is, and so assigns it to its proper place in the 'scale of being'. Statements about existence, on this view, play a relatively subordinate role; their function is to indicate whether some type of being actually occurs or crops up among the phenomena of our world. Modern existentialism can well be understood as a reaction against this type of thought; by laying its stress on existence, it tries to persuade us to see things in the actual context in which they occur, to give full recognition to their individuality and to refrain if possible from classifying them and so losing our grasp of their authentic character in the interests of a spurious demand for order and comprehensibility. For this school, then, that x exists is, roughly, that x makes its own unique impact on the world; while, on the practical side, we are urged to live our own lives and make our own choices, there being no objective standards to which we should conform.

A rather different treatment of the notion of existence has been developed by some philosophers who write in the tradition of Christian scholasticism. On their view, the term 'existence' indicates the fundamental reality or activity of things in virtue of which they are what they are. Thus the grammar and logic of 'is' is not unlike that of 'lives' or 'acts'; it is a very general predicate whose content varies with the subject to which it is attached. What makes the difference, it would appear, is the range of activity that the subject enjoys; thus as ape-like creatures evolved into men, so their existence was gradually enhanced. It is clear that on this view there is a close link between the notions of 'being' and 'being-so-and-so'; since the manner of being that things display springs from their fundamental activity of being themselves.[3] We might say that, on this view, all existential pro-

---

[3] See, e.g., E. L. Mascall, *Existence and Analogy*, 42–3, 79; E. Gilson, *Being and Some Philosophers*, 175, 184–6.

positions have some predicative force; while it is also claimed that, in normal cases at least, predicative propositions have some existential force.

Meanwhile a much more radical approach to the notion of existence had been developed by philosophers of the empiricist tradition. Adopting Kant's dictum that existence is not a predicate, and concerned to give a satisfactory account of fictitious entities, like Kant's 100 imaginary dollars, they have argued that statements of the form '*x* exists' are not really statements about *x*, as one might suppose, but rather statements about the *term* '*x*'; namely that '*x*' refers to a class which is not empty, but has examples. For otherwise, when we say that mermaids do *not* exist, to what does the statement apply? Not to mermaids; for we say, and say truly, that there are no such beings. So long as we construe 'mermaids do not exist' on the analogy (however remote) of 'fishes do not walk', there is a standing temptation to suppose that mermaids must possess some kind of reality in order that true statements may be made about them. The solution offered is to suggest that we are really talking about the *term* 'mermaids'; and this term is real enough; moreover, its reference is reasonably precise; we know what sort of characteristics the creature would have, if it existed.[4]

In its own field this explanation offers some decisive advantages. There are cogent reasons for giving a meaning to '*x* exists' such that a precisely corresponding meaning can be given to '*x* does not exist'. If, then, 'to exist' is construed as 'to exercise one's characteristic mode of being', then 'not to exist' can only mean 'to fail to exercise it'. This provides a reasonable account of things *ceasing* to exist; dodos, let us say, ceased to exist in that they failed to maintain their way of life in adverse conditions. But no such account can be given of mermaids; if the whole tradition about mermaids is based upon misapprehensions, then there never were such beings as mermaids who could either succeed or fail at anything. These embarrassments are certainly relieved by the empiricist explanation.

On the other hand, I believe this explanation is often presented

---

[4] An alternative form of the theory replaces ' "*x*" is predicated of something' by 'something is *x*'. The two forms are clearly equivalent, just as Aristotle's common formula '*P* is predicated of *S*' corresponds to the later and more usual '*S* is *P*'.

in a form which involves unnecessary assumptions and divergences from common usage. In the first place, it is sometimes presented as a doctrine about the correct sense of the words 'exist' and 'existence'. But this is not the crucial point. The crucial point is that the question, what things there are, is a question in its own right; it must not be prejudged by arguments about how things, ostensibly, behave. But this rule does not dictate a policy about the use of the word 'to exist'. If clarity demanded the sacrifice, we could probably dispense with the term altogether. The empiricist could say what he wants to say in terms of 'there is such a thing as x', or similar phrases; the existentialist would not have to sacrifice very much, that I can see, if he were limited to speaking of things 'living' and 'acting'; and as a last resort, if he still required a term so general as to cover the entire range of beings from God to inanimate stones, it would be safe (for the moment) to allow them to 'persist'. But an alternative policy is simply to note that the term is ambiguous, while carefully exploring the logical errors to which its ambiguity may lead. This is in fact the course I shall adopt with the older term 'being', and seems indispensable in a historical study of the kind I have in view. I shall try to note some logical errors made by ancient writers in their discussions of being: but this can be done as required; it would only complicate an already difficult subject if one insisted on corrective paraphrases at every turn.

Secondly, the theory was devised in the light of simple examples such as mermaids, where the reference of the term is fairly clear-cut. Will it work equally well where the reference is less precise? We are in no doubt about mermaids: they are simply fictitious; symbolic figures of sea-gods were mistaken for portraits, and the belief in such beings was confirmed, it may be, by hasty glimpses and confused accounts of porpoises or dugongs; and a dugong, though real enough, cannot count as a mermaid. But dragons are not equally fictitious—or not so clearly fictitious; since there are giant lizards which correspond fairly well with the usual picture of dragons—as well, perhaps, as real whales correspond with medieval pictures of whales. And supermen are hardly fictitious at all, since exceptionally gifted individuals do exist, though they do not perhaps fulfil all the conditions we associate with supermen. Thus if we decide to construe 'exist' in the linguistic mode, as asserting the factual reference of terms, we may be driven to admit that terms have a greater or less degree of factual reference.

Thirdly, the theory has often been presented in a form influenced by symbolic logic, so as to suggest that when we say 'x exists', or 'x's exist', we mean that there is an object answering to the description 'x', or that there is at least one member of the class of x's. But this is to put a restriction upon our use of 'exists' which we do not always observe in practice. If I say 'ozone exists', no doubt I signify that 'ozone' is a term which stands for something that is really there (unlike 'phlogiston'); but I am not saying anything about its distribution. So my statement cannot fairly be forced into the mould 'there is at least one x'. I certainly do not mean 'at least one molecule of ozone exists'; I should not be voicing a contradiction if I said 'ozone exists' but denied the molecular theory.

But if this is what is meant by 'ozone exists', can one give a similar account of self-deception? or patriotism? Suppose, further, that one introduced a time-qualification, and said 'Patriotism does not exist nowadays', or, 'There is no such thing as patriotism nowadays'; can we still construe this as a statement about the *word* 'patriotism', indicating that 'patriotism' denotes a kind of behaviour of which there are, at present, no examples? This may well seem artificial; is a man really *mistaken* if he claims that he is talking about a phenomenon which flourished for a period but has now decayed? Consider, finally, 'There exists' (or 'there is') a revolutionary mood among the students'. Are we crossing a logical boundary if we pass from 'exists' to 'obtains', or 'prevails', or 'flourishes'? Obviously I shall not seek to prove important points by so brief a discussion; but it seems to me that there is a large and ill-defined class of cases where it is by no means clear how we should construe the term 'to exist'; whether as asserting that a term refers to something real, or whether as presuming this and making some minimal further statement about the thing in question. For an account of the presuming, we shall have to wait till we have discussed some of the other senses of the word 'to be'.

Our second illustration, 'Albion is Britain', shows the word 'to be' used to express an identity. For the present we are concerned with identities in the limited sense defined by logicians, as formulae which indicate that two expressions have the same force; we exclude statements of identification whose meaning depends upon their context, e.g. 'the man I saw last night is Smith'. If we reverse our chosen example by saying 'Britain is Albion', we obtain a sentence which is theoretically equivalent, though its function in discourse may well be rather different. We could make up similar examples using common nouns, e.g. 'a sphere is a globe'. Example (2a), 'a triangle is a three-sided polygon' also expresses an identity, but has the further feature that the predicate defines the subject: that is, it exhibits the distinct notions which the subject implies. We may note in passing that defining is not the same as explaining; we might indeed explain the technical term 'dodecagon' by saying 'a dodecagon is a twelve-sided polygon', but it would seldom be natural to use the term 'polygon' to explain a common word like 'triangle'.

Suppose, however, that we say, 'a triangle is a polygon'. Here the subject and predicate are clearly not equivalent, for 'polygon' is a more general term than 'triangle'. This sentence, then, does not entail the definition, 2a; but it follows from it; given the definition, it cannot be denied without contradiction. Sentences of this type have been labelled 'analytic', to suggest that their predicate expresses part of the meaning of the subject, and so can be disclosed simply by analysing the subject; whereas in the contrasting class of 'synthetic' sentences the predicate expresses something 'added to', or other than, what is implied in the subject. The distinction between analytic and synthetic sentences, or formulae, has been closely studied by logicians, and in practice the use of the terms has been widened, so that a sentence or formula is said to be analytic if it follows by the principle of non-contradiction from a definition already accepted.

In making this sharp distinction, it can be said, formal logic is setting up idealized cases for its own purposes; in practice, we cannot always be certain which diagram to apply; for if the relevant definition is not known, or not agreed, it may be uncertain whether a given statement about it is analytic or synthetic. (Thus we may say, 'Water boils at 212° F.' without knowing whether or not the unit 'one degree Farenheit' has actually been defined in terms of the boiling-point of water.) On the other hand, common usage affords a strong presumption for accepting certain definitions without question; and it is easy to overlook this prior acceptance, and to regard any sentence which necessarily follows from such a definition as itself expressing a necessary truth. Putting these two facts together, one sees how it has been tempting to conceive of philosophy as a process by which —in principle at least—it is possible to establish propositions which are both necessarily true and genuinely informative.

Modern logic, therefore, has set up a sharp diagrammatic distinction between analytic and synthetic propositions. The former simply rest on conventions already established in our language or other notation; the latter alone make statements about the 'external' world. The distinction may be fluid in practice, but we can never have it both ways; no sentence can at the same time be logically necessary and genuinely independent. It follows that no existential proposition can be analytic. Common usage, however, gives no hint of any such sharp discontinuity; it seems as if there is a natural transition from the self-evidently true (e.g. 'seeing is perceiving') to the evidently true (e.g. 'seeing is believing'). Aristotle's position here is ambiguous. On the one hand he partly anticipated the modern view by drawing a clear distinction between true, or false, premises and valid, or invalid, deductions; on the other hand he confused matters by laying such weight on the distinction between propositions which naturally *and necessarily* hold good and those that do not. One sign of this was his doctrine that natural objects possess certain 'properties' which necessarily belong to them, over and above those given in (or following from) their definition, which are sharply distinguished from their variable attributes, or 'accidents'. For the traditionalist, of course, the modern logician is simply in error in giving no recognition to such 'properties'. On the traditional view, however, the ideal case of a necessary truth is the identity in which subject and predicate are *verbally* identical, $A = A$; indeed ancient logicians found it difficult to discard the idea that ordinary predications are some kind of by-form of statements of identity; thus Aristotle includes even the statement 'C is musical' in his list of the different types of unity (*Metaph.* v. 6, 1015 b 16 ff.).

We have used a discussion of identities to introduce the important distinction between analytic and synthetic propositions as modern logicians understand it; but it becomes clear that this latter distinction, in its widened sense, is quite general in scope. A sentence may be synthetic even if it is of the identity type (so, perhaps, '212° F. is the boiling-point of water'); or it may be analytic and yet be assigned by modern theory to a quite distinct logical form. It remains to examine these forms, so far as they are expressed in sentences involving the word 'to be'. I have collected some instances under heading (3); and must now consider, first, the differences of logical form; secondly the function of the verb 'to be' in asserting that the statement holds good; and thirdly the question whether, and how, such sentences imply the existence of the things to which they refer.

First, as to the distinct forms. In 'S is rational' the word 'is' connects the adjectival predicate with its subject to give a description of S. But the sentence 'S is a rational being' does not merely describe S as rational, but assigns S to the class of rational beings; and though the two operations stand or fall together, they are logically distinct. (The distinction was established by Peano, who symbolized the relation of belonging to a class by the letter ε.) In some cases the practical importance of the distinction is slight; it hardly matters whether we say 'S is circular' or 'S is a circle'. In others it is significant; partly, I think, because the class of beings which have the property p in common is apt to have others in common besides. Thus 'S is rational' draws attention to one property possessed by S; 'S is a rational being' suggests that S possesses all the properties which rational beings possess.

Aristotle's account of predication ignores this distinction, which indeed is less easy to indicate in Greek, or Latin, than in English. But further, Aristotle expressly asserts an analogy between 'S is a man' and 'man is an animal'. Modern logic distinguishes them: the class of men does not *belong* to the class of animals, as the singular noun 'man' so easily suggests, but is included in it. It is a sub-class, not a member; just as the committee of a club, though composed exclusively of members, is not, itself, collectively a member. Classes may be mutually exclusive, or they can overlap, or one can include another, as the class of animals includes that of man; in 'man is an animal' the verb 'is' indicates this inclusion. Similarly with 'all men are animals'. If, however, I say 'some men are parents' I point to a case of partial inclusion, where two classes overlap. An oddity of modern theory is the convention that takes the statement-form 'some x's are y's' to imply that there actually are some x's which are y's, but takes 'all *x*'s are *y*'s' merely as excluding the case of an *x* which is not *y*, so that the latter statement is true if there are no *x*'s at all. This convention has some theoretical convenience, but conflicts rather sharply with ordinary usage.[5]

As one might expect, the relations which hold between classes are mirrored by corresponding relations of predicates; thus to inclusion of classes there corresponds the relation of implication between predicates: if *S* is *P*, then *S* is *Q*, or more briefly, *P* implies *Q*. This relation can also be indicated by the verb 'to be', as in the sentence 'seeing is believing'. In most of the cases we have considered, the truth or falsity of the statement follows directly from the meanings of the terms employed; but one could also state it as a mere matter of fact that one class is included in another, e.g. 'All my children are girls'; and here the relation between the two predicates is called 'material implication', in contrast to the 'formal implication' of the earlier examples.

We can therefore set out four cases:

S is rational: simple predication.
S is a man: class-membership, often symbolized by ϵ.
Seeing is believing; implication of predicates, often symbolized by $\supset$.
Man is an animal: inclusion of classes, sometimes symbolized by $<$.[6]

When we speak of 'inclusion', it may be noticed that while the class of animals includes the class of men, there is another sense in which the predicate 'man' includes (as part of its meaning) the predicate 'animal'. In this case 'includes' mean 'formally implies', and we can easily relate it to the 'identity' sense of 'is'; for if the relation $\supset$ holds good simply by the definition of the terms, we have an analytic proposition, like 'seeing is perceiving'; if it holds good in both directions, so that $p \supset q$ and $q \supset p$, p and q are logically equivalent.

---

[5] For a discussion of this point, see P. F. Strawson, *Introduction to Logical Theory*, 163 ff.

[6] I give the traditional symbols ϵ and $\supset$; for $<$ see e.g. S. K. Langer, *An Introduction to Symbolic Logic*, 135. (It is suggested by the ordinary mathematical symbol for 'is less than', but has a different meaning; men are more numerous than eagles, but eagles are not men.) But many logicians have adopted radically different notations; see W. and M. Kneale, *The Development of Logic*, 521; more details in G. E. Hughes and D. G. Londey, *The Elements of Formal Logic*, 368–70.

It may perhaps seem anomalous that the table offers no symbol corresponding to the 'is' in '*S* is rational'; for should not the word stand for some relation of 'having' or 'owning' which connects the subject *S* and the property of being rational? The answer is: We can indeed use an expression of this form, but there is no need to do so; simplicity is best, and the simplest form of this statement can be indicated by a two-term symbolism, as it is in the sentence '*S* thinks'.

The different functions of the word 'is' could still be seen if our examples were not plain statements, but (e.g.) suppositions, 'If Jones is clever', 'If Jones is a member', etc. But in the former examples, where no qualifying word appears, the word 'is' has a further function to perform; it indicates that the state of affairs described by the sentence is not merely wished for, demanded or supposed, but actually obtains: the sentences claim to be true. This may indeed simply follow from the meanings assigned to the words; but if the truth of the sentence stems from its correspondence with actual states of affairs, a further consideration arises; for since states of affairs are liable to change, a sentence of this type may be true at one time but not at another. We have therefore to distinguish between cases where 'is' simply asserts a proposition without regard to time, and those where it indicates that something, not was the case, or will be the case, but is the case now. Ancient logic partially recognized this point by distinguishing certain predicates as 'contingent'—the *accidentia* or συμβεβηκότα; but it is sentences or propositions, and not simply predicates, that are contingent. Socrates was young, was a soldier, was taller than Theaetetus, cared for Xanthippe, and some Greeks were philosophers, were wiser than any barbarian, etc., at some time but not at others. In such cases we may perhaps say that 'is' shows a certain preference for indicating the stable features of a changing situation; the nuances of 'Socrates is young' seem rather different from those of 'Socrates grows up'.

Now for our third point. For all we have said so far, it might appear that the only way of indicating the existence of *x* is to say directly '*x* exists', or in the archaic idiom '*x* is'. At least we may have suggested that empiricists take this view (apart from the odd exception of propositions about 'some *x*'s'). But this was not intended. We can of course use alternative phrases which directly indicate *x*'s existence, e.g. 'there is such a thing as *x*', or 'there are x's'. But in ordinary speech these are often unnecessary, since the things we say about x are such that its existence need not be separately stated. The context of discourse itself makes our meaning clear; to use the technical phrase, we make statements with existential import.

But there is an alternative theory to which we have briefly referred; namely that sentences of the form 'x is . . .' always, or at least normally, indicate that x exists, just because they contain the word 'is'. Thus in saying 'x is so-and-so', we assert that x is, or exists, with a further determination which explains what it is or how it is. This is the opinion of most of the ancient writers we shall deal with, as well as some moderns;[7] but in my view it rests on a mistake. Admittedly, I do not usually say 'x is so-and-so' unless I mean it to be thought that x is a real being; but the same will apply to other sorts of statement about x. To take an informal example: if I say, 'the McEwleys have sold their house', you will of course assume that I am talking about real people; just as much as if I said 'the McEwleys are Jews'. Or if it be thought that 'is' normally indicates something more than mere actuality, namely a mode of life and action, I suppose that 'Angus passionately hates hypocrisy' will convey this sense as well as 'Angus is passionately sincere'.

(Philosophers may perhaps be reminded of P. F. Strawson's well-known article 'On Referring', which criticizes Russell's theory of 'definite descriptions'.[8] Russell had argued that the statement (e.g.) 'The present King of France is wise' contains a statement that there is a present king of France, and is therefore false. Strawson argues that it does not state, but implies this, and therefore as a whole is not false, but inapplicable. But the arguments either way do not depend on the fact that the example chosen is a simple predicative statement involving the word 'is'; they would apply equally well if the example were, say, 'The present King of France loves roulette'—as is apparent from Strawson's footnote in his § IV.)

Our giving and inferring of existential import in statements is no doubt governed by conventions, and the conventions may be

[7] So e.g. A. M. Farrer, *Faith and Speculation*, 112. But cf. also Aristotle, *Metaph.* v. 7. 1017 a 25 ff.
[8] *Mind*, 59 (1950), 320–44; repr. in G. H. R. Parkinson (ed.), *The Theory of Meaning* (Oxford, 1968).

difficult to summarize; a full discussion would have to deal with irony, sarcasm, poetic fancy, and the like. But the notion that it belongs peculiarly to statements of the form '*x* is . . .' appears to be no more than a survival from the days—not so long past—when it was thought that '*S* is *P*' is the correct and normal form to which all statements should be reduced.

This brief review of modern logical theory as it affects the concept of being may well appear too hasty and insensitive an introduction to a study which will have to reckon with the thought of Plato, Aristotle, Plotinus, and their Christian interpreters. It does indeed raise some difficulties of interpretation by proposing a framework of thought so far removed from theirs. Theologians in particular are understandably attracted by traditional interpretations of the term 'existence'. To construe 'God exists' as referring to an unique mode of being, whose very splendour and remoteness is symbolized by the abstract description, seems to give the predicate a meaning which is appropriate to divine reality; to render it 'our word "God" is a fact-denoting word' seems to deprive it of illuminating content. And it is, I think, possible to use the term in the former way without offending against empiricist canons of logical rigour. We have to say, that 'God exists' is a statement about the life of God which normally carries existential import, and so normally conveys the much more commonplace judgement that there is a God; since what the *empiricist* wants to convey by 'existence' can be paraphrased in terms of the formula 'There is an *x*'. But care is needed so as not to prejudge the down-to-earth question. For suppose we could establish merely that there cannot be a weak or ineffective god. We could then properly infer that God, if there is a God, is active and powerful; but it would be wrong to argue 'therefore God is active and powerful, and therefore *a fortiori* he is real'. And it must be admitted that the use of 'exist' which I have tried to defend could easily encourage false inferences of this kind.

But whatever adjustments have still to be made, and whatever the break with the past, it seems to me that modern logic has established certain distinctions which must henceforth be respected. All too often it will appear that ancient writers have reinforced their convictions about men's life and prospects by invalid reasoning, to which primitive uses of the verb 'to be' have largely contributed. It seems reasonable to ask at each stage

whether what they say about being can reasonably be paraphrased in such terms as 'life' or 'action'. One must try to dispel
the confusions that cluster round the term 'being' without reducing the whole topic to a commonplace level. But life and action
are not commonplace words, and to speak of God's life or God's
action does him no dishonour.

(iii) *Modern Discussions of Substance*

I have already referred to the problem of translating the Greek
word οὐσία. The first requisite is to find some English word which
gives the modern reader some idea of the range of associations
conveyed by the ancient term. But there is a further point to be
considered. In the course of time the Greek word gathered to
itself a number of synonyms or partial equivalents (ὑπόστασις,
ὕπαρξις, φύσις, and others) and was variously translated (as by
the Latin words *essentia, substantia, existentia, natura*); and the discussion of these terms uncovered a number of new problems
which, however, were studied in the light of older texts embodying
the word οὐσία. It follows that, by choosing to render οὐσία by
'substance', one is pointing to the philosophical tradition which
leads on to the discussions of substance, e.g. by Locke and Kant,
and at the same time pointing away from the (perhaps equally
important) tradition which explored the distinction between
'essence' and 'existence', and indeed gave point to modern
existentialism: and again, pointing away from the discussions
about the mind and its place in the physical universe. Indeed the
choice of a rendering may well reflect the writer's own philosophical standpoint, since one naturally desires to claim a respect-
able ancestry for those problems which one feels to be especially
important and worth reflection.

However, if 'substance' is to be the chosen rendering, it may
be well to make a brief sketch of some contemporary discussions
of it, among philosophers and theologians.

Most of the problems traditionally associated with the term
'substance' have arisen out of the deceptive flexibility of our
language; so the modern empiricist believes. Philosophers in the
past too readily assumed that there is a simple correspondence
between the real world and the forms of ordinary speech. Next,
they focused their attention on statements of the subject-predicate

form, which can be symbolized by '*S* is *P*', and neglected the various other forms of statement, not to mention the many varieties of sentence which are not statements. They also tended to think that the permanent and most important features of our experience are those which are naturally expressed in the subject of a sentence. At the same time they did not appreciate the adaptability of even the stereotyped formula '*S* is *P*'; all kinds of notion can in fact be expressed as a subject, and qualified by predicates; but since this was not fully realized, the concept of substance was given a number of conflicting interpretations. Thus a sentence like 'Socrates is wise' puts forward an in-dividual existent for the role of substance; a sentence like 'man is mortal' suggests a class of beings (if construed as 'men are mortal'), or again, a set of properties (if construed as 'humanity implies mortality'); and so on. There is yet another complication: the sentence-form '*S* is *P*' looks as if it should be convertible, and so equivalent to '*P* is *S*'; it looks, again, as if it were a qualified form of '*S* is', or '*S* exists'. So the notion of substance not only inherits a complex of meanings deriving from the functions of the grammatical subject, but also takes over others corresponding with the kinds of predicate which can be applied to a subject, or with the nuances of the term 'being' itself.

The empiricist view, therefore, is that a number of problems have traditionally been associated under the heading of substance which are better separated and studied piecemeal. They are not indeed entirely unrelated problems; but the relations between them are not what the traditional theory suggests. A modern brief survey[9] has suggested that there is one problem concerned with the dependence of things on one another, and so with what can be said to exist independently; another problem concerned with analysis, and so with the question whether there are 'things' which can be defined as sets of properties; another problem again concerned with the question, What is it to which descrip-tions attach, or to which changes occur?—is it enough to answer, 'The actual concrete individual thing', or must we look for some necessary unifying factor which associates its various descriptions

    [9] D. J. O'Connor, s.v. 'Substance and Attribute' in *The Encyclopedia of Philosophy*, ed. Paul Edwards (New York and London, 1967). But I have restated and very much simplified his summary. See also A. M. Quinton, *The Nature of Things*, Chapter I.

and links its successive phases? It will be convenient to begin with the last-mentioned points, which for present purposes can be treated together.

Ask yourself this question: Suppose something changes in respect of some of its attributes, what remains unchanged? The common-sense answer would seem to be, 'Its other attributes'. Clearly if it is to count as the same thing at all, there must be some continuity; and this ought to be describable by saying that some at least of its attributes must remain at least relatively constant. Why then was this simple answer not thought to suffice?

Partly, we answer, because of the fascination of language. In our common form of words, S represents the thing to which changes occur, and P its various states or changing attributes. From this point on, there are two possible lines of argument. First we can argue that by talking of a thing at all, we are positing at least a minimum structure of *unchanging* attributes; and this may lead us to think that things fall into natural classes, each of which has its own distinctive structure of unchanging attributes. Alternatively, we may be led to admit that a thing might conceivably change any single one of its attributes and yet remain in some acceptable sense the same thing; and this may in turn suggest that a thing may persist independently of *all* changes in its attributes; finally we arrive at the notion of an x which has in itself no attributes at all—which simply acts as a centre to which an indefinitely variable set of attributes may be attached.

It is easy to condemn this latter notion, and it has already been pilloried most effectively by Miss Anscombe: 'It would be almost incredible, if it had not happened, that anyone could think it an argument to say: the ultimate subject of predication must be something without predicates' (*Three Philosophers*, 11). It is not quite so easy to steer clear of it; but as a rough guide, at least to the problem of change, we may say that the theory presupposes too formalized a notion of continuity. There must be some continuity in our experience, since there could be no knowledge at all if there were no recognition; and there must be some continuity in each individual thing if we are to be justified in calling it a single persistent reality. But this continuity does not require that some one feature of that thing persists without change throughout its existence; just as—to use an illustration of Wittgenstein's—if a rope is continuous from end to end, this does not require that one or more of its fibres must reach from end to end. The parallel is not exact; and we can freely admit that some properties of each thing *may* persist unchanged. But to postulate something that *must* persist unchanged because it is not a property leads to the self-contradictory notion of an *x* which does not change, and yet changes—since it is that very *x* to which changes occur!

But apart from the special problem of change and continuity, is there not a problem about predication itself?—for we may still feel some hesitation in admitting that a complex of properties is sufficient to define a thing. This hesitation is probably based on a miscellaneous collection of difficulties, which vary in their relative importance from case to case. One is that if we consider common objects, such as chairs or tables, our names and classifications for such objects depend upon a loosely assorted set of criteria, some geometrical, some functional, and so on. We could call this a chair even if its shape were most unusual, provided it were meant to be sat upon; or, even if its function were quite different, provided it were shaped like a common type of chair—and so on; but there is no set of properties which applies to all chairs and to nothing else. Another difficulty is that the phrase 'a complex of properties' easily suggests the notion of a mere *list* of properties; and this is clearly not sufficient: we must be allowed to specify the manner in which the properties are associated. To take the simplest possible example: although for the reason just given we cannot make a list of characteristics which apply to all chairs and to nothing but chairs, we could certainly describe an object that must pass for a chair, if we were allowed to specify its material and its shape; but we must also insist that the material is disposed *within* the shape we have prescribed. A block of wood with a chair-shaped cavity scooped out of it displays both the appropriate material and the appropriate shape; but it is not a chair.

The example of an artefact such as a chair is of course extremely unfavourable to the other form of substance theory mentioned above, namely that things fall into natural classes, each of which has its own distinctive structure of unchanging attributes. It might be thought, nevertheless, that this form of the theory could find a limited application, for instance within the range of animate beings. But this view is untenable; it involves a number of false analogies which I hope to expose; in particular it involves thinking of natural species as if they were mathematical constructs like geometrical figures, which can be completely defined, sometimes in a whole range of varieties, in terms of a few basic properties. And no one is entitled to think of species in this light if he accepts the theory of evolution and sees animal species as slowly modifying in response to a changing environment. Indeed the more informal notion of continuity described above has in any case tended to break down the traditional distinction between things and processes of change. This now appears to be a matter of degree; and this observation has been given point by the study of very short-lived particles in modern physics.

To avoid confusion, it may be well to mention here a quite different distinction between two classes of attributes, namely Locke's well-known distinction between primary and secondary qualities. This is not founded on the grouping of things into species, with a related distinction between permanent and variable attributes, but rather on the assumption that everything, and so each individual thing, has some qualities belonging to it at any given moment which in no way depend upon the manner in which this thing is observed or the other things with which it is compared. Locke is here influenced by the current scientific theories of matter; in practice his primary qualities—solidity, extension, figure, motion or rest, and number[10]—are those which were recognized by contemporary physics as the basic properties of matter; and an element of continuity is provided by the doctrine of the conservation of matter, which can enter into new combinations but not be destroyed. On the other hand Locke still retains the metaphysical notion of substance as an unknown somewhat in which the primary qualities inhere.

All these forms of substance theory now appear crude and outdated. The idea of an unknown, unqualified substratum is beyond defence. But there may be at least some residual value in the distinction between essential properties and accidents; it is no doubt too rigid and has other drawbacks as well; but it does at least encourage us to reflect that the various attributes of things cannot be assigned to them at random, but that there is a logical order among them; some of them cannot be predicated without presupposing others. And there is some value in the

[10] *An Essay Concerning Human Understanding*, Book ii, esp. Chapter viii.

distinction between primary and secondary qualities; it does at least encourage us to look for those qualities of things which are relatively independent of particular observers or particular circumstances of observation; and this quest has been fruitful, even if, as we now think, no ultimate success is possible.

II

PLATO

(i) *General Outline*

PLATO, though not its originator, was the first considerable writer to use the term οὐσία in a philosophical sense,[1] as distinct from that of 'wealth' or 'possessions'. In his early works he introduces it sparingly, leading up to it by some alternative expression involving the word εἶναι or adding a note of apology; in his later writings from the *Republic* onwards it occurs fairly frequently and without qualification.[2] A total of nearly 200 instances can be found,[3] including a number of cases where Plato describes philosophical views which he does not himself adopt.

However, although the word is a novelty, its usage is largely influenced by the established uses of εἶναι; indeed it is often synonymous either with τὸ εἶναι or with τὸ ὄν. This means that Plato's usage very largely reflects the confusions and sophistical arguments which contemporary philosophers had already attached to the verb. Some of these he was to detect and expose, and by the time he wrote the *Sophist* he was able to make important progress towards clarifying the senses of the verb 'to be'. But the correction came too late to be fully effective; as an influence upon the general reader, the *Sophist* has never been

---

[1] The Ionic form οὐσίη is so used in the speech *de Arte*, assigned to the late fifth century; see Hippocrates, Loeb edition, ii. 192. The Doric forms ἐσσία and ὠσία, mentioned in Plato's *Cratylus* 401 c, have no early attestation; the fragments of Philolaus containing the latter cannot be authentic, though the alternative ἐστώ occurs in the more probably genuine fr. 6. See J. Burnet, *Comm. on Phaedo*, 34; H. Thesleff, *Introduction to the Pythagorean Writings* (Åbo, 1961), 41–5, 93; W. Burkert, *Weisheit und Wissenschaft* (Nuremberg, 1962), 222–56 (and review by J. S. Morrison, *Gnomon* 37 (1965), 344–54); C. H. Kahn, *The Verb 'Be' and its Synonyms* (Dordrecht, 1973), 457–60. [2] See E. S. Thompson, *Comm. on Meno*, 255–8.

[3] A complete list is given by H. H. Berger, *Ousia in de dialogen van Plato* (Leiden, 1961), who includes 193 philosophical instances and six semi-philosophical, and reckons 'not less than 66' non-philosophical instances (p. 16). See also D. Peipers, *Ontologia Platonica* (Leipzig, 1883), 526 ff.; and R. Marten, *ΟΥΣΙΑ im Denken Platons* (Meisenheim am Glan, 1962). The article in Asts's *Lexikon Platonicum* is very incomplete.

able to compete with the great dialogues of the middle period, whose sublime conceptions are often poetically phrased and loosely argued.

It follows that in discussing Plato's use of the term it is particularly important to avoid the mistake of imposing precision on what is imprecise. One can indeed sometimes infer the sense of οὐσία from a verbal form which is used in parallel with it. In some cases 'the οὐσία of *x*' corresponds to the question 'What is *x*?', so that οὐσία represents the predicate in the sentence '*x* is . . .'; it means 'that which *x* is'. In other cases it represents the subject of the sentence, or the verbal idea itself, and so is equivalent to τὸ ὄν and to τὸ εἶναι respectively. In these latter cases it seems that the existential sense of the verb 'to be' is always prominent; one can hardly point to a case where οὐσία means 'thing-of-a-kind' in Plato, without any suggestion that the thing in question is real; and it does not normally convey the verbal sense of 'the-having-of-a-character', or 'being-so-and-so' as distinguished from simply 'being'.⁴ However these analyses should not be pressed too far; for Plato may not have noticed all that we detect; and conversely, when we, with our highly sophisticated logical apparatus, approach one of the pioneers of its development, it is hard to be sure that his imaginative and intuitive mind is not seeing nuances that would strike us as forced if we detected them.

Plato was probably influenced by the assumption that 'is' always indicates some kind of identity. He may never have accepted the extreme version of this view (which he criticizes in the *Sophist*),⁵ namely that 'is' can only connect two identical *terms*, so that it is never legitimate to say that *a* is *b*, but only that *a* is *a*; indeed his own theory of Ideas was partly intended to meet this point. But the theory sprang out of a search for definitions; in asking, for instance, 'What is justice?', Plato makes it clear that he is looking for a definition, rather than some illustration, of justice, and seeks an answer of the form 'Justice is . . .' rather than '. . . is just'. He hopes, then, to discover some revealing but equivalent expression. Yet in looking for an expression that has the 'same' meaning, it seems that he also meant to find a criterion

---

⁴ The latter sense is however given by *LSJ* to the famous passage in *Rep.* 509 b where the Good is described as ἔτι ἐπέκεινα τῆς οὐσίας.

⁵ 251 a 8–c 6; cf. Ross, *PTI*, 112.

for '. . . is just' that is objectively valid and so is 'the same for everyone', in opposition to the view that all judgements are subjective and have equal validity; and one that is constant or 'the same at all times', as against the view that everything is in process of change.[6]

The demand for something intelligible is thus bound up with the demand for something stable and permanent; for if experience is just a succession of sensations, if all we encounter is a mere flux, no knowledge is possible.[7] But in developing this case, Plato is able to appeal to an accepted contrast between εἶναι (and its cognates) and γίγνεσθαι and φθείρεσθαι and theirs.[8] After all, though εἶναι has past and future tenses, its tenses never have *inceptive* force; nor is there any form of the verb which corresponds to the Latin *fuit*, 'it has ceased to be'. Thus οὐσία is felt to be the appropriate word for permanent being; we find it already contrasted with πάθος ('state') in *Euthyphro* 11 a, *Hipp. Maj.* 301 b, and very commonly with γένεσις ('becoming': *Rep.* 525 b etc., *Soph.* 246 c, 248 a, *Phileb.* 54 a, *Timaeus* 29 c). Not that this contrast is always suggested; thus in *Soph.* 219 b εἰς οὐσίαν ἄγειν means 'to bring into existence', and its passive would be equivalent to γίγνεσθαι.[9] Sometimes, however, the contrast dominates to the extent of blanketing further inquiry into the sense of οὐσία; it now means simply 'permanence' or 'permanent reality' as contrasted with change and flux. Again, when Plato reached the conclusion that real knowledge is only possible if there are perfect unchanging objects of knowledge, the 'Forms' or 'Ideas', existing apart from the changing world, he could refer to these forms collectively as οὐσία; and the notion of permanence is still present in this use of the word.

Although there are passages where 'existence' seems the natural translation for οὐσία, it does not seem that Plato drew a clear distinction between a thing's simply 'being' (or 'existing') and its 'being what it is'; he has no true parallel to the later distinction

---

[6] The two views are closely associated; see e.g. *Theaet.* 152, esp. d–e. 'Change' for Plato includes a thing's changing relationships to other things; see e.g. *Phaedo* 74 b, *Rep.* 524 a. In certain cases these may change whereas the thing itself does not.

[7] *Cratylus* 386 d–e, 439 c ff., *Theaet.* 182 a ff.

[8] Γίγνεσθαι means both 'to become' (such-and-such) and 'to come into being'; φθείρεσθαι means 'to decay' or 'to perish', but is not used with a predicate.

[9] Cf. also *Phaedo* 101 c, *Parm.* 156 a, *Phileb.* 26 d.

between the two questions 'whether x is' and 'what x is'; hence he can argue that a thing can only come into being by partaking of its proper 'substance' (or 'manner of being'), whatever that may be (*Phaedo* 101 c, cited below, p. 36). We do, however, find a distinction drawn in rather similar terms between a thing's being 'itself' and its being 'such-and-such' (*Crat.* 439 d, πρῶτον μὲν ὅτι ἐκεῖνό ἐστιν, ἔπειτα ὅτι τοιοῦτον; cf. also *Ep.* vii 342 e). Plato has seen some important ambiguities in the verbal form 'x is . . .'; it can be used to express the essential features of x, but also to indicate mere temporary states of x, as when we say 'he is cold'; a third case, discussed in the *Phaedo*, is that of something having a property which is not part of its essence or definition but is nevertheless inseparable from it, like the coldness of snow. When Plato talks of a thing's οὐσία, he normally means to exclude at least the second of these cases; so that x's 'being', its οὐσία, is given a more specialized sense than the verbal form 'x is . . .'. Thus where οὐσία does not mean 'existence', it tends to be reserved for those predicates, or properties, which belong to a thing as long as it exists; there is only a small minority of passages in which οὐσία refers to a character which can be acquired or lost, and then it usually means a thing's normal state or con-stitution.[10] Plato is here exploring the distinction which Aristotle was to formalize, sometimes using Plato's terms οὐσία and πάθος, sometimes the more technical οὐσία and συμβεβηκός, 'substance and accident'.

Plato does not always very clearly distinguish his demand for permanent factors underlying our experience from his search for objectivity; and this passage of thought is helped by the common use of the verb εἶναι to express the contrast between being and seeming. Ἔστι τοῦτο can mean quite generally 'that is the case'[11] and τὸ ὄν can mean 'the fact' or 'the truth'. It is indeed easy to associate the truth of a suggestion or statement with the reality of what it represents, owing to the easy confusion of representations with things represented. Thus at *Phaedo* 71 e εἴπερ ἔστι τὸ ἀναβιώσκεσθαι may be interpreted either as 'if rebirth is real, if it actually occurs', or 'if (the suggestion of) rebirth is true'. A distinction begins to be outlined in the *Sophist* (236 d ff.), where it is argued that unrealities (i.e. untruths) are in some sense real

---

[10] *Phileb.* 32 b is perhaps the clearest instance.
[11] Ἔστι ταῦτα can indicate assent even to a negative statement: *Crito* 43 c.

(i.e. exist or occur), since errors and deceptions are facts of our experience.

It does not appear that οὐσία is used in the *Sophist* in the sense of truth; but in the *Republic* it is frequently coupled with 'truth', ἀλήθεια.[12] In such contexts οὐσία unquestionably suggests notions of value; and the underlying thought is illustrated by the passage in which Plato compares the Idea of good with the sun. 'Just as the eye sees most clearly when its object is bathed in sunlight, the mind apprehends most clearly when it views its object in the light of the Idea of good;' so Socrates claims that it is the Idea of good 'that gives to objects of knowledge their truth and to him who knows them his power of knowing.'[13] In this context of thought τὸ ὄν does not suggest that which incontrovertibly exists, but rather that which completely satisfies our need for something orderly and reliable; and similarly τὰ οὐκ ὄντα came to mean, not non-existent things or fictions, but rather 'non-entities', 'good-for-nothings', a meaning that is found in St. Paul.[14]

It appears from this brief account that Plato's use of the term οὐσία displays two kinds of imprecision. One of them is mainly grammatical. An important and characteristic use of the term is that in which it corresponds to the question 'What is *x*?', and so means 'What *x* is'; this is a predicative use, and οὐσία serves to denote *x*'s essential character, ὅ ἐστιν. In other passages, however, οὐσία seems to represent the notion of being as such, and to be equivalent to τὸ εἶναι; in others, again, it seems to veer towards the meaning 'something that is', τὸ ὄν or ὃ ἐστιν. The second imprecision is mainly conceptual; it is that the notion of being which is presupposed is sometimes attenuated to mean mere existence or occurrence of some fact, sometimes developed to mean 'being so-and-so', with special emphasis on those characteristics which most properly and permanently belong to the thing in question; and here it tends to pass over into the notion of permanence, or again into that of reliability or truth.

Some impression of Plato's usage can be given by a table; provided that this is not designed to pin it down by rigid subdivisions, but rather to indicate certain focal points and lines of transition

---

[12] See 521 d ff. as cited on pp. 37–8 below; cf. also *Timaeus* 52 c.
[13] Ross, *PTI*, 40; *Rep.* 508 e.
[14] 1 Cor. 1 : 28. Cf. the use of οὐδενία, 'nothingness', to mean 'worthlessness', *Phaedrus* 235 a, *Theaet.* 176 c; imitated by Athanasius, *c. Ar.* ii. 15.

along which his thought was apt to move. To aid comparison with a table to be given later, I put the predicative uses in the second column.

Verbal (τὸ εἶναι)	Predicative (ὅ ἐστιν)	Substantive (ὅ ἐστιν)	
		Inclusive ←	→ Specific
Being, existence (*Soph.* 219 b, 250 b)		Reality, the real. (e.g. sensible reality, *Phileb.* 27 b)	
Being so-and-so (? *Rep.* 509 b)	Essential nature Constitution[15] Normal state (*Phileb.* 32 b)		
Permanence		Unchanging reality	Thing as opp. to its states
Truth		Reality, fact	A reality, as opp. to a mere name, *Protag.* 349 b.

Two remarks may be added. First, there is at least one important use of οὐσία which it is almost impossible to locate on such a table. Plato makes use of phrases like 'intelligible reality' (νοητὴ οὐσία) in contexts which suggest a concrete sense, 'that which is real' or 'something which is real', rather than the abstract 'realness', 'the property of being real'. An example might be 'justice itself'. But this conception fits almost equally well on any of the four levels; since in Plato's view 'justice itself' is more real than any individual instance of justice; yet it belongs to them all, as their prototype or their common characteristic; and again, it alone is always just, and it alone is truly just. Only the context in some particular passage can indicate which of the nuances predominates.

Secondly, it may be worth noting some important senses which are seldom or never found in Plato. He does not use it in the sense of Aristotle's πρώτη οὐσία to denote a particular individual entity; the phrase ἴδιος οὐσία καὶ πρᾶγμα, 'a distinct existence or thing', in *Protagoras* 349 b could easily suggest this sense, but in fact the 'distinct entities' envisaged here are five virtues. Nor is it, I think, used to mean simply 'a species', 'a kind of thing', like Aristotle's δευτέρα οὐσία. Another important absentee is the use of οὐσία to mean 'matter'. Plato does use it to mean 'perceptual reality', or 'the perceptual world'; and this is sometimes loosely

---

[15] μελίττης, *Meno* 72 b; ἁμάξης, *Theaet.* 207 c.

called 'matter' by later philosophers. What is missing is the explanatory concept of an underlying substance out of which perceptible things are made.

(ii) *The Early Development*

To complete the picture, some account must be given of the way in which Plato's conceptions developed. It seems convenient to distinguish three stages in the development. The early dialogues exhibit the Socratic method of seeking definitions without attributing to such definitions a transcendent reality. In a second stage, however, great emphasis is laid on the transcendence of the Ideas, which alone can be truly known, and of which the sensible world is held to be an imperfect copy; to this period belong the great 'classical' dialogues, of which the *Phaedo*, the *Republic*, and the *Phaedrus* are the most important for our purposes. In the third stage the transcendent reality of the Ideas is still strongly upheld, but there is more disposition to see them reflected in the world of time and space, so that changing phenomena can be truly known, and show real though not perfect evidence of rational order. From this period, the *Sophist* is important as marking an advance in Plato's logical theory, though its later influence is slight compared with the *Timaeus*.

We shall try to discuss the following points:

(1) How did Plato's conception of οὐσία develop in his early and middle periods, and what logical steps are implied?

(2) Did he later retract or seriously modify the positions assumed in his most influential dialogues?

(3) What picture results, in Plato's view, of the world of pure form, or eternal substance?

Plato began by asking, through Socrates, 'What is *x*?',[16] usually referring to some moral quality, as temperance in the *Charmides*, courage in the *Laches*, piety in the *Euthyphro*, beauty in the *Hippias Major*. The interlocutor is apt to reply by furnishing examples (e.g. *Hipp. Maj.* 287 e, 289 e, 291 d, *Meno* 71 e, *Theaet.* 146 cd); to which Socrates answers that what he wants is not an example or list of examples, but something single and unique,

---

[16] R. Robinson points out that the question is striking rather than especially frequent: *Plato's Earlier Dialectic*, Chapter 5 *init*. For some of the problems connected with it, see the essays by R. C. Cross and R. S. Bluck in R. E. Allen (ed.), *Studies in Plato's Metaphysics*, 13–41.

that which so-and-so really is. Thus in the sentence, 'What is *x*?', the interlocutor takes 'What' as the subject; whereas Socrates insists on making it the complement, thereby asking for some sort of further description or definition (*x* is . . .) rather than for instances (. . . is *x*). Rather less frequently, and less early, the inquiry is directed, not to some undefined general term, but to a plural noun denoting a group, as when Socrates is shown looking for 'that by which the just are just' (*Hipp. Maj.* 287 c, cf. *Phaedo* 100 b–c).

Οὐσία, then, first appears as a counterpart to the phrase 'what *x* is'. It is several times explained in the early dialogues. Thus in the *Meno* (72 b) Socrates suggests, εἴ μου ἐρομένου μελίττης περὶ οὐσίας ὅτι ποτ' ἐστίν, which should be rendered, 'If, when I asked about the being of a bee, what it (the bee) is . . .' At *Euthyphro* 11 a the word is taken up by the similar phrase τί ποτε ὄν; again at *Phaedo* 65 d it is paraphrased by ὃ τυγχάνει ἕκαστον ὄν; at *Cratylus* 423 e 'imitating the being of each thing', μιμεῖσθαι ἑκάστου τὴν οὐσίαν, is how a man δηλοῖ ἕκαστον ὃ ἔστιν (I print Burnet's accentuation, but the meaning must be 'shows what each thing is').[17] The same question form appears with the important phrase '*x* itself', for instance at its first introduction in *Hippias Major* 286 d 8, where καί με δίδαξον ἱκανῶς αὐτὸ τὸ καλὸν ὅτι ἐστί clearly repeats the question of d 1, ἔχοις ἂν εἰπεῖν τί ἐστι τὸ καλόν;[18] In the *Charmides* (168 d) οὐσία figures in a comparison between what a thing is and what it does (ἐκείνην ἕξει τὴν οὐσίαν πρὸς ἣν ἡ δύναμις αὐτοῦ ἦν), which is closely related to the contrast made at *Euthyphro* 11 a between what a thing is and what happens to it. At the same time the confident way in which οὐσία and πάθος are here contrasted perhaps suggests that the philosophical use of οὐσία was not a coinage of Plato's invention, but was already common currency.

So far, then, ὅτι ποτ' ἐστίν and similar phrases merely ask the question 'What is so-and-so?', and the verb is predicative.[19] But

---

[17] Berger (p. 45) rightly refers also to the explanations of οὐσία by ᾗπερ πέφυκεν, 386 e, cf. 387 c, and ᾗ ἔχει, 388 b. Cf. also *Laws* ii. 668 c, where it is equivalent to the previous ὅτι ποτ' ἐστίν.

[18] 'Show me clearly what beauty itself is.' 'Could you say what beauty is?'

[19] R. Loriaux (*L'Être et la forme selon Platon*) argues that even in the early dialogues ὃ ἔστι has an existential sense, with ὃ as the subject. I think this unlikely, and suppose that Plato's thought gradually developed so that the existential sense came to the fore. Cf. the review by K. W. Mills in *Gnomon* 49 (1957), 325–9.

a new development is foreshadowed in the *Hippias Major* (287 c), where Socrates is made to argue from the admission that it is by justice that the just are just to the conclusion, Οὐκοῦν ἔστι τι τοῦτο, ἡ δικαιοσύνη, where the emphatic ἔστι suggests the meaning 'Justice, then, is a reality'. Here, however, Plato does not proceed to interpret ἔστι in an existential sense, but simply uses the statement, 'Justice is something', to prepare the way for the question, 'What is justice?' A similar phrase, 'that there is such a thing as beauty itself, etc.', occurs near the end of the *Cratylus* (439 c: φῶμέν τι εἶναι αὐτὸ καλὸν καὶ ἀγαθὸν καὶ ἓν ἕκαστον τῶν ὄντων οὕτω, ἢ μή;) but here both its manner of introduction and the use made of it are rather different. The general context of argument is that names, even when suitably chosen, are an imperfect guide to reality;[20] they are only images of things, as opposed to the things themselves. Should one therefore study the image to see whether *it itself* is a good image, and learn the truth whose image it is; or should one learn from the truth both *it itself* and whether the image is right? The latter course is approved, and the conclusion follows that 'it is not from names, but rather from *the realities themselves* that learning and inquiry must begin'. It seems as if the phrase 'it itself', which is first introduced simply as an emphatic method of reference, prepares the way for the mention of 'beauty itself', meaning that which truly corresponds to the term 'beauty', as opposed to imperfect and changing examples (439 d). This looks like a literary artifice; on the other hand Plato is no doubt arguing deliberately when he proceeds from the admission that there is such a thing as beauty itself to the claim that such reality must be permanent and unchanging.

Thus we have found Plato passing from '. . . is just' to 'justice is . . .', i.e. from a predicative sentence to a definition (with the possibility of an existential statement about justice already suggested); and again from the notion of fact-as-opposed-to-names to that of definition, which in turn is held to imply an unchanging reality corresponding to the definition.

The step which was suggested in the *Hippias Major* seems to be firmly taken in the *Phaedo*, where once again we find οὐσία playing a minor part in an argument in which the verb εἶναι is all-important, namely the well-known argument for the pre-existence of the soul based on the doctrine of recollection. At an early

---

[20] For the contrast οὐσία–ὄνομα cf. *Protag.* 349 b.

stage (65 d) we find the question, 'Is there such a thing as justice itself . . . beauty, goodness?', which being agreed the questioner continues, 'Did you perceive such things with your eyes, or other senses?—I mean size, health, strength and in short the being of all things, what each of them is?' (λέγω δὲ περὶ πάντων, οἷον μεγέθους πέρι, ὑγιείας, ἰσχύος, καὶ τῶν ἄλλων ἑνὶ λόγῳ ἁπάντων τῆς οὐσίας ὃ τυγχάνει ἕκαστον ὄν.) ; in this case it is difficult to suppose that οὐσία *merely* implies the definition of the terms, and does not carry over some suggestion of 'reality' from the previous admission that 'there is such a thing as justice'. When the argument is resumed, the example discussed is that of equality. It is first agreed that 'there is such a thing as equality itself', which now seems to be conceived as a perfect standard to which particular instances only approximately conform (see esp. 74 d–75 a: the particular things 'want to be' like equality itself—βούλεται, ὀρέγεται—but are 'inferior'—φαυλότερον—and 'fall short', ἔχει δὲ ἐνδεεστέρως). The argument continues that we cannot have discovered the perfect standard from the imperfect sensible particulars, but must have known it before we began to perceive such things at all, and therefore before birth in a previous existence. The same reasoning is applied (75 c) to cover not only equality but absolute beauty, goodness, justice, piety, and 'everything on which we set the seal of being itself' (περὶ ἁπάντων οἷς ἐπισφραγιζόμεθα τὸ "αὐτὸ ὃ ἔστι").[21] It may therefore be said that our souls 'were' before they 'were in human form' (76 c).

Two features in this argument are to be noted. First, there is a new development in Plato's conception of the Idea, which now seems to be conceived not simply as the thing to which abstract expressions most properly refer, nor as the common factor in a class of things, but as an ideal standard to which particulars do not exactly correspond. Secondly there is the transition from '. . . is just' to 'justice is'; and the latter expression now seems to involve both (a) that there is something distinct from the particulars to which the name 'justice' uniquely applies, and (b) that this, not 'seems', but 'is'; and, not 'becomes', but 'is': i.e. is objective and unchanging. From these perfect objective standards is deduced the previous existence of the soul, unencumbered by the body and *ex hypothesi* itself perfect.

[21] But N.B. this text (Burnet's) is not that of the manuscripts. Berger, p. 61, prints: ἐπισφραγιζόμεθα τοῦτο "ὃ ἔστι".

This train of thought does not, of course, depend wholly on the terms 'to be' and 'being'. Plato introduces a number of alternative expressions to refer to the Ideas, and we have already noted the importance of the phrase '*x* itself', whose logic is similar. He seems to have begun by reflecting that 'the *x*' (e.g. τὸ καλόν, 'the beautiful', *Hipp. Maj.* 286 ff.) may either refer collectively to the many things that we call '*x*', or designate the one 'thing' that they have in common; this latter, then, is the proper sense of '*x*', and is called for emphasis 'the *x* itself'. He then added the thought that the things which we call (e.g.) equal may be sometimes, or to some extent, unequal, whereas it is absurd to suppose that 'the equal itself' ever changes or deviates. Hence 'the equal itself' is always equal, exactly equal, and the cause of equality in other things. (Plato's language can easily suggest that these three characteristics necessarily go together, and are necessarily present in the ideal world, and absent from the world of phenomena; but (i) not all concepts admit of ideal forms; there is no perfect *inequality*; (ii) exact equality is not confined to the ideal world; if Theaetetus outgrows Socrates, they must at some time be exactly equal; what is lacking in the phenomenal world is what is always and necessarily equal; (iii) there are special difficulties in the thesis that equality is equal, or more generally, *x*-ness is *x*; for if 'equality' simply means 'that which is equal', the thesis is vacuous; but if it refers to something which has to be invoked to *explain* 'is equal', the thesis is circular.[22] Plato himself seems to have had some suspicion of the first objection (cf. *Parmenides* 130 c–d: there cannot be 'forms' of hair or mud, yet the theory requires this), and perhaps admitted the possibility of perfect particulars (cf. Ross, *PTI*, 19, on *Cratylus* 389–90); but apparently overlooked the third objection; so he can write (*Phaedo* 100 c) 'if anything else is beautiful besides beauty itself, it is beautiful for no other reason than that it partakes of that beauty'; cf. *Protagoras* 330 c–e.)

The sense given to οὐσία in the *Phaedo* conforms to this pattern of argument. It reappears twice (76 d, 77 a) as a collective designation for the ideal standards whose reality the argument has assumed, and in the latter case at least it seems that the suggestion of 'reality' is intended. A little later (78 c–d) it appears in an argument designed to show that what is real must be immune

[22] Cf. p. 82 below.

from change, again referring collectively to the Ideas; once again there seems to be a passage from 'what each thing is' to 'what is', or 'reality': αὐτὴ ἡ οὐσία ἧς λόγον δίδομεν τοῦ εἶναι . . . αὐτὸ τὸ ἴσον, αὐτὸ τὸ καλὸν, αὐτὸ ἕκαστον ὃ ἔστιν, τὸ ὄν, μή ποτε μεταβολὴν καὶ ἡντινοῦν ἐνδέχεται; A possible rendering might be: 'Reality itself, which we define as being . . . the Equal itself, the Beautiful itself, each thing itself as it really is, true being—does this ever admit of any kind of change?' After an interval, the word reappears at 92 d, where Simmias refers back to the theory of recollection and of the pre-existence of the soul, which (he now admits) disproves his suggestion that the soul is a harmony: ἐρρήθη γάρ που οὕτως ἡμῶν εἶναι ἡ ψυχὴ καὶ πρὶν εἰς σῶμα ἀφικέσθαι, ὥσπερ αὐτῆς ἐστιν ἡ οὐσία ἔχουσα τὴν ἐπωνυμίαν τοῦ ''ὃ ἔστιν'': 'We said, I think, that our soul exists before it enters the body, just as it possesses that reality which is entitled "that which is".' This recalls a passage (76 e–77 a) in which absolute reality is said to have been 'ours' in the sense of having been known by us in a prior existence; hence the soul is 'akin' to what is invisible and unchangeable rather than to visible and changeable things. The one remaining occurrence of οὐσία in the *Phaedo* (101 c) gives it a rather different sense. The argument is that things become two (or perhaps rather, 'twoness comes about'), not by addition or by division, but by twoness or duality: Τί δέ; ἑνὶ ἑνὸς προστεθέντος τὴν πρόσθεσιν αἰτίαν εἶναι τοῦ δύο γένεσθαι ἢ διασχισθέντος τὴν σχίσιν οὐκ εὐλαβοῖο ἂν λέγειν; καὶ μέγα ἂν βοῴης ὅτι οὐκ οἶσθα ἄλλως πως ἕκαστον γιγνόμενον ἢ μετασχὸν τῆς ἰδίας οὐσίας ἑκάστου οὗ ἂν μετάσχῃ, καὶ ἐν τούτοις οὐκ ἔχεις ἄλλην τινὰ αἰτίαν τοῦ δύο γενέσθαι ἀλλ' ἢ τὴν τῆς δυάδος μετάσχεσιν etc. Here the central phrase, 'you know no other way in which each thing can come into being, except by partaking of its own manner-of-being (οὐσία), whatever that may be' is paralleled by 'you can assign no other cause for two coming into being, except the partaking in twoness'. This parallelism suggests the meaning 'essential nature' (viz. twoness) for οὐσία; but the phrasing also suggests that twoness 'comes to be' or 'begins to *exist*' (cf. p. 28 above). However, this is clearly a special case in which the notion of coming-to-be is loosely applied. A pair may result from addition or division; it does not *result* from twoness, but is constituted by it. Plato is in fact using the metaphor which Aristotle was to describe as the 'formal cause'.

Turning to the *Republic*, we shall find that οὐσία plays a more prominent part in Plato's thought about unchanging reality, but that the underlying logic is essentially the same as we have found in the *Phaedo*. It first appears in Book II, in a reference to 'the origin and nature (οὐσίαν) of justice'; this calls for no particular comment, but it does serve to introduce a pair of terms which play an important part in the discussions in Books VI and VII. Here there is a development of the language of *Phaedo* 76–8; οὐσία is no longer phrased with a dependent genitive, as if it stood for a definition or attribute of something, but is used absolutely as a collective singular denoting reality, or the sum total of real beings; and in this absolute use it always denotes 'eternal reality'. This usage is exceedingly characteristic of the *Republic*, and left its mark on later Platonism, though one cannot say that Plato himself maintained it consistently. In the later dialogues οὐσία is still used in a collective sense to mean 'phenomenal reality' or some part of it, though never without some qualifying phrase.[23] And in the *Sophist* 251 ff. οὐσία figures in the rather abstract discussion whether being can 'combine with' motion (etc.); this hardly suggests that Plato has eternal reality particularly in view, though one cannot be sure that a reference to it is *excluded*, in view of possible changes in Plato's judgements about the real world, which will be examined in due course (pp. 45–6 below).

In the *Republic*, then, we find Plato using οὐσία to mean the type of being which he also calls ἡ ἀλήθεια and τὸ ὄν, the truth, as contrasted with changing appearances, referred to as γένεσις. These equivalences may be conveniently shown by a group of passages in Book VII, where Plato begins to inquire how the knowledge of this world of perfect beauty and unchanging reality is to be produced, and argues that the study of mathematics is the best way to draw the soul towards it; it 'draws' or 'leads' or 'converts' the soul towards 'being', or 'reality' (οὐσία), or 'truth':

521 d Τί οὖν ἂν εἴη ... μάθημα ψυχῆς ὁλκὸν ἀπὸ τοῦ γιγνομένου ἐπὶ τὸ ὄν;

---

[23] e.g. *Phileb.* 27 b, μεικτὴν καὶ γεγενημένην οὐσίαν: *Soph.* 246 a (quoted opinion). A possible exception is a small group of passages where 'the whole of reality' may perhaps include both temporal and eternal; so perhaps *Rep.* vi. 486 a, *Ep.* vii. 344 b.

523 a <u>ἑλκτικῷ</u> ὄντι παντάπασι πρὸς οὐσίαν.

524 d–e οὐκ ἂν ὁλκὸν εἴη ἐπὶ τὴν οὐσίαν.

524 e–5 a τῶν <u>ἀγωγῶν</u> ἂν εἴη καὶ <u>μεταστρεπτικῶν</u> ἐπὶ τὴν τοῦ ὄντος θέαν.

525 b ταῦτα δέ γε φαίνεται <u>ἀγωγὰ</u> πρὸς ἀλήθειαν.

525 b φιλοσόφῳ δὲ . . . τῆς οὐσίας ἁπτέον . . . <u>γενέσεως</u> ἐξανα-δύντι.

525 c <u>μεταστροφῆς</u> ἀπὸ <u>γενέσεως</u> ἐπ' ἀλήθειάν τε καὶ οὐσίαν.

When Plato speaks of 'intelligible reality', what is the phrase meant to include? A short answer is to say, the Ideas; while 'the soul'—understood as 'the virtuous soul'—is described in similar terms as 'akin to the divine' (*Phaedo* 65–7 and esp. 80) and has some claim to inclusion, together with 'the gods'. But the details of the scheme are far from clear, and even this short outline runs counter to interpretations of Plato which developed and gained currency in our period.

First, it is generally accepted by modern critics that the Ideas or Forms are conceived as eternal, objective realities; they are not mere thoughts in the mind of God or of men, as the name 'idea' might suggest; nor are they mere conceptual models.[24] The former possibility receives a brief but destructive criticism in the *Parmenides* 132 bc, and probably Plato himself never seriously entertained it, though he does occasionally speak in terms which suggested the theory to his successors.

Next, there has been much discussion as to what sorts of Ideas Plato claimed to have established. In our view, he seems to be embarrassed by his attempt to make the Ideas sustain two distinct roles, (a) as a counterpart to every general term, and (b) as a ideal standard, which many general terms appear to disallow. On the whole it seems safe to conclude that in spite of admitted difficulties he clung to the belief that there was an Idea corresponding to every common name (*Rep.* 596 c 6). 'The most catholic list of classes of Ideas Plato anywhere gives us is in one of his latest writings (*Ep.* vii. 342 d 3–8) where he recognizes Ideas of shapes and surfaces, of the good, the beautiful and the just, of all bodies natural and artificial, of fire and water and the like, of every animal, of every quality of character, of all actions and

24 Cf. R. S. Bluck, *Plato's Phaedo*, 174–8.

passivities' (Ross, *PTI*, 85: cf. 79, 171–5 and *Parm.* 130 c: the great man meets the objections to this view by saying that the mature philosopher will be bold and consistent). At the same time it is the moral and mathematical Ideas which first engaged Plato's attention and which he upheld with the greatest confidence; the theory seems to have developed out of Socrates' inquiries into the nature of moral virtue, and to have been influenced by the attempts of the Pythagoreans to explain things in terms of numbers. This may be shown by a list of the examples discussed in the *Phaedo*:

equality 74 a 78 d
greatness 65 d 100 b, c, e   smallness 100 e
number 101 b
odd number 103 e–104 a   even number 104 b
individual numbers 101 c, 104 a–c

beauty 65 d, 74 a, 76 d, 78 d, 100 b, c
goodness 65 d, 74 a, 76 d, 100 b
justice 65 d, 74 a
piety 74 a
health 65 d   disease 105 c
strength 65 d
heat 104   cold 104

This diagram shows the prominence given to positive qualities or values, those of which an ideal degree is possible, and to mathematical forms which suggest them (as equality suggests equity); also, even allowing for the normal Greek admiration for orderliness in conduct and symmetry in design, the important place which Plato gives to those ideal qualities which can be expressed as some kind of proportion, a clear sign of Pythagorean influence.[25] This is suggested again by the 'kinship' which obtains between the Ideas and the rational soul, whose typical activity is described as 'computation' (λογίζεσθαι, *Phaedo* 65 b). It is the union of mathematical studies with religious and ascetic devotion, as practised in the Pythagorean brotherhoods, which best accounts for Plato's approach to the world of Ideas. The ideal world is devoid of all sensible qualities; yet it is described in the highest terms, as the only reality which merits the love and regard

---

[25] Cf. the suggestion, *Phaedo* 65 d, e, that the truth about *health* and *strength* can be most accurately known by the mind, not the senses.

which we commonly pay to earthly beauty and acknowledged divinity; it is

Pure, everlasting, immortal and consistent (79 d);

Noble, pure and invisible, along with the good and wise god (80 d);

A converse with the divine and pure and uniform (83 e).

Plato's pictures of it in the *Phaedo* might be influenced by the setting of the dialogue, and owe something to the picture-language of common beliefs about the life after death ('invisible', ἀιδής, is a pun on 'Hades', Ἀΐδης, cf. 81 c); but a similar conception underlies the famous description of the 'supercelestial region' in the *Phaedrus*, where the allegory by which the soul is compared to a chariot is balanced by phrases which are meant to be taken literally:

'Uncoloured, unformed, intangible reality that is truly real, perceptible only to the mind that governs men's souls' (247 c).

Thus in the classical dialogues of his middle period, Plato had come to think of the Ideas as perfect prototypes, which together comprise a perfect world. The climax of this development is the passage in the *Republic* (509 b) where he relates them to the Idea of the Good: 'Objects of knowledge derive from the Good . . . their very existence and being (οὐσία); and the Good is not the same thing as being, but even beyond being, surpassing it in dignity and power' (. . . οὐκ οὐσίας ὄντος τοῦ ἀγαθοῦ, ἀλλ' ἔτι ἐπέκεινα τῆς οὐσίας πρεσβείᾳ καὶ δυνάμει ὑπερέχοντος).

This passage is one of outstanding importance in the history of Platonism; but it is difficult to interpret, since Plato seldom returns to this train of thought.[26] A possible reason is that the position reached in the *Republic* is unstable; there is a conflict between the notion of an Idea corresponding to every common name and the conception of the Ideas as perfect prototypes,

[26] The principal exception is an ἀκρόασις, a lecture or course of lectures, on the Good, reported by Aristoxenus (*Harm. El.* ii. 30–1) and other writers. There is much disagreement here; scholars influenced by H. F. Cherniss think of a single lecture; at the other extreme are those who argue for a continuous course for advanced pupils, to which the dialogues were merely preparatory. Literature and full discussion in J. Wippern, *Das Problem der ungeschriebenen Lehre Platons*; brief English discussion in Ross, *PTI*, 142–53, cf. 242–5. Main Greek texts, i.e. those reporting *Aristotle's* lost work *On the Good*, which referred to it, in Ross, *Aristotelis Fragmenta Selecta*, 111–20; some also in C. J. de Vogel, *Greek Philosophy* i. 273 ff.; larger English collection in J. N. Findlay, *Plato: The Written and Unwritten Doctrines*, 413–54. Cf. pp. 49–54 below.

which is needed to explain their dependence upon the Good. It has already been shown that in his early dialogues Plato did not precisely define his objectives; he was looking for permanent and objective standards of judgement, and it was something of an accident that he came to associate these with mathematical expressions, where the exact or regular form is simple and primary, and with moral virtues and other kinds of things that can be idealized. But disease and injustice (or worms and thumbscrews) present much the same logical and epistemological problems as health and justice, bees and waggons. Before long, in the *Parmenides*, Plato was to raise the question, 'Are there Ideas of mud and hair and the like?', which suggests that he partly realized the difficulty, so that his speculations on the Good suffered a check; though he continued to hope that the theory of Ideas could somehow be restated with all its values upheld.

Nevertheless when he says that the Good is 'beyond being', Plato manifestly does not mean that it is too excellent to be real; in his view it is more real than any of its instances. Most probably the term 'being' carries the implication of 'being so-and-so'. Ideal justice is good, but the kind of goodness it displays depends on the kind of thing justice is. It cannot exhibit the quite different type of goodness displayed by the ideal waggon. The Good itself is on a higher level than such Ideas, which are particular types of goodness; it is the prototype of them all.

In the *Republic* there is no suggestion that the Idea of the Good is itself an intelligent, rational being. Plato was to pave the way for this view much later, in the *Timaeus* (30 b), by pronouncing that a being possessed of intelligence must be superior to one that lacks it. In the *Republic* the Good is the supreme reality and the highest value, and as such it fills the place which later theism assigns to a personal God. But Plato does not think of it in theistic terms; and usually, when he does refer to a supreme ruler of the universe, conceives him as contemplating ideal patterns of perfection which exist independently of himself.[27] We must therefore distinguish Plato's position from two main types of view which were developed by later Platonists; one simply identifying the World-Ruler with the Good of the *Republic* (and

---

[27] An exception occurs in the *Republic* itself, at 597 b, where Plato speaks of God making the Idea of a bed—a remark which later commentators probably took more seriously than Plato intended.

the One of the *Parmenides* and Plato's later speculations); the other interpreting the Good, or the One, as an ultimate unknowable divinity, the original source from which the Ruler and Creator of the world was himself derived. It is only in these later developments of Platonism that we find the Ideas interpreted as thoughts originating in the mind of a deity.

It is probable that later theology was more influenced by Plato's conceptions of the intelligible world, the Good, and the soul, than by his directly theological pronouncements, apart from the picture of the world's creation given in the *Timaeus*. It seems that, for much of his life at any rate, he envisaged an ultimate perfection distinct from, or even superior to, the Maker and Ruler of the world. However, this divinity is referred to in dialogues of all periods[28] consistently enough and often enough to make it reasonably clear that Plato is not merely imitating Socrates' half-humorous conformity with the beliefs of popular theology, but means to be taken at his word.

(iii) *Some Later Analyses*

In the preceding pages I have shown in some detail how Plato's concept of intelligible reality was influenced by undetected ambiguities in the use of the word 'to be'. I shall conclude this chapter with a much slighter outline of some leading Platonic themes, intended not so much to assess Plato's achievement in its own right as to illustrate those aspects of his thought which most effectively influenced his philosophical successors. We need, therefore, to summarize the suggestions offered by the later dialogues on the concepts of being, of immaterial reality, and lastly of material reality.

How far, then, was Plato able to correct his faulty assumptions and refine the doctrine of being in its logical aspect? We have already noted (above, p. 26) that he rejected the notion that the verb 'to be' can only connect two identical *terms*; this is made clear in the *Sophist*, a dialogue which is of great importance for professional philosophers, though it has tended to be overlooked by the general reader.[29] In this dialogue it is evident that Plato

---

[28] *Rep.* 507 c, 530 a, *Soph.* 265 a, *Pol.* 270 a, 273 c, *Phileb.* 28 de, besides *Tim.* 28 c etc.

[29] Of the earlier Christian fathers, perhaps only Clement read the *Sophist* for himself. Eusebius cites a doxographic passage, probably drawn from a manual, but has little else; Hippolytus, Origen, and Methodius still less.

is giving serious attention to the problems raised by the notion of being, but it is not agreed whether or not he was successful in distinguishing two or more senses of the verb 'to be';[30] it is clear, however, that if he did so, his grasp of the essential points was insecure, and they were never presented in an authoritative form.

The dialogue begins by describing a series of attempts to define the sophist; but a much more important question is raised in Chapter 24 (236 d ff.), namely how can one say without contradiction that falsehood really 'is' (or 'is there'), since this seems to entail the conclusion which Parmenides constantly denounced, namely that 'not-being is'. The ensuing discussion raises both logical and cosmological questions; under the latter heading Plato gives an outline of several competing doctrines about the universe, including the doctrines that all things are in motion, and that all things are at rest. This leads to the conclusion that both motion and rest *are*, or are real; yet they are not the same as each other, but different. From this he concludes again that some of the Forms 'mingle with' others;[31] but there are also incompatibilities. He illustrates this from the case of the five 'greatest kinds' ($\mu\acute{\epsilon}\gamma\iota\sigma\tau\alpha\ \gamma\acute{\epsilon}\nu\eta$) that his argument has established, namely being, motion, rest, sameness, and otherness; and finally uses the notion of 'otherness' to formulate his theory of falsity.

In the course of this discussion Plato makes some important clarifications in the notion of being. In the first place, he seems to have grasped that the 'is' of identity is a special case, and incorporates this point in his scheme of 'greatest kinds', where 'sameness' and 'being' are distinguished. Secondly, and rather less clearly, he seems to have understood that the existential 'is' is a special case, as distinct from the 'is' which simply serves to attach a predicate; in the latter case he offers a philosophical paraphrase in terms of 'participation'.[32] But here it needs a perceptive reader to grasp the point that is being made; as an

[30] Largely favourable verdict: Cornford, 1935; Ackrill, 1957; Taylor, 1961; Moravczik, 1962; Runciman, 1962; Crombie, 1963. Largely adverse: Frede, 1967; Malcolm, 1967; Owen, 1971; Gosling, 1973. See the Bibliography.

[31] This notion is not very clearly expressed; it could mean either '*x* and *y* are (or may be) compatible', where *x* and *y* are interchangeable, or '*x* qualifies *y*', i.e. '*y* is *x*', where they are not.

[32] See J. L. Ackrill, 'Plato and the Copula: *Sophist* 251–259', *JHS* 77 (1957), 1–7.

example, we may cite a passage from 256 d, lightly paraphrased:
'Let us then fearlessly contend that motion is other than being ...
and therefore clearly motion really is not, and also is, since it
partakes of being.' (In saying 'motion is other than being', the
copulative 'is' is implied; but in 'motion is', the existential;
though this can be paraphrased again with the copulative 'is' by
saying 'is an existent'.)

Thirdly, Plato appears to have caught fugitive glimpses of the
point that truth and falsity are to be defined as agreement and
disagreement with the facts of the case; but he often obscures
this point by referring to falsity as 'not-being', which suggests
that he has not clearly grasped the distinction between false
statements and negative statements, or perhaps negative existential statements. Near the end of the dialogue (p. 263) he offers
an explanation of truth and falsity, taking as examples the two
statements 'Theaetetus sits' and 'Theaetetus flies'; he points out
that both are grammatically correct, and adds that 'the true
one states the things that are (so) as being (so) in your case',
whereas 'the false one (states) things other than those that are',
it 'states things that are not (so) as if they were (so)'. Two brief
comments may be suggested. In the first place, a charitable critic
might well say that here at least Plato has clearly distinguished
falsity from negation, since he offers us two positive statements,
one true, one false. But the point would have been much clearer
still if he had added two corresponding negative examples, say
'Theaetetus does not fly' and 'Theaetetus does not grow'; which
in turn should have led him to recast his more general pronouncements on 'being'. Secondly, although the definition 'it states
things that are not (so) as if they were (so)' is satisfactory, it is
satisfactory only because it makes an advance, which Plato seems
not to have noticed, on the preceding statement, 'it states
things other than those that are'. For clearly if this means '. . .
other than the truth', it merely defines falsity in terms of its
opposite; but if it means '. . . other than the facts', it needs to be
read as '. . . other than all the facts', since a true statement may
say something 'other than' any particular set of facts; 'Socrates
talks' says something other than all the facts about Theaetetus,
apart from a few exceptions like 'Theaetetus is addressed by
Socrates'.

How far was the *Sophist* successful in instructing Plato's successors? Oddly enough, it appears that, in the short run at least, the points which we have found to be least clearly made were the most clearly grasped. Aristotle at least seems to have understood the distinctive character of 'being as truth', to judge from the brief reference in *Metaph.* v. 7, 1017 a 31 ff., and the discussions in vi. 4 and ix. 10. On the other hand the distinctions between existence, identity, and character were not sufficiently pressed, and in Aristotle we shall find many traces of the opinions that a proposition of the form '*S* is *P*' represents either a qualified form of an existential statement, or else a kind of identification falling short of absolute identity.

So far I have tried to describe Plato's attempts to clarify the logic of the verb 'to be'; but there is, secondly, a small group of remarks about being in the *Sophist* which fall rather under the heading of metaphysics.

In 247 e Plato throws out the suggestion that a thing 'really is' if it has any power of affecting something else, or being affected by it; and he sums up this contention in the rather cryptic sentence, τίθεμαι γὰρ ὅρον ὁρίζειν τὰ ὄντα, ὡς ἔστιν οὐκ ἄλλο τι πλὴν δύναμις, which Cornford renders 'I am proposing as a mark to distinguish real beings, that they are nothing but power'. This may perhaps be little more than a debating-point advanced against the materialists,[33] designed to show that some immaterial things are real, since they produce effects; but the aphorism 'being is power' was taken out of context by Plato's successors, and is very likely presupposed by Aristotle's counter-argument that actuality, ἐνέργεια, is prior to power, or 'potentiality', as it is usually translated by Aristotelian scholars. The Stoics are said to have revived Plato's suggestion that 'being is power', and in later philosophy there seems to be little agreement; professional philosophers no doubt had to decide for or against Aristotle's subordination of 'power' to 'actuality', but the common usage of these terms is extraordinarily fluctuating and confused.

A little later, at 248 e, Plato seems to suggest that real being (τὸ παντελῶς ὄν) is endowed with motion, life, soul, and thought; a startling suggestion in view of his emphatic statements, in the great dialogues of the middle period, that motion at any rate

---

[33] So Burnet, *Greek Philosophy*, 280; Taylor, *Plato*, 384; Cornford, *Plato's Theory of Knowledge*, 239; on the other side are Lutoslawski and Ritter, cited by W. G. Runciman, *Plato's Later Epistemology*, 77, n. 2.

belongs solely to the perceptible world, which cannot be described as 'real being', whereas the world of Forms is strictly unchanging. This passage has been much discussed. There seems to be fairly general agreement that Plato is here maintaining, *at least*, that motion, life, and changing souls are to be regarded as truly real; he is thus criticizing the dualistic theory which makes an absolute distinction between 'becoming' and 'being'; and indeed criticizing his own earlier views, if the reference to 'the Friends of the Forms' in 248 a is to be taken as disguised self-designation.[34] The majority of critics, I think, believe that this is all that Plato intended;[35] but there is a minority who go further, and argue that Plato meant to ascribe motion, life, and soul to the ideal world itself;[36] in fact, that he is here recasting his concept of ultimate being.

Without embarking on a full discussion, it seems reasonable to suggest that the truth lies somewhere between the two views. The Stranger's question in 248 e is too striking to be regarded as a mere move in an argument; the phrase τὸ παντελῶς ὄν so naturally suggests 'ideal reality' that it seems artificial to make it mean no more than 'what is indisputably real'; again, one must expect some degree of innovation in the *Sophist*, where Plato has already put forward a respectful but uncompromising criticism of Parmenides, whose reasoning contributed so much to the doctrine of an unchanging ideal world. Such arguments tell in favour of the minority view. On the other hand it must be admitted that this view is not strongly supported by the evidence of the latest dialogues. If Plato's thought on the ideal world had really undergone such a radical revision as Dr. de Vogel suggests, one would expect to find the point made unmistakably clear; whereas it actually rests on rather fine-drawn inferences made by scholars. The *Timaeus* clearly portrays a divine Craftsman who works in imitation of an unchanging model; the alternative, 'non-mythical' notion that the Ideas themselves bring order into the world is much less clearly suggested, as at 50 d, where they are said to play the role of 'Father'. And the world-controlling mind (and

---

[34] So Ross, *PTI*, 105–7, q.v. for other views.

[35] So e.g. Cornford, 245–8; Ross, *PTI*, 110–11; Cherniss, *American Journal of Philology* 78 (1957), 238–9.

[36] So F. Solmsen, *Plato's Theology*, 77 ff.; C. J. de Vogel, *Actes XI Congr. Phil.* (Brussels, 1953), 61 ff., reprinted in her *Philosophia*, 176–82, together with a restatement of her position, 183–209.

soul) which Plato envisages in indisputably late dialogues such
as the *Philebus* and the *Laws*[37] is more easily identified with the
Craftsman than interpreted as a collective term for a system of
living and intelligent Ideas.

Probably, therefore, the Stranger's suggestion is to be regarded
as an *obiter dictum* which Plato put forward quite seriously, but
without realizing its full implications, and which he later qualified
in some degree. Nevertheless the doctrine that life and soul belong to the ideal world was to play an important part in the later
Platonic tradition. It underlies the theory, commonly ascribed to
Antiochus, that the Ideas are to be understood as thoughts of
God;[38] and also the much less familiar theory that they are themselves intelligent.[39] Finally, it appears in the Trinitarian philosophy of Plotinus, whose supreme principle participates in life
and soul, even though his dominant characteristic and proper
title is the One.[40]

The subject of material reality can best be approached by
making a distinction which can be stated quite briefly. Plato, as
we have seen, uses the term *ousia* to denote 'phenomenal reality';
some philosophers, he tells us, hold that this is the only reality
there is; and although he himself introduces the concept of
intelligible reality, that is, of a system of unchanging Forms which
lend to the world of appearances some measure of order and
consistency, his concept of this world remains recognizably
similar to that of the sensationalists. It will not be misleading to
call this a descriptive concept.

Plato further attempts to show, in the *Timaeus*, how the unchanging Forms come to be embodied in the world of appearances.
He postulates a divine Artificer, or Demiurge, who devises the
rational structure of the universe as a copy of the world of Forms.
But to account for this actual universe as we perceive it, he has
to introduce a third principle, which he calls the 'receptacle' and
'nurse' of Becoming (πάσης . . . γενέσεως ὑποδοχὴν αὐτὴν οἷον
τιθήνην, *Timaeus* 49 a). Plato expressly tells us that he thinks this
a difficult and obscure concept which only reason can disclose
(νῦν δὲ ὁ λόγος ἔοικεν εἰσαναγκάζειν χαλεπὸν καὶ ἀμυδρὸν εἶδος

---

[37] *Phileb.* 28 de, 30 cd; *Laws* x. 902 c ff.

[38] See W. Theiler, *Vorbereitung*, 15–17; P. Merlan in *LGP*, 55.

[39] Below, p. 172; cf. E. R. Dodds, *Proclus, the Elements of Theology*, 215.

[40] See P. Hadot, 'Être, vie, pensée chez Plotin et avant Plotin', in *Les Sources de
Plotin* (*EH* 5, 107–41).

ἐπιχείρειν λόγοις ἐμφανίσαι, ibid.) ; we may call it an explanatory concept. It is, he says, not to be identified with any of the four elements; it is 'a form (of being) which is invisible and indefinable (ἄμορφον), all-receiving, and partaking in some very puzzling way of the intelligible, and extremely hard to apprehend' (ibid. 51 a). A little later he gives it the name of χώρα, 'space'.

It seems agreed that Plato's 'receptacle' must not be identified with matter;[41] to quote Cornford (p. 181) 'The Receptacle is not that "out of which" (ἐξ οὖ) things are made ; it is that "in which" (ἐν ᾧ) qualities appear, as fleeting things are seen *in* a mirror.' On the other hand, in introducing this concept Plato uses the comparison of a man moulding and remoulding figures out of gold. The point he is making is that the gold is permanent whereas the figures are not; but the comparison very strongly suggests Aristotle's theory of matter and form, and indeed may well have suggested it to Aristotle himself. Aristotle clearly intends his 'matter' to be that *out of which* things are made, by the imposition of form; and he also improves on Plato by introducing a 'cause of motion', that is, some explanation of why any particular combination of matter and form occurs at one time and not at another. There is, therefore, a real difference, as well as continuity, between Plato's 'space' and Aristotle's 'matter'.

In antiquity, however, the distinction was very soon obscured. Much of Plato's language—the simile of the goldsmith, the description of the Receptacle as 'mother' and 'nurse' of the Forms, and as 'all-receiving'—applies equally well to Aristotle's concept of matter, quite apart from the general disposition to make Plato the authoritative source of all philosophy, which prompted men to reinterpret his teaching in the light of later developments. Plato's 'receptacle' and 'nurse' was soon identified with Aristotle's 'matter'; indeed Aristotle himself credits Plato with this equation.[42] And this confusion soon led to another. Plato, as we have seen, uses the term οὐσία to refer to the phenomenal world, the datum which he sought to account for; he does not use it for the

---

[41] The classical discussion is that of C. Bäumker, *Das Problem der Materie*, 151–88.

[42] See *Physics* iv. 2, 209 b 11, 210 a 1 ; *de Gen. et Corr.* i. 4, 320 a 3, ii. 1, 329 a 13, and discussion by J. B. Skemp in Düring and Owen, 209–10. In Plutarch's *de Animae Procreatione* it appears that χώρα = ὕλη (1024 c) and ὕλη = σῶμα (1023 a) ; cf. also 1014 b–d and 1015 d.

'receptacle', the explanatory concept which forms part of the account. But Aristotle quite commonly uses οὐσία with reference to matter. And this reference can easily, though incorrectly, be read back into Plato, as at 52 c, where he speaks of an image 'clinging to being', οὐσίας ἀντεχομένην, which could be read as 'clinging to matter'. So the identification of Plato's 'receptacle' with Aristotle's 'matter' led to a confusion between two senses of οὐσία, 'reality' (i.e. the phenomenal world) and 'matter'; so that in Hellenistic philosophy phrases like 'perceptible substance', αἰσθητὴ οὐσία, can be used indifferently of the phenomenal world and of the matter which, in theory at least, is postulated to explain it.[43]

In this chapter I have looked at some of Plato's dialogues and have tried to explain the different senses in which he used the word *ousia* within the developing perspective of his theory of Ideas. But a brief note must be added to what has already been said (at p. 40 n. above) on Plato's unwritten doctrines, which can to some extent be recovered by careful study of the allusions and criticisms made by Aristotle, partly in works which survive, but partly in texts which are now lost but can themselves be inferred from statements in later commentators. Not surprisingly, this is a highly controversial subject. In my view, it does not suggest any redraft of the basic senses of *ousia* as already set out; but it does affect the reference of the word. For we have seen that one of the uses of *ousia* was to refer collectively to the realm of Ideas; we must therefore investigate Plato's conception of that realm in its latest form, which the dialogues do not fully reveal. We can also touch on two subjects which will concern us later; the theory of categories, which introduces the largely new and important use of *ousia* as a technical term corresponding to 'substance'; and the origins of the later doctrine of three divine hypostases, or the Neoplatonic Trinity.

In his earlier dialogues Plato was primarily concerned with the contrast between Ideas and sensible particulars; in his later ones he attempted the task of establishing relationships between the Ideas themselves, and deriving them from their source. In the *Republic* he had suggested that they all depend, both for their existence and for their being known, on a single transcendent

---

[43] So e.g. Philo speaks of 'perceptible matter' (αἰσθητὴ ὕλη, *Ebr.* 61) though he also calls it 'obscure, without qualities' (ἄσημος, ἄποιος, *Fuga* 8–9).

Form of the Good; the indirect evidence however suggests that Plato finally came to envisage his ultimate principle under the aspect of unity. What is more surprising, he concluded that this ultimate unity has to be associated with a second principle, which accounts for the diversity of things in the world. These two principles are already foreshadowed in a late dialogue, the *Philebus*, which speaks of 'limit' and 'the unlimited' (16 c–e, 23 cd); the second is commonly referred to as 'the great and small' or 'the indefinite Dyad', though the latter seems to be a shorthand phrase of the Platonic school which cannot be certainly attributed to Plato himself;[44] it represents undefined quantity, which is quantified or calibrated by the imposition of a unit. It must I think be assumed that this arithmetical theory did not spring from a mere shift or contraction of Plato's interests to the problem of the origin of number, but from some sort of prophetic glimpse of the possibility that the derivation of the mathematical Ideas from ideal unity might be the formal pattern which would explain the interrelation of all forms of perfection.

Aristotle tells us that in constructing his chain of derivation Plato assigned a special role to the ideal numbers; that he distinguished these from the mathematical numbers; and that he assigned to the latter an intermediate place between the Ideas and perceptible things.[45] We are also informed, though much less clearly, that Plato sought to derive the ideal numbers from the One and the indefinite Dyad; and again, to make them the source of the other Ideas. This indicates a scheme which can be represented as follows:

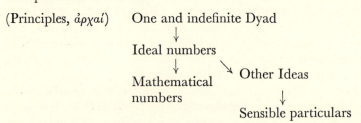

(Principles, ἀρχαί)   One and indefinite Dyad
                           ↓
                      Ideal numbers
                        ↓   ↘ Other Ideas
                   Mathematical
                   numbers   ↓
                            Sensible particulars

But Aristotle's account of Plato's theory is obscured by his polemical aims. In particular, he shows that the distinction between the ideal and the natural numbers was revoked by two

---

[44] Aristotle, *Metaph.* i. 6, 987 b 26, cf. Ross, *PTI*, 184–5.
[45] Ibid. 987 b 14–18; vii. 2, 1028 b 20–2.

eminent Platonists, of whom Speusippus simply denied the existence of the former, while Xenocrates identified the two classes.[46]
Aristotle condemns this last theory;[47] nevertheless many of his
criticisms of Platonism presuppose just such an identification. In
point of fact the distinction seems reasonably clear. The mathematical numbers are timeless realities, like the Ideas; but they
are repeatable, and admit of mathematical operations, addition,
multiplication and the rest, and so can generate other numbers.
The ideal numbers, e.g. duality, as opposed to the number two,
do not allow of repetition or of mathematical relationships.

The derivation of the ideal numbers from the One and the
indefinite Dyad has been studied by a number of eminent
scholars, including Robin, Stenzel, and Ross; it is an austere
subject, and one is inclined to sympathize with the auditors of
Plato's lecture on the Good, who looked for more enlivening
fare. More intriguing, and equally difficult to disentangle, are
the lines of connection leading from the ideal numbers to the
other Ideas. It seems safe to say that a number of different suggestions were advanced by various members of the school, but
never worked into a coherent system. One line of thought which
seems reasonably clear is the derivation of geometrical forms
from numbers, e.g. by connecting the numbers 1–4 respectively
with points, lines, planes, and solids;[48] this could lead naturally
to the mathematical theories of astronomy and of harmony,
whose interest for the school can be divined from *Republic* vii.
524 ff. Another theory, much less attractive to modern critics,
sought to connect the numbers 1–4 with the four mental operations of intellect, knowledge, opinion, and sensation; it was also
suggested that the Idea of living being is compounded of ideal
unity and the three spatial dimensions.[49] Aristotle sometimes
criticizes Plato as if he had thought that the Ideas had a one-
to-one correspondence with the integers from one to ten, and
makes the obvious objection that the Ideas must be far more
numerous.[50] But it seems unlikely that Plato himself can have

---

[46] Evidence and good brief account in Ross, *PTI*, 151–3.

[47] *Metaph*. xiii. 8, 1083 b 3.

[48] *Metaph*. xiv. 3, 1090 b 20–4; cf. vii. 2, 1028 b 25–8 ('others' = Xenocrates?)
and Sextus Empiricus, *adv. Math*. x. 258 (?).

[49] *de Anima* 404 b 20.

[50] *Metaph*. xiii. 8, 1084 a 12 ff.; but note the qualification 'some say'; cf. xii. 8,
1073 a 18–21.

entertained so naïve a view; he may indeed have given a primary place to the simple integers, but explained other significant numbers as multiples or ratios of them;[51] an example might be the explanation, given in the *Timaeus* 35 b–36 b, of the musical tone by the ratio 9:8 and of the semitone by 256:243, i.e. $2^8:3^5$.

Aristotle also propounds, among his series of objections, an argument that, on Plato's reasoning, the Ideas ought to be substances; yet if they are to fulfil the role which Plato assigns to them, they must also be Ideas *of* substances; in other words, only substances can have Ideas corresponding to them.[52] It is fairly clear that this imposes a restriction which Plato never intended; we have seen that he posits Ideas such as that of cold, which later theory would class as a quality; of twoness, a quantity; of equality, a relation; of disease, an affection or state. It is also clear that the objection is invalid; it may perhaps be set out in a somewhat simplified form as follows:

1) Particular *x*'s participate in the *X* itself.
2) The *X* itself is accidentally eternal (i.e. *qua* Idea, not *qua X*).
3) The *x*'s participate in the eternal only accidentally.
4) But they participate in the *X* itself non-accidentally (i.e. *qua X*).
5) Therefore they participate in the *X* itself as a substance.
6) Therefore each *x* must be a substance.

The fallacy depends upon using the term 'accidentally' ($\kappa\alpha\tau\grave{\alpha}$ $\sigma\upsilon\mu\beta\epsilon\beta\eta\kappa\acute{o}s$) in a specialized sense, in which it is *not* opposed to 'substance' as a category-word, so that 'not accidentally' does not point to substance rather than to the other categories;[53] but the concluding steps also involve and illustrate the ill-defined sense of the word *ousia* at this stage of its history. As we have shown, Plato uses it to denote the Ideas, which he sees as the 'true being' of all kinds of phenomena, things, qualities, actions, what you will; thus if a man walks, he participates in the Idea of walking, which is the 'true being' and pattern of this behaviour. But Aristotle passes lightly from this sense of *ousia* to

---

[51] *Metaph.* i. 9, 991 b 13–22; xiv. 5, 1092 b 13–15.

[52] Ibid. 990 b 23–991 a 8.

[53] It seems to apply to everything except the genera etc. to which its subject belongs; thus e.g. trios participate in number, in an Idea, not accidentally; but in properties of numbers, of Ideas, accidentally.

that other, in which it is used to distinguish the permanent *this-worldly* factor in the situation, the man, from his behaviour, the walking. In the chapter that follows, we shall find that his question 'What is it?' shows a similar duality of use. But the objection does nevertheless show up a weakness inherent in Plato's conception. If there is to be an Idea of, say, disease, it should be a timeless reality like the other Ideas; but it cannot also be a perfect and prototypical *example* of disease unless it is occasional and accidental and parasitic.

Among the texts which bear on Plato's unwritten doctrines there are two which describe a primitive categorial theory:[54] realities are divided into Absolutes, Opposites, and Relatives. This theory throws some light on the origins of Aristotle's own treatment of the categories, although his system is quite differently constructed. Plato's first class evidently corresponds to Aristotle's 'substance', and 'man' and 'horse' are in fact among the examples given—though perhaps through later comparison with the *Categories*. But in Aristotle's system Opposites are not treated as a category, but as a feature to be observed, or noted as absent, *in* various categories, the first four being discussed in detail, and two others in brief. The Relative, for Aristotle, is a category; but the criteria for belonging to it are extremely ill defined; thus it seems that what is 'more or less', i.e. indefinite in quantity or degree, belongs *eo ipso* to this category; though Aristotle also wants to make 'allowing of more and less', or not doing so, into a feature of various categories. And in general, the Relative is an extremely miscellaneous and elastic category; it overlaps[55] with substance (8 a 13 ff.), with quality (5 b 30, 6 a 10), with quality (11 a 20 ff., cf. 37) and with position (6 b 11), which is what we should expect it to do if it were a 'feature'. Aristotle's work thus shows traces of two different principles of division, so that the one which he ostensibly adopts is not fully disentangled from an earlier Platonic scheme.

The Neo-Platonic Trinity can be given only the briefest mention at this stage. Understandably there has been much debate on the degree of support it can claim from Plato's genuine writings, and rightly or wrongly some critics have claimed that

---

[54] Simplicius, *in Phys.* 247. 30 ff.; Sextus Empiricus, *adv. Math.* x. 263–5.

[55] 'Overlaps' covers two cases: either it is uncertain whether some *x* belongs to one or the other category, or it is agreed that it belongs to both.

texts which seem to support it cannot be genuine. I believe my-self that the conception comes from a convergence of several distinct lines of thought, one of which connects with the topics just lately reviewed. Plato, as we have seen, sought to derive all reality from the One and the indefinite Dyad; but in later writers we find the view that this pair itself presupposes the existence of a prior, non-relative One, distinct from the One contrasted with plurality. This theory clearly draws upon the double treatment of the One given by Plato, probably for quite different purposes, in the *Parmenides*; it claimed support from texts in which Plato spoke of a single, not a dual, ultimate source; and it allied itself with some other indications of a three-level structure of transcendent reality. But I am convinced that the whole development is more complex than has ever yet been recognized; I may hope to try to describe it on another occasion.

III

ARISTOTLE: THE *CATEGORIES* AND THE *METAPHYSICS*

(i) *The* Categories

ARISTOTLE's views on substance have to be gathered mainly from two works, the *Categories* and the *Metaphysics*. These two contrast very strikingly in scale and treatment, the *Categories* being brief and deceptively simple in style, whereas the *Metaphysics* is long, complex and obscure. Both of them, however, raise important problems of interpretation and criticism, and each has to be considered in the light of the other.

Commentators seeking a consistent body of doctrine in the *Metaphysics* have puzzled for centuries over the apparent diversity of views it expresses. More recently it has seemed possible to find at least a partial solution on historical lines, the most notable exponent of this theory being W. Jaeger. Jaeger claimed that the *Metaphysics* was put together piecemeal over a number of years and never fully revised, so that in different parts it records Aristotle's thought at various stages of development. This development is seen as a fairly straightforward progression away from the Platonist standpoint of his early years, leading from idealist philosophy via critical metaphysics to a final stage at which Aristotle abandoned philosophy for science. The *Metaphysics* then belongs to the middle range of this development; in Books I and II, indeed, Aristotle can still write as a rather radical member of the Platonist school, whereas in some other contexts he is clearly arguing from the opposite camp. This hypothesis promised to illuminate the study of the *Metaphysics*; on the other hand it brought the *Categories* under suspicion; for the doctrine of substance found there is far removed from Platonism, yet there are good reasons for thinking it a fairly early work.

Jaeger seems to have been largely right in the relative dating which he assigns to the several books of the *Metaphysics*, but to have given too simple a picture of Aristotle's philosophical development, especially in its later stages. On his view the whole of the *Metaphysics* has to be assigned to the middle period of Aristotle's career (say 348–334 B.C.) and the biological works to the final period (334–323). Various reasons combine to discredit this chronology, and some modern scholars have practically reversed it: the biological works, except the *de Generatione Animalium*, belong in the main to the middle period, and the *Metaphysics*, apart from Books I, II, and XIV, to the latest.[1] This suggests that Aristotle retained his interest in metaphysics to the end, and that his latest pronouncements made some important concessions to Platonism; and it may also be right to regard the *Categories* as a genuine work, but one which belongs to a phase of abrupt reaction against Platonism which Aristotle later modified.[2] For our purpose it remains to note that the doctrine of substance found in the *Categories* appears to differ from what is found in the other works; it is in fact unique in expressing the distinction between individual and universal as a distinction between two senses of οὐσία.

In antiquity the authorship of the *Categories* was not disputed; but its interpretation was already a matter for controversy in early Christian times, and the controversy has been revived in the past two centuries. The book was adversely criticized by Eudorus, Lucius, and Nicostratus and, more notably, by Plotinus. On the other hand its more sympathetic interpreters could not agree whether it belongs primarily to metaphysics or to logic; whether it deals with the fundamental divisions of reality, or with the divisions of words and terms (φωναί, λέξεις). Porphyry proposed what was in effect a compromise solution which held the field for many centuries, though one cannot say that it is consistently maintained; the *Categories* is concerned primarily with words, though not in the same way as grammar or literary criticism; rather, it considers the natural divisions of our language as reflecting a corresponding division in the order of nature; indirectly, therefore, it contributes to our theory of the universe.

An attractive suggestion thrown up by the revival of this controversy is that the critics have attributed to Aristotle a decision

---

[1] See Ross in Düring and Owen, *Aristotle and Plato in the mid-fourth century*, esp. 10–16.

[2] De Vogel, ibid. 255–6, dates it *c.* 347. But its relationship to the early books of the *Metaphysics* remains puzzling on this view. I. Düring (*Aristoteles*, 49) puts it much earlier, 360–55; cf. also G. E. L. Owen in Düring and Owen, 164.

which he never envisaged. An excellent summary by Professor Kneale[3] concludes that 'Aristotle was almost certainly unaware of the ambiguity which puzzles his commentators. He had almost certainly not asked himself the question, "Does the sign ἄνθρωπος ... stand for the Greek word ἄνθρωπος or for some extra-linguistic entity?".' Kneale continues, 'If, however, he had been able to ask the question, Aristotle would almost certainly have answered that he was dealing with things and not with words.' This, I think, is a good estimate of Aristotle's general position; but it might be more accurate to say, not that he never asked the question, but that he frequently ignores it. Thus we find a fairly clear distinction suggested at 1 a 16–20, between 'things which are' and 'things which are said'; but we also find ambiguous expressions like 'a substance is said'; and passages in which substances are said to 'signify' something, as if they were words or expressions; examples occur at 2 a 31 and at 3 b 10, where Professor Ackrill comments, 'It was careless of him to speak as if it were substances (and not names of substances) which signify.'

For our present purpose the most important passage in the book is that in which Aristotle distinguishes between the so-called primary substance and secondary substance, which must be set out in full:

Οὐσία δέ ἐστιν, ἡ κυριώτατά τε καὶ πρώτως καὶ μάλιστα λεγομένη, ἡ μήτε καθ' ὑποκειμένου τινὸς λέγεται, μήτε ἐν ὑποκειμένῳ τινί ἐστιν, οἷον ὁ τὶς ἄνθρωπος ἢ ὁ τὶς ἵππος. δεύτεραι δὲ οὐσίαι λέγονται, ἐν οἷς εἴδεσιν αἱ πρώτως οὐσίαι λεγόμεναι ὑπάρχουσι, ταῦτά τε καὶ τὰ τῶν εἰδῶν τούτων γένη· οἷον ὁ τὶς ἄνθρωπος ἐν εἴδει μὲν ὑπάρχει τῷ ἀνθρώπῳ, γένος δὲ τοῦ εἴδους ἐστὶ τὸ ζῷον. δεύτεραι οὖν αὗται λέγονται οὐσίαι, οἷον ὅ τε ἄνθρωπος καὶ τὸ ζῷον.

Substance—what is most properly and primarily and especially so called—is what is neither said of a subject nor in a subject; e.g. this man, or this horse. What are called secondary substances are the species in which are the things primarily called substances, together with the genera of these species; for instance, this man belongs in the species, man, but the genus of the species is animal; these, then, are called secondary substances—for instance, man, and animal.

The imprecision we have mentioned is clearly present in this text; it would be easy to render the opening words: 'The term "substance", in its most proper ... sense is ... said' etc. But the

3 *The Development of Logic* (Oxford, 1962), 25–32.

context shows that Aristotle intends to speak about things rather than words. His meaning, then, is that *what is most properly called* οὐσία is the individual entity, for instance this man, So-and-so; not the phrase 'this man', nor the name 'So-and-so', nor indeed the character or individuality of So-and-so (though this will need further discussion), but simply the man himself. The phrases 'neither said of a subject nor in a subject' are meant to distinguish these individual entities, or 'primary substances', from the species and genera to which they belong (which are 'said of them') and from other attributes, states, and the like (which are 'in them'). The species and genera, called 'secondary substances', can both be described (e.g. 'man is rational') and be used for description, as when they are 'said of' individuals; e.g. 'Socrates is a man'. Used in this latter way they are, in Aristotle's view, a means of saying *what* Socrates is, that is, of determining his place in the fundamental classification of things; and this, of course, is fixed and invariable. The categories other than substance are used to state facts about Socrates (or 'things which are "in" Socrates'), many of which are true at one time but not at another, e.g. 'Socrates is pale', 'is lying down', etc. But Socrates has other characteristics which do not vary (e.g. 'two-footed', 'snubnosed'), which Aristotle calls 'differentia' or 'properties';[4] and he does not draw satisfactory distinctions between secondary substances, properties, and some other attributes which he assigns (e.g.) to the category of quality. Thus sweetness is a quality, and honey is invariably sweet, though wine need not be; why then is sweetness not a 'property' of honey? Would this mean that it could not be called a quality? And why is 'man' not a 'quality' of Socrates, if it can be described as 'the sort of thing' (ποιόν τι) that Socrates is?[5]

These problems show that Aristotle has not been wholly successful in establishing the system of categories as a watertight classification. Part of the trouble is that he fails to give a satisfactory account of quality; he *enumerates* four kinds of quality, but the only criterion he proposes for this category (11 a 15 ff.) is that things *resemble* one another in quality; and this is unhelp-

---

[4] These seems to be alternative terms in Aristotle's early works; in the later system, differentia help to classify things, properties do not.

[5] *Categ.* 5. 3 b 15. For 'quality' used to refer to species, or its differentia, cf. *Topics* iv. 2, 122 b 16; iv. 6, 128 a 26; *Physics* v. 2, 226 a 27; *Metaph.* v. 14, 1020 a 33.

ful, since it merely makes the verbal point that things are 'like' (ὅμοιοι) because they are 'suchlike' (ποιοί). But similar problems arise with other categories, which we cannot hope to consider in this condensed account. And there is the standing difficulty that Aristotle uses the same phrase 'What is it?', sometimes as a distinguishing mark of one category, namely substance, sometimes to assign items to any category; he further explains, in some other works, that an answer in terms of substance is the best and proper answer—which presupposes that others are possible; but, as we shall see (p. 68 below), he does not clearly acknowledge that the question can be asked in cases which exclude this kind of competition.

Aristotle's general description of substance seems at first sight fairly clear. 'Substances do not have degrees or contraries; a man is not more a man at one time, less at another, as something is now hotter, now colder; and there is no antipode to man, as black is the antipode of white, or hot of cold'; its truly distinctive feature, however, is that a substance is capable of contrary qualifications: 'a man can change from being good to being bad without ceasing to be that man.'[6] But objections could be made. Thus the condition of having no degrees might be thought too restrictive. It is of course true that 'x is a man' is a statement to which we should never add 'very' or 'fairly'; yet it may depend on criteria (such as rationality) which are matters of degree, even if there is a critical point at which it becomes proper to make the unqualified statement. Aristotle no doubt had biological species in mind, and considered them fixed and distinct; he writes as if the answer to the question 'Is this an x?' should always be a clear 'Yes' or 'No'; whereas we have grown up with theories of evolution and intergrading, and are prepared for such answers as 'Yes, but not a very typical case', or again, 'The criteria are still under discussion.' On the other hand, it may be that the condition of admitting contrary determinations is not peculiar to substance; for it is certainly allowable to say, 'This place is hotter (colder) than it was'; and I am not clear that this has to be construed, 'The things in this place are hotter than they were', or, if necessary, '. . . are hotter than the things that used to be here used to be.'[7]

[6] *Categ.* 3 b 24 ff., as summarized by Anscombe and Geach, *Three Philosophers*, 9.
[7] Cf. J. L. Ackrill, *Aristotle's* Categories, 89–90.

On one point, however, Aristotle's suggested distinction between substance and the other categories has been commonly misunderstood. As we have noted, predications in the category of substance are held to characterize a thing by predicates which invariably attach to it; the other categories include large classes of predicates which apply only 'accidentally', which are not necessary or invariable. But not all of them can be accidental; for a statement such as '*x* is a man' ascribes a character which can be analysed and defined; and in defining it we have to use the other categories. If '*x* is a man' means '*x* is a featherless biped', then the category of quantity has to be brought into the definition; it is an essential predication that *x* has two feet. This point was obscured by some of Aristotle's early commentators, who treated the system of categories as divisible into substance and accidents.[8] Taking 'accidents' in its normal sense,[9] this implies that the other categories are *always* used to refer to variable conditions or states, with the absurd result that a substance now appears to have no properties at all in its own right; it becomes merely the abstract notion of a possessor of accidents. Undoubtedly some of the modern objections to the whole concept of substance are aimed at this caricature; but we cannot pursue this further at present.

We may therefore return to the passage I have quoted from *Categories* 5. Aristotle is here contrasting the individual with the species and genus. But in what respect are they contrasted? Is there an implied contrast between two subjects of the verb εἶναι, or between two predicates of it? Between two orders of things-that-are, or between two orders of what-things-are? The predicative interpretation would suggest that the πρώτη οὐσία is the perfect answer to the question 'What is it?' If, say, we are trying to identify an intruder in a darkened room, then 'a man' is a better answer than 'an animal', but 'Socrates' satisfies us completely. And this thought is not far from Aristotle's mind, since he says that the species is a better characterization of the individual than the genus (2 b 7 ff.) and also (misleadingly) that the individual is related to the species as that is to the genus (2 b 17–18)—which might well suggest that the πρώτη οὐσία is that which perfectly characterizes an (unknown or imperfectly known) individual, that which exactly states what a thing is. On the other hand we have what seems to be an explicit statement at the outset of the chapter that the primary substance does *not* function as a predicate; and later, that all other determinations are either contained in it or predicated of it (2 b 5–6); so that 'if there were no primary substances it is impossible there could be anything else' (Μὴ οὐσῶν οὖν τῶν πρώτων οὐσιῶν ἀδύνατον τῶν ἄλλων τι εἶναι). Here I think we must take οὐσῶν and εἶναι in an existential sense; and, although Aristotle's thought is far from clear, I am inclined to think that this is the consideration which most influenced him in describing the individual as πρώτη οὐσία. So far as this is accepted, we can express his point by saying that individuals *exist* in their own right whereas universals in some sense depend upon them; or even that the individual exists in the true sense of the word, whereas ὁ ἄνθρωπος, Man, exists only in the secondary sense that instances of it exist. In any case it is clear that Aristotle is criticizing the Platonic view which treats the universal as a timeless transcendent being which is more real than its instances.

The concept of 'secondary substance' has a further ambiguity. If we say, 'Man is predicated of Socrates', the statement may be interpreted either to mean that Socrates has the characteristics which constitute him a man, or that he belongs to the class of beings so constituted. Clearly in this instance there is no practical advantage in deciding which interpretation to choose, since the two propositions entail each other. But there is every reason for disliking a terminology which blurs the distinction between 'human characteristics' and 'the human race'; and while the English word 'humanity' can mean either, we rightly feel that there is a difference of sense. It might be added that this distinction could well have been brought out by the use of the words γένος and εἶδος. In their normal usage γένος (genus) stands for a broader classification, εἶδος (species) for a narrower; for instance 'animal' and 'man'. But neglecting this distinction, which Aristotle himself often ignores, it seems that γένος, 'race', is well adapted to stand for a class of beings, who are marked off by possessing a distinctive εἶδος, or specific form. And Aristotle makes some approach to this usage in *Metaphysics* vii, since γένος is used for 'genus *or* species', and εἶδος, when identified with τὸ τί ἦν εἶναι, means 'specific character'. But this convention was not followed up; and we shall continue to use 'genus' and 'species' in their conventional senses, which on the whole come down in favour of a collective interpretation.

The *Categories* does not use the phrase 'the οὐσία of *x*', and it is not obvious what purpose the phrase would serve within its system of assumptions. We can keep close to Aristotle's expressed thought if we say that the species, man, is the οὐσία of Socrates; so, less properly, is the genus, animal. But on the interpretation we have given, the context 'οὐσία of *x*' *precludes* us from taking οὐσία in the sense 'πρώτη οὐσία'. In this sense of οὐσία, Socrates *is* the οὐσία in question, and 'the οὐσία of Socrates' would be merely a misleading equivalent for 'the individual, Socrates'. But it must be admitted that Aristotle is not perfectly consistent; he says, for instance, 'All substance appears to *signify* that which is individual' (πᾶσα δὲ οὐσία δοκεῖ τόδε τι σημαίνειν, 3 b 10), where the use of the term 'signify' shows that he is now thinking of a name or a term, for instance the name 'Socrates', which does signify the individual man Socrates. Further, even if one proceeds on the assumption that the *Categories* is concerned with things and not with words, it is still *possible* to argue that by πρώτη οὐσία Aristotle means not merely the individual Socrates, nor the name 'Socrates', but the individual character of Socrates, his 'essence' or 'quiddity', which is in the requisite sense a thing.[10] As we shall see, Aristotle does use the phrase πρώτη οὐσία in the *Metaphysics* in a way which lends colour to this suggestion, and makes it attractive to those who think it important to harmonize the two works. And it has this much justification, that we do use 'thing-language' for what is strictly speaking a determinate set of characteristics which can be realized in different media. 'Shakespeare wrote Hamlet' has important similarities with 'Brutus killed Caesar'.

Before leaving the *Categories* it may be worth noting a few loose ends in Aristotle's argument. First, he explains the distinction between individuals, species, and genera only in connection with substances. Yet there are passing references to individual items in other categories (e.g. 'this colour', 4 a 14); and, as we shall see, there is no reason to doubt that they can be generalized. But Aristotle does not explain what kind of classification they

---

[10] So, apparently, B. Jones, 1975, esp. pp. 168–9.

would admit; and one would think that the prospects of success are very varied; thus diseases, in the category of 'affections', could be classified more easily than tastes, in that of quality; or, working from the other end, a category such as 'posture' seems uninterestingly narrow, while that of relation seems embarrassingly ill-defined.

Again, the *Categories* does not present the classical scheme of differentia, properties, and accidents; these too, one might think, need not be confined to substances. Aristotle does indeed suggest, in effect, that only substances have accidents; but we have seen reason to query this; the same place may be, now hot, now cold; the same disease may be, now acute, now slight. There are, of course, some defects in his terminology which were never corrected; thus he has no word which refers unambiguously to attributes which are invariable but *not* peculiar to their possessor.

Once again, Aristotle does not recognize the existence of varieties within a species; and he does not comment on differences between individuals; so far as I can see, his remarks would be perfectly applicable if all individuals within a species were indistinguishable, or at any rate if they had only a minimum of distinguishing marks, like a numbered series of rifles or cars. Aristotle's choice of commonplace examples, and his use of the term 'primary substance' to denote the individual, might perhaps have suggested a view of the *Categories* as a sober, non-speculative work which could be a deliberately simplified primer written by a mature thinker. But its rather crude terminology suggests immaturity rather than deliberate simplification. There is little sign that this book represents a more considered view than appears in the *Metaphysics*, or one influenced by the scientific enterprises of Aristotle's later years; though such assumptions have occasionally been made by empiricists who wish to claim Aristotle as their ally and precursor, not to mention those scholars whose sense of symmetry disposes them to see in him the polar antithesis of Plato.

(ii) Metaphysics *VII–VIII: Structure and Vocabulary*

In passing from the *Categories* to the *Metaphysics* one encounters whole new ranges of problems. The literary structure of the book is complex and hard to establish; the theories of substance presented in the several parts of it vary greatly in subtlety and power; the terminology employed is far from consistent; and a further complication is introduced by Aristotle's dialectical method of argument, which leads him not only to report, but to develop, theories whose value he suspects. It has to be remembered that he was not merely investigating at leisure; he was attempting to reach his conclusions by means of a criticism of Plato's views, and to uphold them in debate with rival interpretations and developments of Platonism, which from the first was anything but a static body of doctrine. Plato, the rival Platonists, and Aristotle himself were all subject to change; and differences of standpoint are detectable in the various parts of the *Metaphysics*.[11] It follows that though this is a work of fundamental importance, which Christian theology later recognized, it is almost impossible to present it in outline; and we should be prepared to find that it had little direct influence on the early Christian fathers. Nevertheless acquaintance with it is indispensable if one is to understand the notion of substance as explained in the simplified metaphysics of the Stoics and Middle Platonists, whose works they preferred.

We must first give some impression of its over-all structure.

The *Metaphysics* is clearly not a work prepared for publication; but neither is it a mere posthumous collection of philosophical papers. Four books of it can indeed be set apart as separate fragments or occasional pieces, namely II, a brief report of a lecture; V, a philosophical dictionary; XI, a briefer version of III, IV, VI; and XII, a synopsis which contains a valuable section on theology. These are all authentic, but have been incorporated by later editors. The rest display some sort of sequence, and probably contain the notes used by Aristotle for his lectures on metaphysics towards the close of his career. I, III, and IV belong together, I being a critical survey of previous work on the subject, III outlining the problems of the 'first philosophy', and IV beginning to discuss them. Aristotle's reflections on substance,

---

[11] Note also that there are two methods of referring to its fourteen books:

I	II	III	IV	V	VI	VII	VIII	IX	X	XI	XII	XIII	XIV
= A	a	B	Γ	Δ	E	Z	H	Θ	I	K	Λ	M	N

Occasionally the Greek letters are named; thus *Beta* = III (N.B.), *Gamma* = IV, *Delta* = V, *Lambda* = XII.

however, are best displayed in Books VII, VIII, and IX,[12] which form a sequence in themselves, but have only a sketchy connection with the earlier books. I am inclined to think that Aristotle developed this part of his work into a separate course of lectures, making use of older material but not exactly following the programme outlined in III. These three books are by no means homogeneous; but taken as a whole they represent a more critical approach to 'first philosophy' than III–IV, and may well have displaced an earlier discussion. Subsequently they were incorporated in the larger work, and the short Book VI was added in an attempt to provide a transition. Of the remaining books, X, on being and unity, overlaps in its subject matter with VII–IX, but has no literary connection with them; while XIII and XIV contain two parallel criticisms of Plato's theory of Ideas; the second of these, beginning at XIII. 9, 1086 a 21, is really the earlier, and resembles I in that Aristotle appears to be criticizing the Platonist school from the inside; in the later discussion of XIII. 1–9 he adopts an independent standpoint.

These conclusions are in the main those of Jaeger; and I would accept his judgement that Books VII–IX were developed independently (see his *Aristotle*, 194–204)—unless perhaps they were introduced by material which has not survived.[13] But his conception of the three books themselves seems oversimplified. Apart from three chapters (VII. 12, VIII. 6 and IX. 4) and some briefer passages, which can easily be detached as later additions (*Entstehungsgeschichte*, 49–62), he seems to have regarded them as a unified composition, although VII and VIII were originally separate from IX.[14] It also appears that he thought of Book VII, minus Chapter 12, as a unity (ibid., 59, 61: 'ein zweiteiliges, grosangelegtes Vorlesungswerk über die Substanz'). I would argue that this book, though it has been given a presentable

---

[12] But see also the 'dictionary article', V. 8, and some remarks in the 'theological' Book XII. These books may have been consulted by writers who did not use the *Metaphysics* as a whole. They are likely to have circulated separately, since we hear of an edition of the *Metaphysics* in *ten* books, presumably excluding II, V, XI, and XII.

[13] There is some force in the argument of J. Owens that VII–IX *presuppose* introductory matter such as is now found in V, even if V was only incorporated in the *Metaphysics* long after Aristotle's time; see his *Doctrine of Being*, 86–8 (35–6).

[14] Op. cit., 109: 'Bücher Ζ–Θ, die zwei ursprünglich selbständige Abhandlungen bilden', presumably VII+VIII and IX; *Aristotle*, 201: 'Books Z and H, which form a single whole'.

arrangement, embodies materials of various dates and origins. Even Fr. J. Owens, in general a conservative critic, concedes that Chapters 7–9 'may have been written earlier than or independently of' 1–6;[15] but 10 and 11 have some stylistic similarities with 7–9; 13–16 seem to form a discrete block; and 17, as Aristotle himself remarks, makes a new beginning independent of the immediately preceding matter.

Not all these conclusions are generally accepted, and there is certainly no agreed outline of Aristotle's philosophical development in its later phases. So it will be necessary to look closely at the text of *Metaphysics* VII–VIII in the discussion that follows, which will be arranged on this plan:

The setting of Aristotle's discussion of substance (pp. 66–71).
Explanation of the most important terms (pp. 71–7).
The argument of VII and VIII in outline (pp. 77–9).
Critical discussion of VII. 4 ff.; individual and specific form (pp. 79–86).

In the *Metaphysics* Aristotle sets himself to investigate 'being'; but he does not seem always to have conceived his task in precisely the same manner. In some passages, notably in Book III, his question 'What is being?' could be paraphrased 'What does reality comprise?', and his main problem seems to be whether there is a world of eternal realities set over against the perceptible world. Alternatively, we might say that he considers a particular kind of being whose status is debatable. But in the following books Aristotle seems to have altered his programme, and to be investigating, not a particular kind of being, but the general notion of being as such. Jaeger saw this contrast in treatment as reflecting a change in his point of view; the young Aristotle was preoccupied with questions about a transcendent world which arose directly out of Platonic philosophy; the more independent and theoretical discussions belong to his middle or later life.

Recent research has suggested that this contrast may have been too sharply drawn. In his most thoroughgoing discussions it does not seem that Aristotle is working with the notion of being as a pure universal which is equally well represented by any of its instances; rather, there are some entities which are beings *par excellence*. On the other hand it is not obvious that Aristotle used

---

[15] *Doctrine of Being*, 358 (392), n. 45.

such criteria to single out divine being for a supreme position; so there is still much to be said for the view that he moved from an earlier conception of his work, in which theological concerns were relatively dominant and pervasive, to a later one, more occupied with problems of logic and categorial theory, in which the gods were assigned to a limited enclave. Certainly the work as we now have it does not fulfil the promise of being a theology;[16] theological discussion is almost confined to Book XII, which falls outside the main scheme and is a masterly but brief sketch of Aristotle's philosophy as a whole.

On the other hand, at some comparatively early period Aristotle seems to have thought that there can be no science of being as such, arguing that there is no class of things which simply 'are'.[17] In recent years Professor G. E. L. Owen has argued most persuasively that Aristotle met this objection by developing a theory of 'focal meaning', so that some things can be said to 'be' par excellence, and others can be considered in relation to them. On this view the 'programmatic' books IV and VI represent a phase of renewed confidence in the possibility of a science of pure being, but without showing any sustained intention of putting theology back in the centre of the picture; and it remains true that these books envisage a rather more specialized role for first philosophy than do the books which are arranged to follow them and which develop the argument.

Aristotle therefore devotes his most painstaking analyses, not to inquiring what sort of things there are, but what may be meant by saying that something 'is'. In the *Metaphysics* he produces several roughly similar classifications of 'being' (v. 7, vi. 2, xi. 8–9), from which it appears that the most important use of 'is' is in sentences which declare the 'substance' of things. A typical scheme (cf. v. 7) is:

(1) Accidental being (e.g. 'The builder is cultured', in that X is both cultured and a builder).

(2) Absolute being
    (a) in the category of SUBSTANCE (e.g. 'X is a man').
    (b, c, d . . .) in other categories (e.g. 'X is white', 'X is tall').

---

[16] See xi. 7, 1064 b 3. XI is probably an early book. Cf. also vi. 1, 1026 a 19.
[17] See e.g. *Metaph.* i. 9, 992 b 18–24; xiv. 2, 1088 b 35 ff.; *EE* i. 8, 1217 b 25–35.

(3) Being as truth (e.g. 'That is so').
(4) Potential *versus* actual being (e.g. '*X* is keen-sighted' *versus* '*X* is now seeing clearly').

This table is a little surprising both for what it includes and for what it omits. The third and fourth items are important, but need not detain us here. The first involves a tiresome inconsistency, since Aristotle often applies the phrase 'accidental being', not to cases where two predicates accidentally coincide, but to cases where one predicate is possessed 'accidentally', e.g. '*X* is cultured', which is hard to distinguish from 2(b); though again the *commonest* use of 'accident' is to refer to variable or non-necessary predicates, which would not fall within 'absolute being'. Item (2) is clearly the heart of the table, and may be compared with passages like the opening paragraph of Book VII, where Aristotle says that the question 'What is it?' is answered by identifying the object in question or saying what kind of thing it is, rather than by stating its size, condition, relations, etc. But the distinction drawn in the *Categories* between πρώτη οὐσία and δευτέρα οὐσία is not mentioned; nor is the fact that predications in *other* categories may be more or less specific. And this leads to a complication which will concern us later;[18] for the statement (e.g.) 'it is green' might refer to 'this gate' or to 'this colour' or to 'viridian'. The second possibility is ill defined; but in the first case 'it is green' fails to show 'what it is' in the strictest sense, in which 'it is a gate' succeeds. But '*viridian* is green', or 'is a green', though Aristotle calls it a predication of quality, does 'show what viridian is'; and so again do the more general predications '. . . is a colour', '. . . is a quality'. It is the best available designation, and as such presents some analogy with 'it is a gate'; indeed on occasion Aristotle will even use the word 'substance' to indicate the category to which something belongs, *whatever that may be.*

On the other hand, the table ignores some important distinctions which modern logicians would certainly wish to stress, and which Aristotle himself partly recognizes in other works. It is disconcerting to find no separate place assigned to the 'is' which indicates an identity, nor to the 'is' which represents 'exists', 'is real'; and these omissions are fairly characteristic. Aristotle never

18 See p. 137 below.

makes a complete break with the theory that 'is', *wherever* it occurs, denotes some kind of identity; this is very clearly illustrated in v. 6, where he includes examples of 'accidental being' as part of his article on *unity*. On the other hand he also tends to argue as if all predications have some kind of existential significance, so that 'being so-and-so' is regarded as a qualified form of 'being' absolutely, that is, of existence.

Thus when Aristotle talks about οὐσία, the noun is sometimes roughly equivalent to ὅ ἔστι, with ὅ as subject: 'something that is', or 'that is so-and-so'; but sometimes roughly to τί ἐστι, with τί as predicate, i.e. 'what something is'. And 'the οὐσία of *x*', though apparently it seldom means simply 'the fact of *x*'s existence', can mean something very like 'the manner of *x*'s existence', which on Aristotle's assumptions is difficult to distinguish from 'the kind of thing *x* is'.[19] Indeed 'the οὐσία of *x*' sometimes seems as if it derived from some non-existent causative tense of εἶναι; it is a vaguely defined ἀρχή τις καὶ αἰτία, that which *makes x* be what it is.[20]

Book vii begins with the statement that being, τὸ ὄν, has several senses; it may signify τί ἐστι καὶ τόδε τι (literally, 'what-it-is and this so-and-so'), or it may signify quality or quantity or one of the other categories. Its primary sense, however, is τὸ τί ἐστιν, which signifies substance, οὐσία. We have noted the imprecision involved in saying that being 'signifies' something, and have also seen that the phrase 'what-it-is' cannot be interpreted exactly; but it is worth also remarking at the outset that a 'τόδε τι' by no means always means, as one might suppose, a particular individual object; it can mean a particular shape or form or character.[21] This verbal point reflects the much wider standpoint of the *Metaphysics* as compared with the *Categories*; whereas the latter concentrates on sensible particulars and the classes into which they fall, the *Metaphysics* gives much attention to pure forms and mathematical objects; see, for instance, vii. 10, 1036 a 1 ff.: the circle; the soul; this circle (in geometry); this circular object.

Aristotle next follows his usual practice by reviewing the

---

[19] See below, p. 74; Aristotle identifies *x*'s οὐσία as its ἐνέργεια, understood as the pattern of action displayed by the species as such; for criticism, see pp. 87–8.

[20] See vii. 17, 1041 a 9; cf. p. 70 below.

[21] See Bonitz, *Index Aristotelicus*, s.v. ὅδε, and cf. Ross, *Aristotle's Metaphysics* i, p. lxxxviii.

opinions commonly held about substance; his treatment in vii. 2 is broadly similar to those given at v. 8 and in the recapitulation in viii. 1. Combining these accounts, one can set out the possible claimants to the title 'substance' in a table:

> *Those generally accepted*
> Physical elements
> Physical structures (plants, animals, etc.)
> Parts of these
>
> *
>
> *Those accepted by some*
> Component 'parts', e.g. in mathematics
> The Forms, conceived as separable particulars
>
> *Those established by argument*
> The following conceptions, very variously treated:—
> 'Essence' and 'substrate'
> Matter, form, concrete whole
> Individual and universal

* At this point v. 8 inserts 'cause of being, e.g. soul', which is lacking in vii. 2 and viii. 1; but for substance as cause, see vii. 17, 1041 a 9, viii. 2, 1043 a 2, etc.; for soul as substance, vii. 10, 1035 b 14–15; 11, 1037 a 5; viii. 3, 1043 a 35; and cf. *de Anima* ii. 4.

Clearly the third group of conceptions embodies Aristotle's own views; but in Book vii these conceptions are handled in a peculiar sequence. We are told in vii. 3 that 'substance' may mean:

(1) 'Essence', τὸ τί ἦν εἶναι
(2) 'Universal', τὸ καθόλου
(3) 'Genus', τὸ γένος
(4) 'Substrate', τὸ ὑποκείμενον, which may be identified, (a) with the matter, ὕλη, e.g. bronze; or (b) with the shape, μορφή; or (c) with the combination of the two, τὸ σύνολον, e.g. the bronze statue.

The argument that follows is basically a process of elimination, but is complicated by digressions and changes of plan. Aristotle begins with the fourth claimant, 'substrate'; but 4(a) is the only case which he considers at length (1029 a 10 ff.); then both this and 4(c), the concrete whole, are summarily dismissed, and the argument seems to be leading to a discussion of 'shape', 4(b); but instead there follows, in Chapters 4–12, a long and inconclusive discussion of 'essence'. In 13–16 Aristotle disposes of the second claimant, the universal, and it appears that his criticisms are meant to exclude the genus also, since it is not separately discussed; and in a final chapter he attempts from a different starting-point to show that it is essence which is substance, this line of argument being continued in Book viii. Here, however, when he resumes the discussion of concrete objects, the concepts of essence and form are largely displaced by that of actuality, ἐνέργεια.

Something must now be said about the series of terms which have just been set out, and which have passed into the common tradition of Aristotelian philosophy.

Sensible substances, on Aristotle's view, can be analysed into matter and form. This antithesis, exceedingly common in his writings of every period, no doubt derives from Plato's distinction between the material οὐσία of things and their immaterial οὐσία, which itself reflects the different principles of explanation adopted by the physicists and by teleologists like Anaxagoras. Aristotle incorporates it into two other well-known groups of conceptions: by adding the opposite or negation of the form he develops an explanation of change in terms of matter, form, and its 'privation' (στέρησις) (*Physics*, i. 8–9, cf. *Metaph*. v. 22, vii. 7, 1032 b 3–5); alternatively, by adding the agent and the end in view he arrives at the well-known 'four causes', which play a prominent part in *Metaph*., Book i. The product of matter and form is called τὸ σύνολον or τὸ ἐξ ἀμφοῖν, the composite or concrete whole.[22] The formal element is usually denoted by εἶδος; but Aristotle sometimes avoids this renowned but ambiguous term; thus he substitutes μορφή, as we have seen, in vii. 3, and φύσις in xii. 3, the former word having the more restricted sense of geometrical shape, while the latter suggests an immanent formative principle that controls the development of living things. The material element is fairly consistently called ὕλη, but the use of this term is elastic; it sometimes means little more than the medium, whatever it is, in which a form is realized.[23] Thus the geometer often deals, not with material objects, nor yet with pure concepts like 'the circle', but with configurations like two circles in a spatial

---

[22] Best regarded, not as a combination of this matter *and* this form, but as a disposition of this matter *in* this form (see vii. 17, 1041 b 16 ff., viii. 3, 1043 b 4–14), or its organization *according to* this form.

[23] Cf. *de Anima* ii. 1, 412 b 20: the eye is the 'matter' of vision.

relation; and here Aristotle postulates a νοητὴ ὕλη, 'intelligible matter', as a medium in which there can be such configurations.

In the light of this distinction we can proceed to the perplexing term τὸ ὑποκείμενον, which as we have seen plays an important part in determining the structure of *Metaphysics* vii. The conventional renderings 'subject' or 'substrate' are hardly illuminating; the term can indeed mean the subject matter of a discussion, or the premiss of an argument; but these senses are hardly relevant here. Literally translated it should mean 'that which underlies'; hence it can mean a subject 'put down' for discussion, or the permanent reality which 'is subject to' varying states or qualities; but since Aristotle appears to believe in a natural order of speech and thought which (at least roughly) reflects the natural order of reality, it sometimes seems that the associations of the term are primarily grammatical or lexical; it means that which should be expressed as a grammatical subject,[24] that to which predicates attach. When applied to individual things, compounded of form and matter, its application is straightforward; the predicates refer to states or accidental qualities, while the ὑποκείμενον is the thing itself which undergoes or possesses them,[25] and is naturally denoted by a substantive word. But the contrast between subject and predicate sometimes seems to correspond to the distinction between form and matter; and here at first sight it seems that either element may be made the subject of predication; for we talk of a bronze statue, but also of a hollow stone;[26] the noun represents the form in the first case, the matter in the second. Equally, it would seem that either element can be regarded as the subject to which changes occur; thus in the much-discussed case of the bronze statue it seems that we can either begin with the form, which is then embodied in matter (vii. 10, 1035 a 13–14; 11, 1036 a 31–2) or with the matter, which then receives a distinctive form; in fact the artist would naturally take the former view and the bronze-founder the latter. But at this point Aristotle runs into difficulties caused by a false analogy. In the case of the thing and its states we have a reality, an οὐσία, which is denoted

---

[24] As is well known, Aristotle concentrates on the logic of subject-predicate sentences; so 'subject' for him implies noun, not adjective. The grammatical object is not considered.

[25] See e.g. vii. 13, 1038 b 5–6: ὥσπερ τὸ ζῷον τοῖς πάθεσιν. 'Sick animal' is the proper description; 'animal patient' is not.

[26] Not Aristotle's example; but cf. 'level sea' (viii. 2, 1043 a 24).

by the grammatical subject, not by predicates (*Physics* i. 7, 190 a) ; or, more loosely, the οὐσία can be identified with the ὑποκείμενον. But where matter and form are contrasted Aristotle still wants to say that *one* of these elements is the οὐσία of the thing, in the sense of answering the question 'What is it?'; and on the whole he prefers to say that the οὐσία is the form, since this implies a definite character, and so seems more nearly analogous with the concrete whole ;[27] very often one word (e.g. 'house') will serve for either.[28] On the other hand the ὑποκείμενον is more naturally identified with the matter, probably because it is easier to conceive of a quantity of matter persisting through various changes of form, as when bronze is melted and cast, than of a form persisting in a changing material embodiment (though a wave might serve as an example of this, or indeed a human body, whose form changes relatively slowly, whereas its matter is continually replaced). In other words, where matter and form are contrasted Aristotle cannot maintain both his two presumptions, (a) that substance (sc. reality) corresponds with the grammatical subject, and (b) that substance (sc. what it is) is something definite, τόδε τι ; since the grammatical subject, the ὑποκείμενον, now denotes that which is *contrasted* with the form. In the event we find that οὐσία is freely used with reference to the concrete whole, or again to its form, and rather less freely with reference to its matter; ὑποκείμενον, however, commonly refers to the concrete whole or else to its matter, and is only very rarely applied to the form. But it is so used, as we have seen, in a crucial passage at the beginning of Book vii, and in the corresponding passage at viii. 1, 1042 a 28–9.[29]

A far more crucial term for Aristotle's theory of substance is εἶδος, one of his principal legacies from Platonism. (For simplicity's sake I shall not discuss the related term ἰδέα.)

(i) The fundamental sense no doubt is that in which it is

---

[27] So in the *Categories* the εἶδος (= species) is (δευτέρα) οὐσία.

[28] viii. 3 *init.*, cf. vii. 15 *init.*

[29] Aristotle would clearly like to make the senses of οὐσία and ὑποκείμενον correspond; a curious instance occurs at ix. 7, 1049 a 27 ff., where the correspondence is secured by making οὐσία *include* matter and *exclude* form, giving up the presumption that οὐσία is always τόδε τι :

$$\text{ὑποκείμενον} \begin{cases} \text{Matter} \\ \text{Concrete Whole} \\ \text{Form} \end{cases} \quad \begin{array}{l} \text{οὐσία ὑλική (not τόδε τι)} \\ \left.\begin{array}{l} \text{οὐσία} \\ \text{εἶδος} \end{array}\right\} \text{τόδε τι} \end{array}$$

synonymous with μορφή; a geometrical shape or configuration. It has to be noted that words denoting shapes, like 'circle', are used in several distinct connections, referring to the pure concept, or to the idealized particular considered by mathematicians, or to physical objects which conform, more or less, to the shape in question.

(ii) Εἶδος is used as a *terminus technicus* to mean 'the form as Plato understood it'. Aristotle usually distinguishes himself from 'the exponents of the Forms' (οἱ τὰ εἴδη λέγοντες, vii. 16, 1040 b 27–8), and in polemical passages can even say 'the Forms do not exist' (τὰ μὲν γὰρ εἴδη ὅτι οὔκ ἐστι, δῆλον, xi. 1, 1059 b 3). A leading criticism, expressed in a fairly early passage, is that the doctrine postulates entities which are both universals and separately existing particulars (xiii. 9, 1086 a 31–4). This criticism is later rephrased (vii. 14, 1039 a 24 ff., xiii. 4, 1078 b 30 ff.) for the very good reason that Aristotle himself had come to take up a position which, verbally speaking, is open to the same objection.

(iii) Aristotle nevertheless develops Plato's conception of a hierarchy of natural kinds, ranging from what is technically called the *summum genus* (the most comprehensive class) to the *infima species*, e.g. the various kinds of animals. Aristotle's use of the term εἶδος in this connection is complex and inconsistent, though it may one day be possible to trace a pattern of development. Sometimes the whole hierarchy of classes is lumped together and called indifferently 'species' (εἴδη) or 'genera' (γένη);[30] when, however, the terms are contrasted the species is the less inclusive and more distinctive term, a familiar example being the kinds of animals which do not normally interbreed, the ἄτομον εἶδος of Plato's *Sophist* (229 b).

(iv) In a number of important passages εἶδος means neither precisely 'shape' nor precisely 'species' but something more like 'the shape or form characteristic of a species', which Aristotle regards as the principle of growth and production in changing and perceptible things. In artificial productions the form of the article pre-exists in the mind of the craftsman; in natural reproduction the form of the offspring is present in the body of the parent. The development of a living creature is regarded as an

---

[30] Cf. iii. 1, 995 b 29–31 : τὰ γένη . . . τελευταῖα ἢ τὰ πρῶτα apparently means '*summa genera* or *infimae species*'. But εἶδος is not, I think, ever used for a *summum genus*.

endeavour to realize this characteristic form, which in its complete articulation is called ἐντελέχεια or ἐνέργεια, 'actuality'.

This bold conception requires the greatest care if it is to be stated without contradiction, and Aristotle does not always insert the necessary qualifications. He lets it appear that the εἶδος in this sense is both capable and incapable of separate existence, and that it is both universal and particular. The former contradiction can be resolved fairly easily. As far as sensible things are concerned, the εἶδος must have *some* material for its embodiment (it is not separable absolutely); but it may be transferred from one individual to another; again, it may be *considered* separately (it is separable in thought). There is, however, the problem of non-sensible substances; and here Aristotle's position, though complex, seems to me to be consistent. He regards their existence as debatable, and he clearly sees that many of the proofs offered by the Platonists are invalid: thus we can explain the resemblances of things without postulating eternal exemplars which they imitate; we can explain the generation of things without postulating eternal archetypes or models. But his conclusion is that some non-sensible beings can be shown to exist, namely the pure intelligences which account for the movements of the heavenly bodies. In their case at least the form constitutes their individuality; there is no grouping of them in species, no two of a kind. In fact they are pure forms, and the only pure forms which enjoy a completely independent existence.

Before discussing the second contradiction mentioned above there is one further derivative of the Platonic εἶδος to be considered. In his early work *de Ideis* Aristotle seems to have discussed the so-called 'argument from knowledge', which sought to prove that there are 'things other than particulars', and identified these latter with the Ideas.[31] The discussion showed, however, that a simple contrast between Ideas and particulars is untenable, since there cannot be forms, or Ideas, corresponding to all classes of things; see *Metaph.* i. 9, 990 b 8 ff., xiii. 4 and 5, 1078 b 32 ff., 1079 b 31–5.[32] It was therefore necessary to introduce a more generalized conception, the universal, as a logical counterpart

[31] ἄλλων δέ τινων παρὰ τὰ καθ᾽ ἕκαστά εἰσιν αἱ ἐπιστῆμαι . . . ἔστιν ἄρα τινὰ παρὰ τὰ καθ᾽ ἕκαστα, ταῦτα δὲ αἱ ἰδέαι. Fr. 187 Rose, ed. W. D. Ross, p. 122.

[32] It has been argued (e.g. by Henry Jackson) that Plato himself adopted this view; but the argument has not generally carried conviction. See Ross, *Plato's Theory of Ideas*, 165–75, and works there cited.

to the particular which carried no metaphysical implications. In the *Categories* it appears that Aristotle already distinguished between the genera and species and a broader class of universals. For the genera and species, like the individuals, are assigned to the category of substance: they are 'secondary substances'. But the distinction between particulars and universals extends outside the category of substance; and although the example given ('this white' as against 'every colour') does not specially emphasize the point, there would be no difficulty in exhibiting it; thus the question 'Where?' might be answered universally, 'Outdoors' or 'At sea', as well as 'In the Lyceum'. Again, when Aristotle refers to universals as τὰ κοινῇ κατηγορούμενα, there is no suggestion that such 'general categorizations' must be in the category of substance.[33]

But even within the category of substance, Aristotle can represent the class of 'universal terms' as including terms which cannot be called εἴδη. There are, for instance, distinguishing characteristics which serve to determine the hierarchy of classes, but are not included in it, the differentiae (e.g. 'two-footed'). Again there are characteristics which necessarily belong to an εἶδος (and to nothing else), but are not included in its definition, namely the 'properties' (ἴδια). Sometimes, again, the universal is positively contrasted with an εἶδος; thus 'man' considered as a universal term means human *matter* combined with human form, considered generally (vii. 10, 1035 b 28–30);[34] but we can hardly say that the human *form* includes the matter, though it may in some sense presuppose it. Again, 'wooden box' (ix. 7, 1049 a 22–4) is for Aristotle a perfectly good universal expression, although it is a compound expression of which only the second element refers to a form.

It is in the end impossible to give a consistent account of Aristotle's views on the relationship of the εἶδος and the universal, even if we assume the analysis of εἶδος given above, and further restrict ourselves to Aristotle's special and characteristic sense (4). For Aristotle does not enable us to decide whether the εἶδος is to be called a 'this', a τόδε τι, or a 'such', a τοιόνδε. He is still

---

[33] Cf. Ross, *Metaph.* i. lxxxvii and refs., apparently correcting his *Aristotle*, 24.

[34] Presumably 'all men are mortal' does not mean 'everything in human *form* is mortal'; it does not deny the existence of Gods in human form, understood as 'bodily shape'.

struggling, without entire success, to free himself from the Platonic confusion according to which the εἶδος is both a 'this', in the sense of a transcendent model for imitation, and a 'such', the likeness derived from it. And associated terms assist the confusion; for γένος can mean either a class of things, i.e. a species, or a class of species; ἄτομον can mean either a true individual or a not-further-divisible species. And among 'things' or individuals Aristotle includes things like 'this syllable', of which instances are possible and which can therefore be regarded as species.

Is the form a 'this' or a 'such'? I hope to show that the question itself is too vague to be answered precisely; but so long as it remains unanswered, it is clearly impossible for Aristotle to say whether he regards εἴδη as a privileged subclass of universals, exempt from limitations which normally apply to them, or whether they are not universals at all.

(iii) *Individual and Specific Form*

We will now revert to the argument of *Metaphysics* vii–viii. As we have said, the main bulk of vii is devoted to an examination of the question, whether 'essence' is substance (most of 4–12) and whether the universal is substance (13–16). At 17 Aristotle makes a fresh start, and though this chapter stands rather by itself, its main point is incorporated into the reconsideration of the whole question of substance in viii. 1–3.

The discussion of essence falls into three distinct sections of approximately equal length; these sections were certainly written and put together by Aristotle, but I do not think they were written consecutively. The first section (vii. 4–6, beginning at 1029 b 12) apparently starts from the assumption that in some sense the οὐσία of *x* is identical with *x* (cf. 1031 a 15); it leads up to the question whether the *essence* of *x* is identical with *x*, and Aristotle answers that this is so in the case of 'primary and self-existent terms'. However it appears from some later references that this phrase does not apply to composite and material objects; in their case, therefore, it seems that the claim of essence to be substance must after all fail.

The second section (7–9) apparently starts from the assumption that the οὐσία of *x* must in some sense be the cause of *x*, or the first manifestation of *x* (cf. vii. 8, 1033 b 26 ff., also v. 8, 1017 b

14–16, and with this the third sense of ἀρχή discussed in v. 1);
it therefore considers whether the form or essence does in fact
fulfil this role in the case of material things which come into
being. The conclusion appears to be negative in their case; the
essence does not function as cause, or at least not as 'cause' has
been commonly understood; nor does it come into being, so it
cannot be the first manifestation. It should be noticed, however,
that though this section is incorporated into the discussion of
essence, its connection with 4–6 is by no means obvious; in some
ways it forms a more natural sequel to the end of 3, where
Aristotle proposes to discuss sensible substances. Its subject
matter also overlaps with vii. 17 and viii. 1–3. I think it probable
that this section is a survival from an earlier draft of the *Metaphysics*, which Aristotle retained because its criticism of the
Platonic conception of the εἶδος as cause of phenomena still held
good; but it is corrected and supplemented by vii. 17–viii. 3, in
which Aristotle first redefines the notion of 'formal cause' (vii.
17 *init.*) and then proceeds to a reinterpretation and development of the concept of essence, making use of the term ἐνέργεια.

The third section (10–11, ending at 1037 a 20) apparently
starts from the assumption that the οὐσία of x is to be found in the
system of 'parts' which constitute its structure (cf. iii. 1, 995 b
27–9; iv. 3; v. 8, 1017 b 17–20). Aristotle seems to take it for
granted that both the matter and the form of x are in a sense
'parts' of it (cf. vii. 10, 1035 a 1 ff.); but to test the thesis that the
form of x is its οὐσία, he has to ask whether the parts of the form
correspond to the parts of the thing, x, of which it is a form (cf.
i. 6, 987 b 18, xiii. 10). Once again the conclusion seems to be
negative in cases where x is a material object: the parts of the
form are logically prior to the whole which they compose, but the
parts of a composite object are logically posterior to the whole. It
turns out, then, that the material components of a thing are not
'parts' of it in the sense required. Further, a general description
of a composite object implies the same sort of composition as is
found in its instances; thus 'man' implies human matter in
human form, taken generally (vii. 10, 1035 b 28–30).

In the next main section (13–16) Aristotle draws the conclusion that no universal term is substance, and that no substance
is composed of substances. It should follow from the latter point
that *any* attempt to explain the οὐσία of x in terms of its parts must

fail; and from the former, that we cannot sustain the claim that the εἶδος of x is its οὐσία, *unless* we can show that the εἶδος is in some sense τόδε τι, not a universal, and is distinguishable from the kind of universal described in vii. 10.

The chapters subsequent to the 'new beginning' at vii. 17 are distinguished, first by an attempt to redefine the notion of the 'formal cause' (17, 1041 a 26–7, b 5–6: we are seeking the cause, i.e. the form, in virtue of which these bricks constitute a house); secondly, by a transformation of the terms matter and form, which are now defined in terms of 'the potential' and 'the actual'. The concept of matter is thus enlarged and made less precise; anything which is potentially x can be called its matter. On the other hand the concept of the 'actuality' of x, as I shall argue, is still limited; being still tied to the notion of definition, it cannot be conceived as fully individual.

Aristotle's discussion of substance leads almost immediately[35] into an examination of the obscure and elliptical phrase τὸ τί ἦν εἶναι, which is conventionally rendered 'essence'. The phrase seems to have arisen from the need to distinguish between predicative sentences like 'X is white' and identities or definitions of the form '(the) white is X'—the distinction which Plato attributes to Socrates. Hence 'that which is white' has to be distinguished from 'that which white (or whiteness) is', especially because τὸ λευκόν in Greek is ambiguous, and can mean either 'white things' regarded collectively, or 'whiteness'. Clearly τὸ τί ἦν εἶναι means something closely related to 'that which whiteness is'; it may be compared with the simpler τί ἐστι, 'what is it?', which occurs in vii. 1 but has a broader application;[36] but it is more closely related to phrases like τὸ σοὶ εἶναι (your essence or being, what you are), τὸ ἀγαθῷ εἶναι, etc., where a particularizing word is supplied in the dative case.

But how exactly is the phrase to be construed? I shall not review the detailed philological studies which have sought to answer this question.[37] My impression is that while some suggested

---

[35] Cf. p. 70 above.

[36] See esp. *Topics* i. 9. Cf. J. Owens, *The Doctrine of Being etc.*, 180 (93) : 'which can denote matter and composite as well as form, and the genera as well as the species'.

[37] For a good recent survey see E. Buchanan, *Aristotle's Theory of Being*, 30–9. I think we can exclude the first two senses he distinguishes, namely 'What it has been given to each thing to be' (Robin) and 'Its being what it was' (R. D. Hicks and Ueberweg–Praechter).

answers can clearly be ruled out, we are left in the end with two, which both represent genuine elements in Aristotle's thought, and which he probably failed to distinguish. τὸ τί ἦν εἶναι λευκῷ, then, can mean either 'What it is for . . . to be white' or 'What it is for white to be, or exist'. In the first case Aristotle would be pointing to something like the meaning of the *term* 'white', i.e. what it connotes or conveys (*not* what it denotes or applies to, namely τὰ λευκά); this reading roughly corresponds to the traditional rendering 'essence', and is supported by the close connection which Aristotle makes between 'essence' and definition. In the second case it would mean something more like '*X*'s mode or manner of being', or 'of existing', relating not to the term '*X*' but to the actual individual or species *X*. It is this construction of the phrase which makes it natural for Aristotle to connect it with phrases like τὸ σοὶ εἶναι, where any notion of definition is out of place.

As I think the first sense predominates on the whole in the chapters we are discussing, I retain the conventional rendering 'essence'; but it has to be used with caution, remembering that Aristotle certainly does *not* intend to contrast it with the notion of 'existence', in the manner of the medieval logicians.

In these chapters, vii. 4–6, Aristotle asks two main questions. The first is, what sort of things have an essence? In general terms, Aristotle answers, 'Those that are said *per se*', or perhaps 'named without qualification'; but the actual discussion is rather more complex. It explains that there is no essence corresponding to a compound expression, such as 'white man', which refers to an accidental condition; nor again to other compound expressions like 'white surface', 'female animal', 'odd number', even though it is no accident that *this* number is odd etc.; nor again to words which imply a compound, like 'snub', which refers both to shape and to noses. It also considers whether an essence is found for categories other than substance; if there is no essence of white man, is there an essence of white? Aristotle is not quite consistent here; but he states with some assurance that essence belongs to substances only (1031 a 1, cf. 1030 b 5). Various possible examples are given, including individuals (you, Socrates, 1029 b 14, 1032 a 8), species (horse, 1031 b 30), and entities like goodness, being, unity, which he now seems inclined to call 'primary substances', meaning that there is nothing prior from which they can be derived (1031 b 14, 32, 1032 a 5). But a further restriction is suggested by two phrases in Chapter 4: 'only things that can be defined' and 'only species of a genus' (1030 a 7, 12); these exclude the possibility of an essence belonging to an individual. We can indeed see what led Aristotle to take this line. He takes essence to be that which is stated in the definition; and he emphatically asserts that the individual cannot be defined (1036 a 2 ff., 1039 b 28 ff.). Thus when he speaks of 'the essence of each thing', it seems that 'each thing' can only mean 'each kind of thing', e.g. the circle, the soul;[38] in which case the examples first mentioned are not meant to be taken seriously, and the restricted answer, 'only species', represents Aristotle's considered view.

(His pronouncements on the question of individual forms, however, are so inconsistent that critics disagree as to which view, on the whole, he supported. Ross (*Metaph.* i. cxv–cxix) reviews most of the relevant passages and concludes that in spite of phrases like τὸ Σωκράτει εἶναι etc. Aristotle on the whole concludes that there are no forms of individuals. D. J. Allan (*Aristotle*, 41–3) holds that he recognizes individual forms in the case of *animate* beings, but pronounces against them in the case of inanimate things, both natural and artificial. But cf. also R. Albritton (*Journal of Philosophy* 54 (1957), esp. 707: 'This is a point of unclarity and conflict in the Metaphysics, not fully resolved even in the special case of animate things.')

The second question is, 'What sort of things are identical with their essence?' The answer seems to be, 'each individual thing' (1031 b 19), provided we exclude things qualified by accidental predications, e.g. 'white man'. This discussion is by no means easy to follow. Aristotle's language partly suggests his earlier question, whether there are realities distinct from individual realities (above, p. 75); but the examples he gives make it clear that he is now taking 'each thing' in a very general sense; the examples are 'man', 'animal', 'goodness', and even 'being'. Nevertheless he still conceives his discussion, in part at least, as a criticism of the Theory of Ideas; for this purpose he wants to show that 'the *x*', or 'the *x* itself', is not something over and above

---

[38] We do quite normally and properly refer to the circle, or Hamlet, or the four-stroke engine, as things; nevertheless instances of these are possible. We cannot speak of instances of Socrates.

the 'what it is to be *x*'; for instance 'the animal itself' is to be
identified with 'what it is to be an animal', and in general the
Ideas must be assimilated to his own concept of immanent form.
But before very long he appears to be upholding the quite different thesis that 'what it is to be *x*' is *x*; and this is a fertile source
of misconceptions. It may seem plausible to say that goodness is
good; but this is partly because 'goodness' can stand for 'that
which is good' (pp. 1–3, 79 above) and partly because of special
features of this example. We cannot hope to maintain the *general*
thesis that '*x*-ness is *x*', if only because many qualities can be displayed only by concrete particulars, and therefore not by themselves. We shall not argue that concreteness is concrete, nor that
wealth is rich.[39]

But the most troublesome problem presented by these three
chapters is that of fitting them into the rest of Aristotle's argument.
They are professedly a discussion of *ousia* 'from the standpoint of
logic' (λογικῶς, 1029 b 13). Aristotle emphasizes the correspondence of the essence with the definition, and assumes that in
stating the essence we must follow the rules which apply to definition, and offer neither more nor less than is implied in the
definiendum. In fact the argument is so much swayed by logical
considerations that Aristotle sometimes appears to be talking
about expressions themselves rather than the realities to which
they apply, and the essence appears to be, not so much a set of
characteristics which determines a class, as the formula which
states them.[40] Hence, I have argued, the phrase τὸ τί ἦν εἶναι
should be interpreted 'What it is for . . . to be so-and-so', which
easily suggests that 'so-and-so' is a general predicate of which
an analysis is to be given; in any case the whole argument points
strongly away from individual essences. If one asks, why then
does Aristotle not allow essences to all classes of things in every
category, I think the answer is partly that he is following his
general principle that a thing's substance indicates 'what it is'

[39] I have had to deal summarily with the problem of self-predication. For
fuller discussion see R. E. Allen (ed.), *Studies in Plato's Metaphysics*, 231–91 (G.
Vlastos, P. T. Geach); and for bibliography of recent articles, G. Vlastos, *Platonic
Studies*, 361–2. Cf. p. 35 above.

[40] Cf. H. Bonitz, *Aristoteles Metaphysica*, 307–8: Aristotle says that τὸ τί ἦν εἶναι
belongs to τῶν καθ' αὑτὸ λεγομένων whereas he should have said τῶν καθ' αὑτὸ ὄντων.
Cf. also vii. 10, 1035 b 26, where λόγος and οὐσία are coupled together as though
synonymous.

in the most proper sense, and partly that he is misled by a fallacious argument about compound expressions, which indeed he shows some disposition to retract.[41]

But when he takes up his argument again in Chapter 11, Aristotle seems to reinterpret his conclusions. He has been arguing that x = the essence of x in the case of 'things said *per se*', though not in the case of qualified things (e.g. white surfaces). This leads him to think that the principle applies in the case of forms (e.g. spheres) but not in that of forms embodied in matter (e.g. bronze spheres); and from this again he concludes that it applies to men if we think of them simply as souls, but not if they are considered as souls-in-material-bodies. At the same time the concept of essence undergoes some modification; whereas formerly it seemed to stand for something which determines a class in the sense of giving criteria for including things in the class, it now seems to represent a characteristic from which other characteristics follow, or which determines the functioning of the being in question. There is no plausibility in arguing that 'man' can be understood as 'soul' and 'soul' can be equated with 'essence of soul', if the latter phrase represents merely a formula or a set of criteria; the argument becomes plausible only if 'essence of soul' is interpreted (as was suggested above) as 'what it is for the soul to be', or less formally, 'the soul's characteristic pattern of action'.

At the same time, there are undoubted drawbacks in the thesis that soul = essence of soul, even if we are right in our interpretation of the latter phrase; since this equation can do justice only to the *permanent* features of the soul. The case becomes still clearer if we allow ourselves to speak of individual essences, and suppose that you are identical with your essence. *Some* of the things we may wish to say about you can be translated into phrases involving 'your essence', 'your characteristic pattern of behaviour'; but clearly not all. For you have a biography; you perform various actions; it is indeed a perfectly allowable use of 'you' if we say, 'You are acting out of character'. All talk of individual essences (or 'quiddities', as the schoolmen called them) is frustrated by the 'once-for-all-ness' of many human actions.

At various points in this discussion Aristotle gives the impression of blurring the distinction between what is strictly an

---

[41] See vii. 5, 1031 a 6 ff. The argument depends on interpreting (e.g.) 'This man is a white man' as 'In this case, man = white man'.

individual and what is strictly a determinate universal. One reason, I think, is that he is still influenced by the Platonic ideal of knowledge as a process of deduction, as is shown by his dictum that 'all knowledge is of the universal'. This evidently conveys something more than the blameless doctrine that all knowledge involves recognition of common characteristics;[42] it suggests that there is genuine (i.e. demonstrative) knowledge only of those sets of common characteristics which necessarily and permanently inhere in every member of a species. The individual cannot, in this sense of the word, be known;[43] the characteristics which distinguish individuals are fleeting and impermanent and hence 'unworthy of the name of form'.[44] And once the assumption is made that the *ousia* of *x* is that which *x* cannot lose without ceasing to be *x*, it becomes easy to suppose that the *ousia* of Socrates is simply 'man'.

Aristotle assumes, then, that scientific observation and intuition should enable us to reach a definition from which the properties of *x* can be deduced; that is, our procedure in the case of natural species like the horse is analogous to that in the case of geometrical figures like the circle. Hence (vii. 6, 1031 b 21) to know *x* is to know the essence of *x*, and this means knowing *x*'s definition. A short reply is to say that we can find a formula which is completely descriptive of circles; in the case of natural species or artifacts the most Aristotle ever attempts, or could attempt, is to find a formula (e.g. 'two-footed animal') which states what belongs solely to men, and so serves to distinguish men from not-men. We can at least find a definition of 'circle' such that anything corresponding to it *must* be a circle; but any conceivable definition of 'man' still leaves us free to imagine beings which answer to this definition and yet are not men. *This* kind of definition, in fact, will not even distinguish men from possible not-men; still less will it tell us what we want to know about men.

---

[42] This doctrine *is* perhaps suggested by the more cautious phrase 'we cannot acquire knowledge *without* the universal', xiii. 9, 1086 b 6; cf. iii. 4, 999 a 28 and perhaps xiii. 10, 1087 a 11.

[43] For Aristotle's attempts to explain how individuals are known, see Ross, *Metaph.* i. cviii–cx.

[44] Indeed this is not always a disadvantage. One of the admirable characteristics of Socrates is that the old man is always surprising us; there is a certain consistency about him, but no predictability.

When we turn to consider Aristotle's account of change and production (vii. 7–9, 17, viii. 1–3) we find that the 'essence' of vii. 4–6 is equated (mechanically, as I hold) with the 'form' that controls the production of artifacts and the development of living begins. But the only form which can plausibly be equated with the essence, and can be given a definition, is the form of the species. It seems, then, that the literary improvisation which we have detected in *Metaphysics* vii is directly responsible for Aristotle's pronouncing, at this important point, against the possibility of individual forms.

Something must be added on this much-debated point, leaving fuller discussion to the next chapter. The difficulty may be set out by a diagram which represents the discussions of vii. 8 and 10 and xii. 3:

Animal form × animal matter = animal	Genus
Human form × human matter = man	Species
Human form (*sic*) × this matter = Socrates	Individual

What then is 'this matter'? In one sense, the four basic elements, earth, fire, etc.;[45] in another, the tissues, flesh, bones, etc.; in another, and head and the other limbs and organs, which are the 'proximate matter' of Socrates.

Now it is clear that if we allow Aristotle to use the term 'matter' in this somewhat sophisticated way, he has avoided the crude mistake of suggesting that the imposition of the same form on *quite featureless* matter can result in distinguishable individuals.[46] Nevertheless I think his convention merely distributes the difficulty about individuals without resolving it. It would be possible to have exactly the right *amount* of flesh, bones, etc., and give them a form which was indisputably human without making them into a head and limbs like those of Socrates. Again, although the head and limbs, the 'proximate matter' of Socrates, are no doubt highly characteristic, and an acute observer could recognize the *disjecta membra* of Socrates on a battlefield, it would be possible to animate them in a *human* manner without producing the inimitable gestures and movements of Socrates. Therefore the question, 'What is the substance, the reality of Socrates?', ought to be answered, 'It is his characteristic form, his individual

45 I have expanded the cryptic phrase 'fire, flesh, head', xii. 3, 1070 a 19.
46 Cf. D. J. Allan, op. cit., p. 42.

pattern of behaviour, which cannot be realized in any matter whatsoever, but which nevertheless is not completely bound to this matter, and which is different from that of any other individual'.

One reservation may be suggested here. Should we not say that the form of Socrates—his outward shape plus his whole pattern of behaviour—is determinate rather than strictly individual? That it remains a 'such' (τοιόνδε) and is in theory reproducible? For Socrates might have a double, or an identical twin. The answer, I think, is that this is logically correct, and should be borne in mind when we consider inanimate objects;[47] but the possibility becomes more and more academic when we come to the higher forms of organism, and when we extend the concept of form, as Aristotle extends it, to cover not only physical structure but the pattern of behaviour exhibited by living beings. In such complex varieties of behaviour the likelihood of *complete* coincidence is negligibly small. There is, moreover, an ultimate reason why *sentient* beings cannot be exact duplicates; for since they must occupy different positions in the world, their perceptions at least cannot coincide.

If this point is taken, it will appear that there is a genuine difficulty underlying Aristotle's hesitation whether to call the εἶδος (form) a 'this' or a 'such'. Any completely determinate characteristic (say, the colour sodium-yellow) is a 'this' in the sense that no further determination is possible; it is not a 'kind of colour' such that there are various *colours* of that kind, as there are various shades of red; but it is a 'such' in the sense that it is a quality which can be possessed by any number of individual objects. And the same should be true of those combinations of characteristics which constitute a personality. There should be no *logical* objection to exact duplication. But one can readily excuse Aristotle for not seeing his way clearly through this puzzle, since he was still struggling to clear his reader's minds on a quite different point which these phrases might suggest, namely

---

[47] Hence I think Ross is mistaken in approving Stout's remark that each billiard-ball has an *individual* roundness (*Aristotle*, 24, n. 1); if this implies 'a distinguishable sort of roundness' it could be false, for given the correct size, weight and composition, perfectly round billiard-balls must be indistinguishable, and roughly round ones might be. If it does not, it is trivial. Ackrill rightly notes (*Categories*, 74) that by Aristotle's definitions 'only this individual generosity—Callias's generosity —is *in* Callias'; but it need not be an individual *brand* of generosity.

the theory that all resemblance results from imitation of a transcendent form, a particular 'this' which (as imitated) is also a
'such'. He may also have been misled by his habit of taking
examples of simple geometrical figures, such as the circle or
sphere, in which no subspecies are possible. All accurately
drawn circles are ταὐτὰ τῷ εἴδει in the rigorous sense that they
are indistinguishable as regards their shape; but triangles or
ellipses are not, still less men.[48]

We may perhaps round off this discussion by asking how far the
reformulated account of substance given in vii. 17 and viii succeeds in avoiding the criticisms just made. Aristotle does in fact
introduce some important modifications. The static conceptions
of matter and form give way to those of potentiality and actuality,
which are better adapted to explain the growth and development
of living things. The concept of matter is generalized; since anything that is potentially x can be called the matter of x, it will
apply in cases where x is partially though not completely formed,
and again in the (quite different) cases where we choose to consider only certain aspects of the form. Aristotle conceives of the
actuality as a structure pattern or arrangement, and finally
clears his mind of the notion that it is one of the constituents to be
arranged. But he does not, I think, see clearly that his conception of a formal cause is double-sided: the form of a house seems
to be the arrangement by which these bricks constitute a house,
but also a formative principle which is the cause of this arrangement.[49]

And in all these chapters Aristotle does not seem to recognize
a form of this-or-that man, or of this-or-that house, which could
confirm the passing references to 'your essence' etc., made in
Chapter 6. We are left with the impression that the development
of a human individual is controlled by a tendency to become a
man, but not by the tendency to become any particular sort of
man (e.g. for X to resemble his father); or again (what no one
but a philosopher would suppose) that the construction of a
house is determined solely by the materials available, together
with the pattern or definition of a house in terms of its function—

---

[48] In his scientific works Aristotle of course recognizes the existence of varieties
within a species; but they do not influence his metaphysics. Is this persistence of
habit, or does it really suggest that the *Metaphysics* is not his latest work?

[49] See esp. vii. 17, 1041 a 28–30: the essence is in some cases identified with the
final cause, in others with the mover.

'a shelter'. In practice, of course, an architect will normally be working with specific, or perhaps individual, needs in mind; the theory will only suit the case of a party of castaways who struggle to shape their scanty and intractable material into some semblance of a shelter. And the artist will normally envisage some definite figure or posture; only the most primitive tribesman could have so limited an ambition as to shape his material into a merely human form.

Nevertheless much can be learnt from these final chapters, in which Aristotle identifies the substance of a thing with its realization or actuality. The question, what is x?, now leads us to inquire what x does, attending not to any and every activity of the subject in question, but to that which fully develops all its potentialities. There is here a certain tension in Aristotle's mind, which may be related to the development of his ethical theory and of his psychology. His early writings are dominated by an antithesis between soul and body, which suggests that perfect human development means pursuing goods of the soul while opposing and excluding those of the body, a conclusion quite in the manner of Plato in his earlier writings. In Aristotle's mature work we find a different psychology; the soul is now regarded as the principle of life pervading all the functions of the body from the simplest and humblest, which men share with plants and animals, to the highest activities of the mind where human beings approach most nearly to the divine. And to some degree his ethical scheme is modified to correspond with this doctrine; for while the highest human achievement is still 'contemplation' ($\theta\epsilon\omega\rho\iota\alpha$), an activity of the mind, as the 'highest' part of the soul, Aristotle tries to show that this activity is in some measure a fulfilment also of humbler ethical ideals (*NE* x. 7) and is an activity to which other elements in our make-up have their own contribution to make.

IV

ARISTOTLE AND THE UNITY OF GOD

(i) *Immaterial Being*

THE *Metaphysics* does not deal with theology at any considerable length. The discussion of substance in Books VII and VIII is mainly concerned with material and sensible objects; and it is not at once obvious how Aristotle intended his analysis to apply to immaterial and non-sensible reality. However, the principles of his theology have been often described, and we may begin by outlining their main features as they are usually presented.

The clearest impression is that given by the compact account found in *Metaphysics* Book XII. Here Aristotle bases his doctrine of God on his cosmology. He conceives of an unmoved mover or first cause, eternal, invisible and unchangeable, who initiates all change in the universe by his attractive power, by arousing the desire to be like him in those heavenly beings which most nearly resemble him. He is therefore the supreme perfection, to whom the noblest attributes of human life can be ascribed; and in a well-known passage Aristotle argues that he must be intellect, and further must be intellect engaged with itself; the contemplation of lesser objects would impair the divine perfection.

A modern reader will naturally ask, Is this god personal, and is he one? On the latter point, it has been noted that Aristotle's use of the singular ὁ θεός is not to be taken as a declaration in favour of monotheism;[1] 'ὁ θεός' could mean 'god' in much the same sense as ὁ ἄνθρωπος means 'man', and in this sense would be hardly distinguishable from 'divinity' (τὸ θεῖον). On the other hand, his statement that god is indivisible (ἀμερής) suggests a monotheistic view; and he quotes a verse from Homer against polytheism (xii *ad fin.*), and argues that there is only one prime mover (xii. 8, 1074 a 36, cf. *Physics* viii. 6). It is natural to

---

[1] Cf. P. Merlan, *Traditio* 4 (1946), 17, 25–6; J. Owens, *Doctrine of Being*, 171 (350), n. 47. This is borne out by such passages as *de Caelo* ii. 3, 286 a 9 ff.

conclude that he recognizes one supreme divinity which he calls ὁ θεός, even if the phrase is sometimes more general in its meaning. In one chapter of the *Metaphysics* (xii. 8, perhaps added later) he argues on astronomical grounds for a plurality of unmoved movers, which might suggest a retreat from monotheism; even here, however, he includes the remark that 'one of them is first, and another second.'[2]

As to personality, it appears that Aristotle attributes to his God at least one ingredient of this complex notion, namely self-consciousness. And, in *Metaph.* xii at least, he allows himself to describe his divinity in language which applies to other rational beings; so that alongside his formal description of God's activity as 'a thinking of thought' we find attempts to give substance to the statement that God is the perfect being whom we imperfectly desire to resemble. So the ethical doctrine which makes θεωρία, contemplation, the highest good and the goal of our imperfect aspirations, is matched by a theology in which God, the pure embodiment of θεωρία, satisfies and surpasses our ideas of perfection. God is devoid of evil and error, simple, indivisible, un-affectable, and unalterable; moreover, he is an eternal living being (καὶ ζωὴ δέ γε ὑπάρχει . . . ζῷον ἀΐδιον ἄριστον), enjoying unbroken felicity, who himself supplies the fullness of perfection which he delights to contemplate.[3] And the suggestion that all such phrases ultimately fail to do justice to the reality is made in a fragment which recalls Plato's description of the Idea of the Good: God is 'either mind or something more eminent than mind.'[4]

When he pictures divinity in these terms, Aristotle seems to have formed a clear impression of the quality of divine life, but not to have finally determined whether that life is concentrated in a single centre or distributed in a society. A divine society could in some senses accommodate the claim that 'God is one.' It would be a unique reality. It would no doubt be harmonious, and thus could avoid the Homeric objection to polytheism, which is based on the possibility of conflict. Again, if it forms a hier-archy, as Aristotle once suggests, it must include members which

---

[2] 1073 b 2, reading καὶ τούτων τις πρώτῃ (so Ross, Tredennick, Jaeger).

[3] *Metaph.* xii. 9, 1074 b 33; 7, 1073 a 3 ff., 1072 b 24 ff.; *Eudemian Ethics* v (ii). 12, 1245 b 16–18.

[4] *On Prayer*, quoted by Simplicius *In De Caelo*; fr. 49, Rose[3]; fr. 1, Walzer; Ross, *Select Fragments*, p. 57.

though subordinate are not defective; indeed Aristotle tends to think that all imperfection results from defects in the material medium, so that all immaterial beings are *eo ipso* good; he does not envisage demons or gods who are wicked or contemptible. At this point he is still influenced by the Platonic doctrines that the soul as such is good compared with the body, and that the immaterial coincides with the ideal; though he has largely discarded the view that the ideal coincides with the universal. And so far as he conceives of divinity in this way, there is an easy transition to the Christian doctrine of God in at least one of its main historic forms, as a Trinity of persons identical in nature though differing in rank, yet each perfect and coeternal.

But it is also possible to interpret Aristotle as arguing that God is one in a much more radical sense. This interpretation, I shall argue, has a much slighter basis in Aristotle's writings and was mainly developed by neo-Platonist commentators; but some modern scholars, such as P. Merlan, contend that it is an integral part of Aristotelian thought.[5] Merlan's main theme is that Aristotle does not distinguish very sharply between *metaphysica specialis*, the study of pure being as ultimate spiritual reality, and *metaphysica generalis*, the study of pure being as the most abstract of logical categories; he therefore implies that spiritual reality is absolutely simple. I myself would rather point to the repercussions of Aristotle's dictum that matter is the source of plurality, which was bound to suggest, *per contra*, that immaterial reality is absolutely simple. Matter, as we have seen, is a word of many meanings. It means physical stuff; it is also conceived as the, possibly recalcitrant, medium in which a form is realized, as well as being identified as the source of individual differences. As a counterpart to it, Aristotle links together the three notions of disembodied mind, of completely realized perfection, and of universality or unity. In the cosmological theology we first considered, it is the first two notions which take control; divinity is conceived as perfect mind, without any stringent requirements as to how it is focused or deployed. The alternative course is to take up the third notion and expound Aristotle as arguing, on strictly metaphysical grounds, that divinity must be absolutely one.

Aristotle several times asserts, with slight variations, that things

5 *From Platonism to Neo-Platonism*, 2nd edn. (1960).

that are many in number have matter.[6] In Book xii the context shows that the word ἀριθμῷ is meant to be stressed: matter is required wherever there is the *merely* arithmetical plurality of several individuals having a common form; thus there can be many distinct immaterial realities, provided there be no two of the same form. But in Book viii—in fact in its concluding words— the word ἀριθμῷ is omitted, and the dictum is reversed to read, 'things without matter are essentially one'.

In what sense 'one'? The context of argument shows that Aristotle is not here concerned with the fact that a form, e.g. man, is a *single* reality, as against its numerous instances, but with the fact that it is a *simple* reality, although its definition involves two or more elements. This problem has already been introduced in vii. 10–12; and Aristotle's solution, in both cases, is to distinguish between the elements, so that one of them can be regarded as matter in some extended sense, while the other is more properly the pure form. But the attempt seems to lead to conflicting results; in vii. 12 it is the generic element which is regarded as 'matter', so that the pure form is that which is completely specific, the ultimate differentia; whereas in viii. 6 the form is identified with what is completely generic—'substance (τὸ τόδε), quality, quantity'. These look like verbalistic arguments of very little value; but the latter is of great historic importance, since it points towards neo-Platonism in its suggestion that the divinity— *qua* pure form—must be regarded as simple on the analogy of a completely simple abstract term.

We find, therefore, that the same dictum can be used to support two diametrically opposite theologies, one monistic, the other pluralistic and hierarchical; and it may be well to take a brief look at the history and interaction of these two theologies before returning to examine Aristotle's doctrine of individuation by matter.

It need hardly be said that the peculiar brand of cosmic polytheism suggested in xii. 8 had little appeal outside the Peripatetic school. And so far as Aristotle exercised any influence on Jewish or Christian theology it was through the support he gave to the doctrine that the supreme reality must be absolutely one. This doctrine can probably be traced back to Pythagoras'

---

[6] ὅσα ἀριθμῷ πολλά, ὕλην ἔχει, *Metaph.* xii. 8, 1074 a 33–4, cf. viii. 6, 1045 a 36 f., *de Caelo* i. 9.

derivation of the cosmos from number, and number from the monad. It is to some extent supported by Plato's concept of the Form as a unifying principle, coupled with the doctrine that the Forms themselves are united by their participation in the supreme principle, the Form of the Good. But it hardly seems to become dominant until the neo-Pythagorean revival. Philo, however, can state it as a commonplace that God is completely simple, most generic, a pure monad. But even by Philo's time the monistic theology could no longer be maintained in its original purity. Aristotle's dictum might have led to the conclusion that beyond the material world there is only one, perfectly simple, spiritual being. But a plurality of Forms was already admitted; the most that could be claimed was that a pure unity, identified with the Form of the Good, stood at the head of the hierarchy of Forms. Further, it proved impossible to escape the demand that the supreme reality must understand and control this world of multiplicity and change, and must therefore himself give rise to changing purposes and relationships. Hence it became necessary to interpolate intermediary powers, and so to reintroduce the notion of a divine hierarchy; and, in the best-considered versions of this theology, to maintain that the supreme God, who is absolute simplicity, knows and acts through a second god, who inherits his attribute of unity, but in a modified form which can admit a plurality of acts and functions. This theology was probably supported by an interpretation of Plato's *Parmenides*,[7] which isolated the first two of its eight theses, and took them as arguing positively, first for a purely simple spiritual unity, a One, and next for a complex unity, a One who is also many; but it is noteworthy that Philo, who accepts the doctrine of an ultimate divine simplicity, shows no consistent preference for a single secondary power, rather than two or six. His Alexandrian contemporary Eudorus was possibly the first to use the argument, which later became so familiar to Christians, that the perfect simplicity of the first God is mirrored in the uniqueness of the second. Finally the doctrine of divine simplicity became conventionalized; attempts were still made to define and defend it, but in the main it was protected from attack by the elusive character of the term 'simple', which could mean either 'excluding all differentiation'

---

7 See E. R. Dodds, 'The Parmenides and the neo-Platonic One', *Classical Quarterly* 22 (1928).

or 'comprehending all differentiation' or merely 'not composite', 'not constructed out of parts'.[8]

The second type of theology assumes the Aristotelian principle that things which differ must either be of a different species, or else differ 'numerically' within a species; and holds that only material things can differ numerically. Immaterial beings, therefore, if they differ at all, must differ in species. This doctrine was fully worked out in the medieval Christian theology of the angels, each of which was held to be a unique instance of a separate species; or, more properly (since it is necessarily unique), to be a different species, which exists in this one individual. As regards the persons of the Trinity the position was more complex. They could hardly be regarded as distinct species, in view of the Nicene doctrine that they are consubstantial. Nor could they be regarded as individual members of the same species, if this is possible only with material beings. They must therefore be numerically one. How then was it possible to give any meaning to the distinct existence of the persons? A possible line of escape, still commonly attempted, is to say that their *substance* is numerically one. But this is no real solution, so long as the medieval and Aristotelian assumptions are accepted; for if 'substance' is interpreted as 'secondary substance', it reintroduces the rejected conception of three instances of the same species; if as 'primary substance', it fails to exclude the Sabellian conception of a unitary godhead with no real and permanent distinctions.

It is, I think, possible to show that the basic embarrassment for Christian trinitarian doctrine derives from conflicting theological pressures to maintain that the three Persons are identical and that they are distinct; the Aristotelian doctrine of matter, individual, and species is not decisive, though it does introduce some misleading assumptions. Thus it assumes an artificially formalized view of reality. Even within the natural world, it is not always possible to reduce phenomena to individuals grouped in species and genera. But if the phenomena cannot always be classified in this way, then differences cannot always be classified as either numerical or specific, and identities cannot always be classified as

---

[8] For a striking example see the letter of Gregory Thaumaturgus to Philagrius, [Greg. Nyss.] *PG* 46. 1101–8. Gregory argues (1105c) that a ray of sunlight is inseparable from its disc 'in being impassible and incorporeal (!) and simple and undivided', even though he adds at once that the sun 'pours out its rays'. Athanasius often uses the same illustration of divine 'simplicity'; cf. pp. 262–4 below.

either numerical identities or identities in respect of species. I have argued these points in another context[9] and need not repeat them; though it may also be said that the expressions 'numerically the same', 'numerically different' are in themselves unsatisfactory.[10]

But the doctrine that immaterial beings must differ in species contributes no real difficulties of its own to the Christian trinitarian doctrine; the terms used are so loosely defined that apparent difficulties can be easily avoided. Thus the statement that angels each constitute a separate species tells us nothing about the actual extent of the difference between them; one could not infer, for instance, that angels differ one from another in the manner and degree in which horses differ from men or men from lions, a condition which would seem to preclude any society of spiritual beings. All that is required is some difference of form; for if non-material beings are constituted by their form, and if there are more than one, they must differ in some formal respect: this is the only kind of distinction that such beings allow. Furthermore, such formal distinctions could be greater or less, and non-material beings could be grouped and classified accordingly. Thus if any formal distinction is to be recognized between the persons of the Christian Trinity, there seems to be no valid objection, once the terms are correctly understood, to describing the three Persons as distinct species within the common genus of deity. If, on the other hand, they ought to be conceived as formally identical, it is not difficult to accommodate this demand within the Aristotelian framework of ideas: for Aristotle freely admits pluralities of identical things which are not material in any ordinary sense of that word, for instance mathematical figures; indeed some such figures cannot be conceived at all without admitting a plurality of identical components: the equilateral triangle comprises three equal straight lines, the tetrahedron comprises four equilateral triangles. In practice, therefore, Aristotle has to extend the sense of 'matter' so that it comes to mean no more than a medium of any kind within which a single form can be repeated; and in this sense it clearly does not

[9] 'The Significance of the Homoousios', *Studia Patristica* iii = *TU* 78 (Berlin, 1961), esp. 405–8.

[10] Anscombe and Geach, *Three Philosophers*, 46: 'At any rate as used today they are bad expressions, because they suggest that counting of itself implies that individuals and not kinds are being counted.'

involve either variation or imperfection among the several instances. Thus if the persons of the Trinity are to be regarded as identical, there seems to be no valid objection, once the terms are correctly understood, to postulating an appropriate spiritual 'matter' as the medium for the distinctions.

I have argued that from a critical point of view the Aristotelian dictum should exert no decisive pressure on the Christian doctrine of God. There is, of course, no doubt of its historical influence; but there is one historical point which I have so far bypassed; when did Christian theologians become acquainted with the concept of immaterial beings as individual species? Professor H. A. Wolfson has stated with some confidence that this view was commonly accepted by the Christian fathers;[11] but he quotes no clear allusion to Aristotle's dictum earlier than St. Basil, assuming he was indeed the author of 'his' Letter 38. And both this, and such other evidence as I have been able to gather, suggest that Aristotle's dictum was still being applied to show that number, in the sense of plurality, is inadmissible in the spiritual sphere—i.e. to support the monistic point of view, despite the problems it posed for Christian theologians. What seems lacking is evidence that the dictum was being used in the other sense, to show that there is a plurality of heavenly beings but that no two are alike. Athenagoras does indeed argue that there cannot be two similar gods: οὐ γὰρ εἰ θεοὶ ὅμοιοι, ἀλλ' ὅτι ἀγένητοι οὐχ ὅμοιοι· τὰ μὲν γὰρ γενητὰ ὅμοια τοῖς παραδείγμασι τὰ δὲ ἀγένητα ἀνόμοια, οὔτε ἀπό τινος οὔτε πρός τινα γενόμενα (Leg. 8). But this makes no clear reference to Aristotle, and in any case can hardly have been a general Christian view. Thus Origen has no difficulty in supposing that God created a multitude of rational beings who were all exactly alike until they fell in various degrees from their original perfection.[12] Even less probable is Professor Wolfson's suggestion that the Christian fathers tacitly assumed

---

[11] The Philosophy of the Church Fathers, 308–9, 338.

[12] Princ. i. 5. 3; i. 8. 2; ii. 1. 3. Cf. also Clement, Excerpta 10. 3: the Protoktistoi are numerically distinct, but the similarity of their action shows their equality. The doctrine of individual species is indeed suggested in a homoeousian argument reported by Sozomen (HE iii. 18) for the period c. 340–50: τὸ μὲν γὰρ ὁμοούσιον ἐπὶ σωμάτων κυρίως νοεῖσθαι, οἷον ἀνθρώπου καὶ τῶν ἄλλων ζῴων καὶ δένδρων καὶ φυτῶν, οἷς ἐξ ὁμοίου ἡ μετουσία καὶ ἡ γένεσίς ἐστι, τὸ δ' ὁμοιούσιον ἐπὶ ἀσωμάτων, οἷον ἐπὶ θεοῦ καὶ ἀγγέλων, ἑκατέρου πρὸς ἑαυτὸν νοουμένου κατ' ἰδίαν οὐσίαν. But Sozomen may have improved this argument, which does not appear in the extant documents of 358.

that the persons of the Trinity were distinct individual species grouped within a common genus; since the three persons are constantly compared with three individual members of the same species, man; and in all the numerous fourth-century discussions of this analogy—including 'Basil's' 38th letter and Gregory of Nyssa's *Not Three Gods*—there is no hint that I can discover that the relation of individual men to manhood has to be transposed into a higher order of generality. The most that can be said is that these fathers assumed that the three persons belong to the class of incorporeal beings; but they are by no means convinced that species as such are incorporeal realities; in their view, the nearest parallel to the divine persons would be incorporeal rational creatures such as angels and immortal souls.

The concept of the three persons as distinct individual species also seems to conflict with the view held by Philo and the neo-Platonists that God is not only completely simple but completely remote from all particularity; he is 'most generic', γενικώτατος, pure being. The notion of God as the most general form of being certainly exerted some influence on Christian thought even before St. Augustine; it certainly has some basis in Aristotle; and it certainly calls for evaluation. But before attempting this, I have some further comments to offer on the view which connects particularity with matter, and so suggests that complete generality is the proper attribute of pure spirit.

(ii) *A Theory of Individuation*

In the previous chapter I attempted to show how Aristotle's treatment of being and substance is affected by some very persistent confusions. Perhaps the most general account that can be given is to say that he asks, 'what is οὐσία?' without sufficiently realizing that the question should have been 'what is the οὐσία of *x*?' and that the answer must vary with different types of *x*'s. The main line of argument leads to the conclusion, 'the οὐσία of *x* is its specific form', an answer which is only appropriate where *x* is a species; and, by a further mistake, the form of the species is assimilated to a formula, i.e. a definition. As the chief underlying confusions I have identified:

(i) The confusion of names with things (pp. 57–8, 62, 82 above), which is the immediate source of the last-named mistake.

(ii) A confusion in the senses of the word 'to be' (pp. 68–9, 80, 83 above), which assists it.

(iii) A confusion of species, as classes of beings, with specific forms which are thought to define those classes (pp. 61, 74).

(iv) The confusion of subclasses with true individuals. This shows itself (a) as a logical doctrine (pp. 60, 82), (b) in an ambiguous use of expressions like 'each thing', 'this thing' (pp. 81, 86–7, 101), so that 'this *x*' means in effect 'this sort of *x*', whether because 'this' means 'this sort of' or because '*x*' means 'sort of *x*', (c) in arguments based on merely specious individuals like 'this syllable', which can be exemplified in truly individual cases.

But besides (quite justifiably) taking form as the principle of classification and (misleadingly) supposing that it belongs uniquely in the species, Aristotle also treats matter as the source of individual differences. We have noted two sophisticated variants of this doctrine. One of these dilutes the sense of 'matter' and postulates an appropriate matter wherever plurality is required; this has the effect of making 'things that are many in number have matter' an analytic proposition. The other makes 'matter of *x*' equivalent to 'partly formed *x*', or 'that which is potentially *x*'. Aristotle's reasons for making this second move may be set out briefly as follows. So long as εἶδος means strictly 'shape', it is possible to give a natural account of ὕλη; it has the property of being plastic or in some way workable, and so of assuming a shape. But if εἶδος is generalized to cover every kind of property (e.g. the property of being bronze), then there is nothing left to characterize pure ὕλη divorced from εἶδος; it has to be defined relatively to some εἶδος or other, and so comes to mean that which is ready to receive, but still lacks, a (definite or perfect) form. I have argued above that this usage fails to account for the differences between human individuals.

But it is not enough to disprove Aristotle; we need to trace the source of his error; and this is best done by reconsidering his doctrine in its least sophisticated guise. In accordance with the view that things are naturally classified by their form or structure he several times observes that the same word can be used either for the form or for the form-in-matter (viii. 3 *init.*, cf. vii. 10, 1035 b 1, and 15, 1039 b 20); and in some very well-known passages he seems to imply that '*x*-in-matter' is the same as 'individual *x*', and is individual because it is material. If, then, ὕλη is taken in its straightforward sense, as physical stuff—which is, I think, its dominant sense in vii. 7 and *de Caelo* i. 9—then the particular object, 'this bronze circle' is a product of 'this bronze' and 'circular form'; and Aristotle himself compares this case with the more complex case of the individual man, Callias or Socrates, consisting of 'such-and-such a form in this flesh and these bones' (vii. 8, 1033 b 24–6, 1034 a 5–7).

Aristotle's views can therefore be represented by the diagram:

Universal: Circle
                                                   ↓
Particular: This bronze → This bronze circle.

Some objections to this view seem very obvious indeed. Thus (a) this bronze circle is not an individual circle *because* it is bronze; for if it were, the expression 'bronze circle' by itself would necessarily specify an individual. But this it does not, as Aristotle himself points out (vii. 8, 1033 b 25–6: we can speak of 'bronze sphere in general'; cf. 10, 1035 b 27–8: 'man' and 'horse' apply to individuals, but universally; ix. 7, 1049 a 18–24: 'wooden box' can be a general expression). And (b) the theory that all individuality is due to matter is embarrassed by the counter-examples, already noted, of pluralities involved in mathematical figures, which can only be accommodated by artificially widening the sense of ὕλη.

It seems, then, that Aristotle's diagram should be corrected as follows:

| Universal: | Bronze | Bronze circle | Circle |
| Particular: | This bronze | This bronze circle | This circle |

Here the expressions on the upper line are general descriptions; those on the lower line, distinguished by 'this', refer to, or suggest the case of, a particular example; and such an example may be referred to as 'this bronze circle', or as 'this bronze', or as 'this circle', or indeed simply as 'this'.

The revised diagram suggests, against Aristotle, that form-denoting words and matter-denoting words are used symmetrically; neither class has any special connection with universality or individuality. Are we correct in this view? We have still to account for the fact that 'this bronze' can naturally refer to the mass of matter before it assumes, or after it loses, the circular form; whereas it seems difficult to suggest any analogous use for 'this circle'. This might suggest that there is a genuine asymmetry which Aristotle's diagram, for all its deficiencies, has correctly displayed. Again, the logic of 'same form' seems to be different from that of 'same matter'; for it certainly looks as if 'exactly similar in form' is indistinguishable from 'having the same form'; but 'exactly similar in matter' seems distinct from 'having the same matter'. The last-mentioned phrase might apply to two statues of which the first was melted down to provide material for the second. No two things 'having the same matter' in this strict sense could coexist; whereas it might seem that two things 'having the same form', however closely defined, could do so; as we have said, there should be no logical objection to exact duplicates. This certainly suggests that there is something inherently general about form and something inherently particular about matter.

Nevertheless this Aristotelian view is mistaken. The mistake can be shown if we consider the use of the phrases 'this form', 'this matter' (and 'same form' . . . etc.) *together with* a variety of more specific phrases, e.g. 'this circle', 'this polygon', 'this syllable', 'this bronze'. We first note that in a good many cases 'this (same) x' can mean either 'this individual x' or 'this type of x'; and sometimes, though one meaning is decidedly the commoner, the other is by no means unnatural. We next ask, what are the circumstances in which 'this x' can *only* mean 'this individual x', 'this instance of x, which itself has no instances'? Aristotle offers us the answer, 'when x involves matter'; though this answer in fact covers two quite distinct cases; first, when the word 'x' is itself a matter-denoting word, like 'bronze', or indeed 'matter'; secondly, when 'x' is a form-denoting word like 'circle', but is reapplied to mean 'form-as-embodied-in-matter'. Let us begin by considering the word 'matter' itself. Certainly 'this matter' commonly means 'this individual mass of stuff'. On the other hand it is perfectly good English to say 'this material' (or, 'this stuff') can be got cheaper elsewhere'; and this certainly does *not* mean that we might transfer this individual bolt of cloth to another shop and there pay their price for it. Greek usage appears to be similar.[13] It seems, then, that Aristotle has not succeeded in correctly describing our use of matter-denoting

---

[13] Ὕλη is I think used in this way when Aristotle speaks of the four elements as 'four matters' (τέτταρες ὕλαι, de Caelo iv. 5, 312 a 20).

words; his apparent success with 'this matter' perhaps only shows that his theory has continued to influence our usage of this particular word.

The explanation I suggest is simply that the word 'this' is used to single out an x from other x's; but that the meaning of 'this x' depends upon the kind of subdivision which the class of x's allows. If there are distinguishable types of x, then 'this x' can mean either 'this individual instance of x' or 'this type of x'; but if differences between types of x are important to us, and differences between individual instances of them relatively unimportant, we may refer to a type as 'an x', just as if it were an individual. Many form-denoting words show this characteristic; thus we think it quite natural that Aristotle should cite 'BA' as an example of 'this syllable', rather than 'this BA here, on this tablet', even though he recognizes this latter sort of example (vii. 10, 1035 a 15). I shall argue that the word 'form' itself behaves like the word 'syllable'. However, there is an important minority of form-denoting words which behave differently, namely those denoting forms which have no sub-types, such as the words for some very simple geometrical figures; in these cases 'this x' cannot be used to single out one subtype of x from another, and therefore has to mean 'this individual instance of x'. A great many of Aristotle's perplexities arise from his failure to see that the word 'circle' does not behave like the word 'form'.

By speaking of 'form-denoting words' I mean no more than that certain words show a preference for denoting form; but this preference is a matter of degree, and depends upon the context. We may consider the following series of expressions:

This number
This polygon
This diagram
This map.

It seems clear that 'this number' would normally mean, e.g., 'seven', rather than 'this particular seven'; but the preference progressively weakens in the examples that follow: 'this map' could well mean 'the one in my pocket'.

The case is similar with matter-denoting words. 'This iron' normally means 'this particular mass of iron', or possibly 'this iron implement here'; but if anything prompts us to reflect that there are various types and compositions of iron, then 'this iron' will refer to a type or composition of iron, and there can be two or more specimens of it. In the case of the phrase 'this alloy', the second usage is undoubtedly the normal one.

On the view I have stated 'this man' will normally mean 'this individual'; not (as Aristotle suggests) because manhood is a universal that needs matter for its embodiment, but because we normally assume that men are members of a single species whose varieties are relatively unimportant; but if we had to consider the distinctive features of (say) Neanderthal man, 'this man' could equally mean 'Neanderthal man', and it would be permissible to say 'this man is found in other districts', just as we could say 'this monkey is found elsewhere'.

If these arguments are sound, they should lead us to conclude, against Aristotle, that individual reference and general reference attach to words irrespective of their reference to form and matter. This conclusion consorts well with modern conceptions of matter, whereby differences of matter *are* differences of form, in the disposition of the minute structure of things. But to confirm it we have to show not only that there is a sense in which two things may simultaneously be composed of the 'same' matter (e.g. of the 'same' cloth, in the example above), but also conversely that there is a sense in which two bits of matter *cannot* simultaneously exhibit the 'same' form. This I think can be shown with form-denoting words such as 'wave'. As we said above, the 'same' individual mass of matter can assume different forms, but only at different times; conversely the 'same' individual wave can incorporate and inform different masses of sea-water during its progress or 'life'; but it cannot incorporate them simultaneously. 'This wave' is a kind of individual existent; and what can be said of it could be said more abstractly of 'this form'.

What makes us think of this wave as an individual being, despite the fact that its material content is constantly changing? One reason is clearly its continuity: there are no idiosyncrasies about waves, and so there are no circumstances in which it would be natural to speak of this wave as repeated, revived, or reconstituted on another occasion. It is identified by its constant or slowly changing shape, which occupies a continuous series of positions. It is at this point, I think, that we see why it is unnatural to speak of 'this circle' obtaining bronze material. Circles again have no idiosyncrasies; so we have to reason for saying 'this circle is cast' as we might say 'this statue is cast' or 'this house is (first planned, then) built' or 'this design is (first projected then) executed'. And triangles, though they may indeed differ in shape, do not exhibit repeatable peculiarities which are sufficiently interesting for us to refer to them as 'this triangle'. But in actual cases it may be difficult to decide whether 'thisness' is determined by formal idiosyncrasies or by context and historical relationships. Suppose X devised a theory, or wrote a piece of music, and it was then discovered that an *exactly* similar theory or an identical piece had already been produced; it would be hard to choose between 'Y's theory was rediscovered by X', and 'X's theory corresponds exactly to Y's theory'; it would not matter whether we said that the *same* theory was reproduced, or that an exactly *similar* theory was devised.

However, if a thing's 'thisness' *is* determined simply by its formal idiosyncrasies, it is in principle like 'this syllable'; it is in theory repeatable, however unlikely this may appear. To count as a true individual, a thing must be uniquely located in the world of our experience. Such a location is often implied when we use the word 'this', but not always, as we have seen. 'This syllable' usually refers to a repeatable pattern, 'this iron' to an individual mass, but in both cases exceptions are possible; even 'this wooden box' might be generalized to refer to a distinctive type of wooden box used (say) by some ancient culture. Aristotle's assumption of an absolute bond between form and universality cannot be upheld; the most we can say is that our loose conventions of speech and thought approximate in some degree to his theory.

(iii) *Unity and Generality in God*

We can now return to theology. I have argued that it is possible to develop an Aristotelian doctrine of the substance of God along two distinct lines. In the first place, we can conceive of God as a being who enjoys the highest and purest activity of intellectual life. Such a being could be described as 'without matter' in the sense of not belonging to the physical universe, and again in the sense of having no imperfections or unrealized possibilities; and he could be described as 'pure form' (or 'a pure form') if that phrase can stand for a pure or perfect activity or energy. But if I have argued correctly, the phrase need not commit us to giving him the status of a universal in the logician's sense of the word, or even comparing him with one. He could be a unique particular. An individual 'pure form' might perhaps be illustrated at the lowest and simplest level by a perfect wave, for instance one produced by uniformly acting forces in pure water. Such a wave, of course, would be not only individual but dependent upon matter; but its matter would be perfectly adapted to produce the ideal. One might improve the analogy by considering a human personality, in which a certain characteristic pattern of behaviour is maintained by being superimposed on the continually changing material constitution of the body. One would note in this case that a human personality is to some extent self-perpetuating: it tends to choose, control and dominate its environment and select the matter which it needs. One could then go on to conceive of God as a perfect personality who not only controls but creates whatever environment is perfectly adapted to his state; this condition is already outlined by Aristotle in his requirement that divinity must be αὐτάρκης, self-sufficient; he cannot be limited by or dependent upon something not subject to his control. In tracing this path we have not, I think, encountered any factor which is logically incompatible with the Christian doctrine of the Trinity. If we wish to argue that such a divine personality must be organized about three distinct centres; or alternatively, if we wish to conceive of a divine society formed by the primordial being exalting two others to share the same dignity, the way is so far open for such developments.

In the second place, we must try to evaluate the very different conception which results if God is described as 'pure being' in the sense of 'unqualified being', 'being-in-itself', or 'nothing but being'. Such descriptions are usually associated with the Platonic doctrine that *all* universals are eternal realities, and that each of them is regarded as one, as opposed to its many possible instances. Although Aristotle took the lead in criticizing this view, it remains true that he was influenced by it in his early writings; and it is not unlikely that he wished to retain and develop it, in case it should prove possible to restate it in a form which would escape his own criticisms. Hence, no doubt, his continued interest in the doctrine that being in every context is a form of unity. This framework of thought, accordingly, associates the notions of being, unity, and eternity, and lays it down that God is eternal, pure, and simple Being.

Yet under this general heading there are several distinguishable types of theology, which need to be separately examined. First, 'pure being' looks as if it should designate an unique reality; but the same phrase can stand for something which appears very different, namely the abstract notion of being, which attaches to everything that is, or exists, or is so-and-so. In fact some writers find 'being' an appropriate designation for God precisely because of its lack of any definite content. Philo is clearly familiar with the argument that God, who describes himself in Exodus as 'He who Is', or 'I am' (ὁ ὤν) is thus comparable to the more abstract notion of 'something', the ultimately general category according to the Stoics (*Leg. All.* ii. 86, iii. 175, cf. *SVF* ii. 329, 332–3). God is thus 'the most general being' (τὸ γενικώτατον); paradoxically, God is unique precisely *because* he assumes a description which is perfectly commonplace, which attaches to everything, good, bad and indifferent alike; as Philo puts it, God is the universal which comprehends all things (ὁ πάντων ἐστὶ γένος).[14] But at the same time God is compared to the manna in the desert, whose name means 'What is it?' (Exod. 16: 15), or otherwise accented, 'It is something'; and this suggests the rather different picture of a divine nature which is hidden from us, and about which nothing can be said, not because there is in principle nothing to be said (which is what 'something', taken literally, would suggest) but because there is nothing that our human reason can apprehend.

Again, Clement of Alexandria states that by a process of geometrical abstraction one can reach the concept of a point, defined as 'a monad having position'; a further abstraction yields the concept 'monad' unqualified, which is a fitting description of the godhead, about whom nothing positive can be said; we can say not what he is, but what he is not.[15] Once again it is clear that the notion of complete absence of content, suggested by the term 'monad', is not meant to be a definitive description of the

---

[14] 'Being is common to all things; but only being is common to all things; in this respect, being is unique' probably represents Philo's argument; he does not emphasize the Stoic point that 'something' is a more general category than 'substance' or 'being'.

[15] *Strom.* v. 71. 2. Cf. Plotinus, *Enn.* v. 3. 14 and 17.

godhead, but is a striking way of suggesting an unfathomable mystery which cannot be characterized in ordinary human terms; hence Clement introduces the terminology of the mystery cults to supplement his *theologia negativa*: 'if therefore, stripping off all that belongs to bodies and to things termed incorporeal, we throw ourselves into the greatness of Christ, and thence go forward into the void in holiness . . .'[16] A rather similar impression is given by descriptions of God which use pairs of opposed predicates, sometimes negating both, as in Albinus, for whom the godhead is 'neither evil . . . nor good . . . nor indifferent . . . neither qualified . . . nor without quality' (*Didasc.* 10, p. 165, 6–10), sometimes affirming both, as in 'Monoimus the Arabian', as reported by Hippolytus (*Ref.* viii. 12. 5).

However, if the abstract notion of being fails to prescribe any particular qualities, it also fails to exclude any; so one might expect writers for whom the indeterminate concept of being suggests an infinite multiplicity of actions and forms which God can adopt. Many of the Stoics taught that God is a single power who appears to men in innumerable different guises; and thus, incidentally, were able to explain the innumerable cults of polytheism as simply revealing different aspects of his nature. So Posidonius (fr. 101) is said to have defined God as 'an intelligible fiery spirit, devoid of form, but changing into whatever he wills and conforming himself to all things' (πνεῦμα νοερὸν καὶ πυρῶδες, οὐκ ἔχον μὲν μορφήν, μεταβάλλον δὲ εἰς ὃ βούλεται καὶ συνεξομοιού-μενον πᾶσιν); and similar views were held much earlier by Heraclitus (fr. 67 = Hippolytus, *Ref.* ix. 10. 8; see also *SVF* ii. 1049 ff., though these are mostly hostile reports of doubtful value). Such conceptions appear clearly enough in the Nassene saying quoted by Hippolytus (*Ref.* v. 7. 25), 'I become what I will and am what I am', which looks like a conflate version of the great I AM text of Exodus 3: 14.[17] Hippolytus' Nassenes seem to have thought of their supreme principle as persisting immutably, though assuming many forms ('for it remains what it is while making all things and does not turn into any of the things that come to be', μένει γὰρ ὅ ἐστι ποιοῦν τὰ πάντα καὶ οὐδὲν τῶν

---

[16] Εἰ τοίνυν, ἀφελόντες πάντα ὅσα πρόσεστι τοῖς σώμασιν καὶ τοῖς λεγομένοις ἀσωμάτοις, ἐπιρρίψαιμεν ἑαυτοὺς εἰς τὸ μέγεθος τοῦ Χριστοῦ κἀκεῖθεν εἰς τὸ ἀχανὲς ἁγιότητι προιοῖμεν . . .

[17] γίνομαι ὃ θέλω καὶ εἰμὶ ὅ εἰμί. The first phrase could be paraphrased, 'I will be what I will be', a possible rendering of the Hebrew; cf. Aquila's ἔσομαι ὃ ἔσομαι.

γινομένων γίνεται, loc. cit.); but one can also find Christians conceiving a God whose distinctive character lies precisely in his ability to assume any form (*Clem. Hom.* xx. 7. 6). In Christian circles, however, this theology is usually held in check by the Platonic doctrine that the supreme God is absolutely one, simple and unqualified; thus it is the Second God who is represented as polymorphous.[18] This seems to have been the view of the middle-Platonist Numenius; and among Christians, Origen can say (*in Joh.* i. 119), 'God is completely one and simple; but our Saviour, because of the many—since God set him forth as a propitiation and first-fruits of all the creation—becomes many, or perhaps all of these, according as he is needed by all the creation that is able to be freed.'

We have now considered two possible interpretations of the concept of pure being; there is a third, which will need to be introduced rather less directly.

It seems clear that the language about God's 'generality', considered just now, is often coloured by assumptions derived from Platonism. First there is the well-known identification of the universal with the ideal, to which Aristotle took such strong exception; in practice, the Platonists seem to have constructed their system by concentrating on idealizable qualities, and speaking as if individual instances arose through deviations from such ideals. It was the difficulties connected with this latter point which led some Platonists to maintain a realist view of the Ideas of species while denying reality to genera; for while there is some plausibility in holding that there is a single ideal type of man, and that individuals, Socrates, Plato, Alexander, are what they are because they deviate from it in just *these* respects, it is far less plausible to maintain that lions and tigers are definable simply as deviations from some really existing ideal animal. The theory works only within a limited field; it is, I suppose, a tenable view that particular virtues are modifications or specializations of a general disposition called 'goodness', developed to meet particular circumstances; and this is the view that Philo suggests when he comments on the river that went out from Edom and divided into four branches (Gen. 2: 10), saying that this signifies the

---

[18] Above, p. 93; Gospel of Philip, 26; 'Basilides' in Irenaeus i. 24. 4, Hv. i. 200; other refs. in Daniélou, *Jewish Christianity*, 206 ff., and in Hennecke–Schneemelcher, E.T. Index, s.v. 'Many Forms' (German, s.v. 'Vielgestaltigkeit').

general disposition of goodness which gives rise to the four cardinal virtues (*Leg. All.* i. 63 ff., cf. 59). But it is clear that 'general virtue' in Philo sometimes means 'perfect virtue'—e.g. *Cher.* 5, 7—which as ideal is also eternal; and sometimes again 'comprehensive' or 'all-inclusive' virtue—e.g. *Mut. Nom.* 148.

One can perhaps develop Philo's point by considering the difference between '*x*' and 'an *x*' which has been used already. If one credits a man with 'a virtue', this is to credit him with *one* virtue which is not specified. 'He possesses a virtue' tells us less than, say, 'He possesses courage', just as 'There is an animal in the room' tells us less than 'There is a lion in the room'. But the difference lies primarily in the amount of information conveyed; there is no corresponding difference in the degree of commendation; it might be *more* honorific to be credited with 'a virtue' unspecified, than with some rather unimportant virtue such as punctuality; conversely, 'He has courage' is a powerful commendation only because it explains that an important virtue is involved. On the other hand, if one credits a man with 'virtue', the implication is that he possesses most or perhaps all of the qualities that fall under this description: it implies general virtue or goodness. If indeed one could make the somewhat unrealistic assumption that each virtue is definable as the absence of the corresponding vice, then it might be true that by crediting a man with 'virtue' one implied that he had no vices at all, and so that his virtue was perfect and complete. It is by making similar assumptions on a higher level of generality that one reaches the position that 'pure being' can be regarded, not just as an abstract term implying a minimum predication, but as an inclusive term implying the sum of all conceivable perfections, whether moral, aesthetic, or metaphysical.

'Fullness of perfect being'—the concept just discussed—would seem to provide a fitting close to this chapter; but for completeness there are two further applications of the concept of pure being which need to be mentioned. Such language sometimes appears to be drawn upon *faute de mieux* when the underlying intention is to describe a type of consciousness which has been strikingly characterized by Dr. Rudolph Otto, though not perhaps to the satisfaction of all his readers. The worshipper is presented with an experience which stands out from his normal consciousness, and which arouses emotions both of love and of awe, submission, or even terror; he is confronted with a '*myste-rium tremendum fascinans*'; at the same time the experience is diffi-cult to characterize; sometimes it seems complete in itself: one simply experiences deity as one experiences warmth, or indeed all sense of a distinction between self and not-self may seem to disappear; sometimes a sense of transcendence is strongly felt: the experience may present itself in the guise of an emotional response to a cause or force acting on the personality which remains undisclosed, so that any attempt to comprehend it involves an inference from effect to cause: this must be such, if its effects are such; sometimes, on the other hand, it may seem possible to pass beyond the human response by some process of interpretation, in which case it seems that a reality beyond the self is being apprehended by a process akin to perception; some-thing is 'seen' or 'intuited', or again is 'grasped' or 'touched'. In such cases the language in which this mysterious other reality is described will be extremely various, since the subject tries to categorize it by analogies drawn from other parts of his ex-perience, whether social, aesthetic or philosophical. But it seems probable that the category of pure being is sometimes drawn upon as a pointer to this type of experience.[19]

Lastly, God is sometimes conceived as a sum of positive attri-butes (not positive and negative); but with the proviso that the divine simplicity is unimpaired, so that *verbi gratia* at any rate he may be identified with any one of them taken singly; in Augus-tine's phrase, 'He is what he has' (*Civ. Dei* xi. 10). I must leave this concept undeveloped for the moment,[20] merely noting that it appears in Christian theology at least as early as Irenaeus (ii. 13. 3, Hv. i. 282), for whom God is 'simple and not compounded, uniform and wholly alike in himself, being wholly mind and wholly spirit . . . wholly hearing, wholly sight, wholly light and wholly the source of all good things'.

[19] Cf. P. Merlan, *From Platonism to Neoplatonism*, 185 ff.
[20] See below, pp. 163, 187–9.

V

SUBSTANCE AFTER ARISTOTLE

(i) *Primary and Secondary Substance*

ARISTOTELIANISM, as a distinct and comprehensive system of thought, was already in decline when Christian writers began to interest themselves in philosophy. The Peripatetic school had put much of its best work into specialized researches with a limited appeal; while the general public, whose knowledge of Aristotle rested mainly on his early and popular works, naturally regarded him as an unorthodox Platonist rather than as an important and original thinker in his own right; though we can also trace interpretations of Aristotle which assimilate him to the Stoics[1] and even to Pythagoras;[2] and the Stoicizing interpretation was to continue with Aristocles, and influenced some later Christian writers.

The position began to alter after the new edition of Aristotle's writings by Andronicus drew attention to Aristotle's more technical treatises intended for use within the School, which make up the Aristotelian corpus as we now know it. Some of these, and especially perhaps the *Nicomachean Ethics* and the *Topics*,[3] began to attract the attention of cultivated amateurs; and for the rest we can trace the beginnings of a tradition of learned criticism and exegesis. At first, however, this made little headway outside a small circle of professional scholars; and it may be that, among professed Peripatetics, only Alexander of Aphrodisias was to achieve any real distinction in the double role of scholar and publicist.

---

[1] Antiochus regarded Zeno as a Platonist (!). This probably indicates that he placed Aristotle within a continuous philosophical tradition extending from Plato to 'Zeno', i.e. to contemporary Stoicized Platonism. See Cicero, *Academica*, i. 35, 43; ii (*Lucullus*) 15. Sextus, *Hyp.* i. 235 (cited Theiler, p. 38).

[2] See A. H. Armstrong (ed.), *Cambridge History of Later Greek Philosophy* for notices and refs. to Moderatus (p. 90), Aristoxenus, Critolaus, Ps.-Ocellus (p. 112).

[3] Clement of Alexandria quotes *NE* twenty-nine times; *Topics* thirteen times, allowing for repetitions; no other work more than eight times.

At this time, also, the resources of Stoicism were beginning to run dry. It had hitherto shown considerable elasticity and ingenuity in meeting the attacks of its critics, and it remained a dominant influence in the field of ethics; but the appeal to its 'founding fathers', Zeno and Chrysippus, was still important both for defence and for attack; and the crudity of some of their theories, particularly in physical science, made it an easy target. The decline of the Stoics left the Platonists in a position of dominance that the Peripatetics could not hope to upset; and this reinforced the tendency to subordinate Aristotle to Plato. Indeed some important Aristotelian concepts were kept in circulation by being referred back to Plato himself. This is true for the doctrine of the mean in ethics;[4] it was also suggested that Plato had anticipated the doctrine of the ten categories.[5] And for a time at least the initiative in Aristotelian scholarship passed to men whose primary allegiance was to Plato. It was not until the neo-Platonists had tried, and failed, to halt the progress of Christianity that the originality and intellectual force of Aristotle gained their due recognition.

Accordingly for a period of some two centuries, extending roughly from Justin to Athanasius, Christian writers who can speak respectfully of Plato generally dismiss Aristotle with a somewhat ill-informed contempt. He is accused of inconsistency, a charge which could well be admitted today, but had especial force at a time when the early dialogues were still in circulation, and works such as the *de Mundo* had not been recognized as false attributions. The difficulty of his style and the subtlety of his distinctions were another ground of complaint. Further, he was known to have criticized Plato, and on many points was held to have adopted theories incompatible with Christianity; he taught the eternity of the world; he restricted the scope of divine providence; he commended a worldly and uninspired morality.

It may be thought, none the less, that the evidence for Aristotle's influence on the *logical* methods and terminology of the ancient world is overwhelming, and that the distinctions made in

---

[4] Hippolytus, *Ref.* i. 19. 16, cf. Albinus, *Didasc.* 30.

[5] See Plutarch, *An. Procr.* 23. 1023 e, citing *Timaeus* 37 b; Albinus, *Didasc.* 6 (p. 159, 34–5), referring to the *Parmenides*; cf. R. E. Witt, *Albinus*, 66, n. 8. It is not disputed that Plato has important anticipations of the doctrine of the mean, and of some of Aristotle's categorial distinctions.

the *Categories* were so familiar that it was superfluous to allude to them.[6] This assumption will be especially natural for scholars who approach the ancient writers from the thoughts and tradition of the Middle Ages. But the situation of the medieval writers was peculiar; in their time the Organon of Aristotle was the main instrument of instruction in logic; and in the early Middle Ages only this part of Aristotle's work was known. One cannot assume that the position was similar in the early Christian centuries; and such evidence as I have collected goes to indicate a much more complex picture.

In the first place, we can trace a fairly continuous tradition of comment and scholarly criticism of the *Categories*. Andronicus is said to have been the first to write a commentary; he was followed by Boethus of Sidon and Eudorus, still in the first century B.C. In the second century A.D. we hear of Aspasius, Adrastus, Herminus, Achaicus, Sosigenes, and Alexander as commentators; Galen also tells us that he wrote a commentary, but this was evidently unsuccessful and is otherwise unknown. Interest in the subject certainly extended outside the Peripatetic school; among the Platonists, the theory of the *Categories* was criticized by Lucius, Nicostratus, and Atticus, but endorsed by Albinus and Plutarch; and a neo-Pythagorean writer who took the name of Archytas wrote a systematic treatise on the categories which follows Aristotle in broad outline, though with considerable modifications.[7]

The commentators will hardly have been consulted except by professional scholars, and my impression is that the actual text of the *Categories* was not very widely familiar; it is seldom quoted, by Christian writers at any rate, in the second or third centuries. Non-professional readers seem rather to have gained their impressions of Aristotle's logic from doxographic works or other popular manuals (as Clement did from Albinus); these, I think invariably, credit Aristotle with a list of ten categories, which is in fact only presented in the *Categories* and the *Topics*, and was no doubt commended by its popularity with the Pythagoreans.

Some other ideas presented in the *Categories* passed into common use. The definitions of homonyms and synonyms were

---

[6] See A.-J. Festugière, *L'Idéal religieux des grecs et l'Évangile*, 222–63.

[7] See T. A. Szlezák, *Pseudo-Archytas über die Kategorien* (Berlin, 1972). He dates Ps.-Archytas (the earlier) in the first century B.C.

borrowed by grammatical text-books;[8] other more philosophical notions were incorporated into works on rhetoric, which became the instruments of a general education in the arts of speaking and writing, and taught not only forensic argument but essays and declamations on philosophical themes of general interest.[9] In this way the Aristotelian distinction between essential and accidental predication became widely accepted, since there was an obvious practical importance in arguments which could claim to establish invariable rules which applied to all members of some given class, or conversely could destroy such claims. In a rather more technical branch of the subject a system broadly similar to Aristotle's categories was adopted by some rhetoricians in their lists of *staseis*, or 'stages', i.e. ways of applying a chosen topic of argument. The general plan of such rhetorical schemes is illustrated by the medieval jingle *Quis? quid? ubi? quibus auxiliis? cur? quomodo? quando?*, which contains recognizable equivalents of four of the Aristotelian categories, substance, action, place and time. Quite commonly, however, such schemes are not used to control the whole development of a case, but are applied seriatim to a number of conventional topics; thus the topic, 'His story is unconvincing', may be developed according to a list such as 'the character, the act, the place, the time, the manner, the reason'.[10] Such systems of *staseis*, which vary considerably in detail, have been described by R. Nadeau;[11] but it is worth noting that the systems he describes are mostly influenced by Stoic logic; a partially Aristotelian scheme appears only in one writer of no particular distinction, Theodorus of Gadara.

But we also need to answer the more particular question: was the distinction drawn in the *Categories* between 'primary substance' and 'secondary substance' generally familiar? And in particular, was it generally recognized by Christian writers? Here the point at issue can easily be concealed by careless description. In the

---

[8] Cf. Clement, *Strom.* viii. 17. 1; Hippolytus, *Ref.* vii. 20. 5; Origen, *Hom. Jerem.* xx.

[9] See e.g. Theon, *Progymnasmata*, c. 6 (Spengel ii. 120) for description of the *thesis*, a general theme, 'e.g., should one marry, should one beget children, do gods exist?' (οἷον εἰ γαμητέον, εἰ παιδοποιητέον, εἰ θεοί εἰσι).

[10] Ibid. ii. 94 (πρόσωπον, πραχθέν, τόπος, χρόνος, τρόπος, αἰτία).

[11] 'Classical Systems of Stases in Greek: Hermagoras to Hermogenes', *Greek Roman and Byzantine Studies* 2 (1959), 53–71.

Categories, c. 5, Aristotle distinguishes two sorts of οὐσία (or two senses of 'οὐσία'), and thereby sets down in classical form the distinction between the individual and the species. Accordingly, where οὐσία is found in other writings, one way of saying whether it is being used with individual, or with general reference, is to say that it is used 'in the sense of πρώτη οὐσία' or '. . . δευτέρα οὐσία', as the case may be. But these phrases are ambiguous; it is seldom clear whether they are intended merely to note the logic of the term οὐσία, or whether they are meant to imply that the writer in question had Aristotle's discussion in mind, was conscious of the alternative meanings, and deliberately expressed himself in Aristotle's terminology. These two possibilities are of course perfectly distinct. We may note first that Aristotle's account of primary and secondary substance is a theory based on common usage, in which the same word can have either a narrow or a wider denotation. Obviously the theory could not have been framed unless the usage were established; the usage therefore antedates the theory, and it was always possible to adopt the usage while remaining ignorant of the theory. And it seems that Christian writers did exactly this; at least the question needs to be examined. Furthermore, although Aristotle's theory is framed in terms of the word οὐσία, it does not merely apply to the word οὐσία but to the various expressions for which οὐσία is a compendious term, and the realities they stand for; thus Aristotle illustrates it by giving the example ἄνθρωπος, man. Logically, therefore, a double use of οὐσία does not prove knowledge of the theory any more than a double use of ἄνθρωπος or any similar term; though it is no doubt true that a writer using the term οὐσία would more easily be reminded of the theory, if he knew it.

The question therefore needs to be reopened; and we may begin with a concession. There is one undoubted explicit reference to Aristotle's doctrine of primary and secondary substance in Hippolytus (*Ref.* vii. 16–18). But beyond this, if we exclude mere variation in usage, it is extremely difficult to find evidence for a knowledge of this doctrine among Christian writers before the end of the fourth century.

This conclusion may seem surprising; but some good reasons can be offered in its defence. In the first place, Aristotle does not appear to have used the phrases πρώτη οὐσία and δευτέρα οὐσία as technical terms. The latter phrase, I believe, is peculiar to the

Categories. The former shows an extraordinary variation in usage.[12] Thus in *Metaph.* iv. 3, 1005 a 35, it appears to mean 'being as such', regarded as the most general possible reality; at xiv. 4, 1092 a 8, used in the plural, it seems to mean 'principles from which all else is derived', a role which the Platonists assigned to numbers. At vii. 7, 1032 b 2, it is coupled with 'essence' and associated with the term 'form', and a rather similar usage appears twice in the summary passage in vii. 11, at 1037 a 28, b 1–2; this of course contrasts sharply with its use in the *Categories*. Finally in xii. 8, 1073 a 30 and 1074 b 9, it means respectively 'God' and 'gods'.

Secondly, it is well to consider how the distinction drawn in *Categories* c. 5 would appear to Platonist commentators. *Their* fundamental distinction was drawn between perceptible substances, considered as composite and perishable, and intelligible substances, regarded as simple and immutable. And it was by no means clear whether this coincided with a distinction between individuals and universals; no doubt perceptible substances were normally considered as individuals, but there was a long-standing perplexity about the status of 'the intelligibles' (τὰ νοητά); how far they were to be regarded as universals, how far as ideal prototypes, which would be in some sense individual; and indeed whether there might not be ideas, that is ideal permanent embodiments, of human individuals. But whatever view was taken on such points, such thinkers were hardly likely to countenance a theory which assigns the first rank to perceptible and material entities, such as this (individual, embodied) man, in preference to the intelligible reality or idea of humanity, which they would class as a pure form.

It is not surprising, therefore, that Platonists found the implications of *Categories* 5 an embarrassment. Accordingly, when they do use the phrase πρώτη οὐσία, these implications are set aside; thus there is no difficulty in labelling the intelligibles as 'first substances', for this implies that they are *prior* to the perceptible individuals. On the other hand, when they wish to refer to individuals as such, there is a wealth of alternative expressions which hold no such embarrassments, many of them provided by Aristotle himself; they can be called τὰ καθ' ἕκαστα or τὰ κατὰ

---

[12] See W. Theiler, *Museum Helveticum* 15 (1958) 87, n. 11. I have not followed his treatment of *Metaph.* iv. 2, 1004 a 3.

μέρος or else simply ἄτομα—literally, 'things each-for-each',
'particular things', 'atoms'. Such expressions occur freely in
Christian writers such as Clement, Hippolytus, and Eusebius.
They are also found in writers influenced by Stoicism, though the
Stoics also employ some distinctive terms, based on their convention of treating the characters of a species as qualities, ποιό-
τητες; hence individuals can be called 'uniquely qualified beings',
ἰδίως ποιά, sometimes in contrast with the 'commonly qualified
beings', κοινῶς ποιά, the species themselves. In less technical
contexts the Stoics will refer to an individual quite freely as an
οὐσία; but the phrase πρώτη οὐσία, like πρώτη ὕλη, carries a very
different sense; it refers to the 'primary matter' on which the
qualities are imposed, and as we shall see, it fluctuates in meaning between 'underlying stuff' which is logically presupposed by
its derivatives, and 'original stuff' which was subsequently
transformed into them. Mnesarchus, who identified the divinity
with τὸν κόσμον τὴν πρώτην οὐσίαν ἔχοντα ἀπὸ πνεύματος[13] perhaps
takes πρώτη οὐσία as 'origin' rather than 'original stuff' (Diels,
DG, p. 303) but the latter sense is fairly clear in Galen, de Qual.
Incorp. 4 and 5, SVF ii. 382, 323.

At all events the fluid, non-technical use of πρώτη οὐσία persists in Christian times. The meaning 'most general type of
reality' appears in Calcidius, who uses primae substantiae for the
three summa genera of Platonism, God, matter, and the exemplars
(in. Tim., 330). Apuleius seems to hesitate between the notion of
generality and that of superior dignity; thus the primae substantiae are the νοητά, viz. God, matter (!), the forms, and the
soul, whereas the secundae substantiae are all temporal beings liable
to change (de Platone i. 6). It is the persistence of matter through
its changing embodiments, presumably, that secures its promotion. Next, Aristotle's use of πρώτη οὐσία to refer to God, as
the highest reality, is reflected in Christian writers. Arnobius
considers the possibility that man is God's offspring: si verum est
illum principalis esse substantiae portionem (adv. Nat. ii. 22). There are
also texts which characterize the Father as πρώτη οὐσία in contrast
with the Logos. Eusebius refers to the Logos as 'a second being',
μετὰ τὴν ἄναρχον καὶ ἀγένητον τοῦ θεοῦ τῶν ὅλων οὐσίαν . . .
δευτέραν οὐσίαν καὶ θείαν δύναμιν (PE vii. 12. 2, p. 320 c). The
implication of inferiority appears more clearly in a second

[13] Literally 'the world which gets its first being from spirit'.

passage, too long to quote (ibid. vii. 15); and in both, Eusebius appears to be influenced by Numenius, whom he quotes at xi. 22, p. 544 b. The actual phrase πρώτη οὐσία appears in a similar passage at *DE* v. 1. 24, and again in a polemical passage of Athanasius, at *Syn.* 50. A little later Aëtius, who was thought to be an Aristotelian, uses οὐσίαν δευτέραν . . . προτέραν in criticizing the Trinitarian views of his opponents: God sees his own οὐσία in a twofold form, both as present in his offspring and as subsisting in himself.[14] Gregory Nazianzen also uses πρώτη οὐσία of God, but here the contrast is with the angels (*Or.* 28. 31, ed. Mason, p. 70. 9); and Basil similarly (*c. Eun.* i. 12, *PG* 29. 541 B).

Earlier, Hippolytus had used πρώτη οὐσία, in a description of Naassene theology, to denote an eternal and ideal but formless substance out of which earthly forms are made (Ref. v. 7. 18). The conception recalls the Stoic πῦρ τεχνικόν, but the details are puzzling, since the Naassenes saw a reference to this conception in the ἀσχημοσύνη of Rom. 1 : 27. Hippolytus seems to suggest that the Naassenes took Paul's words to mean that the homosexuals were (not acting indecently but) 'achieving formlessness'; but it may be that he misrepresents his opponents.

On the other hand πρώτη οὐσία can also mean the lowest or simplest form of being. In Hippolytus, *Ref.* x. 33. 4, the πρῶται οὐσίαι are simply the four material elements, earth, air, fire, and water. As a curiosity we may mention also a fragment of Clement (fr. 38, from his *On Providence*, *GCS*. iii. 219) where πρώτη οὐσία is the lowest type of being, the inorganic, whereas δευτέρα οὐσία is that next above it, viz. vegetable life![15]

The relevance of these examples will become clear if I add that the course of reading which discovered them has yielded no instances in which πρώτη οὐσία is used in its normal 'Aristotelian' sense, with the single exception of Hippolytus' account of Aristotle in *Ref.* vii. 16 ff. I cannot be sure that there are none to find, but I do not think they can be frequent, at least in the Eastern Church up to the end of the fourth century.

This point may be most clearly illustrated by considering the case of Porphyry. Porphyry was a professional philosopher, and

---

[14] *Syntagmation* 31, ed. L. R. Wickham, in *JTS*, n.s. 19 (1968), 543; cf. Gregory of Nyssa, *c. Eun.* i. 206.
[15] The *scala naturae* itself is not uncommon; see e.g. Philo, *Immut.* 35, Seneca, *Ep.* 124. 14, and cf. P. Hadot, *Entretiens Hardt*, v, pp. 120–1.

thought well enough of Aristotle to write a commentary on the *Categories*. Yet in the *Isagoge*, his well-known introduction to logic, the phrase πρώτη οὐσία does not occur at all. In the Commentary on the *Categories* it is of course explained and referred to, Porphyry's explanation being that perceptible individuals are called 'first' because they come first in the *ordo cognoscendi* (ed. Busse, p. 91. 10 ff.), so that the supremacy of the νοητά over the αἰσθητά, and so of the universal over the particular, can still be upheld. Nevertheless, when Porphyry writes πρῶται οὐσίαι he normally adds a paraphrase (e.g. ἄτομοι οὐσίαι at p. 88. 26; cf. ibid. 30–1); without such a paraphrase the expression is rarely found (see e.g. 98. 16; 92. 16, 18, 25; 93. 9—contexts in which it would be superfluous to repeat the paraphrase); and even including the paraphrased instances, it is much less common than the alternatives τὰ ἄτομα, τὰ καθ᾽ ἕκαστα, τὰ κατὰ μέρος, which are the ordinary phrases he uses for referring to individuals.

In the light of the evidence just given, it seems clear that πρώτη οὐσία and δευτέρα οὐσία were not in common use as technical terms for 'individual' and 'species'; that οὐσία was not commonly used in just these two connections; and *a fortiori* that a writer who used the word οὐσία would not normally ask himself which of these two senses he meant to convey.

(ii) *Substance and the Stoics*

Plato and Aristotle, taken together, exhibit nearly all the basic senses of *ousia*, so far as these are established by logical distinctions. New *applications* of the term of course appear in the next few centuries; but I shall not attempt to survey the whole development, since the philosophical history of this period is both complex and obscure. However it seems desirable to sketch in the relevant features of Stoicism at any rate, in view of its influence on the thought of the early Christian period.

Stoicism differed radically from Platonism in that it saw the world as an evolving system; instead of an unchanging pattern which controls all events in the material world, it envisaged an orderly process of development, containing of course a number of subordinate regularities and repetitions, but forming over-all a historical process in which a differentiated structure gradually develops out of chaos, and in time will be absorbed into chaos again. As is well known, the Stoics held that this process is repeated indefinitely, so that the whole history of the universe forms a series of cycles, with their alternate phases of evolution and reabsorption or coalescence.

Stoicism is generally described as a monism; not of course in the sense that it discounted all apparent differences in the universe, like the earlier Eleatic systems, but in the sense that it recognized no absolute discontinuities. All forms of reality, matter, mind, and spirit alike, find their places on a single graduated scale which extends from cold, dead, and inactive matter to fiery, active, and intelligent spirit; furthermore, these distinctions themselves have only arisen within the present, evolving, phase of the cosmic process, and will in course of time disappear; the universe has come from fire, and to fire it will return. The Stoic system can also, without too much inaccuracy, be described as materialistic; partly because the Stoics commonly described our thoughts and mental qualities as 'dispositions' of the body, partly because the highest reality they recognized is conceived in material terms; it is identified with the fire from which the other material substances have evolved, and still permeates them in their altered form; and although endowed with intelligence, it nevertheless occupies space and conforms to the principle that only bodies can act on bodies. The term 'materialism', therefore, must not be taken to suggest that intelligence and organizing power develop fortuitously out of lifeless and unintelligent material particles, as in the theories of the atomists and Epicurus; it is an essential feature of Stoicism that the organizing principle, which they call 'constructive fire', was present in the original matrix from which the universe developed.

However, within this general pattern of thought one has to recognize considerable differences of detail and emphasis. Stoicism postulates a single basic constituent material endowed with a constructive organizing power, and similarly considers the universe, in its developed phase, as permeated by a rational principle which is strictly immanent within it. This emphasis on unity and immanence is commonly presented as characteristic of the system in its original form;[16] it is certainly a striking feature of Stoicism, and it persisted well into the Christian era, notably in those

[16] M. Pohlenz, *Die Stoa*, i. 67; cf. *SVF* ii. 306–8, 314.

writers who identify God with the rationally ordered universe.[17]
Some accounts, however, distinguish fairly sharply between the
active and the passive aspects, or constituents, of this divine
world-stuff, and this dualistic picture is also presented as typical
of Stoicism.[18] It would be natural to think of it as a later development,[19] possibly influenced by a revived Platonism which recognized two original principles, the creator-god and unformed
matter, and held that the god himself was the source of the ideal
forms, and so of the rational structure of the world. But in fact
dualistic motifs appear at least as early as Chrysippus, who is
rightly credited with stating a strictly monistic view, but who
nevertheless distinguished the active and passive principles to the
point that he could see them symbolized by two distinct deities in
a myth of Zeus and Hera;[20] indeed Cleanthes already envisages
the directing power of the universe as located in, or proceeding
from, the sun, rather than simply all-pervasive.[21] It seems wise,
then, to recognize the possibility that Stoicism may never have
been completely consistent, but throughout its history admitted
variations in standpoint and emphasis.

We have now to consider the part played by the term *ousia*,
first in the cosmological theories which have just been described,
and secondly in the broader context of the Stoic system of
categories.

The Stoics recognize four material elements, fire, air, water
and earth; but these are not the ultimate constituents of their
universe. The elements themselves are constituted by two pairs of
opposite qualities, hot and cold, dry and wet; and these, we are
told, are applied to a more basic kind of matter which has no
qualities of its own.[22] This is called 'unqualified matter', ἄποιος
ὕλη, or quite commonly ἄποιος οὐσία, and is clearly derived, via
Aristotle, from the 'Receptacle and Nurse of Becoming' which

---

[17] Cicero, *Nat. Deor.* ii. 30–9; Seneca, *Qu. Nat.*, prol. 13; *Benef.* iv. 8; Arius
Didymus, fr. 29, Diels *DG* p. 464 = Eusebius, *PE* xv. 15. 1–4. Cf. Diogenes Laertius, vii. 136–9.

[18] Both von Arnim and de Vogel give a possibly misleading prominence to
Diogenes Laertius vii. 134, which actually speaks of two first principles.

[19] J. M. Rist, *Stoic Philosophy*, 185, 202–11, intimates that dualism seems to
appear with Posidonius and Boethus.

[20] *SVF* ii. 1071–4; cf. Plato, *Timaeus*, 50 d; but also N.B. *SVF* ii. 604–5; in the
original and final states of the universe there is no distinction.

[21] Ibid. i. 502–4; but cf. also 530; Cleanthes' theology seems ill-defined.

[22] For the theoretical difficulties of this concept, see above, pp. 21–2, 98.

Plato introduced in the *Timaeus*. Since the elements are supposed to change one into another, and so to exchange their qualities, the neutral matter appears to be the one perfectly constant factor which persists through change. And although it has no constant quality, it is said to remain constant in quantity;[23] one might compare the doctrine of conservation of mass in nineteenth-century physics. This view of the world-process is not peculiar to Stoicism,[24] though it was adopted by many Stoics; but it does not easily square with the view which we described earlier, namely that *one* of the elements, in fact fire, is the source of all the others; that it initiates their development by changing itself (or part of itself?) into them, and will reabsorb them at the next conflagration.

When they consider the stuff of the universe in its passive aspect, the Stoics often assimilate it to Aristotle's 'formless matter', regarded as a pure product of analysis.[25] But in practice it proved impossible to maintain a clear distinction between ontological analysis and cosmological history; the thesis that unqualified matter is logically prior, or prerequisite, as that in which the qualities inhere and which is necessary for their existence, was easily confused with the quite different thesis that unordered matter, or matter having no permanent structure, was temporally prior, and was the original stuff out of which the universe developed.[26] And this cosmological process could be described in either monistic or dualistic terms. In the one case, the universe arises out of 'constructive fire', which generates an ordered multiplicity by transforming itself into other elements;[27] in the other, the formless matter is conceived as a passive, inert substance on which the organizing principle sets to work.[28]

---

[23] Arius Didymus, fr. 20, p. 457 Diels, = *SVF* i. 87+ ii. 317, and 27, p. 462; Diog. Laert. vii. 150; cf. Galen's criticisms, *de Qual. Incorp.* 5, = *SVF* ii. 323.

[24] Besides matter, Aristotle has qualities prior to elements, e.g. *de Part. Anim.* ii. 1, *de Gen. et Corr.* ii. 3; transmutation of elements, ibid. ii. 4.

[25] Aristotle, *Physics* i. 6 ff.; *de Gen. et Corr.* ii. 1, 329 a 12.

[26] The confusion is present in many of the extracts collected in *SVF* ii. 299–318. Origen perhaps sees the difficulty: the original mass has no quality of its own, though it always has some quality (*Orat.* 27. 8, *SVF* ii. 318, esp. p. 115, l. 3); possibly also Galen, *de Qual. Incorp.* 5 (ibid. 327): it is incomprehensible that something can be neither heavy nor light; cf. Aristotle, loc. cit., 329 a 12, and contrast Philo, *Quis Rerum* 133 ff., who thinks of a mixture that can be separated into light heavy elements, but still describes it as 'unqualified', ἄποιος (140).

[27] Chrysippus, see Plutarch, *Stoic. Rep.* 41; Aetius, *Plac.* i. 7. 33; Plutarch, *Fac. Lun.* 12 (= *SVF* ii. 605, 1027, 1045); Stobaeus, *Ecl.* i. 370, p. 152 W.

[28] Diog. Laert. vii. 135–6; Sextus, *adv. Math.* ix. 11; Galen, *de Qual. Incorp.* 5

It seems, then, that *ousia* can have a very varied application in Stoic physical theory. It can mean the organized universe as a whole.[29] It can mean the passive substratum which is postulated as undergoing change, the ἄποιος οὐσία,[30] though it seldom indicates the active principle.[31] In the context of cosmogony, it can denote the universe in its original (or final) unstructured state, or either of its two principles, though here again the equation with passive matter seems to be much the commoner. *Ousia* can also point to one of the four elements, which are liable to change one into another;[32] again, it can denote compound substances, the constituent material of particular things, or these particular things themselves.[33] In much the same way, the term ὑποκείμενον, 'substrate', can be used either of formless matter, or of specific materials, or or particular individual beings; 'Brass is a substratum, and so is Socrates.'[34]

The Stoic system of categories provides another context for uses of *ousia* which extend outside the field of cosmology. Its main outlines are fairly well known. Simplicius reports that the Stoics reduce the number of categories, or 'first kinds', to four; they divide them into substratum, quality, disposition and relative disposition. (Οἱ δέ γε Στωϊκοὶ εἰς ἐλάττονα συστέλλειν ἀξιοῦσι τὸν τῶν πρώτων γενῶν ἀριθμόν ... ποιοῦνται γὰρ τὴν τομὴν εἰς τέσσαρα, εἰς ὑποκείμενα καὶ ποιὰ καί πως ἔχοντα καὶ πρός τί πως ἔχοντα.)[35] It seems that ὑποκείμενον, 'substratum', is the term commonly used for the first category in formal statements of this theory; but οὐσία can be substituted for it without discernible difference in meaning. Ποιότης, 'quality', is extremely variable in its application; it can denote the four basic physical variables, heat and cold, moisture and dryness, or any one of them; but it can also

(*SVF* i. 102, ii. 301, 323). Aristocles in Eusebius, *PE* xv. 14 (*SVF* i. 98) perhaps reconciles the two pictures.

[29] Cleomedes, *de Motu Circ.* i. 1; Plutarch, *Def. Orac.* 28 (*SVF* ii. 537, 551).

[30] Diog. vii. 134 (= *SVF* ii. 300, which gives wrong ref.); Arius Didymus, fr. 20 (above, p. 121, n. 23); Marcus Aurelius, vi. 1.

[31] A possible example is Philo, *Fuga* 165 *ad fin.*, though the language seems more Platonic than Stoic.

[32] Galen, *in Hippocr. de humor.* 1, *SVF* i. 92.

[33] Diog. vii. 150, *SVF* ii. 316; Plutarch, *Comm. Not.* 44, 1083B, Philo, *Confus.* 184, 186.

[34] Porphyry cited by Simplicius, *in Categ.* 2, p. 48 Kalb.; cf. Dexippus, *in Categ.* i. 22, p. 23 Busse (*SVF* ii. 372, 374).

[35] Simplicius, *in Categ.* 4, p. 66 Kalb. = *SVF* ii. 369; cf. Plotinus, *Enn.* vi. 1. 25 (*SVF* ii. 371); Dexippus, *in Categ.* 1, p. 23 Busse.

refer to species or specific forms.[36] Furthermore the Stoics distinguish between 'common quality' (τὸ κοινῶς ποιόν) and 'individual quality' (τὸ ἰδίως ποιόν or ἰδία ποιότης); hence ποιότης can refer collectively to the sum of properties which characterize an individual. The Stoics were often criticized for holding that qualities are corporeal; but the critics interpreted 'qualities' in various senses, and in some cases the point could have been more fairly put by saying that they are inseparable from matter.

In view of the complexities of both terms, it is not surprising that the relationship of 'substance' to 'quality' is not clearly or consistently stated. Some later Stoics were certainly influenced by the theory that 'quality' is used to refer to temporary states, and it is arguable that some such view was current from the first; for if the Stoics rejected the Platonic view of universals as objective realities, they could regard species as transient patterns which were temporarily assumed by the material substrate, and express this transience by calling them 'qualities'. And even the more fundamental qualities which give rise to the four elements, as we have seen, are not absolutely unchangeable in Stoic theory. But this line of thought, if indeed I have correctly stated it, is overlaid by two others. There is first the general point that *ousia* has to be represented as the unchanging subject of change, remaining constant only in quantity. But there are obvious difficulties in talking about a quantity of x, where x is wholly indeterminate; and it was therefore easy for Platonist critics to represent the Stoics as teaching that material substance accepts every form of change and has no continuity at all. A second point can be made about living creatures; in view of their metabolism, one can say that their material is continually changing, even though their form is at least relatively constant;[37] this led Posidonius to explain that each individual has a dual aspect, a theory which Plutarch dismisses with contempt.[38]

However, permanence and impermanence are relative terms; and qualities can be regarded as permanent in contrast with the third and fourth categories, which are sometimes called

36 Cf. Aristotle's remark (*Categ.* 5, 3 b 15) that secondary substance signifies 'a certain qualification' (ποιόν τι); cf. above, p. 58, n. 5.

37 Plutarch, *Comm. Not.* 44; Methodius, *Res.* i. 22; cf. Plato, *Symp.* 207c ff.

38 In Arius Didymus, fr. 27, p. 462 Diels; Plutarch, loc. cit., cf. ibid. 36.

'accidents' in relation to the first two.[39] (More accurate thinkers envisage a contrast, not between the permanent and the variable, but between necessary conditions and possible determinations: even a permanent quality has to qualify some substance, a disposition presupposes a qualified thing, etc.) The sense of 'disposition' can be conveniently illustrated by a quotation from Sextus: 'Knowledge is the reason (ἡγεμονικόν) in a certain disposition, just as a hand in a certain disposition is a fist'.[40] Similarly Seneca maintains that wisdom is good, and is therefore corporeal; no doubt he equates it with the reasoning organ of the body, if well disposed. But he also refers to a Stoic opinion that 'being wise', on the other hand, is not corporeal, and so not good, since it is merely an 'accident' of the former, i.e. a mental conception which we make of it (*Ep.* 117, 1 ff., 11 ff.); evidently the term 'accident' is used in different senses, which are not entirely covered by the distinction between 'internal' and 'external' accidents (ibid. 7; cf. *SVF* i. 89, ii. 341).

The fourth category is that of 'relative disposition'; and since relatives only appear as a special form of disposition, it might seem that the Stoics afford no place for essential and permanent relations. But Simplicius expressly denies this;[41] and he also knows of Stoic writers who distinguish, as Aristotle did, between permanent and variable dispositions, and do the same with relations; thus if *A* is the son of *B*, this fact is unalterable; what characterizes it as a relative disposition is the fact that it depends on *B*'s existence; whereas *A*'s colour or character, whether unalterable or not, does not depend on a correlative. However, I doubt whether Simplicius' extremely sophisticated distinctions were generally accepted by the Stoics; thus when relations are called σχέσεις, this sometimes seems to mark them off as 'stances', variable poses, in contrast with ἕξεις, 'states', which are relatively permanent; for though the use of ἕξις is also inconsistent, it seems to signify something comparable with 'quality'; it is used of the force of coherence which keeps solid bodies together;[42] and also, with some dissentients, for virtues and vices and similar

[39] So Zeller, iii. 102, and literature there cited; but cf. J. M. Rist, *Stoic Philosophy* 167–71 = A. A. Long, *Problems in Stoicism*, 51–3.

[40] ii. 81. He continues: 'but the reasoning part is corporeal; in their opinion it is spirit'; cf. Seneca, above.

[41] *in Categ.*, c. 7, pp. 165–6 Kalb. = *SVF* ii. 403. I have modified his example.

[42] Plutarch, *Stoic. Rep.* 43; Sextus, *adv. Math.* ix. 81 (*SVF* ii. 449, 1013).

attributes which can increase or diminish.[43] It seems to me that the Stoic theory of categories probably changed and developed to meet the needs of controversy, and its technical terms are not always used with consistency; hence without undertaking a very lengthy and perhaps inconclusive investigation, it is impossible to do more than sketch the main outlines.

(iii) *The Interpretation of the* Categories

Our survey of the senses of *ousia* and its correlative terms will probably have given the impression of extraordinary chaos and incongruity. This indeed was characteristic of the period; with rare exceptions, the writers of the first Christian centuries were scholars and *littérateurs*; they did not command the analytic and constructive power to systematize their ideas and standardize their terminology. In this respect, Christian theologians were not necessarily worse than their pagan contemporaries, though in practice they were often handicapped by a professed lack of interest in questions of logic and philosophical method, not to mention an uncritical respect for the text of their scriptures.

It may nevertheless seem extraordinary that pagan and Christian writers alike should have been so well acquainted with the terminology of categorial theories, both Aristotelian and Stoic, and yet prove so totally incapable of applying either theory in a consistent manner. One reason for this lies in an obscurity and confusion about the function of such theories which goes back to Aristotle himself and which has not yet been completely removed.

The theory of the categories seems to have originated as an exercise in classification. The word *katēgoria* itself means 'predicate'; and the theory, it seems, sought to distinguish the different types of reality which could be denoted by predicates. It was not primarily a theory about the function of the various parts of speech, though it was certainly influenced by the attempts to develop a grammatical science which were then in progress, and were not always clearly distinguished from it; and which probably took the form of distinguishing the various things that can be said about *people*, remembering that the Greeks used

---

[43] Simplicius, *in Categ.* 8, pp. 237–9; ibid. 10, p. 402 (*SVF* ii. 393, iii. 238).

the same word *onoma* to mean both 'noun' and 'name'. It did, however, seem to presuppose that any x, or 'x', can be given an absolute placing in the system; and if so, then it is true to say that 'The categories are the ultimate classes into which whatever exists or is real may be said to fall.'[44]

However, this relatively simple programme was not consistently applied. For since language is flexible, the same facts can be expressed in different grammatical forms; and there is then no compelling reason to suppose that one grammatical form rather than another mirrors the structure of reality. The scheme of categories, as Aristotle developed it, shows some correspondence with grammatical distinctions; thus the distinction between the categories of 'action' and 'passion' seems to be suggested by that drawn between active and passive verbs;[45]—but also much discordance; thus the act of running and the passive state of being ill are expressed by the verbs τρέχειν and νοσεῖν, which are grammatically identical; but also by the nouns δρόμος and νόσος, which resemble each other, but not the former pair. Thus the categorial distinction is not reflected in a grammatical distinction, and the grammatical distinction does not reflect a categorial distinction. The most one could claim is that the theory of categories presents an idealized classification which is suggested by grammatical distinctions, even though the latter do not always conform to it. Thus it might be thought that in Aristotle's view there is a certain natural propriety in a noun's standing for a person or thing, and in a verb's standing for an activity, etc., even though some nouns stand for activities and some for passive states etc.

In particular, it might be thought that there is a basic distinction between referring to things and describing them, which is reflected in a distinction between substantival expressions and predicative expressions. But once again, this does not correspond to the grammatical distinction between nouns and other words. It was already clear to Aristotle, and perhaps to others, that substantive expressions not only stand as subjects of sentences, but also function as predicates; compare the use of 'man' in 'man is an animal' and 'Socrates is a man'. Hence in developing his theory of primary substances, Aristotle puts forward the more limited claim that there is a certain *class* of beings which cannot

[44] G. E. R. Lloyd, *Aristotle*, 114.   [45] Cf. *Categ.* c. 4.

be referred to by predicative expressions, but only by the subjects of sentences; and these are individuals. Indeed, by an extension of language they themselves can be called 'subjects'—though, to be sure, only by neglecting such sentences as 'This is Socrates'. Aristotle therefore argues that 'individuals are substances in the strictest sense, for they are the subjects for all other things, and all other things are either predicated of them or are in them'.[46] We have here the oddity that to say of individuals, 'they are *subjects* for all other things' is equivalent to saying that the distinctive *predicate* (κατηγορία) of substance applies to them alone. Conversely, the other categories, which are *eo ipso* not subjects or substances in this 'proper' sense, can be referred to by nouns and stand as the subject of a sentence, as when we say 'White is a colour'.

How has this come about? There is a clash between a narrower and a wider sense in which a thing may be said to be a subject. Aristotle argues with some force that individuals have a special claim to this privilege; but in a wider sense, it can be extended to anything whatsoever, since anything can be described, and to describe a thing is to qualify it by predicates. (We moderns might not accept this last point; Aristotle believed that sentences were necessarily of subject–predicate form, whereas we are very conscious of their elasticity; yet even a modern, if questioned about an unidentified 'Tom', would probably answer by making 'Tom' the subject of a sentence; 'Tom is my slave' seems more natural than 'I bought Tom'). The ambiguity in question is built into several related terms which Aristotle uses in his logical theory; thus the term ὑποκείμενον, conventionally rendered 'substrate', can mean 'subject under discussion'; but in a more restricted sense it can mean 'subject of predicates', and so tends to be identified with that reality which is most properly the subject of predicates, viz. the individual. Again the phrase τί ἐστι, 'what is it', seems purely general; but Aristotle often takes it to mean 'what are its permanent distinguishing features', thus making it coincide with one interpretation of 'substance'. Meanwhile in its general application it can be used to formulate questions about the other categories, e.g. τί ἐστιν ὁ χρόνος ;, 'What is time?', *Physics* iv. 10, 218 a 31, where no doubt the use of the noun-form 'time' helps to make this formulation acceptable; for

---

[46] Lloyd, op. cit., 115.

one could hardly ask, 'what is *when*?'.[47] A further development is to generalize the sense of οὐσία itself, by applying it to categories other than substance; thus at *Physics* iv. 2, *ad fin.*, Aristotle puts the question, 'What is the οὐσία of space?'

This development was carried further after Aristotle; and the result was that, beside the absolute or classificatory use of the categories, which is presupposed when they are referred to as 'the greatest kinds', there began to emerge what we may call a relative or methodological use, in which one can apply to any subject under discussion the question, what is it?, and then proceed to consider other aspects of it according to some scheme of categories. I have already noted the variant uses of the question, what is it?, and of the noun 'substrate', ὑποκείμενον; and the latter at least reappears in Stoicism, where it can apply either to unqualified matter, or to a species, or to an individual.[48] Where this usage obtains, an individual can be treated *either* as an 'individually qualified being' in relation to the 'substratum', unqualified matter; *or* as himself a 'substratum', or 'subject', when it becomes allowable to open a new range of questions by asking, 'how qualified?'; and in such cases the claim to provide an absolute classification must necessarily fail. Again, we are told that the phrase τὸ ποιόν (the qualified) has three different ranges of application, although it is still claimed that *quality* (ποιότης) is unambiguous.[49]

But perhaps the greatest factor making for imprecision was the semi-popular use of categorial schemes by rhetoricians and lawyers, who naturally tended to adapt them to fit their practical convenience. Thus, since the lawyer often deals with *alleged* facts and incidents, it is understandable that the question 'What is it?' (τί ἐστι) was commonly prefaced by the question 'Is there such a thing?' (εἰ ἔστι), e.g. 'Did the alleged property actually exist?'; this distinction has a basis both in Aristotle (*Anal. Post.* ii, *init.*) and in the Stoics, who introduced an ultimate category of 'things' (τινά) to include both facts and fictions.[50] Other questions are often added along lines suggested by Aristotle's *Categories*; or else by one of the less formal divisions found in Aristotle,

---

[47] Cf. the excellent note in J. L. Ackrill, *Aristotle's Categories and De Interpretatione*, 77–81.

[48] *SVF* ii. 374.

[49] *SVF* ii. 390.

[50] Ibid. 329, 332–4; cf. J. M. Rist, *Stoic Philosophy*, 152–8.

like that of the circumstances of moral action given in the *Nico-machean Ethics* (ii. 6, 1106 a 21–3, 1109 a 27–8, etc.) ; or else by Stoic sources (cf. p. 113 above).

Here then is a large field of thought and usage which so far as I am aware has never been properly explored (though one can refer to R. Nadeau's paper mentioned above; Phillip de Lacy has studied the methodological use of Stoic categories in Epictetus and Marcus Aurelius, and I have given elsewhere a few details of Tertullian's usage).[51] The prevailing confusion is most clearly seen in the familiar distinction of οὐσία/συμβεβηκότα, usually translated 'substance'/'accidents'. This translation of course suggests an Aristotelian scheme, where οὐσία stands either for a possessor of attributes, or for the attributes which belong to it by definition; and συμβεβηκότα stands either (at its most inclusive) for those of *X*'s attributes which do not follow from its definition, or (more usually) for those which *X* may or may not have. But secondly, as already noted, συμβεβηκότα can be used to refer to all the categories other than substance, thus giving the impression that all such predications are non-necessary and that none of them can be used to define a substance, so that οὐσία can stand only for the theoretical concept of a pure subject of attributes; we have already noted the objections to this scheme.[52] But the situation is still further entangled when οὐσία is given a purely existential sense, since even the characteristics by which *X* is identified and defined are now labelled 'accidents'. Here for instance is Quintilian's summary of Theodorus: *Idem Theodorus, qui de eo an sit et de accidentibus ei, quod esse constat, id est* περὶ οὐσίας καὶ συμβεβηκότων, *existimat quaeri*. 'This same Theodorus thinks that what is in question is, whether a thing exists, and what pertains (or 'happens') to a thing which is admitted to exist' (iii. 6. 36).

Such developments may possibly have assisted practical men to conduct their affairs; but they hindered clear any understanding of the categories themselves; in particular, they made it harder to answer the one clearly formulated question which we can trace in antiquity, namely whether the categories are concerned with things or with words. The original classificatory use of the

[51] See (i) p. 113 above; (ii) *Trans. and Proc. Am. Philol. Assoc.* 76 (1945), 246–63; (iii) *JTS*, n.s. 14 (1963), 46–66.

[52] See pp. 21–2, 60 above.

categories preserved some slight connection with discussions of the functions of words, as we have seen. But the connection was soon obscured; even, for instance, by such a simple device as that of introducing a distinctive noun to name each category. In the methodological use of categories it disappeared beyond recall; and it was in any case almost undetectable in the simplified Stoic system of four categories. Aristotle's theory, provisional at best, had been rendered hopelessly obsolete by later developments. Yet his dicta continued to be quoted as authoritative.

THE WORD *OUSIA* IN
LATE ANTIQUITY

THE usage of οὐσία in the early Christian centuries presents more problems than is commonly supposed. This is not because it varies widely from writer to writer; what is striking is the complexity of a generally accepted pattern, modified in some cases by the assumptions of Platonism or Stoicism but seldom controlled by conscious analysis. Certainly the relatively simple distinctions recognized by ancient theory do not match the complexities which are actually found.

Can we tabulate this usage? What is needed is not a mere list of senses, but a diagram which indicates their relationship. But a workable diagram inevitably proves to be a compromise; it seems desirable to reveal some logical distinctions which the ancient writers failed to note; but unless one keeps fairly close to the conventions of ancient logic, one is bound to conceal connections of thought which the ancients observed and which affect their usage.

Most ancient writers were familiar with the distinctions between existence and character, between matter and form, and between universal and individual; and we can make some use of these distinctions in constructing our scheme. To take the first; it seems that we might begin to classify the senses of οὐσία according to the usage of εἶναι that is presupposed; the distinction between existence and character reproduces the familiar antithesis between asking 'whether *x* is' (εἰ ἔστι) and asking 'what *x* is' (τί ἐστι). But we cannot use this distinction as a basis for classifying the senses of οὐσία by a process of simple subdivision; for consider the following case. The question 'whether *x* is' sometimes seems to be asking, not whether there is such a thing as *x*, but whether *x* exists as an independent reality; likewise οὐσία passes easily from the sense of mere existence to that of existence in the category of substance. But for ancient writers, to designate *x* as an οὐσία, in the sense of 'substance', was *both* to declare that *x* is more truly real than states, processes, etc., *and* to give *x* an initial classification in the scheme of things. Put more generally: some of the established senses of οὐσία have links with *both* the main senses of εἶναι; this will be demonstrated in due course.

Nevertheless this first distinction is not without value. If we do take the underlying sense of εἶναι, and consider, how much is said or implied about the subject that is being considered, we can arrange the senses of οὐσία in an order which is roughly that of increasing richness of content. The order which I shall adopt and try to justify is this:

A   Existence,
B   Category or status,
C   Substance,
D   Stuff or material,
E   Form,
F   Definition,
      and finally, in a rather different category,
G   Truth.

But at this point we have to introduce a cross-division, which partly corresponds to the analysis of abstract nouns proposed in Chapter I. The first step is to note that οὐσία may be lexically equivalent either to τὸ εἶναι or to τὸ ὄν. In the first case it will denote some sort of fact or state of affairs; in the second, some object or class of objects, conceived as existing or as being so-and-so. But there is yet another possibility; in appropriate cases οὐσία may stand, not for the verb εἶναι, nor yet for its subject, but for the predicate; and here it means, not ὃ ἔστι, 'something that is . . .', but ὅ ἐστι, '*what* something is'. To formalize these distinctions, for all the basic senses of οὐσία given above, we have to recognize four possible *modes of reference* (or 'modes' for short):

1. Verbal, noting the fact, = τὸ εἶναι, or ὅτι ἔστι.
2. Predicative, = ὅ ἐστι, what *x* is.
3. Subjectival = ὃ ἔστι, considered collectively.
4. The same, considered individually.

The diagram we have just proposed may be attacked on several grounds. First, it invites suspicion by looking much too tidy and symmetrical; and is there not a certain absurdity in a scheme which purports to distinguish twenty-eight different senses of οὐσία? I can answer, that I have indeed constructed an idealized scheme, but one which is useful for critical purposes; in practice, some of the squares in the diagram will be left blank, and some adjacent squares will be hardly distinguishable. (Thus mode 2 will not apply at level A, whereas in the lower levels it tends to supplant mode 1.) And mere complexity can hardly be an objection when one notes that the article in the *Patristic Greek Lexicon* comprises fifty-eight subsections. There is in fact a good reason why my scheme is both tidier and simpler than the classification adopted in the Lexicon. I have classified the senses of οὐσία by considering what it connotes or implies, not what it denotes or applies to; the result is a simpler scheme than that of the Lexicon, which understandably adopts an arrangement based partly on differences of connotation, partly on those of denotation.

It may again be objected that the diagram implies an obsolete logic. I have tried to meet this point; and I doubt if the diagram can be formalized or corrected any further if it is to fulfil its purpose. It *does* of course, defer to ancient logic in assimilating both existential statements and definitions to predicative statements, whereas the modern theory makes the two former relate to the word or term '*x*' rather than to *x* itself. But this is a necessary feature, since one has to accommodate the fact that, for the ancients, mere 'being' shades gradually into 'being such-and-such', and this again into 'being just that'. Further, the diagram can only distinguish what is individual from what is collective by grammatical criteria; and this necessarily ignores a number of complexities which have already been discussed. But we must not introduce further refinements at this stage, especially since we are concerned not only to pin down the various senses of οὐσία, where possible, but also to study its flexibility, the ease with which it moves from one sense to another.

Again, the distinction drawn between modes 2 and 3 in particular may possibly appear forced; someone might object, 'but surely, in the case of the verb 'to be', the predicate must be simply identical with the subject; 'what *x* is' is indistinguishable from '*x*'. This objection would be justified if 'to be' always indicated an identity; but this is certainly not the case. At some risk of anticipating the main discussion, I will give an example to prove my point. St. Clement alludes to the theory that blood is the οὐσία of the soul (*Paed.* i. 39. 2). This clearly does not mean that the soul is the blood and nothing but the blood; it means that it is a product of the blood; similarly he can say that milk has blood as its οὐσία, its basic material (ibid., 1. 39. 5). Yet only a page or two earlier he speaks of 'the life-giving οὐσία of milk, which flows from the kindly breasts' (ibid. i. 35. 3). Here it is equally clear that 'the οὐσία of milk' does *not* mean 'what milk is', i.e. its basic material, namely blood; it means 'that which is milk', and is simply a periphrasis for 'milk'.

It can now be observed that 'what *x* is' frequently represents or demands a generalizing expression. Can you say what man is? A possible answer is, 'a two-footed creature that laughs'—an attempted definition, supposedly equivalent in range of reference. But one could also answer, 'a mammal', 'an animal', etc., assigning man to broader classifications; just as one can say 'the *ousia* of Socrates is (a) man, (an) animal, and so on'. Another possibility might be 'flesh'; man 'is' flesh, just as milk 'is' blood; though clearly there are other manifestations of flesh and of blood. On the other hand, the word 'man' used by itself does not refer beyond the human species (except in by-forms like 'ape-man'); it can however refer to a restricted range within it. 'Man' refers collectively to the human race; but 'a man'—using a distinction unknown in classical antiquity—refers to a human individual; or in special cases, to a class of men, just as 'a monkey' can refer to a class of monkeys (p. 4 above). Such complexities could have been accommodated by further dividing the predicative mode 2, and by modifying the clumsy dichotomy of modes 3 and 4; but for simplicity's sake I have had to forego these refinements. Let us then note that, for any '*x*', 'the *ousia* of *x*' may be more general than '*x*'; and conversely, 'an *x*' may refer to a sub-class, or to a member, of the class of *x*'s.

I pass, then, to consider the levels one by one.

(A)

Oὐσία in the sense of 'existence' considered as a fact or state is by no means uncommon, although it seems to be avoided by some writers, including Philo, who uses ὕπαρξις to express this meaning. It can be found in Clement, Origen, and Athanasius, especially in the contexts of asserting or denying the existence of something, or again of bringing something into existence. Origen can say εἰς οὐσίαν ἔφερε τὰ πάντα and εἰς ὕπαρξιν ἤγαγεν τὰ πάντα without perceptible difference, for 'he brought all things into existence' (*in Joh. frr.* 1 and 2, *GCS*, p. 485. 3, 25.) He also refers to 'the opinion of those who are complete atheists and deny the existence of God' (τὸ δόγμα . . . τῶν παντῇ ἀθεῶν καὶ τὴν οὐσίαν τοῦ θεοῦ ἀρνουμένων, *Orat.* 5. 1). Methodius says that when a statue is melted down its form departs but has no longer any real existence (οὐ μὴν ὑφεστῶσα ἔτι κατ' οὐσίαν, *Res.* iii. 6. 1) as is the case ὅταν χωρισθέν τι ἀπό τινος μηκέτι ὑπάρχοι, ὑπόστασιν οὐσίας οὐκ ἔχον, 'having no reality of existence'. Origen again says that the Greek gods are mere figments (ἀναπλάσματα); let Celsus demonstrate their real existence, οὐσίαν καὶ ὑπόστασιν, or show them κατ' οὐσίαν ὑφεστηκέναι (*c. Cels.* i. 23).

But it is often difficult to be sure that οὐσία means anything so abstract as mere existence, or characterizes something as merely existing; it passes easily into the sense of reality or substance— or indeed is further specified as matter or form—or again, into that of truth. Thus Origen has argued that the goddess Mnemosyne is a mere figment, having no real existence; but he might equally well have said that Mnemosyne is not what she purports to be, a subject or person, but is merely an action personified; or again, that she is a poetic falsehood, an offence against the truth. Athenagoras deals with a similar problem by contrasting the names of pagan deities with their (questionable) 'underlying substances' or 'realities' (οὐσίαι ὑποκείμεναι, ὑποκείμενα πράγματα, *Leg.* 5. 2, cf. Plato, *Protag.* 349 b); but the reality which justifies a name could also be called its 'truth'. In such cases there is a verbal distinction between things (in this case, names) and their 'substances'; in the other group this distinction is absent, and οὐσία is used substantively, in mode three or four. Clement of Alexandria is quoted as saying οὐσία ἐστὶν τὸ δι' ὅλου ὑφεστός (fr. 37, a series of phrases collected from his work *On Providence* by Maximus the Confessor), possibly '*ousia* is the totality of what has come into being'; but the sense may be more restricted if Clement is thinking mainly of substance and tacitly excluding qualities and relations. An unknown scribe copied out Mark 10: 49 to read πᾶσα οὐσία ἀναλωθήσεται, which *could* mean 'everything that exists shall be consumed', sense A4 (since the collective 'all that exists', A3, should be πᾶσα ἡ οὐσία); but other senses are possible, e.g. 'every element', 'every kind of being'. Aetius the Arian attacks the hypothesis that 'every *ousia* is ingenerate' (*Syntagmation*, § 22);[1] but he is not in fact concerned with the metaphysical view which denies all change whatsoever, but with the supposition that the created order (in which he would include the Son) is ingenerate like the Father. 'Every order of being' gives appropriate sense.

In practice it seems clear that ἡ οὐσία can be used inclusively to mean 'the universe', much like ὁ κόσμος or ἡ φύσις. This usage squares naturally with the cosmology of the Stoics, for whom the world-system or cosmos comprises all the *ousia*, or material stuff, that there is, and is surrounded by void. Other philosophers adopt the same usage, sometimes not distinguishing clearly between 'all matter' and 'all that exists', which on materialist theories are of course identified; so Hippolytus quotes Pyrrho's opinion that 'all *ousia* is unstable' (ῥευστήν τε εἶναι τὴν οὐσίαν πᾶσαν, *Ref.* i. 23. 2); and even writers who are not themselves materialists can understand *ousia* as 'matter', taken collectively, in a sense which inclines towards 'the material universe'; so e.g. Philo, *Somn.* ii. 253. With a rather different background, Hippolytus says that in Pythagoras' view being and the universe is one, or a unity (ἔστι γὰρ ἡ οὐσία καὶ ὁ κόσμος ἕν, *Ref.* vi. 25. 2); and Methodius similarly couples οὐσία with φύσις (*c. Porph.* 3, ἐξ ὅλης τῆς πάσης οὐσίας καὶ φύσεως, which must mean 'from the totality of existence and of the natural order'). So also in the speech 'To the Saints', attributed to Constantine, we read ἡ γάρ τοι οὐσία χαίρει μὲν εὐδοκίαις ἀποστρέφεται δὲ πᾶσαν δυσσέβειαν, where the meaning is probably that the world-order, or the order of existence, 'rejoices in acts of grace but rejects all impiety'.[2]

(B)

We have considered a number of cases in which *ousia* could be rendered 'existence'. A second group of usages, now to be examined, is recognizably distinct from these, yet once again shows *ousia* conveying an exceedingly general sense. It now seems

---

[1] Ed. L. R. Wickham, *JTS*, N.S. 19 (1968), 532–69.

[2] Op. cit. 6. 4, in Eusebius, *GCS* i. 160. The parallels quoted above show that there is no need to emend the text. Cf. further Chrysippus, *SVF* ii. 551; Philo, *Vit. Mos.* i. 113, and other refs. given in Index, s.v. οὐσία, 3; Plutarch, *de E*, 21 : τοῦτο συνδεῖ τὴν οὐσίαν καὶ κρατεῖ, Clement, *Excerpta* 19. 4: κτίστης . . . τῆς ὅλης ἐγένετο κτίσεως καὶ οὐσίας.

to serve as the most general *classificatory* term; 'the *ousia* of *x*' means something like the ontological status of *x*, its nature, or the category to which it belongs. In some ancient systems of thought this could be closely associated with the notion of existence, since 'the being of things' could mean 'their distinctive mode of existence', which of course would vary according to the diversity of things considered (cf. pp. 8–9 above). From this meaning, by weakening the implication of diversity one would get back to that of 'the bare fact of actuality', examined above; alternatively, by weakening the implication of actuality one would reach something like 'the status of *x*'; and this might include some cases where one would be doubtful whether '*x*' stands for a real being at all. Thus Hippolytus describes the God of the Docetists as 'himself without solid reality, having darkness as his substance' (αὐτὸς ὢν ἀνυπόστατος, σκότος ἔχων τὴν οὐσίαν, *Ref.* viii. 10. 1); and 'to inquire into the *ousia* of *x*' might indicate a very general inquiry which includes, but does not prejudge, the question whether or not *x* is real.

Clearly, such general inquiries into the nature of a thing could often be satisfied by giving a definition; and sometimes 'definition' may seem to be the most suitable translation for *ousia* in such contexts. But this does not always hold good. Thus Galen tells us that Chrysippus devotes half of his first book On the Soul to discussing its *ousia*, its nature or constitution. *Ousia* cannot mean its definition, since the definition is given without comment in a dozen words at the beginning, which Galen quotes (*de Hipp. et Plat.* iii. 1 = *SVF* ii. 885). I have already noted a similar point about the use of the Latin word *substantia* in Quintilian.[3]

The use of *ousia* for 'category', the general term embracing substance, quality, and the rest, looks like a development of the Aristotelian doctrine that 'being' (τὸ ὄν) applies in all the categories (*Metaph.* v. 7, 1017 a 22–31); in the *Physics* (iv. 2 *ad fin.*), as already noted, he even allows himself to speak of the *ousia* of place, τόπος, meaning quite generally 'what it is'; and the *Topics* vi. 8, 146 b 2, refers to the *ousia* of all relatives. There is of course another strand in Aristotle's thought which holds that being is not a genus (for one cannot think of 'being here' and 'being white' as two species of the same thing, namely being;

---

[3] *Inst. Or.* i, *prooem.* 21; see my paper 'Divine Substance in Tertullian', *JTS*, N.S. 14 (1963), 48.

cf. *Metaph.* iii. 3, 998 b 22–9). Nevertheless a number of later philosophers do treat being (τὸ ὄν) as the *summum genus* (see e.g. *SVF* iii. p. 214, Diog. 25) ; and some extend this treatment to *ousia* itself (e.g. Porphyry, *Isagoge* 2 a 25). In this extremely abstract usage *ousia* stands by itself, without any dependent genitive; whereas the previous instances put it in the context '*ousia* of *x*', which suggests the characterizing sense of *einai* and assigns *ousia* to mode 2. Porphyry's usage could suggest that *ousia* is taken as a general term including all the categories; but there seems to be in this case a prior limitation, so that in practice only substances are being classified.

(C)

The two very general senses of *ousia* just considered lie somewhat outside the main field. More typically, *ousia* indicates the most permanent form of being and the ultimate principle of explanation. But it is easy to advance from this position, and treat other forms of being, not simply as weaker and less permanent, but as aspects', conditions or states of the former. In this case we are beginning to interpret *ousia* as 'substance'; we do this when we assume that:

(i) *Ousia* does not exist in, or as an aspect of, something else; anything else exists in, or as an aspect of, it.

(ii) Consequently *ousia* is the most permanent form of being; it is what persists through change and makes it comprehensible.[4]

Origen's *Treatise on Prayer* contains a discussion of *ousia* which seems to be drawn from a philosophical dictionary.[5] He first alludes to the view that immaterial reality is primary (προηγου-μένην τὴν τῶν ἀσωμάτων ὑπόστασιν εἶναι) so that *ousia* is a collective name for immaterial reality; he then quotes a number of definitions, often with merely verbal differences, which conform to the Stoic view that material reality is primary and the other derivative. Here it is worth noting the grounds on which the case is put for either side, which seldom appear so clearly. Immaterial beings, it is argued, have a 'stability of being' (τὸ εἶναι βεβαίως ἔχοντα) and neither increase or decrease; whereas the Stoics contend that matter is primary, and so can exist independently;

---

[4] Cf. pp. 59–60, 67–9 above. This presumes that Aristotelian *criteria* for *ousia* were widely accepted, even though his identification of it were not.

[5] Op. cit. 27. 8, = *SVF* ii. 318. See R. Cadiou, 'Dictionnaires antiques dans l'œuvre d'Origène', *Revue des études grecques*, 45 (1932), 271–85.

and that while it submits to change it is itself unchanging; so that one definition runs, τὸ πάσας δεχόμενον τὰς μεταβολάς τε καὶ ἀλλοιώσεις, αὐτὸ δὲ ἀναλλοίωτον κατὰ τὸν ἴδιον λόγον.[6]

Origen has here been referring to two claimants to the title *οὐσία* in a way which lets us see what the claim implies. On the one hand, matter; on the other 'immaterial reality' or 'incorporeals', which for Platonist writers include both the Ideas and pure intelligences, whether angels or immortal souls. These two conceptions are very frequently contrasted, sometimes in the collective mode 3 (οὐσία αἰσθητή, . . . νοητή), sometimes pluralized; though I gain the impression that plural expressions for 'kinds of matter' or 'material objects' are rather less common than their counterparts οὐσίαι νοηταί or νοεραί. Where the identification is taken for granted and the qualifying expression is dropped, e.g. where 'the *οὐσία* of *x*' simply *means* 'its matter', or 'its form', it will come under headings D and E; but we may note here the Platonic use of *οὐσία* as a collective term, contrasted with γένεσις, to denote 'unchanging (genuine, and therefore immaterial) reality'. This usage certainly occurs in Platonist writers of the Christian period, including some passages quoted by Christians; though I have not so far found it used by Christian writers on their own account. Examples are Plutarch, *de Iside* 53 fin.; Celsus in Origen, *c. Cels.* vii. 46, Numenius in Eusebius, *PE* xi. 22. 3 = fr. 25, Leemans; Plotinus, *Enn.* ii. 9. 6. However, Clement approximates to the Platonic idiom when he claims that the geometer studies οὐσίαν αὐτὴν ἐφ' ἑαυτῆς, which here means 'pure form' or 'shape' as opposed to bodies having shapes (*Strom.* vi. 80. 2).

Where the technical sense 'substance' is definitely required, the sense of εἶναι which is presupposed begins to pass from the existential to the characterizing sense. For first, to treat *x* as a substance is to presume that *x* is real, or really exists; 'substance' normally excludes 'fictitious substance'. But secondly, to treat *x* as a substance involves determining in the most general terms *what x* is, i.e. assigning it to a category. And thirdly, to assign it to this particular category is to give the best possible account of it, by saying, not how it is, or what it does, but what it is.

Origen provides us with a good example of the use of *οὐσία* where the interpretation 'substance' is clearly required, but no

[6] 'That which receives all changes and alterations, but is itself unalterable on its own account.'

further identification of it is suggested. In his *Commentary on John* (i. 151) he criticizes those who reduce the Word to a mere divine utterance (προφορὰν πατρικὴν οἱονεὶ ἐν συλλαβαῖς κειμένην) and in this way deprive Him of substance: ὑπόστασιν αὐτῷ, εἰ ἀκριβῶς αὐτῶν πυνθανοίμεθα, οὐ διδόασιν οὐδὲ οὐσίαν αὐτοῦ σαφηνίζουσιν, οὐδέπω φαμὲν τοιάνδε ἢ τοιάνδε, ἀλλ' ὅπως ποτὲ οὐσίαν. In this sentence οὐσία should mean something more than bare existence, for the opponents cannot be regarding the Word as a mere figment; nor indeed as unreal in the sense of not fully effective; so we may translate: 'they do not grant him any independent reality . . . or make clear his status as a substance—not to speak of some particular kind of substance, but rather substance of any kind.'[7]

A much simpler example comes from Titus of Bostra, *adv. Manich.* ii. 17: τοῦτο δὴ σκότος καλεῖται μέν, οὐ μὴν ὑφέστηκε κατ' οὐσίαν. Clearly there is no doubt that darkness *exists*; Titus means 'this is called darkness but does not exist as a substance', i.e. an irreducible fact; it is defined as absence of light.[8] A favourite topic of debate was whether evils are substances. Methodius argues against this view, which he states in mode (3) or (4) (τὰ κακὰ οὐσίας ὑπάρχειν τινάς, *Autex.* viii. 4), and proceeds by defining substance in Stoic terms as 'material composition' (σωματικὴ σύστασις), and arguing that only this satisfies the criterion of independent reality. Athanasius, though he would certainly reject Methodius' definition of substance, likewise condemns the idea that 'evil *has* substance' (presumably mode 2): *c. Gentes* 6 and 7: εἴ γε κατ' αὐτοὺς ἡ κακία ὑπόστασιν ἔχει καθ' ἑαυτὴν καὶ οὐσίαν, *et sim.* Both writers of course follow Origen's view that evil is the act or resulting condition of a being who was created good. It might be worth adding that Plato's famous description of the Good as 'beyond being' (ἐπέκεινα τῆς οὐσίας, *Rep.* 509 b) is taken by some commentators to mean that the Good transcends all human comprehension[9] and so transcends the category of substance itself: so perhaps Origen, *c. Cels.* vi. 64, quoted below, p. 152; especially the suggestion that perhaps the

---

[7] For another interpretation, cf. Prestige, *GPT*, 189.

[8] This passage forms an interesting contrast with that just quoted from Hippolytus, *Ref.* viii. 10. 1, ὁ πυροειδὴς θεὸς . . . αὐτὸς ὢν ἀνυπόστατος, σκότος ἔχων τὴν οὐσίαν. The sense is much the same, but the usage of οὐσία quite different.

[9] The variant ἐπέκεινα νοῦ καὶ οὐσίας is common in Platonist writers. See J. Whittaker, Ἐπέκεινα νοῦ καὶ οὐσίας, *VC* 23 (1969), 91-104.

Logos is οὐσία οὐσιῶν etc. but his Father is 'beyond everything of this kind'.

Οὐσία considered as 'substance' takes its place in a system of logical categories which is largely independent of any precise identification of substance. The facts are complex, and only an outline can be given here; but it is probably true to say that there was widespread support for a system broadly resembling Aristotle's, remembering that Aristotle himself is not self-consistent, while there was as yet no disposition to take the *Categories* as the definitive work; and there was no complete agreement on any alternative system, e.g. the Stoic system of four categories. A number of writers were probably influenced by the rhetoricians, whose textbook lists of 'circumstances' (στάσεις) sometimes conform rather loosely to the Aristotelian pattern.[10]

Οὐσία, substance, is very commonly contrasted with συμβεβη-κότα, 'accidents', a term which is often used inclusively to refer to all the other categories, and so conveys the suggestion that all predications of these are variable and contingent (see p. 60 above). Certain other terms behave in much the same way; thus ποιότης, quality, is often used so loosely as to be practically equivalent to 'accident'; Origen says that actions (ἐνέργειαι, ποιήσεις) are called 'qualities' (*Orat.* 27. 8), and Methodius calls the construction (σύνθεσις) of a building a 'quality' (*Autex.* x. 4). Some writers, again, follow Aristotle in using πάθος, 'affection', in the same sense. Another term which suggests accidental being is the verbal noun μετουσία; this appears to be simply a later variant of the Platonic term μέθεξις, participation; but in Christian writers of our period it is seldom used of a thing's relationship to its constituent form or substance; it is commonly contrasted with οὐσία, and indicates a state or condition, or the fact of enjoying it; for Athanasius the presence of the Logos with men is a μετουσία, something they have as a gift, not by nature.

On the other hand what a thing *is* is commonly contrasted with what it *does*, its ἐνέργεια or ἔργον. It is not usual to find ἐνέργεια equated with οὐσία (as it is by Aristotle, *Metaph.* vii).[11] On the other hand ἐνέργεια is often used in a way which cuts

---

[10] See p. 113 above.

[11] In *CH* x. 2 both seem to be equated with God's will: ἡ γὰρ τούτου ἐνέργεια ἡ θέλησίς ἐστι καὶ ἡ οὐσία αὐτοῦ τὸ θέλειν πάντα εἶναι. Julian identifies God's οὐσία with both his δύναμις and his ἐνέργεια; see Festugière, *RHT* iii. 158–9. Cf. also Gregory Nazianzen, *Or.* 29. 16; and p. 171 below.

across the popular division between substance and accidents; it
means a thing's proper and necessary function, what Eustathius
(fr. 81, Spanneut) calls its ἐνέργεια φυσική, as sight is the function
of the eye.[12] Hence ἐνέργεια is sometimes used in theology to describe the Incarnation, as God's proper activity of self-revelation;
but sometimes strongly dissociated from it, as a term which more
properly applies to God's occasional gifts of grace to the saints.

Another contrast which was formulated by Aristotle but never
properly incorporated in a system of categories is that between
οὐσία and στέρησις, absence or privation. This I think raises no
difficulties which need discussion here. We have already noted
Titus of Bostra claiming that darkness is not an οὐσία; no doubt
he defines it as absence of light.

Finally there is the important contrast between an οὐσία and
its various possible ἐπίνοιαι. It seems to have been Origen who
first developed this contrast with some precision; formerly current as a somewhat vague term for a 'notion' or 'conception',
ἐπίνοια in his writings comes to mean a conception formed of
something, or a title given to it, on the basis of its functions or
actions or relationships; and so especially of God or of the divine
Logos. Thus when contrasted with ἐπίνοια, οὐσία can mean 'sub-
stance-designation' rather than strictly 'substance', and sometimes tends towards the sense of 'definition'. On the other hand
the contrast between οὐσία and ἐπίνοια can approximate to that
between οὐσία and ὄνομα, 'name' or 'noun'; in such contexts
οὐσία can be interpreted either as 'reality', 'fact' as opposed to
mere name, or more linguistically as 'truth', 'true designation'.

(D)

We next consider the usage of οὐσία to mean 'stuff'. This usage
goes back to Aristotle and is common at all periods. It is also very
comprehensive; οὐσία can refer to simple substances like gold, or
complex ones, like the tissue of the bones (Methodius, *Symp.* ii. 6)
or to variegated ones, like human 'flesh'. Again, it can be quite
specific or highly inclusive; so that the οὐσία of *x* can be given at

---

[12] The term 'accident', συμβεβηκός, is sometimes used in this way, both by
Aristotle and by later writers, to refer to an inseparable function, συμβεβηκὸς
ἀχώριστον; *Metaph.* v. 30, 1025 b 30; cf. iii. 1, 995 b 20, *Anal. Post.* i. 7, 75 b 1,
al.; see Bonitz's Index, s.v. συμβαίνειν, 3 b; Athenagoras, *Leg.* 24; Origen, *in Joh.*
ii. 124; Eusebius, *DE* iv. 3; [Basil] *c. Eun.* iv. 2.

different levels of generality; this is gold, is a metal, is solid matter. The textbooks tend to mislead us by talking of 'the generic sense' of οὐσία as contrasted with 'the material sense'; for some material descriptions are certainly very *general*, though they are not 'generic' in the sense of following the normal classification of γένη in terms of form. But ancient writers do not always distinguish the language of classification from that of cosmogony; thus ὑγρὰ οὐσία sometimes means 'liquid matter' in general, but sometimes the element, water, from which liquids were thought to be derived. As we have seen, the four elements can be called οὐσίαι, and indeed πρῶται οὐσίαι (Hippolytus, *Ref.* x. 33. 4, cited above); and in Stoic theory they are derived from a primary undifferentiated or qualitiless matter, ἥν τε λέγουσιν οἱ Στωικοὶ πρώτην οὐσίαν καὶ πρώτην ὕλην[13] (Galen, *de Qual. Incorp.* 5 = *SVF* ii. 323); though it is sometimes admitted that this is only an abstraction.

When οὐσία means 'the stuff of *x*', it is easy to detect the underlying sense of εἶναι. To take the stock example, a bronze statue can be regarded as a mass of metal which assumes a certain form; hence one can say that it was bronze, is bronze, and will be (merely) bronze again when it is melted down; bronze is its οὐσία, its permanent constitution as opposed to its existing form. But ancient writers naturally extend this usage, by applying it to beings which they regard as eternal. In such cases the term has a merely comparative force; by saying that the οὐσία of the sun is fire, we emphasize its likeness with other things whose form is different, like the contents of stoves or braziers; we cannot quite properly say that the sun is 'made of' fire if there is no process of making. There are further difficulties where we go on to discuss the οὐσία of beings that are both eternal and *sui generis*, as when we say 'the οὐσία of God is πνεῦμα'; and here some doctrine of analogy has to be employed: God is not πνεῦμα as we ordinarily know it; nevertheless things which embody πνεῦμα are more like him than anything else is.

In the examples just considered, οὐσία is used in the context 'οὐσία of *x*' to mean 'what *x* is', and so is used in the predicative mode 2. But this usage easily exchanges with the other extremely common case in which something is simply designated 'an οὐσία', using mode 3. To designate, say, milk as an οὐσία is to treat it as a reality or substance, as something which has some degree of

---

[13] 'Which the Stoics call first substance and matter.'

permanence but can be altered in certain ways; milk, then, is something that is there, is real, is now hot, now cold; but further, its status as substance does *not* depend on any distinctive form; it can indeed be regarded as the stuff out of which something else is made, for instance cheese—at which point the usage reverts to mode (2): milk is what cheese is made from and what it basically is. Modes (1) and (4), however, are harder to identify at this level: in mode (1) οὐσία would have to mean simply the fact that *x* is material; Plutarch provides a possible example, referring to the wooden E at Delphi: τὸ δὲ πρῶτον καὶ παλαιότατον τῇ δὲ οὐσίᾳ ξύλινον[14] (*de E* 3). Methodius, *Autex.* viii. 10 might be quoted as an example of mode (4); having defined οὐσία as 'material constitution' (σωματική τις σύστασις) and so established it at level D, he says, 'The man who is a murderer is, qua man (an) οὐσία; but the murder he commits is not (an) οὐσία'; this should give οὐσία the sense of 'individual material thing'.

We have so far considered examples in which the sense of 'matter' or 'stuff' is clearly identified; but in some other contexts it is hard to determine whether this sense really predominates over other possible implications. We shall now consider some mixed cases of various types.

First: οὐσία moves easily along the following line of transition: existence—originative principle—material cause—matter. If a thing comes into existence, it is natural, though illogical, to describe the event as if existence were a state, so that a thing passes from non-existence into existence. Athanasius regularly speaks of God as acting on non-existent creatures; so in *c. Ar.* ii. 64, κρατήσας αὐτὰ εἰς οὐσίαν ἤνεγκε (sc. ὁ Λόγος τὰ κτίσματα), 'he took them and brought them into being'. But if things are composed of matter and form, it seems to follow that a thing can be regarded as a notion or project which begins to exist when it acquires the necessary matter: and in practice it is often hard to distinguish between 'bringing a thing into existence' and 'embodying an idea in matter'.

Again, since it is matter which makes the difference between existing merely in idea and existing in reality, the sense 'matter' shades into that of 'beginning', 'cause', 'originative principle', roughly equivalent to ἀρχή. We have seen that Aristotle sometimes regards it in this light (p. 69), and patristic examples can

[14] Literally: 'but the first and oldest, which is wooden in its substance.'

be given: e.g. (perhaps) Hippolytus, *Ref.* i. 2. 13.[15] We have also noted the materialist view which identifies all 'matter' with 'the whole universe' (p. 136 above).

Next, οὐσία can mean 'matter' or 'stuff' and yet also be interpreted through the categorical theory of substance, as in the example given above from Methodius. Another instructive case is the argument that the change of water into wine involves a miracle, since it involves a change of οὐσία (Origen *in Joh.*, fr. 30, *GCS*, p. 506; cf. Athanasius, *de Inc.* 18). If οὐσία meant simply 'stuff', it would not be obvious *a priori* that a miracle was needed, any more than for a change of milk into cheese; the claim to miracle is made by identifying οὐσία as 'stuff' with οὐσία as 'unchanging substratum'.

Thirdly, οὐσία can be used to denote not matter as such, or the four elements, but the distinctive properties of the elements which make them what they are, heat, moisture, and their opposites; for if, as in Aristotle, fire is hot and dry while air is hot and wet etc., then heat and the other qualities are more general than the elements they qualify. A good example is Eusebius *DE* iv. 5. 12 (p. 157): ὁ λόγος στοιχείοις οὐσίας οὔ ποτε διαλιμπάνει παρέχων, καὶ μίξεις καὶ κράσεις καὶ εἴδη καὶ μορφάς, etc.[16]—cf., probably, Origen *in Joh.* i. 115, p. 24. These could no doubt be equally well described as συμβεβηκότα ἀχώριστα (pp. 141–2 above); they are in fact termed ἐνέργειαι in Irenaeus i. 17. 1, Hv. i. 165 = Hippolytus, *Ref.* vi. 53. 1.

Fourthly, the sense of οὐσία can be extended by metaphorical uses based on the sense 'stuff', in much the same way as Aristotle's ὕλη; it then comes to mean something like the English 'content'. An example is Clement's remark that the content or body of knowledge is constructed out of perception and intellect: ἐκ δὲ αἰσθήσεως καὶ τοῦ νοῦ ἡ τῆς ἐπιστήμης συνίσταται οὐσία, *Strom.* ii. 13. 2; though in this case 'the body of knowledge' is perhaps little more than a periphrasis for 'knowledge'.

Fifthly, one has to consider the frontier between 'material substance' and the substance which is variously attributed to

---

[15] For a similar usage unrelated to matter see Philo, *Vit. Mos.* ii. 84 τετράδα τὴν δεκάδος οὐσίαν, whereas at *Spec. Leg.* ii. 40 it is τὴν δεκάδος ἀρχήν τε καὶ πηγήν. Cf. *CH* vi. 1, where it is said of God, οὐσίαν εἶναι δεῖ πάσης κινήσεως καὶ γενέσεως, 'he must be the originative principle of all movement' etc.

[16] 'The word never ceases from conferring on the elements (their) substances and mixtures and blends and forms and shapes.'

souls, heavenly bodies, gods, and (in Platonism) the Ideas. These distinctions are very variously conceived, but can be briefly reviewed as they are fairly familiar. Among the Stoics, spiritual substance is conceived as a purer, subtler, and more vigorous form of the 'fire' or 'vital warmth' which is manifested in living thinking bodies; the stars, they supposed, being wholly composed of fire, must be wholly intelligent. It was not always easy to harmonize the two conceptions of fire as 'constructive vital warmth' and as 'combustion'; but in principle the difference between 'pure fire' or 'spirit' and 'vital warmth' was one of degree. Platonism tended to draw a sharper distinction between the corporeal and incorporeal worlds, but with many variations in detail, according to whether it was the unity and perfection of each Idea that was emphasized in contrast to the diversity and imperfection of its instances—in which case there could, it seems, be a progressive approach to it; or whether its rational and incorporeal nature was contrasted with perceptible matter; though even here some sort of transition was envisaged, since the 'incorporeals' were sometimes held to include immortal souls, which were capable of acting within the material world through visible bodies. Many of the Gnostics, again, offer a distinctive theory which owes something both to Platonism and to Stoicism. In their view the highest reality, and the source of all the others, is spirit. This element is conceived mainly in psychological terms, as opposed to the quasi-physical ones so often employed by the Stoics; it originates in the 'Aeons', which resemble divine personalities; but in some remote past age it has suffered a process of degradation resulting from an impulse akin to human passion, which leads to the emergence of two other substances, the 'psychic', or soul-stuff, and the 'hylic', the matter of the visible universe. This formal recognition of three kinds of being is distinctively gnostic, though the middle class of 'psychic' entities obviously owes a good deal to Platonic and Stoic theories of demons and star-souls.

(E)

This is, perhaps, as much as need be said about the cases where the substance or permanent element in a thing is identified as the stuff of which it is made. We may recall that 'stuff' is often interpreted generally, as 'kind of stuff'; thus to say what *x* is made of is one way of saying what kind of thing *x* is; it gives us a 'generic' description of *x*, in a permissible sense of that term. But there are other kinds of generic description, including those which classify a thing by its form or species or genus proper; and those are comprised in our new heading, E. Where οὐσία is used in this way, it almost invariably points to some permanent or 'substantial' character of a thing; so this heading corresponds, though only roughly, to the textbook category of secondary substance.

Only roughly, because ancient usage is often indefinite. Οὐσία, as we have seen, can mean 'kind of stuff'; it can also mean 'natural kind', i.e. genus or species. But there are cases where it seems to indicate simply some permanent common character or general description, without further specification. Hippolytus refers to philosophers who concerned themselves with the οὐσία of transient things: περὶ τὴν τῶν γενομένων οὐσίαν ἠσχολήθησαν, *Ref.* i. 26. 3. It will not do to translate 'substance', for Hippolytus is certainly not concerned to stress the reality of these phenomena; he means simply *de rerum natura*. Again, when ancient writers refer to questions about the οὐσία of God, or of the soul, it is often uncertain what would count as an answer; οὐσία then simply means 'the sort of thing *x* is'. Indeed, strictly speaking, there is no broader classification within which God, or the soul, could fall; they are *sui generis*. The phrase really suggests an analogical description in terms of some familiar reality. Nevertheless these cases are close to the very general sense of 'category' discussed above, pp. 136–7. But when some definite system of classification in terms of form is implied, οὐσία can refer to a class of beings at almost any level of generality, from species to the most inclusive genera. Athanasius finds it natural enough to cite 'dog' or 'wolf' as an example; at the other extreme we have such highly inclusive phrases[17] as οὐσία θνητή (Origen *in Joh.* xiii. 429, p. 293. 16) or οὐσία σωματική, which shade off into the still more general phrases like οὐσία αἰσθητή which we have discussed under the heading 'reality'. Οὐσία does not commonly refer to varieties *within* a species; and, unlike φύσις, it does not normally refer to the moral character of men, except, significantly, under the influence of the theory that this is predetermined by the infusion of some quasi-physical determinator at or before birth, like the pneumatic (psychic, hylic) οὐσία supposed by Gnostics. On the

---

[17] 'Mortal substance'; 'bodily substance'; 'perceptible substance'.

other hand a thing's οὐσία clearly can imply an ethical valuation of a kind, since no Platonist would dream of denying that some classes of being had, as such, a higher value than others. Οὐσία then can come to imply 'status' or 'dignity'. When Athanasius says that the οὐσία of the mind is not diminished by speech (*de Inc.* 42), his language hovers poised between the two ideas that its content or resources are not diminished, and that its dignity is not impaired; the former is a traditional argument to show that God's being is not diminished when he sends forth his Word (cf. *c. Ar.* ii. 33–4); but the latter squares best with the contrast between dignity and indignity that pervades the whole chapter.

Οὐσία, therefore, normally carries the implication of a character which cannot be lost without the thing in question ceasing to exist. But there are one or two interesting texts which suggest that an οὐσία can be *acquired* by something already in being (cf. Plato *Phileb.* 32 b). Thus Clement describes the case of the disinterested seeker after knowledge, in *Strom.* iv. 136: his activity of thinking becomes an inseparable characteristic, and so passes from the category of action to that of 'substance': τὸ μὲν γὰρ νοεῖν ἐκ συνασκήσεως εἰς τὸ ἀεὶ νοεῖν ἐκτείνεται, τὸ δὲ ἀεὶ νοεῖν, οὐσία τοῦ γινώσκοντος κατὰ ἀνάκρασιν ἀδιάστατον γενομένη καὶ ἀΐδιος θεωρία, ζῶσα ὑπόστασις μένει. This is no doubt an adaptation of the view, more commonly expressed in terms of φύσις, that habit may become second nature;[18] Tertullian is presumably opposing this view in *de Anima* 32, when he argues that moral change effects no change of nature. In another connection Hippolytus speaks of the growing child acquiring πατρικὴν οὐσίαν—not, as I once thought, 'his father's character', but rather 'procreative power', or possibly 'matter' (*Ref.* vii. 22. 1); the puzzling sequence of acquisitions is explained by the doctrine of the successive seven-year 'ages' of man (see, e.g., Philo, *Opif.* 103–5); teeth appear in the first seven years, and semen by fourteen, whereas reason matures during the forties.

Since we have just considered the category of secondary substance, it may be well to review the individualizing senses of

[18] See Aristotle, *Categ.* 8, 9 a 2, imitated by Clement, *Strom.* vii. 46. 9, φυσιοῦται ἡ ἕξις, cf. [Aristotle], *Problems* 879 b 36, τὸ ἔθος ὥσπερ φύσις γίνεται, Philo, *Abr.* 185, *Decal.* 137, *Spec. Leg.* ii. 109, Methodius, *Symp.* iii. 7. 67. The same idea seems to underlie the Valentinian myth in which Sophia's passions become substances; see Hippolytus, *Ref.* vi. 32. 6, Clement, *Excerpta* 45. 2, 46.

οὐσία which are commonly assigned to that of primary substance. Our tabulation distributes them under different headings; and in certain cases at least this division can be justified. We have the following possibilities:

(A) Purely general: individual cases, αἱ ἐπὶ μέρους οὐσίαι (Epictetus, i. 2. 6, 22. 2).[19]

(B) (?) Objects that are *sui generis*.

(C) Individuals exemplifying the category of substance (Origen, *in Joh.* fr. 37, p. 513, l. 17; Athanasius, *c. Ar.* i. 36).

(D) Individual material objects (Methodius, *Autex.* viii. 10, quoted above, p. 144).

(E) Members of a species (Aristotle's ὁ τὶς ἄνθρωπος, e.g. Socrates).

(F) (?) Particular facts.

But it must be admitted that quite a number of cases where individuals are clearly envisaged cannot be classified along these lines. This is probably true of the description of demons as 'psychic entities', οὐσίαι ψυχικαί,[20] which is commonly cited as an example of primary substance. And one hardly knows what to make of St. John's indignant address to Fortunatus,[21] ὦ οὐσία φθορᾶς—perhaps, 'You specimen of corruption!'

(F)

Sections D and E considered οὐσία as matter and as form; of these two, matter is quite commonly, and form nearly always, taken as a universal. This next section is based on the use of εἶναι to convey an identity or definition; and the corresponding notion of οὐσία should be 'special character' or 'individuality'. But the theoretical scheme runs into difficulties at this point; for in saying 'definition of *x*', we are employing a criterion which is only fixed relatively to *x*; and this *x* itself may be either specific or general. This leads to certain overlaps between sections E and F. Thus if 'the οὐσία of man' means a specific character which is common to all men, it should fall under E; but regarded as the definition

---

[19] See however ii. 17. 11–2; although Epictetus is professedly talking about particular cases, his actual examples are fairly general: health, wealth, etc., rather than the circumstances of some particular individual.

[20] Ps.-Plutarch, 882 b; Athenagoras, *Leg.* 23. 2; Eusebius, *PE* xv. 43. 1; Diels, *DG* 307.   [21] *Acta Ioannis*, ed. Bonnet, ii. 192.

of man or manhood it belongs to F; and the distinction is not easy to express in Greek, where ὁ ἄνθρωπος can mean either 'the man referred to' or 'man as such'.

Οὐσία can mean the straightforward equivalence or identity of two general terms. According to Plutarch (*Stoic. Rep.* 18) Chrysippus identified misfortune with wickedness, saying that one is the οὐσία of the other, and thus they are the same: οὐσίαν κακοδαιμονίας ἀποφαίνει τὴν κακίαν . . . διατεινόμενος ὅτι τὸ κατὰ κακίαν ζῆν τῷ κακοδαιμόνως ζῆν ταὐτόν ἐστιν. From this it is an easy step to the notion of definition, in which a term is explained by a formula which is identical in meaning but more explicit, for instance the definition of pleasure as freedom from pain: ὡς γὰρ ἡ ἡδονὴ τὴν τῆς ἀλγηδόνος ἀπαλλαγὴν οὐσίαν ἔχει (Clement, *Ecl. Proph.* 35. 2, borrowed from Plutarch Περὶ ψυχῆς as preserved by Stobaeus) or Xenocrates' definition of the soul as a self-moving number. Plutarch (*An. Procr.* 1) says that in this phrase he was 'expounding the οὐσία of the soul'.

Such expressions, however, seldom attempt to discriminate between defining the term '*x*', and characterizing the reality for which '*x*' stands; indeed for Platonist writers the need for this distinction is hardly apparent, since they held that only species can be defined, and again that the names of species in principle correspond with their definitions (Albinus, *Didasc.* 6, p. 120. 2 ff.). However, it is where οὐσία relates particularly to the term '*x*' that the notion of 'identity' or 'equivalent formula' is really appropriate; in the other case 'the οὐσία of *x*' tends to mean 'the reality named by, and accordingly contrasted with, the term "*x*"', and hence οὐσία takes on the sense of 'reality as opposed to mere name'. A similar ambiguity can be seen in Aristotle's use of οὐσία. He occasionally uses it as a synonym for ὁρισμός, definition (e.g. *Metaph.* vii. 12, 1038 a 19–20); but more commonly he distinguishes the definition as a formula which *expresses* the οὐσία (e.g. v. 8, 1017 b 22); the latter then has to mean something like 'distinctive character', a unique combination of features (*Anal. Post.* ii. 13, 96 a 32–5).

Platonist metaphysics tended to attach particular importance to definition, holding that the whole of reality was predetermined by a fixed structure of patterns or Ideas, descending from the *summum genus* the innumerable *infimae species*, and that this structure could be revealed by correct definition of the corresponding terms. There was in fact a tendency to write as if the definition prescribed *all* the necessary attributes of each species; in Aristotelian terms, as if it revealed not only their essence but their properties as well. It is interesting to find that Clement puts the opposite point of view: a definition (ὅρος) can only reveal the distinguishing features of a species, but not all its properties; but his language is confused, and suggests that he has not clearly distinguished between this contention and the quite different point that the definition cannot reveal features peculiar to the individual. He explains (*Strom.* viii. 21. 4–6) that the briefest possible definition consists of three members, the genus and two of the most necessary εἴδη, or specific characters:

φαμὲν οὖν, ἄνθρωπός ἐστι τὸ ζῷον ⟨λογικόν⟩, γελαστικόν. τό τε ἐξαιρέτως συμβεβηκὸς τῷ ὁριζομένῳ προσπαραληπτέον, ἢ τὴν ἰδίαν ἀρετὴν αὐτοῦ ἢ τὸ ἴδιον ἔργον αὐτοῦ καὶ τοιούτων τινῶν ἄλλων. ἐξηγητικὸς οὖν ὁ ὅρος ὢν τῆς τοῦ πράγματος οὐσίας περιλαβεῖν μὲν ἀκριβῶς τὴν φύσιν τοῦ πράγματος ἀδυνατεῖ, διὰ δὲ τῶν κυριωτάτων εἰδῶν τὴν δήλωσιν τῆς οὐσίας ποιεῖται καὶ σχεδὸν ἐν ποιότητι ὁ ὅρος τὴν οὐσίαν ἔχει.

We say, then, that man is the animal that reasons and laughs; and we must include that which uniquely pertains[22] to the definiendum, its particular virtue or its particular function, and those of similar beings. So the definition which explains the essential nature of the thing cannot accurately comprehend its actual nature, but indicates its essential nature by means of the most important specific characters: so, roughly speaking, the definition presents the essential nature in qualitative terms.

Clement is trying to explain that the definition of *x*, even if peculiar to *x*, cannot tell us all we want to know about *x*. There is, of course, a more obvious point besides, that a description may only profess to give us a partial definition, which is not peculiar to *x*; this shades off into the 'general description' which we have considered in sections D and E. But in some such cases the sense of definition still seems to be present. Thus Hippolytus refers to the Aristotelian view of virtue as a mean, which was attributed in his day to Plato: τὰς μὲν οὖν ἀρετὰς κατὰ τιμὴν ἀκρότητας εἶναί φησιν, κατὰ δὲ οὐσίαν μεσότητας (*Ref.* i. 19. 16 based on *NE* ii. 6, 1107 a 6–8); roughly, 'he says that virtues are extremes in point of value, but moderate degrees in point of definition.'

This is perhaps the place to mention the use of οὐσία to denote

---

[22] Συμβεβηκός can mean inseparable attribute, see above, p. 142.

the Platonic Idea; since this was regarded as the reality underlying a general term, such as justice, though also as the ideal pattern to which members of a species conform. The conception receives a number of theological developments. The Father, and the Son also, could be regarded as the source of the Ideas, but could also be identified with some of them. Origen takes John 14:6, 'I am ... the truth' as a basis for entitling Jesus ἡ τῆς ἀληθείας οὐσία, possibly 'the essence of truth' (*c. Cels.* viii. 12, cf. vii. 16); here the Son, as truth, is contrasted with the Father of truth; and 'truth' no doubt has its rather specialized Platonic sense of ideal and eternal reality. In *in Joh.* i. 186 the Saviour is certainly the embodiment of all truth; and in another passage, commenting on Ephesians 4:20, Origen characterizes Jesus as having 'the archetypal οὐσία of truth' (ἡ γὰρ τῆς ἀληθείας πρωτότυπος οὐσία ἐν τῷ Ἰησοῦ μόνῳ λέγοντι ἐγώ εἰμι ἡ ἀλήθεια, *JTS* 3 (1902), 418). Essentially the same point is made when Jesus is characterized as ἡ αὐτοαλήθεια or in similar Platonic terms. Here too the literal sense of αὐτός, '*x* itself', 'the identical *x*' is displaced by the Platonic convention which makes ἡ αὐτοαλήθεια mean the sole genuine, unmixed embodiment of truth. Indeed the same point is apparent in Plutarch's quotation from Chrysippus discussed above. When Chrysippus says that wickedness is the οὐσία of misfortune, he does not mean, as Plutarch explains him, that the two are identical; his point is that the only real misfortune is wickedness; he certainly does *not* mean that the only real wickedness is misfortune!

In another passage Origen suggests that the Son may be compared, not to the Idea of truth, but to the Idea of the Good itself, which is the source of the being and value of all the other Ideas; while the Father is still further exalted. It is indeed possible, he says, that God is οὐσία though invisible; but 'we would also inquire whether we ought to say that the only begotten and first-born of all creation is being of beings and Idea of Ideas and beginning, and that his Father and God transcends all these' (*c. Cels.* vi. 64, ζητητέον δὲ καί, εἰ οὐσίαν μὲν οὐσιῶν λεκτέον καὶ ἰδέαν ἰδεῶν καὶ ἀρχὴν τὸν μονογενῆ καὶ πρωτότοκον πάσης κτίσεως ἐπέκεινα δὲ πάντων τούτων τὸν πατέρα αὐτοῦ καὶ θεόν). In this case it is particularly clear that οὐσία has moved away from the sense of 'definition' to that of 'ideal form'.

In such cases, therefore, our tabulation is under strain; and that not through logical defects of its own; but because we are trying to deal with a concept, the Platonic Idea, which is itself logically incoherent: the decision to attach it at this particular point has to be fairly arbitrary. We have considered the Idea as a sort of definition; and where it implies a definition, οὐσία is used in the predicative mode (2); it indicates *what 'x' means*, or *what x is*. But other aspects of the Platonic Idea are expressed in the collective use of οὐσία to denote immaterial reality in general—which takes us back to class B3—and in such phrases as οὐσίαι νοεραί, sc. ideas and rational souls—which we have classed as B4; while if considered not in its aspect of reality but as the unifying principle of a class it would be properly assigned to level E.

Possibly, however, class F4 might be the appropriate placing for individual objects which (in ancient thought) are *sui generis*, like the sun or the phoenix.[23] We have already considered whether ancient writers clearly conceived the being of God in such terms; the evidence seems inconclusive. But the analysis of statements about God's being must be reserved for another chapter.

(G)

The notion of truth was briefly introduced in the chapter on Plato; but some further explanation is required at this point. Truth is commonly explained as a relation of correspondence between a set of facts and a set of words. A statement indicates a set of facts, and also declares that its indication corresponds to the facts. Questions, conditionals, etc., indicate but do not declare; an untrue statement both indicates and declares, but the correspondence it claims is lacking. It seems, then, that the logically prior sense of 'truth' is to stand for the relation of correspondence; but this, I think, is rarely found, though it perhaps occurs in phrases like ἐπ' ἀλήθειαν, 'in truth'. In practice the Greek word is commonly specialized in one of two ways. Either it is equivalent to 'true statement'—the older sense, common from Homer onwards; and so, by a natural extension, to 'truth-fulness', 'sincerity'; or it indicates an actual state of affairs in relation to possible statements or beliefs. But this sense too can be extended; instead of contrasting the facts with possibly

[23] See pp. 94 above and 183 below.

misleading statements about them, some writers use ἀλήθεια to
stand for objective reality as they conceive it, in contrast with all
names or statements whatsoever. We have seen Plato making
a move of this kind. Starting from the position that the Idea of
justice (e.g.) is what the word 'justice' really means, he goes on to
affirm that the actions usually signified by 'justice' are only rough
approximations to the Idea. The name 'justice' can therefore
mislead; but Plato does not suggest that any other name is better;
and in some cases—at least, in that of goodness—he clearly indicates that no designation is adequate to the reality.

In dealing with Plato's usage I showed that the sense of οὐσία
sometimes approximates to that of 'truth' (ἀλήθεια). In Aristotle
the convergence seems rather less close; thus the philosophic
dictionary known as *Metaphysics* V mentions 'truth' in Chapter 7,
which deals with the general notion of being, τὸ ὄν, rather than
in 8, under the more specialized, though still very flexible, title
of 'substance'.

In later usage, however, the meanings of οὐσία and ἀλήθεια will
overlap, though the two words never become fully synonymous.
One such overlap has already been considered on pp. 37, 139;
both οὐσία and ἀλήθεια, and for that matter τὸ ὄν, can be used
in a collective mode to denote 'immaterial reality'. It is much
less easy to find cases in which οὐσία means 'truth' in the sense of
ordinary empirical fact, and I am inclined to think this usage is
practically confined to stereotyped phrases such as οὐσίᾳ and
κατ' οὐσίαν; here certainly we have to translate 'in fact' or 'in
reality (as with τῷ ὄντι or κατ' ἀλήθειαν); 'in substance' will not
do. And even the former renderings could be misleading. Thus in
the passage about the Graces quoted above, p. 135, the phrase
κατ' οὐσίαν ὑφεστηκέναι certainly could be rendered 'have truly
existed'; but probably the existential verb influences the sense of
κατ' οὐσίαν and suggests the notion of objective reality; one
would hardly use this phrase if one wished to say that the Graces
were 'in reality' mere figments; that would be τῷ ὄντι. But perhaps we may quote Philo, *Leg. All.* i. 62 for the sense required: 'At
the moment my reasoning faculty (ἡγεμονικόν) is in my body
κατὰ τὴν οὐσίαν, but virtually (δυνάμει) it is in Italy or Sicily,
whenever it thinks about these places . . . so often when people
are in profane places κατὰ τὴν οὐσίαν, they are really in the holiest,
through meditating on virtue'. At its first appearance the phrase

could mean 'in virtue of its essential nature'; but at the second
it must mean 'as a matter of plain fact'. Philo is using Stoic
phraseology (e.g. ἡγεμονικόν), and for the Stoics there is an easy
transition from 'matter' to 'reality'.

On the other hand, as I noted in passing (p. 142 above),
οὐσία can mean 'reality' or 'fact', and so approximate to the
sense of 'truth', when it is used in contrast with names, images,
conceptions (ἐπίνοιαι) and the like. This usage is often influenced
by the commonplaces that one must discriminate between names
etc. and the realities they signify, or conversely, that names etc.
are a reliable guide to reality. Thus Origen argues that although
the word 'wisdom' is feminine, God's Wisdom is not really
female: οὐ γὰρ παρὰ τὸ θηλυκὸν ὄνομα καὶ τῇ οὐσίᾳ θήλειαν νομι-
στέον εἶναι τὴν σοφίαν (c. Cels. v. 39). In the Commentary on St.
John he argues that no one should be offended when he distinguishes the various titles of the Saviour, as if this implied distinctions in his actual being (i. 200); and again: 'They say that
the Word is the Beginning, not distinguishable from it in actuality,
but conceptually and relatively' (οὐχ ἕτερον ὄντα αὐτῆς κατ'
οὐσίαν ἀλλ' ἐπινοίᾳ καὶ σχέσει, fr. 1, p. 485, 12–13). Word and
Beginning are not really two distinct beings; rather, the Word
obtains the title 'Beginning' through his function in the creation
of the world.

In all these cases, however, the word οὐσία does not assume
the exact sense of 'truth', as the characteristic of titles or names
which are just or appropriate, but rather that of 'reality', as that
which such titles represent. It is the latter which is usually important in theological debates which turn on the appropriateness
or otherwise of conventional titles. A well-known example is the
statement of Eusebius to which Marcellus took such strong exception: 'Certainly the image and that which it images is not considered one and the same thing, but two realities, and two facts,
and two powers, to match the (two) expressions' (fr. 72, in
Eusebius, c. Marc. i. 4); this contention was said to support the
view that the Son is distinct from the Father οὐσίᾳ τε καὶ δυνάμει,
perhaps 'in reality and in power'. But it is not always possible
to be certain; when Dionysius of Alexandria proclaims that God
is the absolutely unoriginate, and unoriginateness is, so to speak,
his *ousia* (καὶ οὐσία ἐστὶν αὐτοῦ, ὡς ἂν εἴποι τις, ἡ ἀγεννησία),[24] he

---

[24] Ed. Feltoe, p. 183. 10 = Eusebius, *PE* vii. 19.

may indeed be referring to the essence or true being of God; but considering that οὐσία, without the article, is likely to be predicate, not subject, it is at least possible that he means that the *term ἀγεννησία* is a true characterization or definition of the Godhead, what Aristotle might have called his λόγος τῆς οὐσίας.

VII

GOD'S SUBSTANCE IN THEOLOGICAL TRADITION

(i) *Substance Language in Theology*

THE concept of substance has now been examined in some detail; it remains to consider the question, what is the substance of God? For obvious reasons, I shall not attempt to review all the answers to it that were suggested in antiquity, still less to explore their philosophical and biblical origins. It will be enough to understand the question and to examine one or two of the more important answers, in a way which will help the reader to fill in the details for himself.

Agnosticism, whether religious or otherwise, naturally suggests a doubt whether the concept of substance can be properly applied to God; and in any case, its use in theology involves certain assumptions which may properly be refused by religious and Christian tradition. We may be deterred from asking what God is, for quite different reasons; for instance, because it commits us to describing what is in principle indescribable, to comprehending and so reducing the ultimate mystery; or again, on the grounds that it distracts attention from the more significant and more biblical question of what God does; or indeed, because all such questions seem presumptuous. Our descriptive apparatus may be even more justly suspected when it comes to categorial structures in which the concept of substance plays a part: substance/accident, substance/energy, substance/function, and the like. These seem to have provided valuable means of theological reflection, but also to have been misused, partly in the attempt to score debating-points, partly because they were too readily taken as absolutes which apply to all realities without exception. But the cure for misuse is more reflective use. We have no quarrel with the man who gives up speech for action; but if he wants to *talk* about being and doing, then it is our business to know what is the distinction between them. In clearing up such categorial puzzles, we may be making a modest contribution to the contemporary debate about the relevance of Greek metaphysics to Christian theology; and so, at least indirectly, contribute to theology itself.

Our first concern, however, is the more limited question: What is being said or suggested about God when reference is made to his 'substance', his *ousia*? Since the term *ousia* can be used in a wide variety of senses, it would seem that the phrase 'God's *ousia*' could be explained in different ways which would not necessarily conflict; two apparently conflicting answers might well be compatible, and could be admitted (or intuitively felt) to complement each other and add to our descriptive resources. The question of God's *ousia* seems to be a baffling one, but on two very different grounds; first because God is *per se* so largely beyond our understanding; but secondly, because our theology is avoidably confused, since answers were sought before the question itself was adequately defined.

We have noted that precise distinctions which can be explained to modern scholars were often missed by ancient writers; and this is especially true of the early Christian centuries, in view of some characteristics of later Greek culture which have often been described: its philosophical syncretism, its reliance on tradition, and its lack of original speculation. In particular, we have shown that although the term *ousia* was used in very various senses, the variations for the most part were not detected. Most writers accepted the Platonic distinction between 'intelligible' and 'sensible' substances, or reality; and many assumed that this distinction corresponded, roughly at least, to that between the general and the particular. Few Christian writers were prepared to push the question further; and some believed (or affected to believe) that all such distinctions were logical niceties which theologians could best ignore. A similar situation obtained in theology itself. The early Christian fathers, conforming to the mental habits of their age, had largely come to a common mind on the subject of God's being by a process in which theological statements had lost their original distinctive and exclusive force and were reinterpreted and harmonized, so that verbal contradictions were not always felt to be troublesome. Controversy still could, and did, break out, but not always upon what seem to us the important points: perhaps the most interesting debate we shall notice involved the question whether the Christian experience of God can be concentrated round a single descriptive predicate, which can then have some degree of literal validity, or whether it must be distributed over a variety of terms, which then must necessarily involve large elements of metaphor and analogy.

There is, however, one other difference in approach which does not entirely coincide with that just mentioned. In studying the ancient theologians, we come across two contrasted methods of thought, employed to some degree by every school, which we may call the mystical and the pedagogic, and which it will not be fanciful to compare to the two biblical attributes of justice and mercy. But these are rarely found in isolation. The mystic may be driven by a conviction of God's incomparable power and mystery to reject all descriptions that could in any way assimilate him to the world of everyday. The result is a *theologia negativa*, the type of thought which is perhaps most often studied in this field. Two considerations at least intervene to prevent this method from being pushed to the limit or relied upon exclusively. There is first the danger that it will be self-defeating. To describe God as 'not even indescribable' as Basilides did,[1] begins to look like mere verbal mystification; to refuse him the title 'good' may well suggest, not that he transcends all the good things we can imagine, but that his nature has some of the cruel and repellent qualities of vice. But secondly, the attributes of transcendence and mystery do not exhaust the mystic's consciousness of the divine. In Otto's phrase, he is faced with 'mysterium tremendum fascinans'; and this sense of an inexhaustible sweetness and beauty is readily interpreted as the awareness of a gracious being who wills to disclose himself. So in justice to God it must be acknowledged that he is generous and bountiful, 'not envious', but prompt in bestowing that best of all gifts, the knowledge of himself. The Hermetist can say, 'It is the property of goodness to disclose itself.'[2]

The pedagogic approach, as we may call it, considers not what the divine nature justly demands, but what can reasonably be expected of human beings. Whatever qualifications are needed,

---

[1] Hippolytus, *Ref.* vii. 20. 3; cf. the deliberate use of contradictory predicates by Monoimus (ibid. viii. 12. 5); also Albinus, *Didasc.* 10, p. 165, 4 ff.

[2] *CH* x. 4, based on Plato, *Timaeus* 29 e.

some positive teaching about the divine nature must be conveyed in a form which simple people can appreciate.[3] At its best, this approach is upheld by the theological reasoning which I have just outlined; but it easily degenerates into formalism, for instance, in those textbooks which include the word *theos* along with numerous others in a list of definitions. But once again, such formalism does not always reach its natural conclusion; some writers resort to it only occasionally, and intersperse it with mystical and agnostic pronouncements; and even those who confidently describe God in terms derived in the last instance from everyday life very commonly base their analogies on things which themselves are thought to be in some way mysterious. One of the attractions in describing God as supreme mind (*nous*) is that the mind of man cannot be clearly understood;[4] and the same is true of the mysterious 'spirit' (*pneuma*), the source of life and thought, and the mysterious unity, which is completely simple and yet is the source of all multiplicity.

In theory it should be possible to distinguish questions about God's nature or substance from questions about our knowledge of him. But in classical antiquity the two were closely related, in view of the very wide acceptance of the maxim, Like is known by like. This fact gives a practical relevance to Greek speculations which is not always appreciated; for the maxim can be read, 'Resemble what you wish to know'. The doctrine that God is mind is closely bound up with the commendation and practice of mystical introspection; the doctrine that God is spirit, *pneuma*, prompts one to look for him where spirit is thought to be active as a cosmic or vital force; the mind must study the qualities of the virtuous ruler, or ascend beyond the stars by meditating on the cosmic order. Even the belief that God is perfect unity conveys the moral that unity must be achieved in each human life, through constancy of purpose and avoidance of distractions.[5]

From these rather general considerations we may pass to consider some points of detail.

(1) Most Christian writers take it for granted that God's existence is certain, though many of them hold that his nature is

---

[3] Cf. Philo, *Immut.* 60 f., esp. the striking commendation of useful falsehoods in 64, based of course on Plato, *Rep.* ii. 389 b.

[4] Cf. e.g. Philo, *Mut. Nom.* 10; Eusebius, *ET* ii. 17. 4; W. Pannenberg, *ZKG* 70 (1959), 8–9, 21–3.

[5] Cf. Origen, *Hom. I Reg.*, i. 4; and see pp. 182–3 below.

in some way problematical. But *ousia* is not commonly used to mean God's existence; some instances occur, but chiefly in the context of 'denying . . .' *Hyparxis* is a fairly common alternative, used by Philo amongst others.

(2) Some writers appear to avoid the term *ousia*, while using *hypostasis* in a roughly similar way. Examples are Alexander of Alexandria and Cyril of Jerusalem; and the latter's case is noteworthy, since he has left us, not mere fragments, but a sizeable theological work. It is not quite easy to guess their reasons; for instance, if it were thought that *ousia* would suggest 'material substance', this objection would apply with equal force to *hypostasis*. Imitation of the Latin *substantia* might commend *hypostasis*, but it is hard to see why Cyril should copy Latin usage. A more probable reason is that *ousia*, as a philosophical term, is not found in the Bible, whereas *hypostasis* appears in Wisdom, Paul, and Hebrews; Athanasius finds it necessary to apologize for the use of *ousia* for this very reason (*Decr.* 19 etc.).

(3) Christian writers were also influenced—as were many non-Christians—by the Platonic dictum that the God is *epekeina tēs ousias*, 'beyond substance' (or 'beyond being') in dignity and power.[6] In general the phrase acted as a deterrent against applying the term *ousia* to God; but very different interpretations of it were given in our period, so that it was perhaps too ambiguous to be conclusive. Some examples are 'beyond material substance' (Eusebius, *PE* xi. 23. 11); 'beyond created substance' (implying superiority to angels etc.: Athanasius *c. Gent.* 35, 40, cf. ibid. 2); 'beyond intelligible substance' (and therefore beyond definition: Origen, *c. Cels.* vi. 64, Celsus, ibid. vii. 45, Eusebius, *PE* xi. 21. 6 f.). All these writers are of course influenced by Platonic dualism; whereas Tertullian, who has a poor opinion of Platonism, applies the term *substantia* to God in the directest possible way; in *adv. Prax.* 9 he writes *pater enim tota substantia est, filius vero derivatio* etc. In this passage *substantia* means something comparable to the created (though mysterious) *spiritus*, but distinguished by its purity, subtlety, and power, which was at first concentrated in the Father, then distributed to the Son and Spirit. Tertullian can also assign to 'divinity' a 'substance' in the quite distinct sense of a 'distinguishing property', namely eternity (*adv. Nat.* ii. 2).

[6] Cf. p. 140 above.

(4) Even where there is some reluctance to apply the term *ousia* directly to God, it is clear that no other categorial term is more appropriate; there is no question of God's being described as a quantity, a quality, or a relation. Aristotle cited 'God' and 'mind' as examples of substance (*NE* i. 6, 1096 a 24), and textbook definitions of God as an *ousia* sometimes find their way into Christian writings (e.g. Clement, fr. 37, 39). But such language is also used much more circumspectly. Where Platonic theories of immaterial reality were current, it seemed legitimate, at least as a first approximation, to assign God to the intelligible world as opposed to the perceptible and so regard him as an 'intelligible substance'; so Numenius calls him σύμφυτον τῇ οὐσίᾳ. Even those writers who most strongly assert that God is incomparable and transcends all categories—for example Clement himself, *Strom.* v. 81. 5—do not wholly avoid the suggestion that God not only has, but is, an οὐσία (ibid. iv. 162. 5!). Origen, it is true, seems more willing to allow this in the case of the Son and the Spirit than of the Father; in *c. Cels.* vi. 64 he ventures the suggestion that the *Son* may be described as the 'substance of substances and Idea of Ideas'—i.e. compared with Plato's Form of the Good— but the Father is 'beyond all these'. Of the Spirit he says directly that he is a substance—an 'active substance, not an activity' (*in Joh.*, fr. 37). Eusebius can refer to God as 'the incorporeal . . . and inexpressible substance' (*ET* ii. 6. 2) and Athanasius, as is well known, argues that the phrase 'from God' can be better expressed as 'from the substance of God' (*Decr.* 22, *Syn.* 35).

(5) If, however, the question is not, what God is, but what he has, the case is less straightforward. *Ousia* is commonly regarded as that in which the other categories inhere; but are the other categories applicable to God? I am not aware of a full-scale discussion of this problem by Christian writers; but some prevailing trends can be reported. Greek theologians generally (though not invariably) take it for granted that God is strictly unchanging; he is constant in himself, and is not disturbed by things outside him; hence he cannot be credited with passive states, or with qualities, in their common acceptation of variable qualities.[7] They also assigned him a rather special relationship to

---

[7] God is regularly called ἀπάθης, 'impassible', though contrast Origen, *Hom. Ezek.* vi. 6, *Hom. Num.* xxiii. 2; ἄποιος not before Gregory of Nyssa: but see Athanasius, *Syn.* 53.

the categories of quantity, time, and place, in which the dominant thought is that of all-embracing extent, though without excluding the reverse comparison to a moment, a point, and especially a monad. So God is not in time and space, but they are in him; God was there before time began, and will be there when it has ended; he surrounds or encompasses the whole of space; he is infinitely extended, as compared with the limited extent (or perhaps, the lesser infinity) of time and space; and more generally, infinitely great. It is perhaps unnecessary to go through the whole Aristotelian list of categories; for practical purposes, those which are theologically important are invariable attributes, actions and relations.

(6) Here, however, there arises a problem which can be traced in some detail in surviving discussions, though it will only be briefly outlined at this stage: if God is simple and unchanging, how can he be endowed with a variety of attributes, and a varying succession of actions and relationships? This problem of unity and multiplicity was probably discussed *pari passu* with a similar problem about the soul; if the soul is simple, how can it dispose of a variety of parts, powers, activities, or functions?[8] At least two solutions were proposed. One of them presents a concept of divine unity which, so to speak, digests the plurality. Thus it was held that the various relationships in which God stands to man arise from differences and changes in them, not in him; they give rise to different conceptions of God (ἐπίνοιαι) which do not infringe the divine unity since they are merely partial and human conceptions. This theory no doubt owes a good deal to Stoic justifications of polytheistic cults, as exhibiting various aspects of a single divine reality. A more challenging form of this solution suggests that the various divine attributes are in fact identical, not only one with another, but with their possessor; this view is suggested at least by Irenaeus and Novatian, and was later adopted by Augustine[9] and passed into the common stock of Christian orthodoxy. As formulated by Augustine it seems not only paradoxical in itself, but also inconsistent with the commonly accepted view which distinguishes God's essence from his

---

[8] Philo, *Quis Rerum*, 233 ff. esp. 236. See Tertullian, *de Anima* 14. 3, and Waszink's note, p. 215. Ps.-Plutarch, *Pars an facultas animi sit vita passiva*.

[9] Iren. ii. x. 13. 3, iii. 16. 7, Hv. i. 282, ii. 89. Novatian, *Trin.* 6. Aug. *Civ. Dei* x. 10: 'He is what he has'. id. *Trin.* v. 11. See above, p. 109 and below, pp. 187–9.

energies or activities towards the creation; but discussion of this must be postponed.

The other solution is that which was ultimately adopted by Plotinus and the later neo-Platonists, and ultimately discarded by the Christian church, though only after some centuries of confident use. Traditional exegesis of Plato's *Parmenides* suggested a distinction between pure and absolute unity and a lower unity which allowed of multiplicity.[10] Within the Christian church, the lower unity was identified with the divine Logos, who became the proximate creator and controller of the universe; and it is to him that the theory of multiple designations (ἐπίνοιαι), is most commonly applied. Plotinus, as is well known, came to believe that mind is not the highest form of reality, since even self-consciousness implies a distinction between subject and object which is incompatible with perfect unity.[11]

(7) There is one further problem that needs to be clarified. It seems natural to distinguish between God's substance and his relationships to other beings; and between God's substance and his 'energies', or activities *ad extra*; but can one establish a clear conceptual relationship between God's substance and his attributes? It may be helpful to glance at a solution suggested by Aristotelian theory. This teaches that the substance of natural objects is defined *per genus et differentiam*, adding that a substance can also possess 'properties', which are invariant attributes which are distinguishable from the substance itself, since they do not form part of its definition, and also from its 'accidents', in their ordinary sense of variable attributes. Now there seems to be an obvious unrealism in regarding God as an instance of a genus (though such a conception is sometimes implied; just as the notion that God *is* a genus is used, with some sense of its inadequacy, by the Cappadocian fathers of the fourth century)—or again, in regarding him as in any important sense susceptible of definition. Hence it might seem logical to say simply that God possesses properties; but whether these are regarded as collectively constituting his substance, or as attaching to it, will depend on how the latter term is used. If it simply suggests the notion of existence, or again of reality and power, then a further question arises as to the nature of that existence or power, and the proper-

---

[10] See above, pp. 93–4; below, p. 186.
[11] See Armstrong, *LGP*, 236–7.

ties are conceptually distinct; if it refers to the nature of God, then it is a compendious term for the properties.

I do not think these questions were clearly formulated by Christian writers in our period,[12] and the actual state of discussion will best be conveyed by recalling a few well-known illustrations. Athanasius contends that God is completely simple, has no 'accidents', and needs nothing to complete his 'substance', which is incomprehensible (ἀκατάληπτος: *Decr.* 22); yet he still feels entitled to suggest a *variety* of terms which enable us to 'signify', or possibly 'suggest', his substance; in this sense 'we call him God and Father and Lord.'[13] He is no doubt relying on the theory that such terms are only partial characterizations of a reality which, despite its 'simplicity', is more than sufficient to justify the whole complex of theological and devotional titles. This should suggest a sharp distinction between the term *ousia*, which is simply one of these abstractions, and the reality which it stands for. On the other hand the Anomoean Arians are said to have fixed upon one term, 'ingenerateness', as completely adequate to express the divine nature; they seem to have assumed that a definition sufficient to *identify* x actually corresponds with and expresses all that x is; consequently God's *ousia*, in the sense of his objective reality and character, is reduced to suit his *ousia* in the sense of 'accepted identifying definition'. Again, much perplexity was caused by the Arian argument that since God has no accidents, everything that can be said about him belongs to his substance; therefore the title 'Father' belongs to his substance, and *eo ipso* the Son is excluded from it.[14] Augustine attempts to solve this problem in terms of 'substantial relations'. This is in part a well-justified protest against an over-simplified theory of substance and accidents, whose defects I have tried to expose, on the good Aristotelian ground that some relations can be 'substantial', in the sense of 'invariant', just as properties are; but it

[12] Plotinus of course rejected the Aristotelian system of categories; cf. Albinus, *Didasc.* 10, p. 165, who regards them as inapplicable to God. However, Origen seems to distinguish between God and certain of his attributes; cf. p. 213 below.

[13] Athanasius seldom refers in *general* terms to God's attributes; but in *Syn.* 50, a dialectical passage, he has τὰ τῆς πρώτης οὐσίας ἰδιώματα; cf. πάντα τὰ τοῦ Πατρός, τὰ τοῦ Πατρὸς ἴδια, ibid.

[14] Basil replies that 'ingenerateness' and 'generateness' are not internal to the substance of God, but are 'distinguishing properties'; in Aristotelian terms, they are not properties but differentia, marking off individuals (or individual species?) within a genus.

does not explain how a structure of three distinct persons is compatible with absolute simplicity in the godhead.

(ii) *Attempts to Define God's Substance*

I have suggested that one cannot trace a clear conceptual distinction established in antiquity between the substance of God and his invariant attributes. It may nevertheless be true that ancient discussions of Gods' substance developed in practice along their own distinct lines; at least we can attempt to follow them and discover *ambulando* whether we are traversing new ground. I take three points for granted at the outset:

(1) Christian conceptions of God's substance depend largely on biblical texts of the form 'God is . . .' or 'I am . . .', particularly where the predicate lends itself to philosophical development.

(2) God was seen as both transcendent and immanent; but his action upon the world was commonly ascribed to energies, powers, or intermediaries which are in some sense distinguishable from his substance. We are therefore more concerned with titles which signify God's transcendent being than with those (like 'Creator' or 'Lord') which relate him to the world.

(3) We may legitimately concentrate on positive rather than negative terms, and on nominal rather than adjectival ones.

This third criterion should not suggest that purely verbal tests are adequate; it has been shown that predicates which are negative in form may have positive significance.[15] But if we are dealing with suggestion rather than explicit theory, we must allow for the widespread belief that the structure of language reflects the order of reality. There are no negative substances; and the ancients must have thought it natural to refer to substances by positive terms. Positive terms attempt to state what God is, his *ousia*; negative terms tell us what he is not. The former entail some risks which the latter avoid, as the ancients were well aware; if, for instance, we refer to God as 'light', we are using a metaphor and perhaps encouraging literalistic misunderstandings which easily arise. Yet there are also advantages; by using this metaphor, and expressing it in substantival form, we

---

[15] Prestige, *GPT*, 4 ff.

vividly suggest God's uniqueness and invariance; for after all, nothing does shine but light, and light does nothing but shine! These points would be lost if we merely affirmed that God 'shines' or 'is bright'.

Any representative selection of biblical titles would include the following, to which I have added such proof-texts as were commonly cited by the Fathers; an asterisk indicates direct predication:

Being	*Exod. 3 : 14 LXX ('I am He who Is').
Unity	*Deut. 6 : 4
Source	Jer. 2 : 13 etc.
Fire	*Deut. 4 : 24
Spirit	*John 4 : 24
Light	*I John 1 : 5 etc.
Life	John 1 : 4, 5 : 26, 11 : 25
Love	*I John 4 : 8, 16
The Good	Mark 10 : 18
Father	Matt. 11 : 27
Lord	*Isa. 42 : 8

One might add one or two important titles which rest on philosophical tradition but lack the direct support of scriptural quotations, especially the characterization of God as mind, *nous*; though this is of course indirectly supported by the personal and moral predicates already set down.

It will at once be obvious that the Old and New Testaments together provide a list of theological predicates which cannot naturally and easily be combined. Yet Christian theologians were obliged to explain and justify these texts, and while doing so were bound to defend their scriptures from any charge of self-contradiction; indeed the situation of Platonist philosophers was not very different, in view of the variety of theological suggestions presented by a Platonic corpus of writings which was now regarded as authoritative. Hence it was argued that all predicates attributed to God, being borrowed from the natural world, embody some element of metaphor and suggest only some aspect of the total divine reality. (The attractiveness of divine *proper names* no doubt lay in their apparent exemption from this defect, and the Gnostics were slow to realize that they only acquired significance from their cultic associations, and could easily lose it). In developing such arguments both Christian and Platonist writers were able to exploit the freedom of manoeuvre allowed them by a long tradition of allegorical exegesis. This freedom makes it important not to seize upon isolated pronouncements of any particular writer, but to appraise his contribution as a whole. Nevertheless, there are differences in emphasis. Some writers in practice adopt a particular title, and employ it as what we may call a privileged designation. The majority work with a more or less explicit theory of neutrality, using a wide variety of designations on the assumption that they are compatible, each in itself inadequate, but collectively reinforcing one another. Finally, there is much verbal inconsistency, for reasons already indicated. Thus Athenagoras gives out in a single sentence that God is incomprehensible, but also comprehensible through mind and reason ($\nu\tilde{\omega}$ $\kappa\alpha\grave{\iota}$ $\lambda\acute{o}\gamma\omega$).[16] Philo and Clement abound in similar contradictions; both writers designate God as 'the monad' but also declare that he is 'above the monad';[17] and Origen, who endorses Plato's dictum that God is 'above mind and being' is not in practice deterred from describing God as a simple intellectual nature.[18]

One of the classic ways of expressing divine transcendence and immanence made use of the Platonic contrasts between soul and body, between mind and sense, and between the intelligible and the perceptible. In our period it was no longer possible for Christians to use the term 'soul', or 'soul of the world', to designate the supreme Godhead.[19] Unqualified praise of the soul belongs to an early phase of Plato's thought which he later modified;[20] the *Timaeus* subordinates the world-soul to a creator-god who implanted it; and while later Platonists were able to draw upon Stoic elaborations of the doctrine of the world-soul, they gave it a subordinate place in the divine hierarchy; relics of this conception, combined with that of the demiurge, are built into the Christian concept of the Logos as 'second god'. Meanwhile the philosophic manuals could say tersely that 'mind is

---

[16] *Leg.* 10; W. Pannenberg, *ZKG* 70 (1959), 24.

[17] Philo, *Immut.* 11, *Quis Rerum*, 183; contrast *Praem.* 40, *Vit. Contemp.* 2. Clement, *Strom.* v. 71. 2, at least differs in tone from *Paed.* i. 71. 1.

[18] *Princ.* i. 1. 6, cf. *c. Cels.* vii. 38; similarly Justin, Albinus (below, p. 169, n. 24), and Numenius.

[19] See e.g. Clement, *Protr.* v. 66. 4; contrast Philo, e.g. *Leg. All.* i. 91; and cf. *RHT* iii. 23–4.   [20] See R. Hackforth, 'Plato's Theism'.

better than soul',[21] while Christians, and Christian Gnostics, adopted a scheme which subordinated 'soul' to 'spirit'. Nevertheless Christian theologians continue to use conceptions based on the contrast of soul and body; to assert that the soul of man is in some sense akin to God, even if not consubstantial with him; and that the way towards him is to despise the body and exercise the soul.[22]

Understandably enough, Christian thinkers show some uncertainty about the description of God as mind; since Plato himself, echoed by Aristotle, both endorses and retracts it;[23] though a positive use was common among the middle Platonists and, despite Plotinus' reservations, was adopted by many Neoplatonists as well.[24] Some early Christian writers use this description without reserve;[25] most later writers use it more sparingly, in special contexts and with emphasis on the element of analogy. Two lines of thought in particular kept it in circulation. First, the mere title, the Logos, implies a power that derives from the Father as a word or thought proceeds from the mind that expresses it; Dionysius of Alexandria states this analogy in direct and confident terms;[26] and though Christian writers usually qualify it by saying that the divine Word is not a mere utterance ($\lambda \acute{o} \gamma o s \ \pi \rho o \phi o \rho \iota \kappa \acute{o} s$), it remained indispensable as a corrective to the potentially embarrassing metaphor of physical generation. Both Eusebius and Athanasius insist that the generation of the Son is an inexpressible mystery, but nevertheless use the metaphor of the spoken word (along with that of the light and its radiance), as a partial indication; both, however, are chary of calling the Father 'mind' simpliciter.[27]

---

[21] Albinus, *Didasc.* 10, p. 164, 16; cf. Plutarch, *Fac. Lun.*, 28. 943 a. Tertullian dissents: *de Anima* 12.

[22] Athanasius *c. Gent.* 30–4; he does not appear to distinguish clearly between 'soul', 'rational soul', and 'mind'; cf. ibid. 35.

[23] Contrast e.g. *Phileb.* 28 c with *Rep.* 509 b; and, for Aristotle, the theology of *Metaph.* xii with fr. 46 (Ross, p. 57); 'either mind or something beyond mind'.

[24] Albinus calls the first principle $\nu o \hat{u} s$ (*Didasc.* 9–10, 163. 29, 164. 24–6) despite the extreme negative theology of 165. 4 ff. Cf. S. Lilla, *Clement of Alexandria*, 202, 222–4; J. H. Waszink, 'Porphyrius und Numenius', *EH* xii. 41.

[25] 'Unproblematisch', Pannenberg, op. cit., citing Aristides i. 5, Athenagoras, Minucius Felix. Add Justin, *Dial.* 4 ($\beta a \sigma \iota \lambda \iota \kappa \grave{o} s \ \nu o \hat{u} s$), Clement, *Strom.* iv. 155. 2, Origen, *Princ.* i. 1. 6.   [26] See Athanasius, *Sent. Dion.* 23; Feltoe, pp. 196–7.

[27] Eusebius, *ET* ii. 17. 4–6, clearly recognizes the limitation of the metaphor and does not call the Father $\nu o \hat{u} s$. Athanasius does so in *Decr.* 24, directly following Dionysius, but not, I think, elsewhere; cf. the guarded language of *c. Gent.* 45,

Secondly, the concept of God as mind lives on in the doctrine of universal providence and foreknowledge. This hardly needs illustration or discussion; the doctrine that God made the world with wisdom and intelligence and guides and foresees human history rests on a clear biblical foundation and can easily borrow the language of contemporary Platonic theism; it can appeal to the doctrine that intelligent beings are *eo ipso* better than un-intelligent, and the maker superior to the product; thus no characterization of God is tolerable if it deprives him of intelligence.

I am inclined to think that as time went on orthodox Christians became more discreet (or less enterprising) in their use of this metaphor, and ignored certain characteristics of the mind which are important to Philo and to some early Judaizing Christians, including Gnostics. Philo sees the mind as receptive,[28] nimble,[29] and resourceful,[30] and infers similar qualities in God himself.[31] The mind's quickness is proverbial; it can 'go anywhere' (in imagination) without lapse of time; it understands, but it cannot be understood (thus breaking the rule that like is known by like); it has no form or sensible configuration of its own, yet it can 'assume' or 'contain' perceptible forms and sense-qualities, just as soft wax receives tangible and visible impressions.[32] Philo is careful to avoid any suggestion that God himself is passive, or subject to limitations of time and space; he can be present anywhere, but does not need to 'go' anywhere, since this would entail leaving one place to enter another; and though he acts upon the world, Philo tends to attribute this action to his 'powers' ($\delta v v \acute{a}$-$\mu \epsilon \iota s$), which are sometimes conceived as modes of divine action, but sometimes as rational beings with wills of their own. This latter view closely resembles that of the 'Aristotelian' treatise *de Mundo*, which reproduces the tradition of God as the 'untroubled king' and expressly seeks to avoid any suggestion of his manual or

c. *Ar.* ii. 33. A striking passage in Gregory of Nyssa (*c. Ar. et Sab.* 12) compares the mutual indwelling of the three persons to the coexistence of several sciences in the same mind; but this is conscious metaphor.

[28] $\pi a v \delta \epsilon \chi \acute{\epsilon} s$, *Leg. All.* i. 61; *Immut.* 42.

[29] $\kappa o \hat{v} \phi o v$, *Plant.* 24; $\acute{o} \xi v \kappa \iota v \eta \tau \acute{o} \tau a \tau o v$, *Post. Cain* 19; $\acute{\omega} \kappa v \delta \rho o \mu \acute{\omega} \tau a \tau o s$, *Quod Det. Pot.* 89, cf. *Mut. Nom.* 178, quoting Homer, *Od.* v. 36.

[30] *Plant.* 31 [?]; *Leg. All.* iii. 223–4 (contrast 31!); *Sacr.* 45, 49.

[31] *Post. Cain* 18–20; *Immut.* 48.

[32] *Opif.* 18, *Leg. All.* i. 61, etc. The application to God, *Opif.* 19, of course avoids the *words* $\kappa \eta \rho \acute{o} s$ and $\delta \acute{\epsilon} \chi \epsilon \sigma \theta a \iota$.

mechanical contact with the world. Clement also seems to think that the human mind should share God's immobility, though he follows this suggestion with a warning against inactivity, 'so that a good rhythm may adorn your quietude.'[33]

Some early Christian writers still claim that it is characteristic of God that he can assume any form he wishes;[34] but in general this opinion lost ground before the Platonic doctrine of God's changelessness.[35] It could still be asserted that God is 'active';[36] indeed the biblical phrase 'God worketh' (ἐργάζεται, John 5 : 17) is compatible with the Aristotelian view that the οὐσία of God is perfect activity, ἐνέργεια; but Christian writers came to rely on the Logos (or sometimes the angels) as the proximate instruments of God's activity, and also to distinguish between God's energies and his essential nature; the former limited, because adapted and deployed for special purposes, the latter regarded as the unlimited source from which the special energies proceed. Some interesting Philonic touches reappear in Gregory of Nyssa, who speaks of 'intelligible nature' as residing in a place which is 'nimble' and 'lively'.[37] But the notion of an intelligible realm or world demands a page or two to itself.

Plato's theory of Ideas inevitably prompted the questions, What Ideas are there, and how are they related? Should we postulate Ideas corresponding to every general term, or somehow determine a more limited range? Do the Ideas, some or all of them, qualify each other, as well as their sensible instances? Do they form a connected series, or 'world'? Such questions, already projected in Plato's own writings, were pursued in several rather different idioms. One of these is well represented by the abstract and technical discussion of the 'five greatest kinds' and their relationships, in the latter part of the *Sophist*. Akin to this (though its precise source is difficult to trace) is the theory reported by Aristotle, in which the Ideas are regarded as ideal numbers and thought to be derived from the One and the 'indefinite Dyad'.[38] But in his early works Plato had given a vivid picture of the Ideas

[33] Fr. 44.   [34] Above, pp. 106–7.
[35] Prestige, *GPT*, 12–13. Philo is notably inconsistent here. For God's immobility, see *Post. Cain* 28, *Gig.* 49, *Confus.* 96 *al.* For the reverse opinion, *Immut.* 47–8 (voluntary movement is characteristic of God); cf. *Congr.* 45.
[36] So e.g. Athanasius, *c. Ar.* ii. 29, *al.* Cf. Origen, *Princ.* iii. 5. 3; Marius Victorinus, *adv. Ar.* i. 43.   [37] *Or. Dom.* 4; *Or. Cat.* 6.
[38] See P. Merlan in *LGP*, 15–32.

as forming a connected whole or 'world': suggesting moreover that the human soul had previously known this world of Ideas and could return there after death. In the *Phaedrus* and elsewhere this world of Ideas is given spatial extent and located in a region above the heavens.[39]

Theoretical difficulties in this conception were soon detected by professional philosophers; and indeed it is hard to imagine a world in which there is only one of every kind of thing, as the theory of Ideas required; especially as it was commonly held that there are no Ideas of individuals. Nevertheless the image of an ideal world firmly established itself in popular thought, which readily absorbed the pictorial and mythical elements in Plato's writings. Plato himself had suggested in the *Timaeus* that the creator-god began by making the perfect prototype of the universe, using the Ideas as his model ($\pi\alpha\rho\acute{\alpha}\delta\epsilon\iota\gamma\mu\alpha$, 28 a, *al.*); and it was only a short step from here to regard the Ideas themselves as constituting a 'model universe'.

The Ideas, on Plato's showing, are objective realities, in no way dependent on our minds; though later Platonists came to regard them as thoughts or conceptions of a supreme God. This theory was foreshadowed by the isolated remark in *Republic* x. 597 b, that God makes the Idea of a bed; but its development is unclear. It has been thought to stem from Posidonius, or alternatively from Antiochus, and so in either case from the period around 100 B.C.;[40] but it has also been suggested that it may go back to Xenocrates, a view already outlined by Heinze in 1892.[41] It was no doubt acceptable to the Middle Platonists as presenting a theistic world-view which subordinated the Ideas to the creator-god and also disarmed the purely conceptualist view of them which was taken by many Stoics.

Again, the Ideas as originally conceived are certainly not themselves minds or souls; although Plato described the soul as 'alike' or 'akin' to the world of Ideas (*Phaedo* 79 d), he later came to regard it as something intermediate between the ideal and the visible world; thus it is ever-changing ($\dot{\alpha}\epsilon\iota\kappa\acute{\iota}\nu\eta\tau\sigma$), whereas the

---

[39] $\dot{\upsilon}\pi\epsilon\rho\sigma\upsilon\rho\acute{\alpha}\nu\iota\sigma$ $\tau\acute{\sigma}\pi\sigma$, 247 c; cf. $\dot{\alpha}\lambda\eta\theta\epsilon\acute{\iota}\alpha$ $\pi\epsilon\delta\acute{\iota}\sigma\nu$, 248 b.

[40] Posidonius, e.g. E. Bickel, 'Senecas Briefe 58 und 65'; Antiochus, e.g. W. Theiler, *Vorbereitung* 34–55; further literature in the introduction to the 1964 reprint; see also J. M. Rist, *Eros and Psyche*, 62–5.

[41] So H. J. Krämer, 'Grundfragen', Pt. ii, 'Xenocrates und die Ideen im Geist Gottes', *Theol. u. Philos.* 44 (1969), 481–505; S. Lilla, *Clement of Alexandria*, 202–3.

Ideas are perfectly immobile. But here too the opinion arose that the Ideas should be regarded, not simply as intelligible, but as intelligent beings. Two reasons for this change may be proposed. First, the principle noted above: if intelligent beings are best, the Ideas, which are perfect, must themselves be intelligent. Secondly, the suggestion made in the *Sophist*, that the Ideas must be endowed with intelligence, movement, and life;[42] though indeed the Idea of life already mentioned in the *Phaedo* (106 d) would on Platonic principles be most fully alive; and the *Timaeus* also seems to represent the Idea as a source of life (τὸ δ'ὅθεν φύεται, 50 cd) and so as 'Father'. Suggestions such as these tended to attract the attention of popular writers to those Ideas which they most easily fitted, namely Ideas of living beings, indeed of individuals, as against generalities like equality or justice. So the Ideas were recast as 'ideal living beings' or perfect intelligences, which originate in the mind of God but are endowed with a measure of independent being.[43] We thus account for the fact (which I have not yet seen satisfactorily explained) that Philo can identify them with the 'powers' or 'angels'; though the doctrine is by no means peculiar to Philo; the Docetists described by Hippolytus (*Ref.* viii. 10) envisage the Ideas as 'cooling down' to become incarnate souls in need of salvation, a view which has close affinities with Origen's better-known doctrine of the created intelligences, or λογικοί.

Thus the Ideas, regarded as perfect intelligences, and sometimes equipped with luminous and regular celestial bodies, as star-souls, represent the closest approximation to the divine nature which human minds can attain; and that nature itself can be described in the memorable phrase from the *Phaedrus*, that 'colourless, formless intangible reality which truly exists, which only the mind, the soul's charioteer, can behold.'[44] (The approximation becomes even closer for Christians who adopt Philo's concept of the Logos as either the locus, or himself the totality, of the Ideas.)[45] But it is difficult to establish any precise

[42] 248 e, well discussed by P. Hadot, *Les Sources de Plotin*, EH v, 107–57; cf. pp. 45–7 above.

[43] See, e.g., Philo, *Somn.* i. 127. Philo's 'powers' (δυνάμεις) no doubt derive in part also from Stoic attempts to rationalize polytheism: see *RHT* iii. 153–174.

[44] 247c. 'Formless reality' (ἀσχημάτιστος οὐσία) is used as a theological term, rather disconcertingly, by Hippolytus' Naassenes, *Ref.* v. 7. 18.

[45] Philo, *Mut. Nom.* 180: τὸν ἐκ τῶν ἰδεῶν παγέντα συγγενικῶς. The Logos is 'compacted out of Ideas'.

sense which this phrase, and similar phrases, bore for Christian writers; since by their time they had been subjected to conflicting interpretations, monistic, dualistic, and every form of compromise, which were seldom controlled by scholarly discussion. Thus if God is described as νοητὸν φῶς the phrase could be taken to mean 'ideal light', i.e. the pure and perfect prototype of actual light (cf. Philo, *Opif.* 29, νοητὸν ἡλίου παράδειγμα) ;[46] and a writer of Stoic sympathies would think of this as located on the upper margin of the visible universe. It is not a long step from this to the opinion that, since the heavenly bodies are in fact perfect, the ideal light is actually embodied in the visible sun: see *CH* v. 3, xvi. 12, Exc. II A 14. At the other extreme, a dualist writer would use Platonic phraseology to emphasize the incorporeal and imperceptible nature of the ideal world; in this context νοητός comes to mean, not so much 'intelligible' as 'accessible to the mind alone' by some process of analogy; Origen's νοητὸν φῶς is not something we can understand, in the sense of knowing more about it than the words themselves convey; it is something which, we merely infer, possess properties analogous to those of light in an enhanced and purer form (*in Joh.* xiii. 131–2; below p. 177).

A modern critic might wish to ask, 'What prompts Plato to describe the objects of thought as colourless, formless, and intangible?' What is the relevance of just these denials? A brief answer could be given by pointing to his habit of regarding sense and thought as contrasted opposites. When we perceive, or imagine, something visible or tangible, we are dealing with sense-qualities, with colours, shapes, and resistances; when we recognize, or conceive, equality or justice, we do not find such qualities, or anything analogous to them, playing a similar role. Plato notes their non-appearance by saying that we are now dealing with what is 'colourless' etc. But the modern thinker will not approach the problem with similar expectations; he is removed from Plato's horizon by lessons he has learnt about the power of abstraction, the importance of symbolism, and the role

[46] In Philo, *Opif.* 30–1, νοητὸν φῶς is the prototypal ideal light, purer and brighter than actual light, as mind is better than the senses; it is an image of the Logos, and serves as a model for the stars. In *Abr.* 119 it stands for divine illumination, if not for God himself, since θεῷ περιλαμφθῇ is equivalent to νοητοῦ φωτὸς ἀναπλησθεῖσα.

of the subconscious. Philo describes an architect visualizing his projected city as if on a colourless and intangible, though spatially extended, diagram; a modern writer would regard the process as a set of operations, most of which are preferably (though not necessarily) carried out on the drawing-board; while the architect may 'know' where he is going to put the docks without any explicit internal debate; and if asked his intentions might reply 'on square 49', recording his decision by indirect and conventional means.

If then we still seek to use the human mind as a clue to God's nature, we must find a place for its operational complexity in our theology; even though it be granted that our power of thinking rests on the ability to comprehend a vast multiplicity of operations in relatively simple terms, it will not be so easy as it once was to relate our psychology to the mystical intuition of God as consciousness at rest.

If our thinking is an interplay of symbolic forms which can be transferred from one medium to another, and are independent of any particular medium, there is one ancient conception of the soul which could have pointed in this direction if it had ever been fruitfully exploited, and that is its definition as a 'self-moving number'. But we do not hear of any profitable developments of this formula, which is nearly always quoted by its opponents, and it had little influence on Christian thought. However, there is one further conception which links theology with psychology, which has far greater historic importance, and which does at least attempt to express the dynamic character of our thinking; and that is the concept of Spirit. This was originally developed by the Stoics, and came to have some influence on later interpretations of Plato's descriptions of intelligible reality.

What did the Stoic theologians mean by 'spirit'? An answer is commonly given in terms of a phrase originated (I believe) by James Drummond: a 'tenuous thinking gas'. The phrase is misleading in so far as it presents an apparently bizarre conception without indicating how it could have been in any way persuasive. In fact the concept of spirit was rooted in physical and physiological theories which, though we now think them erroneous, did at least attempt to deal with real problems, and offered an explanation which was in some degree coherent and plausible. We still make use of pneumatic machines, where work is applied through the compression and expansion of air or other gases, and in some cases (e.g. mechanical drills, or automatic railway signals) we can choose between electrical and pneumatic devices. The Stoics assumed that pneumatic forces were at work in nature where we now postulate electrical energy. It was spirit, *pneuma*, which by its varying 'tension' (τόνος) established the various physical properties of matter. The human body was controlled, they thought, by pneumatic 'signals', by rhythmical to-and-fro vibration of the *pneuma* transmitted along the arteries, which the Stoics and others pictured as air channels;[47] in effect the mechanism which we correctly assign to the outer ear was postulated to do the work which we now attribute to electrical nerve impulses. It was only a natural extension of this theory to conceive thought itself as an activity of the *pneuma* in man. A more speculative step was taken by comparing the universe itself to the human body, and postulating a rational principle or *pneuma par excellence* who controls it; for there are difficulties both about the rational principle and about the means of control. For how do controlling impulses act on physical bodies? And what, if anything, corresponds to the arteries? Several possible theories were suggested. A common view was that the consistency or coherence of solid bodies resulted from the pulsating movement of the *pneuma* that interpenetrated them; plants and animals were governed by *physis*, rational men by soul, thus displaying a progressively more flexible movement of the *pneuma*. But it was not easy to develop this theory consistently, since the *pneuma* in solid bodies was often assimilated to the physical elements of air and fire; whereas the *pneuma* in man was given a special source, as breathed into him directly from the rational principle of the universe.[48] Some Stoics seem to have drawn an analogy between the to-and-fro movement of the *pneuma* and the mutual interaction of the heavenly bodies and the earth, by which the former suck up vapours from the ground which both serve them for fuel and moderate their heat. Some thought that

---

[47] S. Sambursky, *Physics of the Stoics*, esp. 21–48; F. Solmsen, 'Greek Philosophy and the Discovery of the Nerves', *Museum Helveticum* 18 (1961), 150–67, 169–97; J. M. Rist, *Stoic Philosophy*, 86–9: C. R. S. Harris, *The Heart and Vascular System*; *SVF* ii. 439 ff., 826 ff. Philo, *Immut.* 84, *Exsecr.* 144. Hippolytus, *Ref.* vi. 14. 9, cf. iv. 51. 12.

[48] See J. M. Rist, *Stoic Philosophy*, 185, 268–9; earlier Stoics however gave a naturalistic explanation; see e.g. *SVF* ii. 806.

the health of living bodies was governed by the air or 'spirit' that they inhaled.

When the concept of spirit was adopted by Christian writers, it was already conventionalized and detached from its original basis in physical theory. The 'spirit' assigned to Sophia by the Wisdom writer (7: 22 ff.) represents an important landmark in this process; of some twenty epithets assigned to it, only two or three clearly require a physical interpretation; as 'finely divided' and 'freely moving' the spirit has properties like those of fire; but the writer's real emphasis falls on its power, serenity, and goodness. Philo, writing at much greater length, shows clear traces of Stoic physical theory; thus it is the 'spirit' in the arteries which enables man's rational principle to control his other parts;[49] and the rational soul itself is both constituted and inspired by divine spirit; but although Philo speaks of this spirit being 'breathed into' the soul, and compares its influence to that of the winds,[50] it hardly seems that he can give an intelligible explanation of the process. Origen also is well acquainted with the Stoic view, and criticizes Celsus for taking John 4: 24 to indicate a corporeal being (c. Cels. vi. 71); his own solution seems to be to fall back upon the Platonic concept of 'intelligible reality'; thus the physical attributes of God have to be explained by 'changing them into allegory' (in Joh. xiii. 131). If God is light, he says, this phrase can be taken in two senses, 'corporeal and *spiritual*, i.e. *intelligible*, which the scriptures would term invisible and the Greeks incorporeal' (ibid. 132).

However, the history of the term 'spirit' in Christian theology is beset with misunderstandings, both ancient and modern. In use from the first as a general designation of the divine nature or activity (John 4: 24), and again for the divine element in Christ, it was also taken to stand for a third power which was in some degree distinguishable from these. As time went on, this third Person was associated mainly with the inspiration of virtuous men, and so conceived as deploying the divine activity within a limited field; and some theologians came to regard Him as subordinate to the Father and the Son, and accordingly to regard the term *pneuma* itself as having limited value and limited scope. Applied to the divine nature, it was liable to suggest the corporeal

<hr />

[49] *Immut.* 84.   [50] *Plant.* 24.

deity of the Stoics; applied to Christ, it would imply that his 'divinity' was no more than a gracious influence comparable to that conferred upon the prophets. To exclude such a view, it was emphasized that the Logos, the second Person of the Trinity, himself took human flesh; and a text such as Luke 1 : 35 came to be regarded, not as an alternative description of the Incarnation, but as an adverbial qualification of it; not as referring generally to 'the divine spirit' or 'the divine power', but specifically to 'the Holy Spirit'. Thus it came to be held that the second Person made himself incarnate through the agency of the Third.

The second-century Apologists tend to emphasize the Logos and keep the Holy Spirit rather in the background; though they do sometimes use the term *pneuma* to denote the divine nature.[51] The Alexandrians, for whom the Holy Spirit is most distinctly a third, and often a subordinate, Person, seldom apply the term *pneuma* to the Father or Son. Clement 'avoids calling God a pneuma; only once in a while does he apply the word to Christ';[52] Origen, as we have seen, adopts the first usage with reservations but seems to avoid the second;[53] Athanasius is almost as reserved as Clement.[54]

Meanwhile it is difficult to gain a clear impression of those writers who use the term *pneuma* more freely. One could make up quite a long list, including Tatian, Theophilus, Irenaeus, Tertullian, Callistus, Lactantius, Eustathius, Marcellus, the Sardicense, Basil of Ancyra, Hilary, Apollinarius, and even Epiphanius. Some of these (Tertullian, Lactantius, and also Phoebadius) are positively attached to the term and accept at least some of its Stoic implications; others, I take it, use it occasionally and without speculative development. But they have all been liable to misjudgement; either they have been accused, perhaps unfairly, of teaching a reduced, humanitarian Christology; or they have been wrongly supposed to have used *pneuma* to refer specifically to the Holy Spirit. Tertullian certainly

---

[51] Tatian, *Or.* 4. 1; cf. 12. 3; Athenagoras, *Leg.* 16. 2.

[52] Grillmeier, *Christ in Christian Tradition*, 105, n. 1. But note that Philo does not call God a πνεῦμα, though he speaks of πνεῦμα θεῖον.

[53] *PGL* gives only citations (Celsus, Heraclides).

[54] He cites Dionysius on John 4: 24 in *Sent. Dion.* 15, Feltoe, p. 187, but does not seem to reproduce him. In *ad Serap.* iv. 19, 23 he uses πνεῦμα of the divinity of Christ.

deserves some notice, as a striking and influential though hardly representative member of this group.

To see his teaching in proportion, one should emphasize that much of his doctrine of God is drawn from the Apologists, and so at least indirectly shows the influence of Middle Platonism; to this strand of it belong the great metaphysical attributes of divinity; God is eternal, invisible, immutable, impassible. But the more characteristic and personal element appears in his doctrine that the *substantia* of God is *spiritus*. In such contexts *substantia* undoubtedly has the sense of 'constituent material';[55] and *spiritus* is conceived as analogous to the controlling fluid or vapour in man; though Tertullian is at pains to make clear that the two are not identical; man's soul is a 'little breeze' (*aurula*), created in the image of God's spirit, and necessarily inferior to it. As is well known, Tertullian asserts that God is a *corpus*; and this, I think, is not merely an attempt to state in Stoic terms that God is real; rather, his language conveys the impression that God's *spiritus* has some form of spatial extent, and something like dynamic properties. He describes God as '*immensus*'; but this can mean 'boundlessly extended'; Tertullian does not explain clearly that God has no location.[56] Indeed the phrasing of *adv. Prax.* 16. 6, *in quo omnis locus, non ipse in loco, qui universitatis extrema linea est*, seems to suggest that God is located at the outer boundary of space. Other writers also suggest that God is coextensive with, or surrounds, the universe, sometimes appealing to Jer. 23 : 24 ('Do I not fill heaven and earth?'), sometimes using arguments presumably borrowed from Stoicism to the effect that there must be only one God since there is no room for any other.[57]

Tertullian also explains the derivation of the Son and of the Spirit by metaphors which imply local extension and configuration: one Person is 'drawn out' from another, though without separation, and given its own distinct 'structure'. In *Apol.* 21 the well-known phrase *nec separatur substantia, sed extenditur* belongs to the metaphor of the sun and its rays; but the parallel phrase *a matrice non recessit, sed excessit* occurs independently. And the notion of structure can be found in *adv. Prax.* 7. 5, adopting C. H.

---

[55] See R. Braun, *Deus Christianorum* (1962), 170–83, and my paper 'Divine Substance in Tertullian', *JTS*, n.s. 14 (1963), 46–66; also G. Verbeke, *L'Évolution . . .*, 445.

[56] Braun, op. cit., 52; contrast e.g. Philo, *Confus.* 134–6.

[57] So Athenagoras, *Leg.* 8, and especially Irenaeus ii. 1. 1, Hv. i. 251–2.

Turner's reading *das aliquam substantiam esse sermonem, spiritu et sophia et ratione constructam?* It seems to me impossible to say how far Tertullian himself accepted these implications of his metaphors; one can only note that he makes no effort to dispel them.

Tertullian's use of spirit as the descriptive term *par excellence* for the divinity was opposed by a theory which we find most clearly stated by Novatian, namely that no predicate suffices to convey more than a partial indication of the divine nature. This view leads to a certain (possibly healthy) agnosticism, particularly if combined with the doctrine of divine simplicity: our minds can apprehend God only under a multiplicity of different aspects; we cannot trace the pure light, so to speak, from which these various colours are refracted. I shall not stay to examine this view, but pass on to consider a particular development of it already mentioned (p. 109 above); namely that the various attributes are in reality identical with each other and with their possessor. This, however, will require a further note on the concepts of unity and identity.

(iii) *The Concept of Unity*

The notion of unity has appeared in Chapter IV, where I discussed some theoretical implications of Aristotle's theology. It remains to consider how this notion was actually treated by early Christian writers and their pagan contemporaries; and this for two reasons; first, because unity was considered to be an important property, or even the distinctive property, of the godhead; and secondly, because discussions of God's 'substance' were increasingly influenced by the claim that *one* substance was common to the three divine persons.

Christians of course discovered the notion of unity in the Bible; the Old Testament claims that God is one; the New Testament endorses this claim, but also lays down that there is only one Lord Christ, and refers to the unity of the Christian fellowship in the Holy Spirit. There is no need to review this biblical material, which is no doubt familiar; in particular, the emergence of monotheism in Israelite and other religions has been thoroughly investigated. But it is perhaps worth noting that there seem to be in principle two ways in which a monotheistic belief can replace an earlier polytheism. Polytheism rarely implies a strictly equal society of gods; some divinities will normally be greater and more powerful than others. Thus it is possible for one divine being to take the lead so decisively that the others are degraded to the status of attendant spirits, or of mere manifestations or powers of the supreme god. He then is 'the one God' in the sense of the only being who can rightfully claim this dignity. Alternatively, a more philosophical approach to polytheism can note the similarities between different deities, and reflect on the drawbacks of a plurality of gods within a single universe; hence comes the suggestion that these may be merely different names or aspects of a single divine reality. This then is 'the one God' in the quite distinct sense of the unitary being who transcends the apparent plurality. It would seem that the first approach to monotheism is much the commoner, and that such was the course taken by the Jews. The second is rarely found in a completely pure form; Stoic theology adopts it in the main, but is nevertheless still influenced by the old Greek belief that Zeus is the head of the Olympic pantheon.

When the Christian fathers began to formulate their doctrines, the Greek philosophical tradition could offer them several theoretical discussions of the notion of unity, some of which came to have a certain influence on Christian thought. But I do not find that such analyses were applied to theology in any clear, consistent, and methodical fashion. Christian thinking on the unity of God remained largely intuitive. Where certain axioms were accepted (as for instance that God is 'simple', ἁπλοῦς) their content was not precisely defined; and where certain important distinctions were clearly grasped (as I think they were by Tertullian and Novatian) they failed to find a permanent foothold in theology.

One can gain some idea of this loosely formulated concept of divine unity by employing a group of terms first known to me from M. J. Rouet de Journel's *Enchiridion Patristicum*, namely *unicus, simplex, immutabilis*. There is only one God (though no doubt his influence may be conferred upon, and found in, other beings); he is undivided (for if one finds in him distinctions of powers, or persons, these are not thought to infringe his wholeness or 'simplicity'); and he is not subject to change (at least, not to moral change, nor to change imposed from without, though he may in some sense respond to changing human needs). It seems that these three great claims were clearly distinguished at least by Novatian who writes (in his *de Trinitate*, 4–5) that God is 'always self-same . . . one, without a rival . . . simple, without any corporeal structure' (*Hic ergo semper sui est similis . . . et unus pronuntiatus est, dum parem non habet . . . est enim simplex, et sine ulla corporea concretione*); and Tertullian, according to R. Braun (pp. 67–8), used the two Latin words *unitas* and *unio* to distinguish between God's simplicity and his uniqueness. *Unitas* excludes division; *unio* excludes rivals.

We should not of course represent these as three properties which are independent and unconnected; and the ancients did in fact trace certain connections, some of them naïve or artificial, but others worthy of note. The popular use of the word 'one' makes no distinction between the senses 'undivided' and 'unique'; the sense 'unique' is uppermost in the adjective μόνος, but once its by-form μονάς came to mean 'unity' or 'unit', the notion of indivisibility came to attach to it; thus Aristotle speaks of the monad as indivisible (*Metaph.* xiv. 2, 1089 b 35 f.), and Philo is only exploiting this line of argument when he contends that the biblical profession of one God points to a being who is absolutely simple.[58] Another verbal link (fortuitous, I believe) connects μόνος and μονάς with derivatives of μένω; thus Alexander tells us that the Pythagoreans associated soul and mind with the number one, since reason is μόνιμον, 'permanent'.[59] It was commonly held that composite things are liable to perish through loss of their distinctive structure, whereas the indivisible is indestructible—a proposition which was given wide currency by Plato's argument for the immortality of the soul, and which appears *ad nauseam* in the later Platonists, who contrasted the 'composite' 'perishable' world of sense and the unitary (or at least unified), imperishable world of the intelligibles. A rather similar contrast obtains between the 'definite' number one and the 'indefinite', 'variable' concept of plurality in Plato's theory of the one and the indefinite dyad; and the notion of 'invariant' is taken up in the Stoic morality which contrasts the unity of purpose which marks the

[58] *Leg. All.* ii. 1–2, cf. *Quis Rerum*, 38, 183; *Spec. Leg.* ii. 176.
[59] *In Met.* 985 b 30, p. 39, 14–15 Hayduck; cf. Eusebius, *Laus Const.* 6. 11, and other refs. in Festugière, *RHT* iv. 22.

wise man with the perpetual change imposed on all men by the circumstances of life.[60]

It is fair to note, further, that even if we establish a clear distinction between the unique and the undivided, which the ancients too readily assimilated, there are cases where it is hard to decide which concept is appropriate. We go to pull up a tulip plant, and find one bulb—but in what sense one, if we were hoping that it had 'divided' and 'made another'? A similar difficulty appears in the case of individual species, and so, presumably, of God; for if we speak of (say) 'one phoenix', it seems that we might develop this conception either by explaining that the phoenix, as species, is undivided, being concentrated in a single individual, or that the phoenix, as individual, is unique and has no fellow. Ancient arguments for the unity of the cosmos and the unity of God were frequently embarrassed by confusions between these two interpretations.

What assistance, however, was actually available from the professional philosophers in antiquity? We may remark on three principal analyses of the concept of unity.

Aristotle's two main discussions of unity are found in *Metaph.* v. 6 and x. 1; these have some similarity, but do not exactly correspond. At x. 1 he gives a compacter and better-organized account; v. 6 however contains a passage, possibly added to the original draft, which offers an independent and clear, though misleading, classification. In each account Aristotle begins by referring to 'accidental unity', which need not detain us here; 'essential unity', which follows, is variously divided, but covers three main types of case, namely that in which a number of beings are physically connected to form a single whole; that in which a number of beings resemble each other so as to fall into a single class (genus or species); and thirdly that of a single being referred to by different names or in different connections. The scheme is as follows (see table overleaf).

This necessarily simplified diagram already suggests that Aristotle's divisions by no means correspond with what I have proposed as natural. One difficulty, familiar by now, is that Aristotle does not clearly distinguish between the unity of

---

[60] *SVF* i. 202, iii. 197–8, 200; Seneca, *Ep.* 58. 19 ff., Plutarch, *De E*, 8. 392a ff., and discussion by W. Theiler, *Vorbereitung*, 13–14; Origen, loc. cit., p. 160 above; cf. Plato, *Rep.* 443 e (ἕνα γενόμενον ἐκ πολλῶν) as possible source.

			v. 6		x. 1
Unity:	Accidental				
	Essential	[Cohesion] (a)	Continuity (1015 a 36) [below]	(1) (2)	Continuity (1052 a 19) Organic connection (1052 a 22)
		[Resemblance] (b)	(i) Material (ii) Generic	— —	
		[Identity] (c)	Specific [? suggested 1016 b 1.] Organic unity	(3) (4)	Specific Numerical

v. 6, 1016 b 31 f.: Numerical, specific, generic, analogical.

individual cases and that of classes of cases. Thus 'organic connection' is exemplified by 'the shin', 'the thigh', which together form 'one leg', referred to quite generally—the individual (Socrates' right) leg is not mentioned. And by 'material unity' Aristotle seems to mean that any wine is like any other wine (!) because they have the same proximate 'substance' (*hypokeimenon*), i.e. wine, and no permanent shape to distinguish them (contrasting the case of wine and oil, which have only the same *ultimate* substance, namely 'water'); but 'same substance' here has to be taken generally; it should be (but is not) sharply distinguished from the 'one matter' (*hyle*; the verbal difference is not significant) which is proposed as the condition of individual identity in v. 6, 1016 b 33.

As a result, the concept of 'arithmetical unity' remains confused. The brief tabulation proposed in 1016 b 31 f. is no doubt intended as a scale of decreasingly close unity; and the first case, that of 'arithmetical unity', is presumably meant to suggest 'individual identity' (e.g. 'Socrates' and 'Xanthippe's husband'); but the tests proposed ('same' matter, form, place, and time) are not adequate to exclude cases where general terms have the same reference; thus 'wine' and 'liquor' (*oinos, methy*) would satisfy these conditions. The table also suggests that individual identity is a sort of limiting case of close resemblance; but this, we have seen, will not do: close resemblance culminates in the case of identical twins. Can we then say that these display a merely numerical difference—whereas a single individual, who lacks even this, can be called 'numerically one'? This no doubt represents the logic of the designation; but we have already rejected the former suggestion.[61]

It should however be noticed that for Aristotle 'arithmetical unity' does not necessarily imply 'a bare unit', 'a monad', something without internal structure; indeed he says expressly that 'one' does not mean 'simple'.[62] The latter equation was presumably suggested by Pythagorean mathematics; since the Pythagoreans did not clearly distinguish between arithmetical units, geometrical points, and physical atoms; again the word *atomon* itself can mean both 'an individual' and 'an atom'. Conversely, a thing which has no internal structure need not be either unique or individual; but this assumption was often made in theological contexts, where the unique simplicity of God was contrasted with composite matter, ignoring the possibility that matter, if composite, may be composed of simple units.[63]

Two further analyses of the concept of unity call for attention. The Stoics adopted a fairly straightforward classification, based on the different degrees of cohesion between material bodies; they distinguished between 'unities' or organisms (e.g. plants and animals), 'structures' (e.g. chairs or ships), and 'collections' (e.g. armies or flocks).[64] This analysis provided the conceptual basis for the claim that the world itself is an organism, a complex whole whose parts mutually affect each other through a relation of 'sympathy', just as all parts of a human body are affected if one member is injured. Further, the opinion was widely held that God himself was either an aspect or part of this material universe, like the rationality of the human being; and where the transcendence of God was more strongly asserted, it was often held that a single divinity controlled the world through a variety of powers, which however involved no separation or division, just as the mind acts as a whole in its various operations. It will appear that this world-view gives the greatest prominence and dignity to the concept of complex unity; though it was also asserted that the

---

[61] Above, p. 86.

[62] xii. 7, 1072 a 32–3; contrast however v. 6, 1016 b 23, and p. 182 above.

[63] This last point is noted by Methodius, *Autex.* xii. 2.

[64] Best account in Sextus Empiricus *adv. Math.* ix. 38 = *SVF* ii. 1013; cf. ibid. 366, 368, 391, and iii. VI. 7 (Boethus, cited Philo, *Aet. Mund.* 15). Sextus uses the terms συνημμένα, ἐκ συναπτομένων, ἐκ διεστώτων; the others vary slightly.

universe is one in the sense of 'one only', since this universe contains all the matter there is.[65]

The other scheme has already been mentioned (above, pp. 93–4, 164), namely the distinction between absolute unity and relative unity which was read into Plato's *Parmenides*. Whatever Plato himself had intended, it was used in our period, not as a general analysis of the notion of unity, but as an explicitly theological scheme; thus the concept of absolute unity is exemplified only in the perfect simplicity of God, who is therefore not only simple but unique. It was of course a commonplace that the ideal world is simple and unchanging, as contrasted with the flux of the material world and of human passions and circumstances; hence it was natural to hold that the supreme God is totally free of multiplicity, a pure monad conceived in Pythagorean terms. But this, as already noted, conflicts with the doctrine that God governs the world and therefore stands in several relationships to varying earthly circumstances. One attempted solution was to say that God, though himself simple, possesses various 'powers', conceived as semi-independent agencies through which he carries on his purposes: this is in practice the position adopted by Philo. But it hardly meets the case; since one can object that if the various powers are in any real sense possessed by the ultimate godhead, they must give expression to various distinct purposes or activities, and he must be variously related to them; it still seems impossible to reconcile the exercise or employment of a number of powers with the theoretical requirement of absolute simplicity.

The alternative solution seems to have been first clearly formulated by Numenius, though of course making use of older material. He distinguished between a first God who is absolutely simple, and a second God who is indeed 'one', but who exercises the complex of powers; Numenius even says that his action on the material world unifies matter but has the converse effect that he himself is 'dissipated' or 'divided' ($\sigma\chi\iota\zeta\epsilon\tau\alpha\iota$) by it (fr. 20 = Eus. *PE* xi. 17). This last point is naturally avoided by those Christian writers who follow his solution, notably Clement, Origen, and Eusebius; and they are able to take over traditional language, found in Philo and elsewhere, so as to describe the Logos as the 'place of the Ideas', or sometimes the 'Idea of

---

[65] *SVF* ii. 528, 529; this agrees with Aristotle, *de Caelo*, i. 9, 278 a 26 ff.

Ideas',[66] corresponding to Plato's 'Idea of the Good', while suggesting that the Father possesses a still greater dignity and remoteness from the material world.

It is obvious that this scheme can only be employed by theologians who can tolerate a fairly pronounced difference in status between the Logos and the Father; and although this subordinationist trend was to continue for some centuries,[67] it conflicted with the tendency, which appears in Alexandrian tradition at least as early as Clement, to assign the same titles and functions to the Father and to the Logos, and so in practice to suggest that they are equal in rank and in nature.[68] Subordinationism was finally discredited through the emergence of a distinctive Nicene theology and the failure of Arianism. But in the mean time it would appear that the concept of divine simplicity was adopted too readily by some Christian writers who did not pause to consider its implications. Thus we find Athanasius arguing that God, being perfectly simple, cannot possess a multiplicity of accidents;[69] but it is not clear why the same argument should not be used to exclude a diversity of divine characteristics (which Athanasius upheld), or even a trinity of persons. Plotinus was perhaps the only philosopher to deal successfully with the problem; though his solution took a form which, particularly after the Arian controversy, Christians were bound to reject.

Meanwhile there appeared yet another solution, a theory which sought to reconcile the divine simplicity with the diversity of traditional attributes without invoking a distinction between Father and Son, but by a drastic and paradoxical step; namely to assert that the divine attributes are identical with each other and with their possessor. This theory is first suggested in Christian literature by Irenaeus, who writes that the Father of all is 'simple and not compounded, uniform and wholly alike in himself, being wholly mind and wholly spirit . . . wholly hearing,

---

[66] χώρα: Philo, *Cher.* 49, cf. *Somn.* i. 127; Clement, *Strom.* iv. 155.

ἰδέα ἰδεῶν: Philo, *Opif.* 25 (*si vera*); Origen, *c. Cels.* vi. 64.

[67] Even Athanasius maintains that the Logos is in some sense knowable; the Father can only be known through the Logos.

[68] See e.g. *Strom.* iv. 162 and vii. 2, cited by Osborn, *Clement of Alexandria*, 40; another striking comparison is that of *Strom.* vii. 37. 6 with vii. 5. 5, two passages to be discussed presently.

[69] *Decr.* 22, cf. *c. Ar.* i. 36.

wholly sight, wholly light, and wholly the source of all good things' (*omnium Pater . . . et simplex, et non compositus, et simili-membrius* (ὁμοιομερής?), *et totus ipse sibimetipsi similis, et aequalis est, totus cum sit sensus, et totus sensuabilitas . . . et totus auditus et totus oculus et totus lumen et totus fons omnium bonorum*: ii. 13. 3, Hv. i. 282). Clement and Novatian write in similar terms;[70] and since Clement elsewhere quotes Xenophanes verbatim, we have good grounds for thinking that Clement's description, and indeed the theory as a whole, derives from Xenophanes, whose long life covers the period *c.* 570–475 B.C. Xenophanes writes: οὖλος ὁρᾷ, οὖλος δὲ νοεῖ, οὖλος δέ τ' ἀκούει (fr. 24), which G. S. Kirk translates 'All of him sees, all thinks and all hears'; this suggests the notion of perception and thought exercised not through special sense-organs but 'by the god's whole unmoving body'.[71]

It should be noticed, however, that Irenaeus, Clement, and Novatian all replace Xenophanes' verbs by nouns: instead of 'all of him sees, hears, etc.' we find 'he is all sight, all hearing' or the like. This strongly suggests some common intermediate source; but it also points towards a difference in the doctrine conveyed. Xenophanes might be said to teach that God is wholly engaged in each of his operations; but he does not suggest that the operations themselves are identical with each other, or with himself. The point may perhaps be explained by a parallel drawn from human activities, despite the importance of our special sense-organs and the like. A man might be said to be wholly occupied in playing the organ, in that all his faculties are engaged in it; his brain, limbs, and lungs active; or again, his dexterity, experience, and attention applied. Similarly he could be said to be wholly occupied in playing chess. But 'wholly' here need not mean 'exclusively'; it would not disallow the feat (which I believe some organists can perform) of playing the organ and playing chess simultaneously. We should misunderstand the term 'wholly' if we concluded that only one activity was taking place, and that the organ-playing was identical with the chess-playing.

How and when did Xenophanes' dictum come to be developed in this form? Irenaeus professes to find it in Scripture (loc. cit.,

[70] Clement, *Strom.* vii. 5. 5 (applied to the Son); vii. 37. 6 (applied to the Father); Novatian, *Trin.* 6.

[71] G. S. Kirk and J. E. Raven, *The Pre-Socratic Philosophers*, 170. K. Freeman's *Ancilla* renders 'sees as a whole' etc.

cf. ii. 28, Hv. i. 354); but it appears several times in the course of a highly abstract and philosophical discussion, and is indeed treated as an acceptable but not completely adequate premiss for his argument against the Gnostics (ii. 13. 8, Hv. i. 285). It is most probably a pre-Christian development; indeed Pliny also quotes the dictum in nominal form, though he constructs the nouns in the genitive: *Deus totus est sensūs, totus visūs, totus auditūs, totus animae, totus animi, totus sui*;[72] one notices the prepared climax in the last phrases, which indeed cannot be expressed in the original, verbal, form. At all events Irenaeus clearly asserts that the divine operations are identical one with another: 'Just as he does not sin, who calls Him wholly sight, wholly hearing (for in the very act of seeing He also hears, and in the very act of hearing He also sees) . . .': *in quo autem videt, in ipso et audit, et in quo audit, in ipso et videt*; this is, in all essentials, the doctrine of Augustine and of Aquinas.

[72] *NH* ii. 14. I owe this reference to Professor R. M. Grant, 'Early Christianity and pre-Socratic Philosophy', *Harry Austryn Wolfson Jubilee Volume*, i. 357–84. Cf. also Plutarch, *Strom.* 4, in Diels, *DG*, p. 580. 16.

VIII

THE WORD *HOMOOUSIOS*

(i) *The Second Century*

THE word ὁμοούσιος, usually translated 'consubstantial' or 'coessential', appears to have been introduced by Gnostic Christians of the second century. It occurs in summaries and criticisms of Gnostic teaching made by Irenaeus; it was used by Ptolemaeus and is attributed to some other second-century Gnostics, and it also occurs once in the *Poimandres*; otherwise it is not found in pagan writers before Plotinus. It originally meant, 'having the same substance', οὐσία; and in the majority of cases at least, the notion of οὐσία that is implied is either material or conceived in physical terms. It thus means roughly, 'made of the same . . . kind of stuff'.[1]

When it first appears it is not used to express the Christian theology of the Trinity. Nor does it convey a sense which is peculiar to Gnosticism, though naturally the Gnostics' use of it sometimes gives it a distinctive colouring. The case is rather that the Gnostics and their opponents introduced the term into commonplaces of debate which go back to pre-Christian times. Of these, the most important concerns God's relationship to the world; in particular, whether it is right to apply the language of physical paternity to God, either in relation to the world itself, or to man as such, or to the rational principle or soul in man.

The surviving instances of the Greek word itself for the whole period down to the outbreak of the Arian controversy are not very numerous, and can be shown by a table (see opposite).

The material is thus by no means abundant; but we can add to it by taking in those Latin texts which can reasonably be supposed to offer translations of ὁμοούσιος, or at least use equivalent expressions in similar contexts. Thus the scanty second-century evidence—one passage in Ptolemaeus and five in Irenaeus' *Adversus Haereses* are the only certain examples—can be supple-

[1] Prestige, *GPT*, 197.

Ptolemaeus	1	
Irenaeus	5	
Hippolytus	7	(two of no independent value)
Poimandres	1	
Clement, *Excerpta*	5	
others	2	
Origen	6	at least
*Plotinus	2	
*Porphyry	3	
Dionysius of Alexandria	1	
Synod of Antioch, A.D. 268	?1	(very poorly attested)
Methodius	?3	(two rather doubtfully attested)
Pamphilus	?3	
Dialogue with Adamantius	2	
Clementine Homilies	2	(not certainly pre-Nicene)
Acta Archelai	1	(Latin text, but Greek word retained)
Eusebius	2	

47 at most, so far discovered.

mented by adding a number of passages in Irenaeus where the Greek is lacking but the Latin has *unius substantiae*; this phrase seems to be a regular equivalent, since it is used in all five cases to render ὁμοούσιος, and is never used, where the Greek survives, to render any other term or phrase. This yields a series of nineteen second-century examples which may be listed in order, (1) being from Ptolemaeus, (2–6) from the Greek of Irenaeus, Book i, and (7–19) from the Latin version of the later books.

Ptolemaeus, writing to Flora, urges her not to be disturbed at the doctrine that the one Source of all, acknowledged eternal and good, gave rise to two other natures, the evil nature of the devil and the intermediate nature of the Demiurge, 'these being non-consubstantial, whereas the Good has a nature to beget and produce things like itself and consubstantial' (πῶς ἀπὸ μιᾶς ἀρχῆς τῶν ὅλων, . . . τῆς ἀγεννήτου καὶ ἀφθάρτου καὶ ἀγαθῆς, συνέστησαν καὶ αὗται αἱ φύσεις, ἥ τε τῆς φθορᾶς καὶ ⟨ἡ⟩ τῆς μεσότητος, ἀνομοούσιοι αὗται καθεστῶσαι, τοῦ ἀγαθοῦ φύσιν ἔχοντος τὰ ὅμοια ἑαυτῷ καὶ ὁμοούσια γεννᾶν τε καὶ προφέρειν : in Epiphanius, *Haer.* 33. 7. 8). The Gnostic character of this passage appears clearly in the character assigned to the Demiurge, who occupies an intermediate position between God and the devil (ὁ διάβολος, ὁ ἀντικείμενος) and in the doctrine of three natures (οὐσίαι, φύσεις) which determines the sense of ὁμοούσιος in this context; though these are defined in moral terms, as good, intermediate, and bad, rather than by the more typical 'spirit, soul, and matter'. On the other hand Ptolemaeus clearly intends the last remark quoted to be recognized as a commonplace, as indeed it is (see Plato, *Rep.* 379 bc, *Timaeus* 29 e, Philo, *Opif.* 140, *Aet. Mund.* 44, Athanasius, *c. Gent.* 6); and this perhaps suggests that the term ὁμοούσιος itself would already be familiar to his readers.

The first four cases in Irenaeus belong closely together, and refer to the Valentinian 'pre-cosmic' myth of the erring lower Sophia, or Achamoth, and the three orders of being, matter, *psyche*, and spirit, which arise respectively from her passion, her repentance, and her angelic vision. We are told first, in example (2), that she could not give form to the spiritual element, since it was *homoousios* with her, being in fact her own offspring;

(3) that she turned to the formation of the psychic substance, and formed from it the Father who is king of all, both of the psychic beings who are *homoousios* with him, and of matter; he is called Father of the former, but Artificer (*demiourgos*) of the latter. This Father is identified with the God of the Old Testament; thus,

(4) the LXX text of Gen. 1 : 26, 'according to our image and our likeness', is explained by saying that man made 'according to the image' is the material ('hylic') man, 'resembling but not *homoousios* with God', while that 'according to the likeness' is the psychic.

(5) The Artificer himself remained ignorant of the spiritual element, which was the offspring of the Mother (Achamoth), conceived through the vision of the angels around the Saviour and *homoousios* with her. The texts are as follows:

(2) Ἀλλὰ τὸ μὲν πνευματικὸν μὴ δεδυνῆσθαι αὐτὴν* μορφῶσαι, ἐπειδὴ ὁμοούσιον ὑπῆρχεν αὐτῇ . . . and cf. above, ὃ ἀπεκύησε, τουτέστι τὸ πνευματικόν (*Haer.* i. 5. 1, Hv. i. 42).

(3) Καὶ πρῶτον μεμορφωκέναι αὐτὴν ἐκ τῆς ψυχικῆς οὐσίας λέγουσι τὸν Πατέρα καὶ βασιλέα πάντων, τῶν τε ὁμοουσίων αὐτῷ, τουτέστι τῶν ψυχικῶν, ἃ δὴ δεξιὰ καλοῦσι, καὶ τῶν ἐκ τοῦ πάθους καὶ τῆς ὕλης, ἃ δὴ ἀριστερὰ καλοῦσι . . . τῶν μὲν δεξιῶν πατέρα λέγοντες αὐτόν, τουτέστι τῶν ψυχικῶν· τῶν δὲ ἀριστερῶν, τουτέστι τῶν ὑλικῶν, δημιουργὸν, συμπάντων δὲ βασιλέα (ibid.).

* MS. αὐτῇ.

(4) Δημιουργήσαντα δὴ τὸν κόσμον, πεποιηκέναι καὶ τὸν ἄνθρωπον τὸν χοϊκόν· οὐκ ἀπὸ ταύτης δὲ τῆς ξηρᾶς γῆς, ἀλλ᾽ ἀπὸ τῆς ἀοράτου οὐσίας, ἀπὸ τοῦ κεχυμένου καὶ ῥευστοῦ τῆς ὕλης λάβοντα· καὶ εἰς τοῦτον ἐμφυσῆσαι τὸν ψυχικὸν διορίζονται. καὶ τοῦτον εἶναι τὸν κατ᾽ εἰκόνα καὶ ὁμοίωσιν γεγονότα· κατ᾽ εἰκόνα μὲν τὸν ὑλικὸν ὑπάρχειν, παραπλήσιον μὲν, ἀλλ᾽ οὐχ ὁμοούσιον τῷ Θεῷ· καθ᾽ ὁμοίωσιν δὲ τὸν ψυχικόν . . . (ibid. i. 5. 5, Hv. i. 49).

(5) Τὸ δὲ κύημα τῆς μητρὸς αὐτῶν* τῆς Ἀχαμώθ, ὃ κατὰ τὴν θεωρίαν τῶν περὶ τὸν Σωτῆρα ἀγγέλων ἀπεκύησεν, ὁμοούσιον ὑπάρχον τῇ μητρὶ, πνευματικὸν, καὶ αὐτὸν ἠγνοηκέναι τὸν Δημιουργὸν λέγουσι (i. 5. 6, Hv. i. 50).

The mythological setting of all this is quite characteristic of Valentinianism; but many of its ideas are not peculiar to the Gnostics, but find a place in philosophical Judaism and its derivatives. Creation is conceived as the forming of things out of formless matter which has a prehistory of its own, an idea which goes back to Plato; and the exegesis of Gen. 1 : 26 which distinguishes 'image' from 'likeness' has a complex history and was adopted by Irenaeus himself. The most puzzling sentence is perhaps that first quoted; but it reflects the common opinions that the man himself must be better than his works (Philo, *Migr. Abr.* 193, *Decal.* 69, cf. Wisdom 15 : 17; contrast Ptolemaeus above), and that only God can form the highest element in man (Philo, *Fuga* 69, cf. *CH* x. 18); hence Achamoth can only operate on the soul-stuff which is inferior to herself. Similarly the 'Father', or Demiurge, is called Artificer of the material things, which are inferior to him, but Father of the psychic beings who are his equals. This again reflects the *communis opinio* that God is Father of rational beings only (Plato, *Timaeus* 69 c, Philo, *Fuga*, loc. cit.; Celsus in Origen, *c. Cels.* iv. 52), but in an adapted form, since the 'Father' and the psychic substance are inferior to the ultimate Source and the element of Spirit which belongs to Him and to the immediately ensuing ranks in the heavenly hierarchy, including Achamoth and her spiritual offspring. *Homoousios* therefore means 'made of the same element' or 'belonging to the same order of beings', whether spirit (examples 2 and 5) or *psyche* (3 and 4) or matter.

The one remaining Greek instance occurs in a discussion of the

* MS. αὐτῆς.

opinions held by an '*epiphanes didaskalos*'; that is, not the Epiphanes mentioned by Clement, but an unnamed 'celebrated teacher', probably Marcus.[2] This man derived the world from four original powers, each denoted by a title expressing some aspect of unity. The first three are Μονότης, Ἑνότης, and Μονάς (Unity, Oneness, Unit); we then read, (6) ταύτῃ τῇ μονάδι συνυπάρχει δύναμις ὁμοούσιος αὐτῇ, ἣν καὶ αὐτὴν ὀνομάζω τὸ Ἕν: 'with this Unit there coexists a power consubstantial with it, which also I call the One.' Too little is known about this author's beliefs to give a firm basis for discussion; though I think they should not too readily be dismissed as frivolous, despite Irenaeus' heavy sarcasm, since there is a legitimate distinction between the principle of unity and the number one;[3] and another between absolute unity and unity which admits of differentiation. Marcus may have been using a recognized terminology; in which case it would be logical to speak of the two mathematical entities as 'consubstantial', i.e. 'belonging to the same order of beings'.

In Book ii of the *Adversus Haereses* Irenaeus turns from what is ostensibly description of Gnostic beliefs to a formal refutation. In the course of it he argues that the Gnostics' opinions are borrowed from Greek philosophers and share their embarrassments. Thus the Gnostics' eschatology makes God subservient to fate, since they hold that each creature must revert to the element out of which it is made (*unumquemque in illa secedit ex quibus et factum esse dicunt*, ii. 14. 4, Hv. i. 294); spiritual beings find their place within the Pleroma, 'psychic' beings revert to the intermediate region, corporeal ones to the dust (*choïcum*); (7) *et praeter haec nihil posse Deum, sed unumquemque praedictorum ad ea, quae sunt* eiusdem substantiae, *secedere affirmant.* The Greek will have run, approximately: καὶ παρὰ ταῦτα μηδὲν δύνασθαι τὸν Θεόν, ἀλλ' ἕκαστον τῶν προειρημένων πρὸς τὰ ὁμοούσια διΐστασθαι φάσκουσιν: 'God, they say, has no further power, but each of the aforesaid reverts to what is consubstantial with it'. As in examples 2–5, the sense of 'consubstantial' is determined by the Valentinian doctrine of the three elements; things are consubstantial with the element which predominates in their constitution. The word is not, of course,

---

[2] I. 11. 3, Hv. i. 102–4, cf. 15. 1, ibid. 144. See the *Dictionary of Christian Biography*, ii. 148.

[3] For the distinction between ideal and mathematical numbers see Ross, *PTI*, 176 ff.; Merlan in *LGP*, 16 and refs.; cf. also Numenius in Eusebius, *PE* xi. 22. 5, p. 544b = fr. 25, Leemans, = 16, des Places.

essential to the eschatological view just described, which is mentioned in less precise terms at p. 359: like reverts to like, *similia ad similia congregari*.[4]

The next nine examples, 8–16, belong to a single sequence of argument.[5] Irenaeus notes that he has been criticizing the Valentinian doctrine of the Pleroma with special reference to the first Ogdoad. He now asks, how were the other Aeons produced? He suggests three possible views of their origin, and then puts three other questions:

A. How were the other Aeons put forth?
    (i) Without any separation, like the sun's rays?
    (ii) Or as separate units, like the offspring of men and beasts?
    (iii) Or as outgrowths, like the boughs of a tree?
B. Were they of the same substance as their origins, or did they derive their substance from some other substance?
C. Were they contemporary or successive?
D. Were they simple and uniform, like spirits and lights, or articulated structures?

Quaeritur igitur, quemadmodum emissi sunt reliqui Aeones? Utrum uniti ei qui emiserit, quemadmodum a sole radii, an efficabiliter et partiliter, uti sit unusquisque eorum separatim, et suam figurationem habens, quemadmodum ab homine homo, et a pecude pecus? Aut secundum germinationem, quemadmodum ab arbore rami? Et utrum eiusdem substantiae *exsistebant his qui se emiserunt, an ex altera quadam substantia substantiam habentes? Et utrum in eodem emissi sunt, ut eiusdem temporis essent sibi; an secundum ordinem quendam, ita ut antiquiores quidam ipsorum, alii vero iuveniores essent? Et utrum simplices quidam et uniformes, et undique sibi aequales et similes, quemadmodum spiritus et lumina emissa sunt; an compositi et differentes, dissimiles membris suis?*

In discussing these points Irenaeus roughly follows the scheme set out under heading (A), but makes changes of detail. He begins with alternative (ii), § 3, *sed si quidem . . . secundum suam genesin*

---

[4] For the doctrine cf. Hippolytus, *Ref.* v. 21. 5–8 (Sethians), vii. 28. 4 (Satornilus), and for its physical basis, Severus, *de Anima* (? 1st–2nd cent. A.D.) in Eusebius, *PE* xiii. 17. 2–3, p. 701a. This suggests an origin in Aristotle, *de Caelo* iv. 3.

[5] All in ii. 17, Hv. i. 306–7. Cf. Sagnard, *Gnose*, 72, 97; though Irenaeus is probably less systematic than he suggests.

etc., and follows it with a comparison which looks like (i) but is in fact a new suggestion: 'if they were like lights kindled from a light, or torches from a torch'. This possibility, like (ii), implies separate units, whereas in (i), the image of rays of light proceeding from a source, Irenaeus is probably influenced by the Stoic theory which regards light not as an outgoing current or stream but rather as an extension of its source which is retracted when the light is cut off.[6] Alternative (iii) comes next (17. 6, *Haec eadem ratio sequetur, etsi velut ab arbore ramos etc.*) and finally (i) in its original form.

The term 'consubstantial' has already appeared in setting out question (B); this question is answered by saying that *whatever* theory of emission is adopted, the product will be 'consubstantial' with its source. This point is made separately for each alternative, so that question B and its four answers account for five of our examples, Nos. 8–10, 12, and 13.

(8) (Question B): *Et utrum* eiusdem substantiae *exsistebant his qui se emiserunt, an ex altera substantia substantiam habentes?* Here the Greek may perhaps be conjectured: καὶ ἆρα ὁμοούσιοι τοῖς προβαλοῦσιν αὐτούς, ἢ ἐξ ἄλλης τινὸς οὐσίας ὑφεστηκότες;

(9) *Sed si quidem efficabiliter et secundum suam genesin unusquisque illorum emissus est secundum hominum similitudinem; vel generationes Patris erunt* eiusdem substantiae *ei et similes generatori, vel si dissimiles parebunt, ex altera quadam substantia etc.*

(10) *Si autem velut a lumine lumina accensa sunt . . . velut verbi gratia, a facula faculae; generatione quidem et magnitudine fortasse distabunt ab invicem:* eiusdem *autem* substantiae *cum sint cum principe emissionis ipsorum, aut omnes impassibiles perseverant, aut et pater ipsorum participabit passiones.*

(12) *Haec eadem ratio sequetur etsi, velut ab arbore ramos, dicant a Logo natam esse emissionem Aeonum, cum Logos a Patre ipsorum generationem habeat:* eiusdem substantiae *omnes inveniuntur cum Patre, tantum secundum magnitudinem, sed non secundum naturam differentes ab invicem, etc.*

(13) *Si autem quomodo a sole radios, Aeonas ipsorum emissiones habuisse dicent,* eiusdem substantiae *et de eodem omnes cum sint, aut*

---

[6] See Marcus Aurelius, viii. 57; Justin, *Dial.* 128. 3; Athenagoras, *Leg.* 10; Epiphanius, *Haer.* 62. 1. 8. The same theory probably underlies Tertullian's language in *Apol.* 21, *adv. Prax.* 8; the light-tentacle is thrust out (*porrigitur, extenditur*) until its tip (*apex*) rests on some solid object.

omnes capaces passionis erunt cum eo qui ipsos emisit, aut omnes im-
passibiles perseverabunt.

No. (11) resumes the argument of (10), after a short digression concerned with question (C), and makes a point which is common to the whole of (9–13) : since on any theory of derivation the Aeons are 'consubstantial' with their source, either they must all be incorruptible, or if any one of them is corruptible, then all, together with their source, must be so too. Virtually the same point is made in (14); while (15) and (16) add a somewhat similar argument: since conflict only arises between things of opposite nature, how could Sophia be confused and endangered through contact with the ultimate Source, if this is 'consubstantial' with herself? We may set down these instances without further comment:

(11) *Labes igitur eius quae est secundum ignorantiam passionis, aut universo similiter Pleromati ipsorum proveniet, cum sint* eiusdem substantiae, *et erit in ignorantiae labe, id est semetipsum ignorans Propator: aut similiter omnia impassibilia perseverabunt, etc.* (ii. 17. 5, Hv. i. 308).

(14) *Necesse est . . . eas quae ex eo sunt emissiones,* eiusdem substantiae *cum sint . . . perfectas et impassibiles et semper similes cum eo perseverare, qui eas emisit* (ii. 17, 7, Hv. i. 310).

(15) *Quemadmodum autem et solvebatur et patiebatur Aeon? Siquidem* eiusdem substantiae *cuius et Pleroma erat; Pleroma autem universum ex Patre.*

(16) *Si igitur ⟨et⟩* eiusdem substantiae *cuius et universum Pleroma, ex eo emissus fuisset hic Aeon, nunquam demutationem perciperet, etc.* (Both in ii. 18. 5, Hv. i. 314–15).

If we now turn from detailed analysis to broader questions of interpretation, we shall find that the arguments which Irenaeus here deploys against the Gnostics were not coined for this purpose, but are adapted from a common repertoire which antedates both Gnosticism and Christianity and could be used against any form of emanation theory. Both Stoics and Pythagoreans were attacked on these lines. The necessary presupposition is to assume some radical difference between the ultimate Creator and the world, whether dogmatically, as by Platonists holding a creation doctrine, or by agnostics simply for the sake of making their point. The disputant then tries to manoeuvre his opponent into admitting that composite, divisible, and corruptible beings emanate from a source that is simple and incorruptible. This can then be attacked, either,

- (a) on the general ground that it breaks the rule that like must be generated from like; or,
- (b) as implying that the ultimate source itself must be composite, etc.; or
- (c) conversely, as implying an illicit promotion of corruptible beings to equality with their source.

Of these arguments, (a) is clearly envisaged by Ptolemaeus in the extract quoted above; he urges Flora not to be disturbed by objections of this kind, and promises to answer them later. The general principle 'like from like' is of course much older, and could presumably be used against any theology of creation; but I have not discovered any such application of it before Christian times. However argument (b) is clearly pre-Christian, since it is presented by Cicero as used in the Epicurean interest against Pythagoras: if human minds are offshoots of the divine mind, this implies division of the godhead; further, if our minds are unhappy, *tum dei partem esse miseram, quod fieri non potest* (*de Nat. Deorum*, i. 27).[7] It seems indeed that the Stoics were trying to counter the first point when they put out the doctrine (which later proved so useful to the Christian theology of the Logos) that the human mind is an offshoot of divinity *which does not involve division*. The second point is echoed by Horace, though he has vice rather than unhappiness in mind:

> *quin corpus onustum*
> *hesternis vitiis animum quoque praegravat una*
> *atque adfigit humo divinae particulam aurae.*
> (*Serm.* ii. 2, ll. 77–9).

It reappears in Marcion's argument that the Creator of the sinful human minds must himself be capable of sinning, and the converse argument of Hermogenes, that corruptible matter cannot have been created by the good God, but must pre-exist; and again in a passage of Clement that will be examined below.

This argument is clearly taken up by Irenaeus, though he does not stress the point about dividing the godhead; he is inclined, like Philo, to accept the Stoic defence that there can be forms of

---

[7] Cf. also H. Dörrie, 'Emanation', in *Parusia*, 126–7, who refers to Lucretius iii. 518–19.

emanation which do not involve either separation or a division of the source. He deprecates inquiry into the manner in which the Logos proceeds from God (ii. 28. 6, Hv. i. 355–6), but he does not object to terms like 'emanation'; thus he can say of matter, *quoniam Deus eam protulit.* He therefore recasts the argument in the form that objectionable consequences follow *whatever* kind of derivation one supposes; and the point about division is relegated to a subordinate place, appearing at 17. 3, p. 307, as a comment on alternative A (ii); the Aeons emerge as distinct units with their own shape and size, *quae propria corporis sunt, et non spiritus.* His main contention is that imperfection in the product entails imperfection in the source; and the obvious retort, that this would equally condemn the orthodox doctrine of creation, has to be met by saying that knowledge of such matters is withheld from us (ii. 28. 7, Hv. i. 356).

The third argument, that of 'illicit promotion', appears in Irenaeus at the passage quoted above as example (7); to say that souls are saved by nature is to deprive God of his saving power. He returns to this point later in the second book, with another use of the phrase *eiusdem substantiae*:

(17) *Si enim propter substantiam omnes secedunt in refrigerium, et medietatis sunt omnes secundum quod sunt animae, cum sint* eiusdem substantiae, *superfluum est credere, superfluum autem discessio Salvatoris* (ii. 29. 1, Hv. i. 359).

This argument embodies three traditional points:

   (i) the argument that any determinist view of human destiny robs God of his power.
   (ii) the theory that some souls at least are saved by nature.
   (iii) the view that all the elements of the human *compositum* return to the source from which they were taken.

The main argument, (i), must be briefly handled; it rests on ancient speculations as to whether or not the gods are superior to fate; and Irenaeus' use of it is anticipated by Justin, who argues (*Dial.* 4) that the mind does not see God because of τὸ συγγενές, its natural relationship to him as his offspring, but because it is good and just. A similar argument is used by Clement against Valentinus, *Strom.* iv. 89. 4. There is, clearly, a certain artificiality in this argument; since if God himself has laid down that some or all men shall be saved according to their nature, his decree is not frustrated, any more than if he has laid down that those who show themselves just and good shall be saved.

Similarly the view that some souls are saved by nature is a polemical adaptation of the view that some souls are naturally good, which can be traced back at least to Plato. Philo regards Noah and Er as actual examples of men who are naturally good and bad, though he also allegorizes them, making Er stand for the corruptible body and Noah for the righteous man's repose; while Eve apparently represents sensation, which is neither good nor bad by nature but can turn either way (*Leg. All.* iii. 65–79)— an exegesis which closely resembles the Gnostics' treatment of body, spirit, and soul. In another passage Philo expresses the view that some men are good by teaching, some by nature, and some by discipline, *ascesis* (*Praem.* 24 ff., esp. 27, 31, 49–51, 59); these three possibilities had already been envisaged by Aristotle (*NE* x. 9, 1179 b 20–1, cf. Plato, *Meno* 89 ab, 98 cd, 99 e) and Philo sees them as typified by the three patriarchs; thus Isaac represents the man who is good by nature. Such claims may possibly not have been contested until the Gnostics asserted that they themselves were the elect, destined for salvation and incapable of falling; when clearly counter-arguments were needed. The doctrine that the several elements in man revert to their original sources has been briefly noted above (p. 195, n. 4) and perhaps does not call for extended discussion here.

Irenaeus uses the phrase *eiusdem substantiae* twice more, in Chapter 9 of Book iv, Hv. ii. 168–9. In the first case, example (18), his general theme is that the Law is not contrary to the Gospel. This leads him to remark, rather strangely, *Unius igitur et* eiusdem substantiae *sunt omnia, hoc est, ab uno et eodem Deo.* Here the Greek may possibly be, as Harvey suggests, ἐκ μιᾶς καὶ τῆς αὐτῆς οὐσίας. Pursuing the same theme, Irenaeus quotes the text *Plus est enim templo hic* (Matt. 12 : 6), and then asserts that the comparatives 'greater' and 'less' do not imply difference of substance, but only difference of degree between things of the same substance, which cannot therefore be opposed to each other: (19) *Plus autem et minus non in his dicitur, quae inter se communionem non habent, et sunt contrariae naturae, et pugnant inter se; sed in his quae* eiusdem *sunt* substantiae, *et communicant secum, solum autem multitudine et magnitudine differunt: quemadmodum aqua ab aqua, et lumen a lumine, et gratia a gratia.* This philosophical reflection hardly fits its context, since it is difficult to see in what sense the Lord can be consubstantial with the Temple; and it proves to be only a misleading version of the treatment of comparison in Aristotle's *Categories*. It may be true to say (with Aristotle) that comparison implies difference of quality; it is clearly false to say that it excludes difference of substance.

We may now collect our findings about Irenaeus' use of the term *homoousios*. He apparently takes over the word from his Gnostic opponents. But the contexts in which they use it are not pure Gnostic inventions, but are applications of common philosophical themes; and so are Irenaeus' replies. Many of them can be paralleled by similar statements expressed in other terms (e.g. (7), and cf. the use of the phrase *eiusdem naturae*, perhaps equivalent to ὁμοφυής).

Homoousios is a word of wide application. It is just possible that Irenaeus applies it to 'everything', i.e. the whole created order (18). In practice he generally uses it to mean 'belonging to the same order of being', following the Valentinian distinction of spirit, soul, and matter. But no doubt this is simply because he is writing against Valentinians; the word can also have a purely general sense (19).

In more than half the instances a thing is said to be *homoousios* with its source (1–5, 8–14); though the widest possible variety of derivation is envisaged (8–14). However, collateral realities are clearly indicated in 6, 17, 18, 19. The word allows, but does not entail, organic connection. And it allows, but does not entail, equality of status. The inequality of consubstantials is positively stated at 10, 12, and 19.

Before leaving the second century there is one other pagan writing to be considered, the *Poimandres*, which though difficult to date may be tentatively assigned to this century, and could conceivably be the earliest text which contains the word ὁμο-ούσιος.[8] The writer describes a revelation given to him by the god Poimandres, which explains the origin of the universe and of man; he draws fairly freely on the book of Genesis, but boldly reinterprets its theology so as to present a fairly complex hierarchy of heavenly beings resembling those of the Gnostics. At the head of the hierarchy stands the supreme God whose name is Mind,

[8] C. H. Dodd, *The Bible and the Greeks*, 201–9 (probably second century, possibly a little earlier).

Nous, and who is also characterized as 'life and light'; next to him comes the Logos, who is described as 'Son of God' (§ 6, ὁ δὲ ἐκ Νοὸς φωτεινὸς Λόγος υἱὸς θεοῦ); after him the supreme God 'brought forth by his word—or Logos—' (§ 9, ἀπεκύησε λόγῳ) another Mind, the Creator or Demiurge, a god of fire and spirit who dwells above the visible world; whereupon the Logos, who had previously been sent down (§ 5) to separate the finer elements from the grosser 'leapt up . . . and was united with the Demiurge Mind, for he was of the same substance' (§ 10, ἐπήδησεν . . . ὁ τοῦ θεοῦ Λόγος . . . καὶ ἡνώθη τῷ δημιουργῷ Νῷ, ὁμοούσιος γὰρ ἦν . . .). The last phrase seems to indicate their common derivation from the supreme God who is intelligence, light, and life; and their 'unification' marks a further step, a close association which however stops short of absolute coalescence; the writer goes on to speak of 'the Demiurge Mind with the Word', a phrase which governs verbs in the singular; but he never makes his thoughts completely precise.

(ii) *The Age of Tertullian and Origen*

The first half of the third century brings no important change in the usage of the term ὁμοούσιος by Christian theologians. In the great majority of cases it occurs in quotations or reminiscences of Gnostic writers; and it is only towards the end of this period that we can trace the first tentative use of the term to formulate the Christian doctrine of the Trinity.

It is especially noteworthy that Tertullian, who relies upon the phrase *una substantia* to express the unity manifested in the three Persons of the Godhead, and is willing to borrow Gnostic terms such as προβολή, 'emanation', nowhere himself appropriates any word coined on the model of ὁμοούσιος. He does indeed introduce two forms, *consubstantialis* and *consubstantivus*; but only to represent his opponents' theories.

Consubstantialis appears only once, in the treatise *adversus Hermogenem* (44, 3): *Cui credibile est deum non apparuisse materiae, vel qua consubstantiali suae per aeternitatem*—perhaps to be rendered, 'Who can believe that God did not appear to matter, supposing it was his equal in rank through its eternity?' R. Braun, who has provided an authoritative survey of Tertullian's theological vocabulary, notes that the sense of *substantia* which is here implied is not that which Tertullian himself most commonly gives to the term; *consubstantialis* does not mean 'made of the same stuff', but rather 'having the same nature, status, or rank'; compare the comment made earlier in the same treatise (6, 2) : *Erit enim et materia qualis deus, infecta, innata, initium non habens nec finem*, 'for matter will be like God, unmade, ingenerate, having no beginning nor end'.[9] It may well be that *consubstantialis* directly represents Hermogenes' language, whether as a straight citation, or as a translation of the Greek ὁμοούσιος—for it is uncertain whether or not Hermogenes wrote in Greek. In this case it is permissible to remark that Tertullian's own use of the phrase *una substantia* is closer to the Valentinians' ὁμοούσιος than is Hermogenes' *consubstantialis*; for in Tertullian's Trinity the *una substantia* represents the stuff or reality, called *spiritus*, which the Second and Third Persons derive from the First; whereas Hermogenes positively denies that matter proceeds from God; it is formed by him, but not created, much less emitted as an offspring.

The term *consubstantivus*, on the other hand, appears only in three passages in the *adversus Valentinianos*, all of which suggest that Tertullian is closely following Irenaeus. At 12. 5 he suggests that the angels which accompany the Saviour may be *Soteri consubstantivos*, in which case the Saviour would have no pre-eminence in rank; here Irenaeus speaks of τῶν ἡλικιωτῶν αὐτοῦ, 'his coevals' (i. 4. 5, Hv. i. 39). At 18. 1 Tertullian reproduces the argument, already noticed above in connection with examples (15) and (16), that conflict only arises between things of opposite nature. Irenaeus' statement of this general thesis is more loosely phrased (*quod enim simile est, in simili non dissolvetur . . . quae autem sunt contraria, a contrariis patiuntur etc.*) and the phrase *eiusdem substantiae* appears in its theological application; Tertullian uses *consubstantivus* to state the general thesis: *fere enim paria et consubstantiva in alterutrum valere societas naturae negavit*. The third instance, at 37. 2, is a straightforward reproduction of the passage cited above as example (6): *huic adest consubstantiva virtus quam appellat Unionem*.

[9] R. Braun, *Deus Christianorum* (Paris, 1962), 197–9, esp. 198, n. 3. For the meaning of *substantia* in Tertullian, ibid., 167 ff. I had independently come to much the same conclusions; see my paper, 'Divine Substance in Tertullian', *JTS*, n.s. 14 (1963), 46–66. The subject has since been fully discussed by J. Moingt, *Théologie trinitaire de Tertullien* (Paris, 1966), 299–430.

Tertullian's use of these two terms has been summarized by Fr. Braun in words which can hardly be bettered:

Ainsi ni *consubstantialis* ni *consubstantivus* n'ont eu de vie dans la langue de Tertullien. Ils font figure d'étrangers, sentent la traduction livresque du terme gnostique ὁμοούσιος dont le sens mal défini, flottant entre les notions de φύσις et d' οὐσία, ne répondait pas en tous cas au concept latin de *substantia* tel quel l'usage de Tertullien permet de l'observer.[10]

So the later Trinitarian use of the term *consubstantialis* is not really anticipated by either of the two compound adjectives, but by the phrase *una substantia*; and this notwithstanding the fact that Tertullian's use of it has much in common with the Gnostic theology which he condemned, but also expressed in terms which proved useful to later orthodoxy.

Hippolytus uses the term ὁμοούσιος seven times in his *Refutatio*, but one case has already been considered, as giving the Greek text of Irenaeus (6). Of the rest, one appears in an account of the Naassenes, the two next concern the Peratae, and the last three Basilides. The first three are similar in that they all treat of the salvation of the elect under somewhat unusual images. The Naassenes, like the Valentinians, seem to have posited three classes of being (v. 8. 2), but to have conceived them rather differently, as including first the perfect archetypal Man, then inferior mortality, and thirdly the elect, who perfectly resemble the primal Man like the two identical statues in Samothrace (v. 8. 10: εἰκόνες δέ εἰσι τὰ προειρημένα ἀγάλματα τοῦ ἀρχανθρώπου καὶ τοῦ ἀναγεννωμένου πνευματικοῦ, κατὰ πάνθ' ὁμοουσίου ἐκείνῳ τῷ ἀνθρώπῳ). If one can trust Hippolytus' account, the three classes of being seem to be defined as the spiritual, the carnal (σαρκικόν, 8. 7), and thirdly what is earthly in origin but destined to become spiritual, and so is called *homoousios* with the first class by anticipation; so in § 4 the three-bodied giant Geryon is fancifully explained as *Gē-rheōn*, flowing from earth, like the Jordan flowing upward at the command of 'Jesus' or Joshua, a tradition which presumably rests on a variant translation of Joshua 3: 16, or else on an eccentric reading of the LXX ἔστη . . . ἄνωθεν.

The Peratae seem also to have used *homoousios* to denote a likeness that could be acquired. In their system, as Hippolytus describes it, the universe comprises the Father, the Son, and matter;

[10] Op. cit. 199.

the Son, also called the Word, is pictured as a serpent which glides up and down (στρέφεται)[11] between the material and the heavenly world, presenting the powers of the material world before the Father's face, and impressing on formless matter the forms (ἰδέας) taken from the Father. This serpent is identified with the life-giving serpent of Numbers 21, and again with the serpent which sprang from Moses' rod; and the word 'rod' has probably suggested the strange comparison of his influence on the world with the influence of Jacob's rods on the lambs conceived at Laban's drinking-troughs. Salvation, for the Peratae, seems to depend on the believer's power to recognize his heavenly destiny (ἀνάγκη) to be *homoousios* with the Father; if it goes un-recognized he is lost, and suffers the fate of unregenerate matter. But 'if anyone of those here below has the power even to realize that he is the Father's imprint (χαρακτήρ) brought down from heaven and rendered bodily, (then) like a conception from the rod he becomes white, (?) entirely *homoousios* with the Father in heaven, and ascends to that place.' And as a magnet attracts iron but nothing else . . . 'so by the serpent there is led back from the world the conformed, perfect race that is *homoousios*, but nothing else.' This use of *homoousios* presupposes the theory, already discussed above on p. 28, of an *ousia* that can be acquired; it does not, I think, imply that the believer becomes identified with, or even equal to, the Father.

The Naassenes and the Peratae seem to have shared a com-mon background of thought; but the system of Basilides, as Hip-polytus describes it, is very different, and raises critical problems which cannot be fully discussed here. Basilides seems to have postulated an ultimate principle described as 'the God who is not', who produced out of nothing a seed of the world from which all its future developments were to unfold. Hippolytus continues, 'There was in the seed itself a threefold sonship, *homoousios* in all respects with the God who is not, generated from what is not' (ἦν, φησίν, ἐν αὐτῷ τῷ σπέρματι υἱότης τριμερής, κατὰ πάντα τῷ οὐκ ὄντι θεῷ ὁμοούσιος, γεννητὴ ἐξ οὐκ ὄντων, vii. 22. 7). A diffi-culty here is that we are told soon afterwards that the sonship is

---

[11] V. 17. 2. Στρέφεσθαι is a suggestive word; it is used of the movement of the heavens; also, in the LXX, of the darting movement of the flaming sword of Eden, which Philo compares to the Logos (*Cher.* 28). In *Leg. All.* ii. 79, Philo speaks of 'another serpent, contrary to Eve's, the word of prudence'.

divided into three grades (τριχῇ διῃρημένης), one being fine-grained, one coarse-grained, and one in need of purification. It is hard to see how the second and third grades of sonship can be *homoousios* with the supreme reality; and it is just possible that the word is interpolated by Hippolytus, who is professedly trying to prove that on this cosmology everything is generated out of nothing, and may therefore have falsely assimilated the sonship created 'from what is not' with 'the God who is not'. But it has to be noted that Basilides assigns to the sonship, even the third grade of it, an unexpected dignity; it is superior to the most glorious of the world-rulers, and even to the Holy Spirit; its place is in the 'hyper-cosmic' region, whereas the Holy Spirit has to remain at the lower boundary of this region: 'for it was not *homoousios*, nor did it share the nature of the sonship.'

Clement uses the term *homoousios* twice in his *Stromateis*, with five further references in the *Excerpta ex Theodoto* and one Latin fragment of some interest. At *Strom.* ii. 74. 1 he contrasts God's mercy with the mercy shown by a righteous man; the latter shows mercy 'through a natural benevolence and relationship, and through the commandments which he obeys; but God has no natural relationship to us, as the heresy-makers maintain . . . unless one will dare to speak of us as part of him and *homoousios* with God' (εἰ μή τις μέρος αὐτοῦ καὶ ὁμοουσίους ἡμᾶς τῷ θεῷ τολμήσει λέγειν). To speak of sinful men in this way leads to the blasphemous conclusion that God is 'sinful in parts', μερικῶς ἁμαρτάνων.

In this passage Clement develops the argument, already discussed, about 'degrading God' (p. 198 above). Later in the *Stromateis* he adopts the complementary argument about the 'illicit promotion' of man. He is criticizing a Valentinian theory of a creator-god or demiurge responsible for death, opposed by a superior race (τὸ διαφέρον γένος) who are bringers of life; but this means, he says, that they usurp the function of Christ: 'if the superior race appears to put an end to death, it is not Christ who did away with death, unless he too be called *homoousios* with them' (εἰ μὴ καὶ αὐτὸς αὐτοῖς ὁμοούσιος λεχθείη, iv. 91. 2); and even this would demean the Creator, since the elect, even if assisted by Christ, would be saving his work from destruction, which he himself could not save. It is not easy to determine the sense of *homoousios* in the context of its amending clause; it is perhaps simplest to take it as equivalent to *homogenēs*, 'belonging to the same (superior) race'; but it is not quite impossible that it implies some closer identity.

In the *Excerpta*, according to Sagnard,[12] Clement comments successively on four separate Gnostic documents which differ slightly in the details of their teaching. One of his references to *homoousios* belongs to Sagnard's 'Section B', the remaining four to 'Section C', which is closely parallel to Irenaeus i. 4. 5–7. 5, Hv. i. 38–65. *Homoousios* is used twice with reference to the creation of man (50. 1 and 2), once referring to the flesh (53. 1), and twice referring to the saving work of Christ; and here 42. 3, from Section B, agrees fairly well with 58, from Section C. We may therefore treat the passages in this order.

In Ch. 50 Clement's account of the Creation narrative, as expounded by the Gnostics, is closely parallel to that of Irenaeus, from which we have already taken the example numbered (4). The Artificer makes man 'after his image and after his likeness' (Gen. 1 : 26). The 'image' is explained by saying that he takes dust from the 'earth', understood as formless matter, and makes an earthy and material soul which is irrational and *homoousios* with that of the beasts; whereas the 'likeness' stands for a psychic element which is breathed in and implanted by the Artificer himself and *homoousios* with him, imparted by means of the angels:

"Λαβὼν χοῦν ἀπὸ τῆς γῆς",—οὐ τῆς ξηρᾶς, ἀλλὰ τῆς πολυμεροῦς καὶ ποικίλης ὕλης μέρος,— ψυχὴν γεώδη καὶ ὑλικὴν ἐτεκτήνατο ἄλογον καὶ τῇ τῶν θηρίων ὁμοούσιον· οὗτος ⟨ὁ⟩ "κατ᾽ εἰκόνα" ἄνθρωπος. (2) Ὁ δὲ "καθ᾽ ὁμοίωσιν", τὴν αὐτοῦ τοῦ Δημιουργοῦ, ἐκεῖνός ἐστιν ὃν εἰς τοῦτον "ἐνεφύσησέν" τε καὶ ἐνέσπειρεν, ὁμοούσιόν τι αὐτῷ δι᾽ Ἀγγέλων ἐνθείς.

Why is the dust of the earth fashioned into a *soul*, albeit of an earthy and material nature? The reason seems to be that the Valentinians could not envisage even the psychic element—the second noblest—coming into contact with actual flesh, which they associate with grossness and corruption; hence the divine soul had this material soul to serve as its 'flesh' (51. 2). No doubt the Valentinians were thinking of a soul having the form of a human body, described as 'a psychic man within the earthy man' (51. 1), so that it can be called alternatively 'a psychic

[12] *Extraits de Théodote*, ed. F. Sagnard, *Sources chrétiennes* 23 (1948).

body' (2. 1 ; 14. 2 ; 51. 3 ; 61. 2). Actual flesh is described as 'the adversary', 'the serpent', 'the seed of the devil', as *homoousios* with him (53. 1). The phrase resembles Heracleon's exegesis of John 8 : 44, to which we shall shortly come.

In the context of Redemption the word *homoousios* occurs in the difficult Chapter 42, which is dominated by the image of Jesus taking up his Cross and commanding his 'brethren' to do likewise. However, the Cross also symbolizes the 'boundary' which separates the unfaithful from the faithful (42. 1) ; hence in carrying his Cross he also carries the faithful on his shoulders and brings them into the Pleroma. But the Valentinian christology of this section distinguishes between Jesus, who is the 'shoulders' of the elect, and Christ who is their head (Isa. 9 : 6, Col. 1 : 18, etc.). The text of 42. 3 reads: Ἦρεν οὖν τὸ σῶμα τοῦ Ἰησοῦ, ὅπερ ὁμοούσιον ἦν τῇ Ἐκκλησίᾳ ; Sagnard interprets this with 'Christ' understood as the subject: 'He lifted up the body of Jesus, which was consubstantial with the Ecclesia', i.e. a psychic body ; 17. 1 has already suggested the theory that Jesus, the Ecclesia, and Wisdom interpenetrate each other.

In Ch. 58, however, the supreme Saviour is called Jesus Christ, and he has to 'put on' a lesser being, the 'psychic Christ',[13] in order to appear in the world (59. 2–3) ; when the time of salvation was come he 'took up in himself the Ecclesia by his power, both the elect and the called, the one spiritual coming from the Mother, the other psychic coming from the Economy (i.e. the work of the Demiurge, cf. 33)—these he saved[14] and bore upwards what he assumed, and through them those that were *homoousios* with them' (τὰ τούτοις ὁμοούσια, for MSS. ὁμοιοῦσα). At first sight this might appear to describe Jesus' saving work, first for his contemporaries, and then for their successors in the Church. But in view of the use of ἀναλαβεῖν in 61. 1–2, it seems more likely that the first 'assuming' applies to the *pre-existing* Ecclesia of angels, pneumatics, and righteous men (cf. Heb. 12 : 23), and the salvation of his earthly disciples is first mentioned in the last three words.

In general, Clement's use of the term *homoousios* agrees with

[13] The manuscripts give the same title 'Jesus Christ' to both (58. 1 ; 59. 2). I am not convinced that this is impossible.

[14] I retain the word ὅ before ἀνέσωσεν (so MSS.), which applies only to τὸ ψυχικόν; cf. 61. 8, which suggests that only the psychics need to be 'rescued' (ἀνασῴζεται).

that of Irenaeus. It means 'belonging to the same order of being'; so it can express the false assumption that man is equal to God or to Christ; more particularly, it refers to the three orders of being postulated by the Valentinians. The fact that it is once used to compare men to Christ gives no ground for thinking that it was already in use to express the relationship between Christ and the Father.

It is therefore in Origen that we find the first suggestion of the Trinitarian use of *homoousios*; but I shall begin by examining the five occurrences of it in the *Commentary on St. John*, two in Book xiii and three in Book xx, which follow the older convention. In all five cases Origen is criticizing Heracleon's exegesis of the Gospel; however the actual word *homoousios* occurs not in quotations from Heracleon, but in Origen's comments.

In Book xiii Origen expounds John 4: 24, 'God is a spirit, and they that worship Him must worship Him in spirit and in truth'. After giving his own exegesis (§§ 123–46) he quotes Heracleon's remarks on the first clause ('for his divine nature is undefiled and pure and invisible'), and then on the sequel ('in a manner worthy of him who is worshipped, spiritually, not carnally; for they too, being of the same nature—τῆς αὐτῆς φύσεως—with the Father, are spirit, who worship in truth and not in error'). Heracleon's language hardly goes beyond the New Testament (e.g. I John 3 : 9); but Origen suggests that it is blasphemy to call those who worship God in spirit *homoousios* with his unbegotten and blessed nature; and he adds, perhaps unfairly, that by taking the Samaritan woman as representing the spiritual nature, Heracleon has made an adulteress *homoousios* with God.[15] This follows a line of argument which we have already traced in Irenaeus and Clement; and it may be that this accounts for Origen's introducing the term associated with it in order to sharpen his criticism of Heracleon.

The second group of passages depends upon John 8: 44, 'You are of your father the devil.' Origen seems to give Heracleon's comments verbatim in § 168 (fr. 44), whereas there are variations and additions in §§ 198 and 211 (frr. 45, 46). Accordingly, Heracleon takes the text to mean 'of the substance of the devil' ("ὑμεῖς ἐκ τοῦ πατρὸς τοῦ διαβόλου ἐστέ;" ἀντὶ τοῦ "ἐκ τῆς οὐσίας τοῦ διαβόλου"). Origen comments: 'He clearly says that some men

---

[15] The text of this second passage is unfortunately defective.

are *homoousios* with the devil, being (as his school suppose) of a different substance from those whom they call psychic or pneumatic.' Once again the sense of *homoousios* is controlled by the Valentinian doctrine of the three classes of men; and the notion of men being *homoousios* with the devil closely resembles the description of the flesh just quoted from Clement's *Excerpta*, 53. 1.

A little later, having given his own exegesis of John 8: 44, Origen returns to Heracleon, and observes that his view implies that the devil is of a different substance from other rational beings. This gives Origen the opportunity to make his familiar point that if the devil is bad by nature, he will not be responsible; the blame will fall on his creator (§ 202). He adds an argument to the effect that if men differ in nature, it becomes impossible to explain how they ever agree. 'For has a similar experience occurred in different substances, or has the experience turned out similar because it happened to a being who was *homoousios*?' (ὁμοούσιον ἦν τοῦτο ᾧ συμβέβηκε τὸ πάθος)—as Origen himself maintains. 'To say that the same types of impressions etc. occur in beings of a different substance is unreasonable; but to say, in beings who are partly *homoousios*, as if there were some further additional substance in them, is absurd.'

The argument smacks of the schoolroom. Heracleon has evidently been taking *ousia* rather loosely, as a mere manner of behaviour that can be acquired or altered; this appears from §§ 213 ff., where he explains that the term 'children' can be used in three ways, indicating either natural offspring, or those who assimilate themselves by an act of will (γνώμῃ, θέσει, as opposed to φύσει), or thirdly those who are similar in moral quality. Φύσις, then, is Heracleon's term for an unalterable character; and as we have seen, there is some precedent for speaking of an *ousia* that can be acquired. Origen's reply depends on pressing the much more usual sense of *ousia* as that element in a thing that is strictly unalterable. But Origen comes badly out of the exchange; for he assumes (a) that where there are several *ousiai*, all their functions (δυνάμεις) must be different, and (b) that each individual has only one *ousia*. The suggestion he condemns as 'absurd' could be the perfectly reasonable one that two beings are 'partly *homoousios*' through belonging to different species of the same genus (since both species and genus are called *ousiai* by

Aristotle). But there is worse to come. For Heracleon goes on to explain that our Lord's condemnation is addressed not to the 'earthy' men who really are devilish by nature, but to the 'psychic', who have become so by their own act. So in regard to the psychics, at least, Heracleon takes the libertarian view that Origen himself favours; but Origen, feeling perhaps that he must oppose Heracleon at every point, unwisely counters with a deterministic quotation from St. Paul: 'We were by nature children of wrath', Eph. 2: 3. The incident is instructive, and suggests that there can be a certain unreality in the customary attacks on Gnostic determinism when deterministic sayings are firmly embedded in the New Testament.

However, Origen also used the term *homoousios* to indicate the Son's relationship to the Father; and so far as we know was the first Greek writer to do so.[16] Several passages from his *Commentary on Hebrews* are quoted by Pamphilus in his *Apology for Origen*, as preserved in Rufinus' Latin translation. In the fifth chapter of Book i, which alone survives, Pamphilus deals with Origen's doctrine of the Incarnation, and mentions a series of objections to it, beginning: *Prima illa est, quod aiunt eum innatum dicere Filium Dei*. This looks like a criticism framed by subordinationists who thought that Origen's doctrine of the eternal generation of the Son did not adequately safeguard the Father's pre-eminence; but in his reply to this objection Pamphilus appears to shift his ground: he quotes six passages designed to exhibit Origen's teaching that the Son is born from the Father, therefore *unius est cum Patre substantiae, alienus vero a substantiis creaturarum*. This sentence, which is in the nature of a heading, could conceivably have been inserted by Rufinus with Arianism in mind; however, the six quotations and the concluding remark are such as to suggest that Pamphilus himself was now concerned to defend Origen against a charge of excessive subordinationism, perhaps because the converse charge had already been sufficiently disposed of in Chapter iii. Three of the quotations are independently attested, one coming from the Commentary on

---

[16] Origen's use of the term *homoousios* in this context has recently been questioned by scholars of note; so M. Simonetti, *Studi sull' arianesimo*, 125, n. 76; R. P. C. Hanson, *Epektasis* (*Mélanges Daniélou*), 293–303; F. H. Kettler, private communication. Admittedly we have only the evidence of translations; and Rufinus had strong reasons for introducing the term to suggest Origen's orthodoxy. But the combination of passages quoted below seems to me sufficient to uphold the traditional view.

Romans and two from that on St. John; so there is no ante-
cedent reason for suspecting the genuineness of the concluding
three, derived from the lost Commentary on Hebrews.

In these three passages Origen begins by criticizing 'those who
are reluctant to confess that the Son of God is God'. A little later
he comments on the phrase *splendor gloriae* (i.e. ἀπαύγασμα τῆς
δόξης, Heb. 1 : 3), and quotes for comparison the description of
Wisdom as 'a breath of the power of God, and a pure effluent—
ἀπόρροια—of the glory of the Almighty', Wisdom 7 : 25. This
leads him to remark that Scripture instructs us by mysterious and
subtle methods; it introduces the metaphor of a vapour, ἀτμίς,
which is a physical reality, in order to show that just as a vapour
proceeds from a physical substance, so Christ, who is Wisdom,
proceeds from the actual substance of God. After referring briefly
to the metaphor of a *corporalis aporrhoea*, he concludes:

> These two metaphors show most plainly that the Son has a com-
> munity of substance with the Father; for an emanation appears to be
> *homoousios,* that is of one substance, with that body from which it is an
> emanation or a vapour. (*Quae utraeque similitudines manifestissime osten-
> dunt, communionem substantiae esse Filio cum Patre. Aporrhoea enim* ὁμοούσιος
> *videtur, id est, unius substantiae cum illo corpore, ex quo est vel aporrhoea,
> vel vapor.*)

Thus if Rufinus has correctly represented him, Origen uses
homoousios when describing the Son's derivation from the Father,
in an argument designed to show that he is superior to every
principality and power and virtue (and therefore to all created
things), and proceeds from the Father while preserving a community of substance, or unity of substance, illustrated by that of
a vapour or effluent with its source. In saying this, we largely
accept the interpretation of this passage offered by conservative
scholars. Nevertheless there are some reservations which ought
to be kept in mind.

First, it can hardly be thought that Origen habitually used the
word *homoousios* in Trinitarian contexts, or it would be impossible
to account for the suspicion of it shown by later Origenists like
Eusebius of Caesarea. It is not found elsewhere in the surviving
Greek texts of his writings. As we shall see, the Latin texts indicate
that he expressed the same thoughts elsewhere, and perhaps used
the same word; but it remains relatively infrequent.

Next, it is clear that Origen puts forward his comparison with some degree of circumspection. Scripture uses metaphors drawn from corporeal things; but the divine realities are incorporeal. The metaphor of a vapour therefore gives only one aspect of a complex truth; it cannot have been intended to mask the conviction that the Son is a *hypostasis*, and therefore necessarily a distinct and second *hypostasis*, on which Origen elsewhere insists with some force. And a fragment of the same commentary, already quoted by Pamphilus in Ch. 3, points to one respect in which they have to be contrasted. Origen explains the metaphor of light and its radiance as showing that the Son is eternally generated and coexists with the Father without beginning; but he is not unbegotten (*agennetos*?) : *non . . . innatus, ne duo principia lucis videamur inducere.*

Thirdly, the passage may be compared with Origen's other expositions of Wisdom 7 : 25; for in one case at least where we possess the Greek text (*in Joh.* xiii. 152–3) Origen interprets the verse in a strongly subordinationist sense. He writes that the Son, though superior to the angels, is in no way comparable to the Father: 'For he is the image of his goodness, and the effulgence, not of God, but of his glory and his eternal light, and the breath, not of the Father, but of his power.' It seems that God's glory, light, and power are conceived as attributes which in some way mediate between the Father and the Son. God's power (*virtus* = δύναμις) is treated in this way in *de Principiis* i. 2. 9, part of which has been quoted by Pamphilus in ch.3 ; and it is not impossible that the same turn of thought lurks beneath Rufinus' rather repetitive Latin phrases in our present passage.

On the other hand, Origen's theological method permits him to use complementary expressions which by later standards appear inconsistent. (Even in his *Commentary on St. John*, 'the effulgence of God's glory' is expounded with a very different emphasis in Book xxxii. 353.) He expresses the distinction between Father and Son in the emphatic form that there are two Gods,[17] and criticizes those who say that they are not distinguishable in *ousia*.[18] At the other extreme he can permit himself to say, *Unus et idem est cum Patre deus et dominus,*[19] or again *Pater et Filius est et in nullo differt.*[20] It is therefore understandable that he also

---

[17] *Dial. Heracl.* 2.
[18] *In Joh.* ii. 149; cf. ibid. x. 246, *Orat.* 15. 1, *in Titum, PG* 14. 1304 d.
[19] *Princ.* i. 2. 10, p. 43. [20] *In Cant. Prol.*, p. 69.

expresses their unity in phrases which involve the elastic term *ousia*. Its elasticity can be shown from the well-known and controversial passage in *de Principiis* iv. 4. 9, where he argues that every mind which participates in intellectual light is of one nature with every other such mind: therefore the heavenly powers and the human soul are of one nature and one substance. Rufinus' translation implies that the 'heavenly powers' are angels who, like men, participate in the Godhead; Jerome makes Origen argue that the human soul is '*quodammodo*' of one substance with the Godhead itself. Here the terms 'substance' and 'nature' are closely associated, and may be meant as equivalents. The same applies to two passages which assert unity of substance between the Son and the Father. In *de Principiis* i. 2. 6 Origen comments on Adam's begetting Seth 'according to his image' (Gen. 5 : 3) and adds, *Quae imago etiam naturae et substantiae patris et filii continet unitatem.* The application to the divine Father and Son follows at once, together with the observation that the Son's derivation from the Father is not physical, but resembles that of will from mind; but the idea of personal distinctness, suggested by Adam and Seth, is not further developed. On the other hand the discussion of the Trinity in the Twelfth Homily on Numbers is dominated by the contrasted themes of unity and plurality, suggested by the image of several wells fed by a single spring (Prov. 5 : 15–16). Origen first gives emphatic expression to the personal distinctions, suggested by the several wells: *Alius enim est a patre filius et non idem filius, qui et pater . . . Alius enim et ipse est (spiritus) a patre et filio . . . Est ergo haec trium distinctio personarum in patre et filio et spiritu sancto.* It is in this context that he adds, *Sed horum puteorum unus est fons*;[21] *una enim substantia est et natura trinitatis.* The unity of substance in the Trinity is its derivation from the Father, who is its single source.

Neo-Platonist writers roughly contemporary with Origen also used the term *homoousios*, but only rather rarely. Plotinus affords two examples; the first, from one of his earliest writings (*Ennead* iv. 7. 10) suggests that the soul is akin to and consubstantial with divine things: 'For prudence and true virtue, being divine, could not settle in any worthless and mortal thing; but such a thing (as can receive them) must be divine, since it partakes of divine things through its relatedness and common substance' (διὰ

---

[21] See p. 249 below.

συγγένειαν καὶ τὸ ὁμοούσιον). Both the thought and the language are commonplace: we have already noticed Justin's objection that the human mind does not see God because of some natural relationship (διὰ τὸ συγγενές) but on account of actual virtue (p. 199 above); but Plotinus could reply that the capacity for virtue is a precondition for its exercise, and only rational beings have this capacity.

In a later work, *Ennead* iv. 4, § 28, Plotinus argues that anger (θυμός) is *homoousios* with desire: 'The proof that it is *homoousios* with the soul's other track (Μαρτύριον δὲ τοῦ ὁμοούσιον εἶναι τοῦτο τῷ ἑτέρῳ ἴχνει ψυχῆς) is that those who are less desirous of bodily pleasures and generally despise the body are less liable to (fits of) anger.' *Homoousios* is used here to compare what are properly two states or accidents rather than two substances; more accurately, two types of state, described in very general and inclusive terms.

Porphyry also appears to have used the term *homoousios* to state the affinity of the human intellect with divine Mind (the second hypostasis of his trinity) if Augustine's evidence can be trusted; see his *de Regressu Animae*, fr. 10, in J. Bidez, *Vie de Porphyre*, p. 37* = Augustine, *Civ. Dei*, x. 29. And the word occurs at least twice in his works preserved in Greek. In *de Abstinentia* i. 19 he mentions the view that it is wrong to kill animals, if indeed their souls are *homoousios* with ours (ἀλλ' οὐ χρῆναι φήσει τις κτείνειν τὸ ὁμόφυλον, εἴ γε ὁμοούσιοι αἱ τῶν ζῴων ψυχαὶ ταῖς ἡμετέραις). Once again the unity asserted cannot be a close one.

In his *Sentences*, 33, Porphyry asks what kind of 'contact' (σύνοδος) can be made by perceptible things which occupy space with intelligible reality which is not in space;

for we are not examining any contact of bodies, but of things which are entirely separate from each other, according to the peculiar character of the *hypostasis*. Hence also their contact transcends what is usually recognized in things of the same order (ἐπὶ τῶν ὁμοουσίων). So it is not blending or mixture or contact or juxtaposition, but another form appearing indeed in the conjunctions of things of the same order one with another, however they occur, but transcending everything that is subject to sensation (φαντάζων μὲν παρὰ τοὺς ὁπωσοῦν γινομένας . . . κοινωνίας τῶν ὁμοουσίων . . .).

I translate ὁμοούσιος here by 'things of the same order', since Porphyry seems to apply it very generally to all perceptible realities, in contrast to the intelligible. All perceptible things, as such, are *homoousios*; Porphyry does not, I think, suggest, or deny, that all intelligible things, as such, are *homoousios*.

(iii) *From Dionysius to Nicaea*

I have given a fairly full account of the use of the word *homoousios* down to the middle of the third century. In the remaining period before the Council of Nicaea it does not seem to have altered its meaning to any great extent; but we can trace the beginnings of controversy over its application to the persons of the Trinity. Evidence for this has been found in two incidents which have been very fully discussed in connection with the Council; I shall describe these as briefly as possible, reserving my comments for another chapter.

Dionysius of Alexandria undertook (*c.* 260 A.D.) to criticize the 'Sabellian' theology which had become popular in the Pentapolis, the Greek-speaking cities of Libya, and did so in terms which emphasized the contrast between the Father and the Son. This in turn provoked a reaction; either the Libyans themselves, or their supporters in Alexandria (it is not clear which) complained to the Bishop's namesake Dionysius of Rome; the latter intervened, and the Alexandrian Dionysius replied with a work in which he revised and defended his position; brief extracts are given by Eusebius and Basil, and a rather larger selection by Athanasius in his *de Sententia Dionysii*. The Bishop refers to the charges brought against him, and mentions a previous letter written to his namesake 'in which I refuted the charge which they lay against me, that I do not call Christ *homoousios* with God. For even if I state that I have not found this word or read it anywhere in the Holy Scriptures, yet my subsequent suggestions, which they have ignored, are not inconsistent with this conception' (op. cit., 18).

Within a decade another patriarch found himself on the defensive; this was Paul of Samosata, Bishop of Antioch *c.* 260–72. He was criticized on a number of grounds, both personal and doctrinal, by bishops whose theology resembled that of Dionysius of Alexandria, and was eventually deposed at a synod held in Antioch *c.* 269, though his deposition was not immediately effective. We are told by Athanasius, Hilary, and Basil that the Synodal Letter of Antioch condemned the word *homoousios*; but

Athanasius and Hilary disagree as to the grounds on which it was rejected, and both rely for their information on a letter, now lost, circulated by the 'homoeousian' party (who themselves distrusted the term) in the year 358, some ninety years after the event. It seems now to be commonly admitted that the condemnation had been ignored in all previous discussions of the term, and it is, I think, an arguable thesis that the whole tradition rests upon an over-literal reading of a tendentious statement by the homoeousians. But more of this anon.

Coming to the period *c.* 300 A.D., we find the word *homoousios* appearing in Methodius' *Dialogue on the Resurrection* (ii. 30), in the course of an elaborate attack on Origen's doctrine. Origen seems to have appealed to the Stoic theory of the transmutation of the elements, as proving that it would be impossible to reassemble the constituents of our physical bodies; the resurrection body must be spiritual, a new creation. Methodius replies that there are no limits to God's power; but that in any case the Stoic theory is false, and the elements must remain permanently distinct; 'for every composite being consisting of pure air and pure fire, and being *homoousios* with angelic beings, cannot have the quality of earth and water, since it will then be terrestrial.' The former phrase is supposed to represent Origen's conception of the spiritual body, and is probably a misrepresentation; but we know enough about Methodius' own cosmology to suggest that *homoousios* is nevertheless used in a manner characteristic of Stoicism, where each element consists of undifferentiated matter endowed with its peculiar quality, and both this matter, and an element derived from it, can be called *ousia*. We are also told by Anastasius that Methodius drew an analogy between our three first ancestors, Adam, his son (Seth), and Eve, and the three persons of the Trinity. The word *homoousios* appears twice in this fragment (ed. Bonwetsch, p. 521), which mentions 'the three consubstantial hypostases' as symbols of 'the consubstantial Trinity'; but these phrases are more likely to stem from Anastasius himself than to reproduce Methodius.

We have already mentioned Pamphilus as our authority for Origen's use of *homoousios* in his lost *Commentary on Hebrews*. It is clear, moreover, that Pamphilus himself was ready to endorse this usage, in marked contrast to the reserve shown a little later by his friend Eusebius. He may have used it three times in all, but the first instance at least is not wholly reliable, and may be an insertion by Rufinus. Pamphilus is rebutting the charge that Origen declared the Son of God to be *innatum* ('ingenerate' or 'underived'), and thus robbing the Father of his unique prerogative; but the reply takes the form of showing that Origen declared the Son to be derived from the Father but consubstantial with him; and in the event it emphasizes the second point more than the first. He begins by quoting a passage from Origen's *Commentary on Romans* which by linking together the texts 'God is love' and 'Love is of God', and identifying the second 'Love' with the Son, pronounces him 'Love begotten of Love, as God of God' (*sicut Deum ex Deo, ita caritatem ex caritate progenitum*). This quotation is prefaced by the heading 'That the Son is born of God the Father, and is of one substance (*unius substantiae*) with the Father, but distinct from the substances of created things'. This certainly stresses those features of the reply which do not fit the accusation, and would be entirely agreeable to Rufinus' interests; but it may be simply a clumsy insertion made by Pamphilus after he had assembled his material and had become slightly confused about its purpose.

Homoousios appears twice more, but now in Greek transliteration; first in the heading which introduces the series of five quotations from Origen's *Commentary on Hebrews*, in much the same terms as before (*quomodo ὁμοούσιος est cum Patre Filius . . . alienus autem a substantia creaturae*); and again in Pamphilus' concluding comment on this section, which Rufinus renders *Satis manifeste, ut opinor, et valde evidenter ostensum est, quod Filium Dei de ipsa Dei substantia natum dixerit, id est, ὁμοούσιον, quod est* eiusdem *cum Patre* substantiae; *et non esse creaturam, neque per adoptionem, sed natura Filium verum, ex ipso Patre generatum.* We may note once again how closely the word *homoousios* is associated with phrases describing the Son's derivation 'from the substance' of the Father.

Pamphilus' apology seems to have been written *c.* 309 A.D., fairly shortly before the outbreak of the Arian controversy; but before dealing with Eusebius and the immediate antecedents of Nicaea, we should notice one or two texts which are more difficult to date.

The *Dialogue with Adamantius*, commonly dated *c.* 300, introduces the word rather prominently into a quasi-credal formula near the beginning: 'I have believed that there is one God, creator and artificer of all things, and the consubstantial Logos derived from Him' (καὶ τὸν ἐξ αὐτοῦ θεὸν Λόγον ὁμοούσιον, i. 2); but the author does not return to the Trinitarian problem so as to make his meaning clearer. The word recurs, but in another context, in a short sentence in which the pagan referee, Eutropius, sums up the opinions of two Marcionite disputants: 'You say that the two substances [good and evil] are ingenerate and imperishable; they must (then) also be consubstantial and similar, which is impossible' (ἀνάγκη καὶ ὁμοουσίους ταύτας ὑπάρχειν καὶ ὁμοίας, ὅπερ ἀδύνατον, iii. 7). The argument is clumsily constructed, but seems to depend on the principle that opposing substances cannot possess the same accidents; hence if it is said that imperishability (which this writer terms an 'accident') belongs both to good and evil, this conflicts with their previous description in terms of opposing substances, viz. light and darkness. The categorial scheme of substance, quality, and accident seems to be borrowed from a Stoic source; the argument leads to the supposition of two beings of the same substance which are both 'ingenerate', and therefore not derived the one from the other; but it is of course intended as an *argumentum ad absurdum*.

The *Clementine Homilies* present a strongly subordinationist theology expressed in rather unusual terms: the Son cannot share the Father's distinctive attributes even if he is begotten from Him and of the same substance (τῆς αὐτῆς οὐσίας, xvi. 16)! This writer cannot use the latter phrase as a distinctive description of the Son, since he applies it very freely (together with the verb 'to emit', προβάλλειν) to God's action in creating imperfect and corruptible beings, as we shall soon see. The actual word ὁμοούσιος occurs twice in a later homily, where the writer discusses the origin of the devil and mentions the possibility that he is 'of the same substance as his source' (τῆς αὐτῆς τῷ προβαλόντι οὐσίας, xx. 5. 2); this leads to an explanation that God's nature is different from man's, since he can change his substance as he wishes; after all, he changed Moses' rod and the waters of the Nile; and the angels who had their feet washed by men as if they were men of like substance (ὧν καὶ τοὺς πόδας ὡς ὁμοουσίων ἀνθρώπων ἄνθρωποι ἔνιψαν, xx. 7. 2) were changed into flesh, though in themselves ageless and composed of fiery substance; *a fortiori* the power of God changes the substance of the body (?) into anything he wills, and emits it 'consubstantial' with the manifestation which is presented, though not equal (i.e. not so limited) in power. It seems that this writer also uses the term 'substance' in a way which owes something to Stoicism (cf. Tertullian, *de Carne Christi*, 3); it clearly does not stand for a thing's characteristic mode of behaviour, but either for its place in the order of nature, or for the material form through which it acts, and which can be a merely temporary embodiment. This work cannot be later than the mid-fourth century, since it was used by the writer of the *Recognitions*, *c.* 360–80, which in turn was translated by Jerome; and its eccentric but quite uninhibited use of phrases which rapidly became notorious in the Arian controversy could be taken to point to a pre-Nicene date; but its whole theology is so extraordinary that this latter argument cannot be trusted.

The *Acta Archelai* present a much better articulated and more orthodox theology than either of the last two works, but are written with similar problems in mind, as a refutation of Manichaeism, which is represented as teaching that every soul and every living creature partakes in the substance of the good Father (τῆς γὰρ τοῦ ἀγαθοῦ πατρὸς οὐσίας πᾶσαν ψυχὴν καὶ πᾶν κινούμενον ζῷον μετέχειν λέγει, ed. Beeson, p. 13). A passage preserved only in Latin presents *homoousios* in transliteration in a context of argument which recalls that of Irenaeus, namely that it is unreasonable to maintain that frail and sinful creatures partake of the divine essence, which is unique, eternal, and invisible:

> For every creature has its own order . . . the human race . . . animals . . . angels . . . but there is one and only one immutable divine substance, eternal, invisible . . . (cf. John 1 : 18) . . . So all other creatures must be visible . . . but God, since he was never seen by any man, what consubstantiality can he have with those creatures? (*Deus vero, cum a nullo unquam visus sit, quid ei potest ex istis creaturis esse homoousion?*) . . . But you say that every animal that moves is made from one (source) and received from God a substance like (his), and that that (substance) can sin and come to judgment; and you refuse to accept the argument which says that the devil was an angel and fell into transgression and is not of the same substance with God (*et non esse eiusdem cum Deo substantiae*, ibid., pp. 51–2).

The last phrase may represent *homoousios* once again; and the writer continues by referring to the view that sinners are *unius cum deo substantiae*, and repeats that the devil *non erat ex dei substantia*. It does not appear that this work used *homoousios* in

Trinitarian contexts; but its theology seems broadly Nicene, if we can judge from such phrases as 'only God is his Father by nature' (p. 55), or again 'Who would dare speak about the substance of God, except it be only our Lord Jesus Christ?' (p. 62). It may in fact have been written after 325, though probably before 348.

Our previous discussion has suggested that Origen was mainly responsible for introducing the word *homoousios* into Trinitarian theology, but did so with reservations and counter-assertions that must have left his admirers in doubt as to the usefulness of the term. Pamphilus apparently upheld it; Eusebius on the whole seems to have avoided it, and to have thought that the independent reality of the three Persons could properly be stated not only in terms of three distinct *hypostases*, but also of three distinct *ousiai*.

One of the few pre-Nicene passages in which he uses the word, *DE* i. 10. 11–13, is concerned with the question of animal sacrifices. Eusebius argues that 'He who taught that blood is the soul of brute beasts (Lev. 17:14) shows that they by no means participate in rational and intelligent being, like men (οὐδαμῶς λογικῆς καὶ νοερᾶς οὐσίας ὁμοίως τοῖς ἀνθρώποις μετέχειν), but rather resemble the plants.' He then quotes Gen. 1: 11, 24, in order to show that the creative words are similar in the two cases, and concludes 'so beasts must be thought to be of the same kind and nature and substance (ὁμογενῆ καὶ ὁμοφυῆ καὶ ὁμοούσια) with plants from the earth, so that sacrificers of animals do nothing that is wrong.' This is clearly a reply to the argument mentioned by Porphyry quoted above (p. 215); it incidentally shows the term *homoousios* being used in an exceedingly general sense, and for two classes of beings that are collateral and not derived one from the other.

In *PE* xi. 21 Eusebius is ostensibly discussing the thesis that the Hebrew scriptures teach us that 'the *ousia* of the Good, and goodness itself, is nothing else but God'. He quotes from Plato the well-known passages *Tim.* 29 d, e and *Rep.* vi. 508 b, c, e, 509 b, understanding the latter to mean that *intelligible substances* (τὰς νοητὰς οὐσίας: Plato has τοῖς γιγνωσκομένοις, 'things that are known') obtain their 'being and substance', τὸ εἶναι καὶ τὴν οὐσίαν, from the Good: 'so that he does not make them *homoousia*, nor consider them unbegotten, because they have

obtained their being and substance from Him who is not a substance, but excels beyond substance in dignity and power.'
Though the passage is not directly connected with Trinitarian
theology, a subordinationist view is suggested by its continuation, which argues that the title of 'gods' must not be given to the
intelligible substances, 'but to Him alone and no other, who is the
only Good'. A little later (c. 22) he quotes from Numenius (fr.
25, Leemans) a passage which says that 'if the artificer of becoming (τῆς γενέσεως) is good, the artificer of being (τῆς οὐσίας)
will certainly be essential goodness . . . thus the first god is essential goodness, and the artificer, his imitator, is good; and the
being (οὐσία) of the first is one, but that of the second, another.'
It seems hardly doubtful that Eusebius accepted this implication
for the persons of his Christian Trinity.

IX

NICAEA

(i) The Son 'from God's Substance'

THE last two chapters have examined the theological applications of the term *ousia* and the use of the derivative word *homoousios* in Christian and pagan writings down to the outbreak of the Arian controversy. It remains to consider the use of these terms in the brief period of at most ten years which led up to the Council of Nicaea in June 325. The events of this period, and of the Council itself, present many problems which Church historians have so far failed to clarify;[1] but their main outlines at least are well known and easily accessible, and I shall take them for granted; my concern is with basic theology as revealed by the available texts, and particularly the contemporary sources. Most of these have been collected by H. G. Opitz, in two fascicles of his unfinished edition of Athanasius; some other important Arian texts, including the *Thalia* of Arius himself, can be found in the work of G. Bardy on St. Lucian of Antioch.[2]

The documents suggest that although *ousia* and *homoousios* came in for discussion at an early stage in the controversy, they were not the original focus of conflict. It seems rather that Arius began by rejecting the teaching of his bishop, Alexander, that the Son is coeternal with the Father; Arius wished to assert the Father's priority, though this was for him not strictly a priority in time, since he was willing to set the origin of the Son 'outside

---

[1] The fundamental studies are those of E. Schwartz, *Zur Geschichte des Athanasius* (*Gesammelte Schriften*, iii (Berlin, 1959), reprinting papers of 1904–11) and H. G. Opitz, 'Die Zeitfolge des arianischen Streites . . . bis 328', *ZNW* 33 (1934), 131–59. See also W. Telfer, 'When did the Arian controversy begin?', *JTS* 47 (1946), 129–42; W. Schneemelcher, 'Zur Chronologie des arianischen Streites', *TLZ* 79 (1954), 393–9; C. Kannengiesser, 'Où et quand Arius composa-t-il la Thalie?', *Kyriakon* (*Festschr. J. Quasten*) i. 346–51. The traditional date for the outbreak of the controversy is 318; Schwartz argued for 323; Opitz gives 315–17 as a *terminus post quem*.

[2] H. G. Opitz, *Athanasius Werke*, iii. 1–2; G. Bardy, *Recherches sur St. Lucien d'Antioch et son école* (Paris, 1936). Bardy's text is however defective and should be compared with Opitz's edition where available.

time' and 'before the ages';[3] he was convinced, however, that only the Father was strictly 'without origin'; hence 'there was—though there was not a time—'[4] when the Father was not yet Father and the Son 'was not'. The terms *ousia* and *homoousios* were drawn into the dispute in view of two consequent points: the Arian claim that the Father is necessarily superior to the Son in status, and the doctrine that the Son derives from the Father by a pure act of will, which would not involve any change or diminution; he is not therefore 'of his substance', nor 'consubstantial with him'. But the issue of the Father's priority seems to be put first by Arius in his letter to Eusebius of Nicomedia (Opitz, *Urk.* 1) and in the creed which he submitted to Alexander (ibid. 6: οἴδαμεν ἕνα θεόν, μόνον ἀγέννητον . . . μόνον ἄναρχον);[5] and equally in Alexander's Encyclical (ibid. 4b, § 7) and in the dogmatic letter which he circulated later (ibid. 14: see § 10, which begins his summary of Arian doctrine; § 15, which begins his reply; and §§ 22–7).

Nevertheless *ousia*, and probably *homoousios*, had become the subject of disagreement before the Council began. And the fathers of Nicaea included in their Creed two clauses embodying *ousia*: the declaration that the Son is 'from the substance of the Father' (ἐκ τῆς οὐσίας τοῦ πατρός) and the anathema on those who held that he was 'from', or 'of', 'another substance or essence' (ἐξ ἑτέρας ὑποστάσεως ἢ οὐσίας). They added also the declaration that the Son is *homoousios* with the Father. I shall review these phrases in the order just given, without ignoring a few other contexts in which *ousia* was used in the controversial writings of both parties. I begin with two brief prefatory notes.

(1) The previous discussion will have suggested that *ousia* was used in a wide variety of senses, which the users themselves largely failed to recognize, by all parties to the dispute. This can certainly be shown in the case of Eusebius of Caesarea, the only participant who has left us a considerable body of writings dated

---

[3] *Urk.* 1, § 4; 6, § 3; for the phrase πρὸ αἰώνων see Ps. 54: 20 LXX.

[4] H. M. Gwatkin, *Studies of Arianism*, 24.

[5] 'We recognize one God, alone unbegotten . . . alone without beginning.' I discuss these documents in their traditional order; however C. Kannengiesser (op. cit.) shows that the *Thalia* was written while Arius was still at Alexandria, after his condemnation, and argues that it is *anterior* to the letters. In this case its polemical tone may reflect Arius' initial dismay, while the letters and the Arian creed illustrate subsequent attempts at a *rapprochement*.

both before and after 325. There is thus no question of 'an' orthodox or 'a' heretical use of *ousia*; the case is rather that *within* this generally accepted and little-discussed structure of usage certain differences of meaning and application acquired importance or began to be recognized.

(2) Some important documents of the period do not use *ousia*. The most notable of these is the dogmatic letter of Alexander, Bishop of Alexandria, to his namesake (*Urkunde* 14). The omission may perhaps be deliberate, since the writer uses ὑπόστασις ten times and φύσις sixteen times,[6] often in contexts where οὐσία would be possible. Moreover οὐσία does occur three times in his earlier and much shorter encyclical letter (*Urkunde* 4b) which is sometimes thought to have been drafted by Athanasius,[7] who uses οὐσία much more frequently than ὑπόστασις in his later writings. Another important text which appears to have used neither *homoousios* nor *ousia* itself[8] is the Synodal Letter of the Council of Antioch, which, it has been noted, closely echoes the language of Alexander.[9]

Yet the term *ousia* was traditionally associated with discussions of the origin and status of the Son, as we have shown, and soon came to play a part in the controversy. Arius considered that the official teaching involved the absurdity of postulating two independent first principles; and also that it suggested a physical process of generation, which implied that the Father was subject to change. He himself seems not to have been entirely consistent in the way he formulated his views; or, possibly, he made some concessions in the hope of reaching agreement. Thus in his letter to Eusebius of Nicomedia he seems to have criticized the doctrine that the Son is 'from God himself' (ἐξ αὐτοῦ τοῦ θεοῦ, *Urk.* 1, § 2); but in his more conciliatory letter to Alexander (ibid. 6) he admits, in slightly different terms, that the Son 'received his being from the Father' (τὸ εἶναι παρὰ τοῦ πατρὸς εἰληφότα)[10] and 'was constituted by the Father' (ὑπὸ τοῦ πατρὸς ὑπέστη); and in the

---

[6] In Opitz, *Athanasius Werke*: ὑπόστασις, p. 22. 10, 18, 24; 23. 4; 24. 5, 8, 10; 25. 23; 27. 8, 19. φύσις, p. 21. 12, 17, 19, 20, 21; 22. 13; 24. 11, 22, 24, 27; 25. 2, 4, 23; 26. 27; 27. 8, 10. Cf. also p. 161 above.

[7] A. Robertson, *Athanasius*, *NPNF*, 68.

[8] ὑπόστασις appears once in Schwartz's retroversion, op. cit. p. 39. 10.

[9] E. Schwartz, *Nachr. Gött.* (1905), 288, = *Zur Gesch. des Ath.* 154.

[10] Contrast Origen, *in Joh.*, fr. 9, where παρὰ πατρός (John 1: 14) implies a *more* intimate relation than ἐκ θεοῦ; cf. also the argument of George, in *Urk.* 13: ἐκ τοῦ θεοῦ is non-committal, and the Arians themselves accept it.

Thalia he says directly that he originated 'from God, from the Father' (ἐκ θεοῦ ὑπέστη . . . τὸν ἐκ πατρὸς ὄντα: Athanasius, *Syn.* 15, Bardy, op. cit., p. 257). Arius did not of course reject the traditional titles 'Father' and 'Son', nor the metaphor of procreation which they imply, for the *Thalia* speaks of the Father's 'begetting' (γεννᾶν, τεκνοποιεῖν, ibid. 256–7); but he wished to define their sense. The only acceptable safeguard, he considered, was the proviso that the Son originated from the Father at a moment (though not in time) and by an act of will which had no association with division or change.

It was in some such circumstances that the phrase 'from the Father's substance' (ἐκ τῆς οὐσίας τοῦ πατρός) attracted the criticism of the Arian party. With slight variations this phrase occurs five times in the letter of Eusebius of Nicomedia to Paulinus, a document which became something of an Arian classic. It was largely reproduced in Latin by the Arian Candidus,[11] and the full Greek text is given by Theodoret. Further, there seems a reasonable probability that it was this letter which was strongly criticized from the Nicene side, and defended by Asterius, who was then himself attacked by Marcellus;[12] this in turn induced Eusebius of Caesarea to write against Marcellus, some years after the original letter was written. Indeed it is not impossible that the letter in question was read at Nicaea, and provided a reason for including the controversial phrase ἐκ τῆς οὐσίας in the Creed itself.

Eusebius begins, much like Arius, by protesting against any doctrine of 'two ingenerates, or of one divided into two or suffering any bodily change' (οὔτε γὰρ δύο ἀγέννητα ἀκηκόαμεν οὔτε ἓν εἰς δύο διῃρημένον οὐδὲ σωματικόν τι πεπονθὸς μεμαθήκαμεν);

---

[11] It has been suggested that Candidus is a literary fiction devised by Victorinus; so M. Meslin, *RHR* 164 (1963), 96–100; P. Nautin, in *L'Homme devant Dieu* (*Mélanges Lubac* iii), 309–20; M. Simonetti, *Orpheus* 10 (1963), 151–7; and P. Hadot, who was formerly doubtful, now agrees (*Marius Victorinus* (1971), 272). But there is some force in the argument of A. Ziegenaus that the letter of Candidus is more coherent than Victorinus' reply to it; see his *Die trinitarische Ausprägung*, 74, n. 98; and Hadot himself admits its merits, op. cit., 274. Meslin's arguments go to show that Candidus, if real, is not one of the common run of Arianizing Western churchmen, but a philosophical colleague of Victorinus who has adopted Christianity in its Arian form. But this remains a possibility; in which case Victorinus has excerpted his second letter. For the diffusion of Eusebius' letter, cf. Meslin, 98; Nautin, 312–13; Simonetti, 156, who cites E. Schwartz, *Zur Gesch. des Ath.*, 118 ff.

[12] Eusebius, *c. Marc.* i. 4 (Klostermann, 19–20).

rather, there is One who is ingenerate, and One who is truly generated by him, and not from his *ousia*, in no way partaking of the ingenerate nature or being 'from' his *ousia* (ἀλλ' ἐν μὲν τὸ ἀγέννητον, ἐν δὲ τὸ ὑπ' αὐτοῦ ἀληθῶς καὶ οὐκ ἐκ τῆς οὐσίας αὐτοῦ γεγονός, καθόλου τῆς φύσεως τῆς ἀγεννήτου μὴ μετέχον ἢ ὂν ἐκ τῆς οὐσίας αὐτοῦ). The two clauses containing *ousia* seem to make two slightly different points: the first is clearly concerned with the origin of the second Person, the second may be intended rather to reinforce the statement that he does not share the nature of the ingenerate first principle. A little later Eusebius quotes Proverbs 8: 22–3, 25: 'the Lord created me the beginning of his ways . . . before the age he founded me . . . before all the hills he begets me.' He argues that the terms 'created' and 'founded' show that the second Person did not proceed 'out of him, that is, from him, as a part of him, or from an outflow of his *ousia*' (εἰ δὲ ἐξ αὐτοῦ, τουτέστιν ἀπ' αὐτοῦ ἦν ὡς ἂν μέρος αὐτοῦ ἢ ἐξ ἀπορροίας τῆς οὐσίας, οὐκ ἂν ἔτι κτιστὸν ἢ θεμελιωτὸν εἶναι ἐλέγετο); while the term 'begets' cannot imply any 'origin from the paternal *ousia* or sameness of nature derived from him' since it is applied to beings who are wholly unlike him in nature, e.g. to men. (The excluded possibility is, ὡς ἂν ἐκ τῆς οὐσίας τῆς πατρικῆς αὐτὸν γεγονότα καὶ ἔχειν ἐκ τούτου τὴν ταυτότητα τῆς φύσεως.) A little later he declares, 'For nothing is from his *ousia*, but all things coming into being by his will, each one exists just as it came into being.'

It is not easy to determine the sense which Eusebius gives to *ousia*, since in all the five cases we have noticed it is used to express a view which he condemns. Further, his two main axioms, namely the uniqueness and the immutability of God, seem to call for slightly different exegesis of the phrase ἐκ τῆς οὐσίας. God's *uniqueness* would be infringed (*per impossibile*) by the mere existence of an exactly similar being, another first principle, who would be ἐκ τῆς οὐσίας in a purely formal sense, as *sharing* his unique position of primacy; his *immutability* would suffer if such a being *issued from* him by some quasi-physical process of generation involving change or loss (σωματικόν τι πεπονθός, ἀπόρροια). The only time Eusebius himself uses *ousia*, it seems to mean 'nature', 'rank', or 'metaphysical status'; he speaks of the Lord as 'created and founded and generated in respect of his *ousia* and his immutable and ineffable nature and likeness to his maker' (κτιστὸν

. . . καὶ θεμελιωτὸν καὶ γεννητὸν τῇ οὐσίᾳ καὶ τῇ ἀναλλοιώτῳ καὶ ἀρρήτῳ φύσει, etc., § 4). Eusebius is clearly expressing a fairly radical form of Arian doctrine, and makes some points which we have no direct evidence for attributing to Arius himself; and it may be significant that he nowhere refers directly to 'the Father' or 'the Son'; but even he stops well short of the later Anomoean position; the second Person, though 'wholly distinct in nature and power', has come into being 'for perfect likeness to the disposition and power of his maker' (πρὸς τελείαν ὁμοιότητα διαθέσεώς τε καὶ δυνάμεως τοῦ πεποιηκότος, § 3); and if it seems disconcerting that the theme of perfect likeness is treated only prospectively, as if it were a task to be fulfilled by the Logos, we still cannot say that Eusebius ranks him with the created order; he is in no way comparable with men, who are 'in all respects unlike him in nature'.

To trace the history of the phrase ἐκ τῆς οὐσίας it is necessary to go back about a hundred years. Tertullian was possibly the first Christian writer to adopt it, though Irenaeus uses the concept of emissions or emanations from a divine spiritual stuff, in comments on Valentinian theology. Tertullian, however, boldly appropriates the Valentinian term 'projection' (προβολή: *adv. Prax.* 8) and declares: 'I derive the Son from no other source than from the Father's substance' (*filium non aliunde deduco, sed de substantia patris*, ibid. 4). Tertullian pictures God as a mind which contains within itself the Word as its 'plan' or 'thought'; yet this latter is sufficiently distinct to be addressed as a 'partner in dialogue' (ibid. 5). At the moment of creation, however, this thought is uttered, and becomes *sermo*, spoken word, in place of *ratio*, and now for the first time can be regarded as 'Son' in the full sense. So Tertullian applies the text 'This day have I begotten thee'; he comments, *haec est nativitas perfecta sermonis*, ibid. 7, an expression that brings together the two concepts of spoken word and begotten Son; and adds that He is not (as '*sermo*' might suggest) a mere utterance, or a mere physical effect, but ranks as a substance himself, proceeding from the substance of the Father: *nec carere substantia quod de tanta substantia processit et tantas substantias fecit.*

Novatian follows Tertullian fairly closely, making a more guarded use of the controversial term 'emission', and teaching that the Word–Son was born from the Father 'when he willed' and in substantial form (*ex quo, quando ipse voluit, sermo filius natus est; qui non . . . in tono coactae de visceribus vocis accipitur, sed in substantia prolatae a deo virtutis agnoscitur, Trin. 31*); he calls him 'a divine substance coming forth from the Father', 'God from God' (ibid.).

Origen differs from these Latin fathers in holding that the Son is eternally generated, and in showing more concern about possible materializing interpretations of the term 'generation'; this leads him to make constant use of the alternative metaphor of an act of will proceeding from the mind, even though this metaphor calls for the further corrective that God's Word and Wisdom is to be understood as a substantive second being, not a mere utterance or act. He also shows a marked interest in the great metaphors of Wisdom 7, especially 'breath', 'radiance', 'image' (ἀτμίς, ἀπαύγασμα, εἰκών, vv. 25–6), which suggest an intangible and mysterious process of generation and avoid the distasteful suggestion of a physical 'effluent' (ἀπόρροια, ibid.).

Both Tertullian and Origen seem to switch rather abruptly between the metaphors of proclamation and procreation; and it may be worth remarking that in the light of Stoic theory the contrast between them would be less extreme than it seems to ourselves. Both writers express the view that the emission of human seed is of itself sufficient to release a fully individualized offspring in germinal form, which only needs shelter and nourishment within the womb. Procreation would then be in principal asexual; would be, like speech, an activity of the 'spirit' in man; and the seed itself, embodying a 'logos', was sometimes thought to proceed direct from the brain by way of the spinal cord.[13] Both Tertullian and Origen of course insist that these human processes offer only the remotest analogy for divine realities; my point is simply that in their thinking the two alternative bases for analogy were less widely separated than they are for us.

I have called attention to the physical associations of the word

[13] Male seed alone sufficient: Aeschylus, *Eum.* 658–61; Sphaerus in D. L. vii. 159; Censorinus, *de Die Nat.* 5. 4; Hebrews 7: 10; Hippolytus vi. 17. 5; Origen, *in Joh.* xx, *init.*; Tertullian, *de Anima*, 27. 8, and J. H. Waszink's Commentary, 324–6.

Seed embodies a 'logos': Philo, *Leg.* 54–5; Origen, loc. cit.; Arius Didymus in Eusebius, *PE* xv. 20, cf. *SVF* i. 128.

Originates in the brain: Alcmaeon acc. to Aetius (Diels, *DG*, p. 417), but cf. Censorinus, loc. cit.; Plato, *Timaeus*, 73 cd, 91 ab; [Hippocrates], *de Genitura*, 1 (ed. Littré, vii. 470); [Galen], *de Defin. Med.* 439 (Diels, *Vors.*⁶ ii. 167); Hippolytus, *Ref.* iv. 51. 10–12, v. 17. 11–12.

'effluence', and indeed 'substance' itself, in order to illustrate Origen's hesitation over accepting the phrase 'from God's substance'. In his *Commentary on St. John* (xx. 157–8) he suggests that it could imply the Father's losing some of his substance in procreation: 'Others explained "I came forth from God" as "I was begotten of God", and these would consequently say that the Son was begotten from the Father's substance, as if God were diminished and lacking in the substance which he had before, when begetting the Son, as in the case of those who are pregnant.' (This is clearly one of the points which Eusebius takes up.) In the *de Principiis* again Origen condemns all materializing notions of the Son's generation, preferring to speak of 'will from mind', though in fact there is a substantive reality, *virtus altera in sua proprietate subsistens*, not a mere act of will (i. 2. 9); but so far as I can discover, he does not use the phrase 'from the substance' in this work. But there are at least three passages elsewhere which accept it. In fr. 9 of the *Commentary on St. John* it is used to emphasize the contrast between the Son and the creatures; these have their being 'from God', ἐκ θεοῦ, but the Son is παρὰ πάτρος, 'from the Father's side'; so 'The phrase " As of the only-begotten from the Father's side" (John 1 : 14) indicates that the Son is from the substance of the Father; for none of the creatures is from the Father's side, but they have their being from God through the Word.' In the *Commentary on Romans* (iv. 10, *PG* 14. 998A) he argues that Christ's death is a proof of divine goodness: *Nisi enim esset hic ex illa veniens substantia*, 'For unless he had come from that substance, and been the Son of that Father [who is good], he could not have shown such great goodness towards us.' These two passages are noteworthy as exhibiting an apparently spontaneous and unforced use of the phrase; in the *Commentary on Hebrews*, as quoted by Pamphilus, a slightly more apologetic note appears when Origen cites Wisdom 7 : 25 and explains that the Scripture uses corporeal metaphors to express spiritual truths: he concludes, *sic et sapientia ex eo procedens, ex ipsa Dei substantia generatur*. There follows immediately the reference to the term *homoousios* quoted above.

Not unnaturally, the followers of Origen were not agreed as to the value of the phrase 'from God's substance'. Athanasius was able to quote in its favour a passage from Theognostus where the writer clearly alludes to Wisdom 7 : 25–6 so as to show that the

Son is not alien to the Father's substance, but emanates from it without causing any division or alteration:

οὐκ ἐξωθέν τίς ἐστιν ἐφευρεθεῖσα ἡ τοῦ υἱοῦ οὐσία οὐδὲ ἐκ μὴ ὄντων ἐπεισήχθη, ἀλλὰ ἐκ τῆς τοῦ πατρὸς οὐσίας ἔφυ ὡς τοῦ φωτὸς τὸ ἀπαύγασμα, ὡς ὕδατος ἀτμίς . . . καὶ οὔτε . . . αὐτός ἐστιν ὁ πατὴρ οὔτε ἀλλότριος, ἀλλὰ ἀπόρροια τῆς τοῦ πατρὸς οὐσίας, οὐ μερισμὸν ὑπομεινάσης τῆς τοῦ πατρὸς οὐσίας. ὡς γὰρ μένων ὁ ἥλιος ὁ αὐτὸς οὐ μειοῦται ταῖς ἐκχεομέναις ὑπ' αὐτοῦ αὐγαῖς, οὕτως οὐδὲ ἡ οὐσία τοῦ πατρὸς ἀλλοίωσιν ὑπέμεινεν εἰκόνα ἑαυτῆς ἔχουσα τὸν υἱόν. (Decr. 25.)

It would perhaps be unwise to infer too much about Theognostus' general standpoint from this single passage; indeed Athanasius' reference to his 'previous discussion by way of an exercise' suggests that the Arians also could invoke his authority,[14] as they certainly did that of Dionysius. On the other hand Pamphilus, who quotes the passage from Origen in support of the *homoousion*, seems to have no hesitation about the phrase 'from God's substance'; his comment is: *Satis manifeste, ut opinor, et valde evidenter ostensum est, quod Filium Dei de ipsa Dei substantia natum dixerit, id est* ὁμοούσιον, etc.

Eusebius of Caesarea gives us much more abundant material for study, having left us at least one major work on dogmatic theology, the *Demonstratio Evangelica*, which was completed before the Council of Nicaea, and largely written before the Arian controversy attracted attention. His teaching on the Son's origin is complex and not entirely consistent. He does not, like Origen, uphold his eternal generation, but regards him as having originated by an act of the Father's will, so that the Father is in existence before the Son (ὁ δὲ πατὴρ προϋπάρχει τοῦ υἱοῦ καὶ τῆς γενέσεως προϋφέστηκεν, *DE* iv. 3. 5); on the other hand he places the Son's generation 'before the ages', and admits—quite shortly after the passage just quoted—that he was *not* 'at some times non-existent, and originating later, but existing and pre-existing before eternal times' (οὐ χρόνοις μέν τισιν οὐκ ὄντα, ὕστερον δέ ποτε γεγονότα, ἀλλὰ πρὸ χρόνων αἰωνίων ὄντα καὶ προόντα, ibid. 13). He constantly emphasizes that the *manner* of the Son's generation

---

[14] Cf. Photius, *Cod.* 106; for 'exercise' (γυμνασία) cf. *c.* 27, on Origen, and the rather similar defence of Marcellus quoted by Athanasius in *Apol. c. Ar.* 47. The source is Plato's *Parmenides*, 135 cd, 136 a. Origen's usage is well discussed by F. H. Kettler, *Der ursprüngliche Sinn der Dogmatik des Origenes*, 13, n. 65; 17, n. 80; 37, n. 159.

surpasses our comprehension, and is decidedly circumspect in his use of the traditional images; in one passage he points out that a ray of light is no true parallel, being coexistent with its source and proceding from it involuntarily (ibid. 5); rather strangely, he takes refuge in the alternative metaphor of a fragrant odour (ibid. 9).

In the course of these discussions on the Son's origin we find a list of objections to materializing theories, which occurs several times in almost standardized form:

iv. 3. 11: οὔτι πω κατὰ στέρησιν ἢ μείωσιν ἢ τομὴν ἢ διαίρεσιν ('not by deprivation or diminution or severance or division').

ibid. 13: οὐ κατὰ διάστασιν ἢ τομὴν ἢ διαίρεσιν ἐκ τῆς τοῦ πατρὸς οὐσίας προβεβλημένον.

iv. 15. 52: οὐ κατὰ προβολὴν ἢ κατὰ διαίρεσιν ἢ τομὴν ἢ μείωσιν . . .

v. 1. 8: μήτε κατὰ προβολὴν μήτε κατὰ διάστασιν ἢ διαίρεσιν ἢ μείωσιν ἢ τομήν . . .

ibid. 9: μηδὲ . . . οὐσίαν ἐξ οὐσίας κατὰ πάθος ἢ διαίρεσιν μεριστὴν καὶ χωριστὴν ἐκ τοῦ πατρὸς προεληλυθέναι τὸν υἱόν.[15]

It will be seen that the phrase ἐκ τῆς οὐσίας, or its near equivalent, occurs twice over in this list of condemned phrases. But a little later, Eusebius embodies it in a cautiously worded positive statement. Beginning from the familiar text 'Who shall explain his generation?' he continues: 'But if anyone ventures to go further and compare what is totally inconceivable with visible and corporeal examples, perhaps he might say that the Son came forth from the unoriginate nature and ineffable substance of the Father (ἐκ τῆς τοῦ πατρὸς ἀγενήτου φύσεως καὶ τῆς ἀνεκφράστου οὐσίας) like some fragrance and ray of light . . .', v. 1. 18; but he almost immediately points out the limitations of all such metaphors, and once again associates the phrase 'from the substance' with the notion of change and division: οὐδὲ γὰρ ἐξ οὐσίας τῆς ἀγενήτου κατά τι πάθος ἢ διαίρεσιν οὐσιωμένος, οὐδέ γε ἀνάρχως συνυφέστηκεν τῷ πατρί etc., ibid. 20. It must be said that Eusebius looks on the phrase 'from the substance' with marked disfavour, even though he does not reject it absolutely, like his namesake of

---

[15] These terms are taken up in Eusebius' *Letter to his Diocese* (Opitz, *Urk.* 22), in § 12: οὔτε γὰρ κατὰ διαίρεσιν τῆς οὐσίας οὔτε κατὰ ἀποτομήν, ἀλλ' οὐδὲ κατά τι πάθος ἢ τροπὴν ἢ ἀλλοίωσιν τῆς τοῦ πατρὸς οὐσίας τε καὶ δυνάμεως. In § 7 he attributes rather similar disclaimers to Constantine, and a similar list reappears in *ET* i. 12. 9.

Nicomedia; so that his reluctant acceptance of it at Nicaea has some support in what he had previously written.

What then was the sense given to the phrase at the Council of Nicaea? We have noted one or two passages in which Eusebius of Nicomedia connects it with the notion of 'partaking of the Father's essence'; but the vast majority of the texts examined above and elsewhere,[16] including those from Athanasius' *de Decretis*, indicate that the phrase was *not* designed to make the directly ontological statement about the Son, that he is 'of' the *ousia* (i.e. rank, dignity, status) which is proper to the Father; but rather to show that he derives from the Father by a process comparable to natural generation, as opposed to some process of 'making', like that of God's created works. The setting of the phrase in the Creed, as appended to 'begotten of the Father, only-begotten', confirms this estimate; (and if μονογενῆ were given the weaker sense, 'unique', this would hardly be confirmed by a phrase which suggested that the Son was ontologically *equal* to the Father, however true this may be). Granted the above interpretation, it can readily be admitted that the phrase does also, though indirectly, elucidate the Son's ontological status: he is equal to, and one with, his Father as a true natural son, and not just a creature adopted or dignified with the name of Son.

(ii) *Not 'of a Different Substance'*

The term *ousia* reappears in the anathema directed against 'those who assert that (the Son of God) is of a different hypostasis or substance', ἐξ ἑτέρας ὑποστάσεως ἢ οὐσίας φάσκοντας εἶναι. In this case it is important to pose the question: 'Can we determine precisely what the doctrine is which this phrase is meant to condemn?' It is of course possible that it was left deliberately vague, or that its sense was never properly clarified in discussion; but if it was intended to bear a precise sense, we shall have to attend not only to the striking fact that *hypostasis* and *ousia* are used as synonyms,[17] but to the force of the preposition ἐξ.[18]

---

[16] See e.g. I. Ortiz de Urbina, *El Símbolo Niceno*, 133–40.

[17] This point is almost universally agreed today, though it was long disputed, chiefly on the authority of St. Basil, who himself distinguished between *hypostasis* and *ousia*, and read back this distinction into the Nicene formula; see e.g. his *Ep.* 214. The discussion in A. Robertson's *Athanasius* (*NPNF*), 77–82, is still instructive.

[18] Sounded like its Latin equivalent *ex*, but spelt ἐκ before consonants.

There are two possibilities here. The first is that generally adopted. We can translate, as above, 'the Son is of a different hypostasis' etc. This is essentially a qualitative description; so construed, the phrase is nearly equivalent to ἑτέρας ὑποστάσεως etc. without the ἐξ; or if we retain and emphasize the ἐξ, and perhaps translate it '*from* another hypostasis' etc., the relationship expressed is a purely formal one, such as the individual has to the species 'from' which it is derived by adding individualizing characteristics, on the common Stoic theory. This is tantamount to condemning the doctrine that the Son *is* another hypostasis, in one possible meaning of that phrase; it can be taken as a lightly disguised attack on the doctrine of three hypostases.

To be strictly accurate, this needs some qualification, since 'another hypostasis' *need* not indicate anything more than distinct individual existence. A son is 'another hypostasis' (ἑτέρα ὑπόστασις) compared with his father; but he would not be described as '*of* another hypostasis' (ἑτέρας ὑποστάσεως), since the genitive case here indicates a distinction *between* the individual and his hypostasis, and the latter term thus naturally takes a generalized sense, e.g. 'physical substance' or possibly 'nature'; in these senses the son is not 'of another hypostasis' compared with his father. The description would apply rather to a being such as a Greek hero, who had a god for his father, and differed from him in nature and constitution. But even the hero would not be described as '*from* another substance' (ἐξ ἑτέρας ὑποστάσεως); this third phrase would aptly qualify a bastard, or a creature like Pygmalion's lady, who was made *by* the sculptor *from* wax or bronze.

But it is not to be expected that the fathers of Nicaea attended to these exact distinctions. The real difficulty with the purely qualitative interpretation is that it breaks the analogy between the phrases ἐξ ἑτέρας ὑποστάσεως ἢ οὐσίας and ἐκ τῆς οὐσίας τοῦ πατρός; indeed the preposition ἐκ (ἐξ) is used five times in the Creed, and consistently suggests an actual or personal derivation: γεννηθέντα ἐκ τοῦ πατρὸς μονογενῆ, τουτέστιν ἐκ τῆς οὐσίας τοῦ πατρός, θεὸν ἐκ θεοῦ, φῶς ἐκ φωτός, θεὸν ἀληθινὸν ἐκ θεοῦ ἀληθινοῦ. It seems reasonable to translate this (with Dr. J. N. D. Kelly) 'begotten from the Father, only-begotten, that is, from the substance of the Father, God from God, light from light, true God from true God'. I shall therefore explore the other possibility,

namely that the preposition retains its full significance throughout, and that the view condemned is that the Son is *derived from*
some other hypostasis or ousia. What could be the relevance of
such a pronouncement in the circumstances of the Council?

We learn from Tertullian that Hermogenes suggested three
possible theories of the origin of the universe: either God made
it from himself, or from nothing, or from something (other than
himself): *aut deum de semetipso fecisse cuncta, aut de nihilo, aut de
aliquo* (*adv. Herm.* 2. 1). Irenaeus envisages the same three possibilities when he says that man cannot make anything out of
nothing, but only out of material lying ready to hand; but God
devised his own material for his creation (ii. 10. 4, Hv. i. 274).
And in Methodius we find a Valentinian speaker discussing three
possible theories of the origin of matter; it comes either 'from
something eternally coexistent with God' or 'from himself alone'
or else (which is impossible) 'from nothing' ((i) ἔκ τινος συνόντος
ἀεὶ τῷ θεῷ (ii) ἢ ἐξ αὐτοῦ καὶ μόνου (iii) ἢ ἐξ οὐκ ὄντων: *Autex.* ii. 9,
p. 149).[19]

We seem here to be in the presence of a recognized cosmological
scheme; and if we revert to the well-known passage quoted by
Athanasius from Theognostus, it will appear that he has simply
adapted this scheme for his discussion of the origin of the divine
Son; thus the Son's being (i) is not introduced from some outside
source, (ii) nor produced from nothing, but (iii) sprang from the
Father's substance:

(i) οὐκ ἔξωθέν τίς ἐστιν ἐφευρεθεῖσα ἡ τοῦ υἱοῦ οὐσία,
(ii) οὐδὲ ἐκ μὴ ὄντων ἐπεισήχθη,
(iii) ἀλλ' ἐκ τῆς τοῦ πατρὸς οὐσίας ἔφυ (Ath., *Decr.* 25).

Theognostus will naturally have had the cosmological scheme in
mind, since his *first* book actually included a cosmological discussion directed against the theory that matter is coeternal with
God (Photius, loc. cit.).

Arius must certainly have read Theognostus, and so could
have known the christological version of this scheme. We may
also assume that he rejected the third of Theognostus' three possibilities, as Eusebius of Nicomedia certainly did. He accepted the
second, which Theognostus denied; so the way was open for
him to agree with Theognostus in rejecting the first. And this is

[19] Cf. also Clement, *Strom.* ii. 74. 1.

what in effect we find. In his letter to Eusebius of Nicomedia the same three possibilities are envisaged. This appears most clearly near the end: 'We are persecuted because we said, he is from nothing. But we said this because he is neither a part of God nor (derived) from any subject' (διωκόμεθα καὶ ὅτι εἴπομεν, ἐξ οὐκ ὄντων ἔστιν. οὕτως δὲ εἴπομεν, καθότι οὐδὲ μέρος θεοῦ ἐστιν οὐδὲ ἐξ ὑποκειμένου τινός). In his more conciliatory letter to Alexander the denial of a quasi-material derivation from God is somewhat amplified (*Urk.* 6, § 3) and the doctrine that the Son is 'from nothing' is tactfully toned down; it is represented by the phrase 'he was not before his generation' (οὐκ ἦν πρὸ τοῦ γεννηθῆναι) and others like it. The third possibility is represented by the proposition, for which he claims Alexander's agreement, that the Son 'was not previously existing and afterwards generated or further established as Son' (οὐδὲ τὸν ὄντα πρότερον, ὕστερον γεννηθέντα ἢ ἐπικτισθέντα εἰς υἱόν); this makes a somewhat different theological point, and could stand as an acceptable criticism of theologies like that of Tertullian, for whom the Word became Son at the creation, or of Marcellus, for whom he became Son only at the Incarnation.

The discussion so far will have suggested a conclusion which some scholars may not welcome; namely, that this Nicene anathema did not bear on the Arian position, since it condemned a view which Arius himself rejected (or at least, was able to disown). But there is another point to be considered. We cannot assume that all parties to the debate kept the three possibilities distinctly in mind. Arius, I think, may have done so; but can we say the same for Athanasius? He certainly attacks the Arian view that the Logos came into being 'from not-being' (ἐξ οὐκ ὄντων), and argues (with some injustice to Arius himself, but perhaps legitimately against his adherents) that this puts the generation of the Logos wholly on a par with the creation of the world. And of course he whole-heartedly accepts the doctrine of creation *ex nihilo*. But his main concern is to establish his positive doctrine that the Son is uniquely generated 'from the substance' of the Father—as is well known, this phrase is constantly repeated in the *Orationes*, where the *homoousios* itself occurs only once; and he lays such weight on the contrast between this view and any alternative that the differences between the various rejected views receive little emphasis. In fact we can find the Son's generation contrasted with at least three possibilities, natural human generation, human workmanship, and the divine workmanship in the creation. Athanasius tells us that the divine Son is not a natural son, nor an artefact, nor a creature; but he does not make it clear that the first two possibilities would entail his coming into being 'from some other substance', and only the third would make him originate 'from not-being'.

Associated with this unspeculative approach to the problem, I think we can detect a certain imprecision in Athanasius' concept of creation itself. For one thing, he allows himself to use the verb κτίζειν, to create, not only of the primary act of creation *ex nihilo*, but for the subsequent stages of creation. Thus he can write (*Decr.* 10) that 'men were created from matter, and passible matter at that' (οἱ μὲν γὰρ ἐξ ὕλης καὶ ταύτης οὔσης παθητικῆς ἐκτίσθησαν); so that verbally at least he allows creation 'from something'. More important perhaps is the fact that even where Athanasius is professedly expounding creation *ex nihilo*, he seems unable to visualize the divine action in its authentic sense, so that things simply begin to be at the divine word. He teaches that God calls things into being out of not-being;[20] but the latter is conceived, not as sheer nothingness, but as a sort of limbo of unreal being. This appears clearly in *c. Ar.* ii. 64, where he argues that in the beginning 'the Logos came down in condescension to the things that were to be (?) so that they might be able to come into being ... condescending in fatherly kindness he took hold of them, grasped them, and brought them into being' (συγκαταβέβηκε τοῖς γενητοῖς, ἵνα γένεσθαι ταῦτα δυνηθῇ ... φιλανθρωπίᾳ πατρικῇ συγκαταβὰς ἀντελάβετο, καὶ κρατήσας αὐτὰ εἰς οὐσίαν ἤνεγκε). Beginning to be is for Athanasius a kind of change;[21] indeed in his time it could be stated as a commonplace that *omnis generatio mutatio quaedam est*.[22]

It seems, then, as if Athanasius has not grasped the point of the three alternatives mentioned by Theognostus; he has read the passage as if the first two were merely alternative expressions of the same possibility. His doctrine that the Son is from the

---

[20] See e.g. *c. Ar.* ii. 22: τῶν μὴ ὄντων καὶ καλουμένων, cf. Rom. 4:17.

[21] Cf. *c. Ar.* i. 36: τὰ γενητὰ ... ὅτι οὐκ ὄντα γίνεται, ἀλλοιουμένην ἔχει τὴν φύσιν. Athanasius here follows Origen (*Princ.* ii. 9. 2 init.). Cf. also *de Inc.* 4. 5.

[22] Candidus, *de Generatione Divina*, init. (Marius Victorinus, *CSEL* 83, p. 1). Cf. Aristotle *de Gen. et Corr.* i. 1–4, and Gregory of Nyssa, *Or. Cat.* 6 (*PG* 45. 28D), 21 (ibid. 57D–60); *Hom. Op.* 16 (ibid. 184CD).

Father's substance is not contrasted with two clearly stated alternatives, but with a number of possibilities vaguely indicated by the phrase 'from not-being', or by the equally ill-defined term ἔξωθεν 'from outside', which can apply to human purchases (*c. Ar.* i. 26) as well as to divine creations. Origen shows a rather similar failure to distinguish between 'from something else' and 'from nothing' at *Princ.* iv. 4. 1 : *Non enim dicimus, sicut haeretici putant, partem aliquam substantiae dei in filium versam, aut ex nullis substantibus filium procreatum a patre, id est extra substantiam suam, ut fuerit aliquando quando non fuerit.*

So far as I can discover, Athanasius never comments *expressis verbis* on the Nicene anathema. He may possibly have it in mind in *Decr.* 27, but does not follow its wording exactly; if we follow the manuscript reading and discard (at * *) Opitz's additions of ἐξ and γέννημα, for which I can see no justification, the allusion is : περὶ δὲ τοῦ ἀϊδίως συνεῖναι τὸν λόγον τῷ πατρὶ καὶ μὴ * ἑτέρας οὐσίας καὶ ὑποστάσεως, ἀλλὰ τῆς τοῦ πατρὸς ἴδιον * αὐτὸν εἶναι;[23] and the passages he quotes from Origen by way of comment relate to the Son's coeternity and status as image of the Father's substance, without any direct reference to alternative theories of his derivation. He follows the wording of the Nicene anathema rather more closely in *Syn.* 40 and 41 ; but in this case he is referring to pronouncements from the 'semi-Arian' side which he has previously quoted, and which endorse it more or less verbatim, as we shall see.

There are moreover some passages in which Athanasius condemns the view that the Son became Son by some form of promotion on account of his merits, a view which he associates with Paul of Samosata. Thus at *Syn.* 45 he writes : 'unless Christ has become God from man' (εἰ μὴ ἐξ ἀνθρώπου γέγονεν ὁ χριστὸς θεός), reproducing what he took to be Paul's argument. This context makes it unlikely that 'from man' is being suggested as an exegesis of 'from some other substance', since Athanasius is arguing that Paul's heresy was different from that of Arius and so justified other tactics (though in other contexts he sometimes assimilates the two heresies) ; and of course this erroneous view is quite distinct from the form of 'promotion theory' which Arius himself condemns, namely that the *Word* became Son by

---

[23] 'But as to the Word's eternal coexistence with the Father, and his being not of another substance and reality, but belonging to the Father's . . .'

some process of 'further creation' or 'establishment'. At *Syn.* 34
Athanasius argues that if the other side do not accept the formula
'from God's substance' they must derive the Son 'from what attaches to God or resides in him' (ἐκ τῶν περὶ αὐτὸν ἢ τῶν ἐν
αὐτῷ), which he thinks would entail postulating qualities or
accidents in the Godhead. In this case he seems to be criticizing
yet another unsatisfactory view, namely that the Son is an image
of God's *power* and other attributes (cf. Origen, *in Joh.* xiii. 249,
Asterius, fr. 1 = Athan. *Syn.* 18, etc.) and not of his essence; he
does not here discuss the possibility of derivation from some other
substance. He reverts to this argument in *ad Afros*, 8–9, and condemns the doctrines that the Son is 'from man' (by promotion),
'from virtue' (i.e. on account of it), and 'from nothing' (as a
creature); but I cannot see that his argument rests on any clear
exegesis of the Nicene anathema.

The case is quite different if we turn to the 'conservative' pronouncements quoted by Athanasius himself. Our only contemporary comment on the Nicene Creed is the letter which Eusebius
of Caesarea addressed to his diocese to justify his subscription to
it.[24] Eusebius clearly alludes to the anathema when he explains
that the Son 'is not from some other hypostasis and substance,
but from the Father' (μὴ εἶναι ἐξ ἑτέρας τινὸς ὑποστάσεώς τε
καὶ οὐσίας, ἀλλ' ἐκ τοῦ πατρός); but this comment appears in a
paragraph in which Eusebius explains the sense in which he was
able to accept the term *homoousios*. This in itself is significant;
Eusebius distrusted this term, and his exegesis of it has often
been criticized;[25] but he seems to have found no difficulty in the
anathema, which he incorporates into his own explanation. And
the sense in which he understood the anathema is both logical in
itself and clearly detectable; the relevant sentence seems to fall
into two pairs of clauses, the first pair dealing with the Son's likeness to the Father, the second with his origin from the Father;
and it is in the latter context that the anathema is recalled.
Eusebius thus declares that the Son

  (i) is entirely unlike created beings
      but completely like the Father
  (ii) is not (derived) from some other hypostasis and substance
      but from the Father.

---

[24] Greek text in Opitz, *Urk.* 22; E.T. in J. Stevenson, *A New Eusebius*, 364 ff.
[25] See, e.g., F. L. Cross, *The Study of Athanasius*, 14.

(. . . τοῦ μηδεμίαν ἐμφέρειαν πρὸς τὰ γενητὰ κτίσματα τὸν υἱὸν
　　τοῦ θεοῦ φέρειν,
　　μόνῳ δὲ τῷ πατρὶ τῷ γεγεννηκότι κατὰ πάντα τρόπον
　　ἀφωμοιῶσθαι
καὶ μὴ εἶναι ἐξ ἑτέρας τινὸς ὑποστάσεώς τε καὶ οὐσίας
　　ἀλλ᾽ ἐκ τοῦ πατρός.)

Construing the phrase in this way, Eusebius is fully entitled to
maintain his opinion that the Son *is* another hypostasis, so that
there are two, and indeed three, divine hypostases; these phrases,
which became the common expression of Eastern trinitarianism,
are still upheld in his later works, the *contra Marcellum* and the
Ecclesiastical Theology; on the other hand he seems to avoid the
phrase ἑτέρας ὑποστάσεως (or οὐσίας), '*of* another substance',
with its suggestion of qualitative distinction; and, so far as I can
discover, he does not again allude to the wording of the anathema
itself.

We can, however, find the same exegesis in the 'conservative'
credal statements quoted by Athanasius in his *de Synodis*. Beginning with the Fourth Creed of Antioch, we find a series of
formulae which manifest a desire to reach agreement with the
West,[26] and *inter alia* conclude with a series of anathematisms
which fairly closely resemble those of Nicaea. In those appended
to the Fourth Creed of Antioch, the phrase ἐξ ἑτέρας ὑποστάσεως
is clearly incorporated into the scheme of three alternatives which
we have been tracing: 'But those who say (i) that the Son is from
nothing, or (ii) is from another hypostasis, and (iii) not from
God . . .' (τοὺς δὲ λέγοντας ἐξ οὐκ ὄντων τὸν υἱὸν ἢ ἐξ ἑτέρας
ὑποστάσεως, καὶ μὴ ἐκ τοῦ θεοῦ . . .), Ath. *Syn.* 25. This same
formula is repeated, with additions, in the Eastern Creed of
Sardica (Philippopolis)[27] and in the so-called 'Macrostich' or
'Long-lined' Creed (Ath. *Syn.* 26); and here it is followed by an
amplified explanation: 'For it is not safe to say that the Son is
(derived) from what is not . . . nor yet from some other substance
pre-existing alongside the Father; but from God alone, etc.'
(Οὔτε γὰρ ἐξ οὐκ ὄντων τὸν υἱὸν λέγειν ἀσφαλές . . . οὔτε μὴν ἐξ
ἑτέρας τινὸς ὑποστάσεως παρὰ τὸν πατέρα προϋποκειμένης· ἀλλ᾽ ἐκ
μόνου τοῦ θεοῦ etc.) In this case the threefold cosmological
scheme is easily recognizable, and the wording closely resembles

---

[26] Cf. Kelly, *Creeds*, 273, 277, 279–80, 282.
[27] Two Latin versions are given by Hilary, in *Frag. Hist.* 3 and *de Synodis*, 34.

that of Irenaeus quoted above (p. 235); its theological intention is presumably to exclude any doctrine that the Son is part of the created order, whether on the orthodox (and Arian) view that creation is from nothing, or on the Platonic and Gnostic-Christian view that it derives from some substance which coexists (or is coeternal) with God. The threefold pattern of anathematisms appears once again (though I think without relevant explanation) in the First Sirmian Creed (ibid. 27); after this it disappears from the series recorded by St. Athanasius as a result of the movement, which is characteristic of the so-called 'Blasphemy of Sirmium', to eliminate the whole terminology of substance.

In these documents, therefore, the phrase 'from another hypostasis' is given a precise explanation, clearly connected with the cosmological scheme which I have traced. The 'conservatives' did not mean to condemn the view that the Son is himself 'another hypostasis' beside the Father, since they themselves were still clearly attached to the doctrine of three hypostases, which they asserted almost verbatim in the Second Creed of Antioch, even though they thought it wise to surrender this phrase for diplomatic reasons in favour of the 'three realities and three persons' (τρία πράγματα καὶ τρία πρόσωπα) affirmed in the Macrostich. For this party, then, the phrase simply denies that the Son had an origin outside, or independent of, the Father; and I think I have shown that this rests on a tradition which was known at the time of Nicaea. It is tempting to go further, and argue that this interpretation of the Nicene phrasing is the correct one, and indicates the intentions of those who inserted the clause. But this goes beyond my submission; it seems to me all too likely that the phrase was inserted without any insistence on its exact exegesis, and that it was from the first understood in somewhat different senses by the various parties in the debate. The most I shall assert is that the 'conservative' interpretation has claims to be respected; it rests on a clear and continuous tradition, and should not be discounted as an attempt to evade the proper sense of the anathematism.

To say even this, of course, is to challenge the orthodox interpretation. Arius asserted with the greatest possible emphasis that the hypostases of the Father and Son are not only distinct, but unequal in dignity;[28] and conservative scholars have

[28] See especially the *Thalia* (Ath. *Syn.* 15), ll. 16–18 in Bardy, op. cit., 256.

understandably taken the Nicene anathema to be a direct attack on the Arian position. My own investigations lead to a rather different assessment. For why did not the Nicene fathers simply condemn the doctrine of unequal hypostases *expressis verbis*, instead of adopting the ambiguous phrase whose background I have attempted to trace? The answer, I think, must lie in the climate of contemporary opinion. It was clearly impracticable to condemn the doctrine of three *distinct* hypostases, which had widespread support in the East and is in fact approached by the language of Alexander himself;[29] it may well have been judged imprudent, in a brief credal formula, to rule out every hint of disparity; a course which could easily be criticized as infringing the Father's unique dignity as ultimate Source and suggesting an inadmissible concept of two Gods. Hence a more widely acceptable formula had to be found; one which Western theologians could develop in the sense defined by modern orthodoxy, but Eastern 'conservatives' could legitimately restrict. There is no need to question the wisdom of the Nicene fathers. But this formula of theirs was essentially a formula of compromise.

(iii) *'The Same in Substance'*

Finally we have to consider the term *homoousios* as it occurs in the Nicene Creed; what were its immediate antecedents, and what was its meaning? These two questions have been repeatedly discussed, but without reaching assured conclusions. Nor are the two questions inseparably connected; the notions of sameness and of substance are so extremely elusive that even if we could establish a clear conceptual scheme of possible meanings, it might fail to clarify the actual developments. There can be no presumption that a strenuous debate, in which personal and political factors played a part, was guided by considerations which strict logic would approve.

There is, moreover, too little trustworthy evidence for the use of the term in the years immediately preceding Nicaea. Scholars have therefore had to rely, partly on certain broad historical projections, partly on the reports of the Council presented by Eusebius and Athanasius; of whom the former has come under suspicion as offering a tendentious account of the proceedings,

[29] Below, p. 244.

designed to excuse his reluctant subscription, while the latter, whether or not he displays an opposing *Tendenz*, records his impressions of the Council after a lapse of twenty-five years.

There are, however, one or two pre-Nicene documents from the Arian side in which *homoousios* appears in a context which gives some reasonable clue to its meaning. The first is the confession of faith presented by Arius to Alexander, which is printed by Opitz as *Urkunde* 6. This takes the form of a credal statement, which however does not proceed beyond its christological section, but elaborates this in considerable detail. *Homoousios* is found here twice; and first in a section intended to clarify the sense in which the Father 'begot' (γεννήσαντα) the Son; certain opinions are set aside, as linked with acknowledged heretics, including the following:

> Not, as Valentinus stated, that the Father's offspring is an emission, nor, as Mani proposed, that the Father's offspring is a consubstantial part of him, nor as Sabellius spoke of a Son–Father, dividing the Monad. (. . . οὐδ' ὡς Οὐαλεντῖνος προβολὴν τὸ γέννημα τοῦ πατρὸς ἐδογμάτισεν, οὐδ' ὡς Μανιχαῖος μέρος ὁμοούσιον τοῦ πατρὸς τὸ γέννημα εἰσηγήσατο, οὐδ' ὡς Σαβέλλιος τὴν μονάδα διαιρῶν υἱοπάτορα εἶπεν.)

It seems plainly right to agree with H. Kraft[30] that the reference to these heretics is an artifice of controversy; so that for present purposes nothing is gained by investigating the actual opinions of Mani; though it might be worth considering what impressions of his doctrine are given in contemporary anti-Manichaean argument. Arius is pursuing a line of thought which is already well established in Origen, namely that the metaphor of paternity needs to be qualified in order to avoid the suggestion of a physical emission of substance, which would conflict with the doctrine of God as simple, incorporeal, and eternal. Without attempting to assemble all the evidence, we recall that the objection that such theories would make God *divisible* is clearly stated in Origen's *de Principiis*, i. 2. 6; *corporeal*, ibid. iv. 4. 1; and *changeable*, in his *Commentary on John*, xx. 157.

This impression of Arius' position is confirmed by the second appearance of *homoousios* in § 5:

> But if the phrase 'from Him' and 'from the belly' (Ps. 109: 3 LXX) and 'from the Father I came forth and am come' (John 8: 42) is

---

[30] 'ΟΜΟΟΥΣΙΟΣ', *ZKG* 66 (1954), 9.

interpreted by some as a part of Him that is consubstantial and as an emission, the Father will be composite and divisible and changeable and a body in their view . . . (εἰ δὲ τὸ "ἐξ αὐτοῦ" καὶ τὸ "ἐκ γαστρὸς" καὶ τὸ "ἐκ τοῦ πατρὸς ἐξῆλθον καὶ ἥκω" ὡς μέρος αὐτοῦ ὁμοουσίου καὶ ὡς προβολὴ ὑπό τινων νοεῖται, σύνθετος ἔσται ὁ πατὴρ καὶ διαιρετὸς καὶ τρεπτὸς καὶ σῶμα κατ' αὐτοὺς . . .)

Two comments may be added. First, Arius does not make the point that *homoousios* would preclude any proper distinction of the three divine Persons (*hypostaseis*, § 4). The necessity of this distinction can indeed hardly have been a point of conflict between Arius and Alexander, who comes very near to endorsing the phrase 'three *hypostaseis*' when he disclaims any suggestion that 'the natures that are two in *hypostasis* are one', *Urk.* 14, § 38. Arius no doubt refers to this mistake when he mentions the Sabellian theory of a 'Son–Father' (above); but it is not suggested that *homoousios* would encourage this mistake; on the contrary, Arius puts forward the puzzling objection that Sabellius' theory would involve 'dividing the monad', which I have briefly discussed elsewhere.[31]

Secondly, Arius does not, in this document, suggest that *homoousios* would preclude the proper distinction in rank and seniority which he wishes to uphold. This distinction is strongly pressed in §§ 3 and 4; but it is not closely associated with the criticism of *homoousios* which precedes and follows it. Arius' objections are based solely on what he thinks are its materializing implications.

The case is rather different when we come to consider the use of *homoousios* in Arius' *Thalia*, as reported by Athanasius, *Syn.* 15. In these verses there is no tendency to avoid the designations 'Father' and 'Son', and the metaphor of begetting (γεννᾶν, τεκνοποιεῖν); these occur fairly freely, along with more abstract terms like 'eternal' (ἀΐδιος, cf. ἄναρχος) and 'invisible'; but the immediate context in which *homoousios* is used is not the anti-materialist argument considered above, but rather the contention that the two persons must not be treated as equal; so Arius is reported as writing

'He has nothing that is proper to God personified in his proper being (?)

[31] 'The Platonism of Arius', *JTS*, n.s. 15 (1964), 18–19.

For he is not equal to him, nor consubstantial either'

(ἴδιον οὐδὲν ἔχει τοῦ θεοῦ καθ' ὑπόστασιν ἰδιότητος
οὐδὲ γάρ ἐστιν ἴσος, ἀλλ' οὐδὲ ὁμοούσιος αὐτῷ).

It seems unlikely that *homoousios* is here intended to introduce a new point (supposing, perhaps, that this was explained in some following lines which Athanasius has omitted). The more natural reading is that *homoousios* now suggests to Arius an inadmissible parity of esteem between Father and Son; and this is confirmed by a later line in which he says that

'The Father is foreign to the Son in substance, because He exists without beginning'

(ξένος τοῦ υἱοῦ κατ' οὐσίαν ὁ πατήρ, ὅτι ἄναρχος ὑπάρχει).

For what it is worth, Athanasius' selection of verses makes this follow immediately after an assertion that there is an infinite difference in glory between the three *hypostaseis*; Athanasius at least must have taken Arius to be objecting to *homoousios* on subordinationist principles.

There is one other pre-Nicene reference to *homoousios* from the Arian side; this occurs in a letter of Eusebius of Nicomedia, which was read out at the Council, and therefore must have been written somewhat earlier:[32] *Si 'verum' dei filium et 'increatum' dicimus,* ὁμοούσιον *cum patre incipimus confiteri* (Ambrose, *de Fide*, iii. 15 (125), Opitz, *Urk.* 21).

I have introduced quotation-marks, since without them it is not easy to understand Eusebius' objection to the phrase 'true Son of God'. I suspect that there is some allusion to the well-known doctrine that the Son is 'God', but not 'true God'; possibly *verum deum* would represent Eusebius' thought more clearly, even if it is not what Ambrose himself wrote. In any case it seems that Eusebius' objections are based on subordinationist principles, like the last-quoted passage from Arius; one should not represent the Son as equal to the Father.

We must now pass to consider the extremely difficult question of the meaning given to the term *homoousios* at the Council of Nicaea. The Council forms a natural watershed, in that it initiates a period in which the term began to come under much closer critical scrutiny. It seems right, therefore, to pause at this

[32] See my paper '"Eusebius" and the Council of Nicaea', *JTS*, N.S. 24 (1973), 100.

point and take a look at the conceptual possibilities in order to clarify the issues involved; and the data so far assembled may perhaps help to indicate how much, or how little, these possibilities were actually distinguished at the time.

It would seem that if two or more things are said to be the same in respect of their substance, this substance can be identified with the things themselves, or it can be pictured as something more, or as something less, than they are. The first possibility amounts to saying that the so-called two or more things are actually one and the same; the reference to 'substance' merely advises us that in calling them 'two' or 'three' or some other number, we are attending to distinctions which are not those of substance; for instance, we are recognizing different names, functions, or contexts of what is really one individual thing. The concept of 'one individual thing' is often explained with reference to Aristotle's doctrine of 'primary substance'; but it is sometimes forgotten that Aristotle employs this concept, as traditionally understood, only in his *Categories*, and here only of embodied creatures like 'this man', 'this horse'; he did not hold that immaterial realities are individuated in the same way, since, as we have seen, he thought that things are individuated by their 'matter'.[33] Furthermore, unless we are dealing with philosophers professedly discussing Aristotle, it is not easy to be sure whether this concept is really intended; since ancient usage allows it to be said that two things are 'identical as regards their substance' when all that is meant is that they are members of the same genus or species; and we have also noted the flexibility of modern usage in speaking of 'one thing', and the complexities presented by individual species.[34]

The second possibility is less familiar. Two or more beings could be called *homoousios* because there is one single *ousia* to which they belong, and of which they are aspects, parts, or expressions; and since 'aspects' and 'expressions', no less than 'parts', imply that other aspects, expressions, or parts are possible, there is a sense in which the *ousia* referred to contains more than any one of its aspects, expressions, or parts. Thus three divine Persons might be described by the term *homoousios* as belonging

[33] For details, including an attempt to maintain the analogy by modifying the sense of 'matter', see pp. 91–103, above.

[34] Above, pp. 4–5, 100–3, 181 ff., esp. 183.

to a single complex *ousia* which needs the three distinct Persons for its full expression.

Thirdly, the term *homoousios* could be applied to two or more beings because they severally have (and not 'jointly constitute') a single *ousia*; that is, if they have the same generic or specific characteristics, or the same material constitution. Most probably ancient writers do not draw the line between this third possibility and the second in the way which would seem natural to us; since to have the characters which identify a species is to belong to that species; and the ancients often refer to the members of a class, species, or genus as 'parts' of it; they also quite commonly attribute to classes, for instance to animal species, a metaphysical status influenced by Platonic theory which we might refuse to concede. Nevertheless it would be natural to think that the notion of 'belonging to an inclusive reality' would be easily suggested where one could claim for this reality some natural unity and structure, or again in the case of a class with a limited number of members; where these conditions are absent, it would be more natural to think in terms of 'sharing some identical feature'. Thus the term *homoousios*, used of angels, might suggest that they all belonged to the same glorious company; used of stones, it might rather suggest that they share those features which inseparably attach to stones, in being inanimate, heavy, and hard. But I do not think the former sense is distinctly presented in pre-Nicene literature. For instance, when Irenaeus discusses the Aeons of Valentinian theology and calls them *homoousioi*, he is thinking of their common constitution as πνευματικοί, beings activated by spirit, rather than of the complex body, the Pleroma, to which they belong.

Critics have often spoken of 'the generic sense of *ousia*', and F. Loofs, in an authoritative article,[35] has made this phrase the basis for further subdivisions. My own examination has, I think, established two points. First, the criteria for a thing's being *homoousios* are much more varied even than Loofs has suggested; which makes me think that 'the generic sense', with its suggestion of uniformity, is a phrase to be abandoned. *Homoousios* guarantees very little; it can be used of things which resemble one another merely in belonging to the created order, or to the category of substance; it can relate collaterals to each other, or derivatives

[35] 'Das Nicänum', *Festgabe für K. Müller*, ed. O. Scheel (Tübingen, 1922).

with their source; it does not exclude inequality of status or power. Secondly, however, the term is often used to indicate a relationship which in fact is closer than mere membership of the same species or similar material constitution, for instance that of a stream to the actual fountain from which it flows, or that of an offspring to his own parent. To call a son *homoousios* with his father implies more than merely their common membership of the human race; and the further implication need not be merely that of their physical linkage; the term can evoke their whole biological and social relationship.

Our examination of the term *homoousios* has shown that all (or virtually all) the theological applications of it in pre-Nicene times fall within this elastic third class; we have found no evidence which clearly points to the first or second. Nevertheless we should pose the question: could it have been understood at Nicaea, by some of those present, along the lines of the first or second possibilities?

Some theologians certainly used phrases which, taken literally, would suggest that Father and Son are identical in the strictest sense. Marcellus can refer to them as 'one and the same thing', 'one Person' (ἓν καὶ τὸ αὐτό, ἓν πρόσωπον, fr. 61, 71 and 76, 78); Constantine's letters occasionally adopt strikingly monarchian expressions, especially perhaps the opening sentence of his *Letter to Nicomedia* (*Urk.* 27), which implies that 'the Lord God and Saviour, Christ' is 'both Father and Son'[36] (though this is almost immediately qualified by phrases which distinguish the two Persons; cf. *Urk.* 34, § 14, where a reference to the 'one substance of the Father-and-Son' follows a clause which draws clear personal distinctions); and a similar sense can be read into the less precise phrase 'a single reality' (μία ὑπόστασις) which was a common Western expression of Christian monotheism. But two reservations have to be made. First, such expressions are not always to be taken literally. Marcellus supports his contention that Father and Son are one and the same by arguing that a man and his reason are one and the same, and this has good Platonic authority in the doctrine that the real man is the inner man, the soul, and especially the rational part of it. Nevertheless this implies that the sense of 'one and the same' is in some degree diluted; against Marcellus it would be fair to argue that *X*'s

[36] For this rendering see H. Kraft, op. cit., p. 17, n. 56.

reason is not absolutely identical with X, but is a particular aspect of his total existence, distinct from his will or his feelings. Secondly, there is no direct evidence which connects the term *homoousios* with the theology of Marcellus, or with that of Constantine apart from the Council; it does not occur in the fragments certainly attributable to Marcellus, or in Constantine's letters.

To consider the second possibility: could it have occurred to some to use the term *homoousios* to suggest that Father and Son are aspects of a single and distinct reality, the Godhead? Once again, we are led to consider the phrase μία ὑπόστασις as a likely expression of this possibility; but a more promising candidate, perhaps, appears in the correlative terms 'monad' and 'triad'. May it have been thought that the Triad of persons is called *homoousios* because they jointly constitute the single complex reality which is the divine Monad? The difficulty here is that although we do encounter phrases which suggest that Monad and Triad are, as it were, complementary aspects of the same divine reality,[37] this scheme is seldom presented in a pure form. The pure form would be a symmetrical scheme in which all three persons play an equal part. What in fact we find is that the divine Monad and source of the Triad is identified with the first person, the Father (just as, in the history of theology, the Father concept is the original nucleus). The one divine substance is therefore, properly and primarily, the Father's substance (πατρικὴ ὑπόστασις as Alexander puts it, *Urk.* 14, § 48); and Marcellus of course goes further and envisages a quasi-historical process, so that the original Godhead, truly and properly described as a Monad, expands into a Triad for the salvation of the world.

All in all, therefore, it seems unlikely that the Nicene fathers should have interpreted *homoousios* along the lines of the second possibility; we do not find clear references to a system in which Father, Son, and Holy Spirit are described as constituting one Godhead which is conceptually distinguishable from each of the three Persons, including the Father. Something of the kind is perhaps suggested in Origen's *Homily on Numbers* (12. 1) already quoted on page 214: 'Thus there is this distinction of three persons in the Father, the Son and the Holy Spirit; *sed horum*

---

[37] So most clearly Dionysius of Alexandria in Athanasius, *Sent. Dion.* 17: οὕτω μὲν ἡμεῖς εἴς τε τὴν τριάδα τὴν μονάδα πλατύνομεν ἀδιαίρετον, καὶ τὴν τριάδα πάλιν ἀμείωτον εἰς τὴν μονάδα συγκεφαλαιούμεθα.

puteorum unus est fons. Una enim substantia est et natura Trinitatis.'
This does *not* mean 'one of these "wells" is the source' (sc. of the
other two), but 'these (three) "wells" have one source'—'for the
nature and substance of the Trinity is one.' Taken literally, this
would imply that the Father himself is derived from the single
substance of the Trinity; and this suggestion may help to explain
the argument put forward by some critics of Nicaea, that if
Father and Son are called *homoousios*, they must be so in virtue
of some third reality from which both are derived (see Athanasius, *Syn.* 51, and cf. Plato, *Timaeus* 31 a). But the suggestion of
a common *source* for the two (or three) Persons, distinct from
each of them, is in fact rather different from the suggestion of
an inclusive reality to which all three belong;[38] and it was correctly answered by saying that in common Christian tradition
the ultimate and unbegotten source of all being is the Father;
which once again shows the unacceptability of any completely
symmetrical picture of the Trinity.

The conceptual analysis which we have just undertaken has
perhaps given some indications of the way in which *homoousios*
was understood at Nicaea; but to exhibit the problem more
clearly, we shall have to consider the very various attempts which
have been made to evaluate the term in the light of the historical
context or the dogmatic interest in which it was proposed. No
argument along these lines commands universal support at the
present time. Perhaps the most widely accepted view, (a), is that
the word reflected, and was intended to express, a Western
theology of *una substantia* which goes back to Tertullian; this is
often linked with the view that Ossius, Bishop of Cordova, the
Emperor's theological adviser, took the lead in proposing it at the
Council. H. Kraft has proposed, (b), what is in some ways a
modification of this view; he also stresses the importance of
Western theology, but points to the Gnostics' use of this and
related terms (e.g. 'emission', προβολή) as helping to fix its meaning; and attributes its appearance in the Creed to a theological
initiative stemming from Constantine. E. Schwartz, (c), had also
thought of Constantine as its principal author, but judged rather
that it was the *absence* of any fixed theological meaning which disposed him to adopt the term; it would serve to isolate Arius from

---

[38] Cf. H. A. Wolfson, *Philosophy of the Church Fathers*, 353–4; though in suggesting
that Augustine initiated the former view, he overlooks Origen, loc. cit.

his supporters without imposing a clearly articulated standard of doctrine; it was therefore adopted on political rather than theological grounds. N. H. Baynes, (d), took up a rather similar position by endorsing the judgement of Ambrose (*de Fide*, iii. 15, *Urk.* 21) that the word was chosen simply because the Arians rejected it. Meanwhile H. Lietzmann, (e), had suggested, in direct opposition to view (a), that the word had a rather local currency in the East, and was used to express a reaction of popular monarchian theology against the pluralistic doctrine of Origen; though he also expresses agreement with Schwartz. Finally, (f), one could suggest that the word was adopted more or less impromptu as a reply to the contention that Father, Son and Spirit are three *ousiai*, which is known to have come to the attention of Ossius shortly before the Council.[39] There is no absolute need to choose only one of these alternatives; some at least can be combined with others. In my judgement (c), (d), and (f) contain the most important elements of truth; (b) and (e) may be partly true; (a) is definitely to be discounted.

I shall begin, therefore, by criticizing (a), which has played a large part in scholarly discussion in the past. Theologians have been rightly convinced that the ultimate effect of Nicaea has been to assert, not merely the equality, but also the essential unity, of the three Persons; and they have attempted, I think incautiously, to represent this as the original and express intention of the Nicene fathers. In support of this view, it has been argued that *homoousios* was adopted at Nicaea to express the form of trinitarian theology prevailing in the West, which from about the time of Pope Callistus appears to have been influenced by popular modalism and relatively untouched by the scholarly constructions of the Logos theology. Attention has been called to the probable influence exerted by Dionysius of Rome, and to the activity of Ossius. In recent years the distinctive interpretation of *homoousios* championed by Zahn and Harnack has been widely criticized, on the grounds that, so understood, it would have provoked a strong and immediate reaction by the Origenist

---

[39] See (a) T. Zahn, *Marcellus von Ancyra* (1867), 23; A. Harnack, *Lehrbuch der Dogmengeschichte*[4], ii. 232, n. 4 = *History of Dogma* (E.T.), iv. 56; J. N. D. Kelly, *Creeds*, 250–1, and many recent studies; (b) H. Kraft, op. cit.; (c) E. Schwartz, *Kaiser Constantin und die christliche Kirche*, 140; (d) N. H. Baynes, *Constantine the Great and the Christian Church*, 87; (e) *Constantine to Julian* (E.T.), 119.

majority;[40] but some eminent scholars, such as J. N. D. Kelly and M. Simonetti, have still attached importance to the theory of Western influence. I shall direct my argument to this point.

1). There is no question of minimizing the importance of Ossius; nevertheless, the evidence that he proposed the term *homoousios* at the Council is by no means convincing. In the case of Constantine, Eusebius clearly states that he both advocated and explained the term. It is the much later Arian writer Philostorgius who alleged, at least a hundred years afterwards, that Ossius and Alexander 'agreed to make the Son *homoousios* with the Father' (ἀνομολογῆσαι παρασκευάσαι ὁμοούσιον τῷ πατρὶ τὸν υἱόν).[41] But Philostorgius represents Alexander, not Ossius, as taking the initiative; and it is not clear that he intends a literal reference to the term *homoousios*; it may be merely a shorthand phrase for 'adopting an anti-Arian theology'. Support for Philostorgius has been found in Athanasius, and in the general presumption that Ossius acted as Constantine's theological adviser. But Athanasius merely indicates in quite general terms that he 'propounded the Creed';[42] and there is at least some reason to credit Constantine with a theological judgement of his own.[43]

2). We have no independent evidence of Ossius' theological position, or of his capacity for taking a theological initiative in the Greek-speaking Church. In particular, it is noteworthy that the Synodal Letter of the Council of Antioch, though it represents the writer, probably Ossius, as taking power to settle ecclesiastical disputes, expounds a theology which is almost identical with that of Alexander.[44] It is hard to suppose that Ossius was responsible for introducing Western theology at Nicaea, when he made no attempt to do so at the much smaller Council of Antioch, in which he enjoyed an undisputed primacy.

3). Eusebius speaks with scarcely veiled irritation of those who, 'on the pretext of adding the term *homoousios*' (προφάσει τῆς τοῦ ὁμοουσίου προσθήκης) put out the final draft of the Nicene Creed; but he goes out of his way to refer to Ossius in complimentary

---

[40] Prestige, *GPT*, 211–12; Kelly, *Creeds*, 254; on Western influence, see Prestige, 219–21; Kelly, 251; M. Simonetti, *La letteratura antica cristiana*, 194.

[41] *Hist. Eccl.* i. 7 (Bidez, p. 9).

[42] *Hist. Arian.* 42: οὗτος καὶ τὴν ἐν Νικαίᾳ πίστιν ἐξέθετο. The context is a series of complaints attributed to the Arian party.

[43] See H. Kraft, op. cit., though I do not follow his reconstruction at all points.

[44] E. Schwartz, *Nachricht. Gött.* (1905), 288, = *Ges. Schriften* iii. 154.

terms, and specifically commends him as a peace-maker, the exponent of a policy of Constantine's which Eusebius warmly approved.[45] This again hardly suggests that he regarded Ossius as having played a significant part in drafting a creed which he accepted with reluctance.

4). Even if it were shown that Ossius was responsible for introducing the term *homoousios*, this would not prove that it was intended as an expression of Western theology; it might have been adopted as a reply to the use of 'two' or 'three *ousiai*' to refer to the persons of the Trinity, which Ossius had certainly encountered in Narcissus and Eusebius.[46]

I now turn to the broader question: is there good ground for thinking that the term *homoousios* was generally current in Greek-speaking circles in the West as an expression of their trinitarian theology? Once again, I shall argue that the case for this view is unconvincing.

1). Any study of the Latin tradition must begin with Tertullian. We have noted the importance of the phrase *una substantia* in his theology; the sense of this has been thoroughly investigated by R. Braun and J. Moingt, and I have myself contributed a short study which substantially agreed with their conclusions.[47] But it has been noted that Tertullian does not make any general use of a Latin expression coined on the model of *homoousios*. This means that Greek-speaking theologians would most naturally represent his teaching on the Trinity by using the phrases μία οὐσία, or the philologically apter μία ὑπόστασις, rather than ὁμοούσιος.

2). Evidence for the Western use of *homoousios* is commonly found in the controversy between Dionysius of Alexandria and Pope Dionysius of Rome, which has been briefly described (above, p. 216). It is clear that the term *homoousios* was used by Dionysius' accusers, whether these are in fact the Libyan group which he accused of Sabellianism, or a party in Alexandria which espoused their cause.[48] It is also clear that they relied on the sympathy of Dionysius of Rome. It has been inferred from this

---

[45] *Vita Constantini*, ii. 63, cf. Opitz, *Urk.* 22, §§ 7, 14.

[46] Eusebius, *c. Marc.* i. 4. 39, 53 f. = *Urk.* 19.

[47] R. Braun, S.J., *Deus Christianorum* (Paris, 1962); J. Moingt, S.J., *Théologie trinitaire de Tertullien* (Paris, 1966); G. C. Stead, 'Divine Substance in Tertullian', *JTS*, n.s. 14 (1963), 46–66.

[48] Cf. E. Schwartz, *Kaiser Constantin*, 118.

that the Pope himself used, or even required the use of, the term *homoousios*.

I find this argument unconvincing. Dionysius of Rome protests in vigorous terms against those who 'divide . . . the monarchy into three powers and separate hypostases and three deities' (Athanasius, *Decr.* 26, Feltoe p. 177, cf. pp. 181–2). The reference to *separate* hypostases may possibly indicate that he deliberately refrains from condemning *every* form of the doctrine of three hypostases (which the Alexandrian bishop continued to defend) ; but the language also suggests that the natural positive expression of Dionysius' belief would be 'one hypostasis'. This, I think, sufficiently accounts for the Libyans' appeal to Rome and their hope of a sympathetic response, without inferring that the actual term *homoousios* was already in use among Greek-speakers in the West in connection with the Trinity. Again, it is easy to think that Greek users of *homoousios* would expect support from Latin exponents of *una substantia*; it is less probable that the latter would translate their Latin phrase by a clumsy and possibly suspect compound adjective, which had no accepted Latin model, when the exact equivalents μία ὑπόστασις and μία οὐσία lay ready to hand. And it is surely unlikely that either party in the controversy made positive use of the term; for Athanasius, who had access to the correspondence, was anxious to produce accredited authority for it; yet the only passage he could quote in its favour was the somewhat unhelpful one in which Dionysius of Alexandria gives his reasons for *not* using it, and adds that he had made use of others with a similar meaning. Unless we are to accuse Athanasius of scarcely credible incompetence, I think we should agree with Lebreton: 'The term was not obligatory at the time and the Pope himself had not made use of it.'[49]

3). If the term *homoousios* really was condemned at Antioch in 268 (pp. 216–17 above), this would suggest that it was not yet officially recognized. But I shall not rely upon this argument, since our evidence for its condemnation is relatively late; it comes (we recall) from a document circulated by the homoeousian party in 358, which has not survived, and of which conflicting accounts are given by Athanasius and Hilary. It seems to me possible that the document which gave this impression was merely enlarging on the fact that the bishops who condemned Paul of Samosata re-

[49] *History of the Primitive Church* (E.T.), iv. 891.

ferred to Christ as himself an *ousia*, which (from the homoeousian standpoint) implied that there were three *ousiai* and so was tantamount to a condemnation of the *homoousion*. And we have some independent evidence that the Origenist bishops at Antioch took this line, since they are said to have complained that Paul spoke of the wisdom of Jesus as something learnt and enjoyed, 'and not a substance substantified in his body' (Leontius of Byzantium, cited in de Riedmatten, S. 33, p. 155: οὐχὶ οὐσίαν οὐσιωμένην ἐν σώματι). Clearly they are thinking of the pre-existent Wisdom of Alexandrian tradition as an *ousia*, and one which is distinct from the Father; so they can be quoted in support of the doctrine of three divine *ousiai*.

4). But if the tradition about the Council of Antioch in 268 is unreliable, there is one further argument of some weight. The Council of Sardica in 343 put out a dogmatic statement[50] which is generally agreed to be the work of Ossius in partnership with the local bishop Protogenes, and which presents a strong, indeed provocative, affirmation of the Western viewpoint. This document makes no mention of Nicaea, nor of the term *homoousios*. Its theology, which I should judge to be surprisingly incoherent and naïve, is drawn from various sources; but in defining the unity of the Godhead it repeatedly uses the phrase 'one hypostasis' (which I have already mentioned as the natural equivalent of *una substantia*), as well as openly attacking the widely held Eastern doctrine of three hypostases. It seems to me incredible that if *homoousios* really were an established expression of Western theology, this council and these authors should have refrained from pressing it upon the Eastern bishops; but if it were deliberately avoided, this may well have been because it was regarded as an ambiguous expression which did not go far enough.[51] Moreover, the reference to 'one hypostasis, which the heretics themselves call *ousia*' might possibly suggest that the Westerners at Sardica were hardly at ease even with the simple noun.

5). This point can perhaps be reinforced by recalling the general ignorance of the Nicene formulae which prevailed in the West until about the year 355, if one may judge from the case of

---

[50] See Theodoret, *HE* ii. 8. 37–52.

[51] Eustathius was clearly dissatisfied with the Nicene formula; hence his complaint that the best theologians had been muzzled: Theodoret, *HE* i. 8. 3.

St. Hilary, who was clearly much above the average in alertness
and intelligence. 'Though I had been baptized some time previously, and had been a bishop quite a while, I did not hear of the
Nicene creed until I was about to set forth into exile (*fidem
Nicaenam nunquam nisi exulaturus audivi*)' : so he informs us in his
de Synodis, 91. It seems difficult to explain such ignorance if the
Council could really be regarded as an important victory for
Western theology; for Rome was not normally slow to celebrate
such triumphs. More probably the West took a little time to
appreciate the merits of *homoousios* as a term which sufficiently represented their own teaching and effectively countered Arianism
without being wholly unacceptable to the conservative majority
in the East.

By way of comment on H. Kraft, it must be said that though
his essay is valuable and suggestive at many points, it is possible
to overwork the evidence for a Gnostic use of *homoousios*.[52] Our
previous investigation has shown that it was used in statements
and criticisms of one particular Gnostic school, the Valentinian,
which had especially close contacts with Greek philosophy; and
that the points made by it had already been expressed in different but similar terms by writers who were not Gnostics. The
Valentinians may have introduced the term into theology, and
given it a distinctive application as related to their theory of
three orders of being; but that is all. It is worth noting that the
Nag-Hammadi texts, which have greatly increased our knowledge
of Gnosticism, have not so far thrown any new light on the
homoousion. On the other hand, the Arian party display an extreme opposition to all material images of the Father–Son relationship, which made them detect Gnostic influence even in the
traditional analogies of light, water, vegetation, etc., which
Dionysius amongst others was prepared to accept; hence at
times Athanasius and other Nicenes can use expressions which
seem, relatively speaking, to be closer to Gnosticism. When
Athanasius says that the divine essence is 'fruitful' (καρπογόνος
ἡ θεία οὐσία), this looks not unlike the Gnostic description of it as
'fertile' (γόνιμος).[53] But any notion that the Nicene theologians

---

[52] So e.g. J. N. D. Kelly, *Doctrines*, 235: 'Christian writers seem to have
borrowed it from the Gnostics' etc.

[53] Athanasius, *c. Ar.* ii. 2; Hippolytus, *Ref.* vi. 29; *CH*, fr. div. 27 = Cyril,
c. Iul. 552 D.

could have regarded the Valentinians with *sympathy* is of course fanciful.

It might perhaps be argued that if the term *homoousios* were intended as a reply to the doctrine that Father, Son, and Spirit are three *ousiai* (possibility (f) above), this fact should afford some clue to its meaning. I would accept this argument up to a point. 'Three *ousiai*', no less than the commoner 'three hypostases', would seem to conflict with the Western *una substantia*. But I do not think it realistic to imagine such a reflection as the following: 'here is a phrase which strongly asserts the distinctness of the divine persons; let us find a counter to it which strongly upholds their unity'; for this would imply that the Council fathers were able to distinguish the equality and the unity of the three persons as two separate issues which could be found by analysis of a single phrase.[54]

Using modern methods of study we can see that behind the phrase 'three *ousiai*' there lies a fairly complex theology. Its champions were primarily concerned to insist that the Word and the Spirit are genuinely existent beings, and cannot be reduced to mere operations of the Father. Having thus asserted their metaphysical parity, they felt bound to introduce some element of subordination in order to avoid the danger of tritheism; but hardly succeeded in stating it in a consistent form; thus Eusebius can protest against any doctrine that Father and Son are 'equal in rank' (*ET* ii. 7 and 23), even though he also asserts that the Son is 'completely assimilated' to the Father (ibid. ii. 14. 21, 17. 3, etc.). In these circumstances, it must have been impossible to determine how far the proponents of 'three *ousiai*' were simply insisting on the metaphysical integrity of all three Persons, and how far they also meant to imply some difference of status, which was so hesitantly expressed as a corollary of the other doctrine. In any case, the Nicene fathers were not perceptive of distinctions in the sense of *ousia*, apart from the well-worn distinction between the immaterial and the material; indeed no such perception emerges in the next few decades. For the controversies about sameness and likeness of *ousia* completely

---

[54] It is true that Dionysius of Rome distinguished between those who divide the Trinity and those who degrade the Son; but his contention is that the true faith opposes both heresies, because it includes the *two* traditional doctrines of the Trinity and the Monarchy: Athanasius, *Decr.* 26.

ignore the vital fact that *ousia* is logically multivalent; and the Cappadocian fathers' distinction between *ousia* and *hypostasis*, which is presented as fixing the 'correct' sense of the two words, draws on textbook logic without mentioning any previous theological analysis of *ousia*.[55]

It would seem, then, that attempts to evaluate the *homoousion* in terms of its probable context of thought have not so far led to assured results. It remains to see whether any more can be achieved by considering the reports of the Council given by Eusebius and Athanasius.

Eusebius' comments are aimed at setting aside all possible materializing implications of the term; in § 12 of his *Letter to his Diocese* he says that the Son is consubstantial 'not in the manner of bodies, or like mortal creatures, for he is not so by division of the substance, nor by severance, nor indeed by any affection or change or alteration of the Father's substance and power; for the unoriginate nature of the Father is foreign to all such things.' These reservations, we have seen (p. 232 above), agree very closely with those which Eusebius had already formulated in his *Demonstratio Evangelica* in connection with the phrase 'from God's substance'; and it is at first sight surprising to find him claiming (§ 7) that the Emperor himself explained the *homoousion* in much the same terms: 'he was called *homoousios* not in view of (any) bodily affections, for he did not originate from the Father by any division or severance; for the immaterial and intellectual and incorporeal nature could not undergo any bodily affection, but it was right for us to understand such things in divine and ineffable terms.' But it is not necessary to suppose that Eusebius is misrepresenting Constantine; no doubt these reservations were urged in the course of the debate, and accepted as reasonable by the anti-Arian party, so that the Emperor could quote them as agreed disclaimers; indeed we find Athanasius making the same points in not dissimilar language (*Decr.* 11 and 24, *Syn.* 41, etc.). In this case Eusebius may have accurately reported Constantine, though no doubt he gives a misleading impression by quoting only those comments which suit his own argument.

On the other side, Eusebius' positive exposition of the *homo-*

---

[55] For some comments on this distinction, which the Cappadocians themselves by no means consistently follow, see my paper 'Ontology and Terminology in Gregory of Nyssa', in the proceedings of the Freckenhorst Conference, 1972.

ousion is decidedly limited; it is comprised in a pair of sentences which we have already discussed (pp. 239–40 above); one explains the qualitative aspect of the *homoousion*: 'the Son is entirely unlike created beings, but completely like the Father'; the other its implications for the Son's origin: He 'is not (derived) from some other hypostasis and substance, but from the Father.' The last phrase is one which Arius himself had come to accept, and which Athanasius was to criticize as inadequate; but the former sentence clearly dissociates Eusebius from the evasive argument that the words 'from the Father' are wholly non-committal, since all things come from God. Confronted with the embarrassing credal term, as he found it, Eusebius is not in the mood for generous tributes to the glory of the Son, such as he freely expresses elsewhere;[56] but he does at least define for him a status which is unique, and relates him to the Father, in terms which Athanasius himself refrains from criticizing, and sometimes adopts.[57]

Although there are known disadvantages in arguing from silence, I think it is also possible to take some account of the things which Eusebius does *not* think it necessary to say. First, his explanation that the Son is 'completely like the Father' accords with his own theology as already expressed in the *Demonstratio Evangelica*.[58] He does not raise or counter the objection that the status accorded to the Son by the Creed would make him 'equal in honour' (ἰσότιμος) with the Father, though this was an issue on which he was, and remained, sensitive. This is at least consistent with the view that *homoousios* was understood in such a way that the Father's primacy was preserved; and such would be the case if it had been expounded in close connection with the phrase ἐκ τῆς οὐσίας, as teaching that the *ousia* of the Father was communicated to and incorporated in the Son. This might raise suspicions of some quasi-material process of emission, such as we find Eusebius trying to allay; but it would not immediately suggest that Father and Son were in all respects equal (since the Father retains his position as ultimate source); still less, that they are in all respects one and the same.

It is particularly significant that Eusebius makes no allusion

---

[56] See e.g. *DE* iv. 13. 9.

[57] *Decr.* 20 and *ad Afros* 9 both make the point that *homoousios* means 'not a creature'. 'From the Father' occurs in *Syn.* 50.

[58] See e.g. iv. 3. 7 (κατὰ πάντα ἑαυτῷ ἀφωμοιωμένον).

to any 'Sabellianizing' exegesis of *homoousios*. He explains, and invokes Constantine's authority for explaining, that it was not intended to convey material implications; and he gives a positive explanation of it, as defining a status for the Son distinct from creatures. This exposition has often been criticized for evading the real point at issue; but we have to remember that Eusebius was writing, not for the instruction of future theologians, but to allay disquiet in his own diocese; and also that his words would be read, not only by priests and laymen who had been absent from the Council, but by like-minded fellow-bishops. If a stronger exegesis of *homoousios* had been clearly set forth, whether by Constantine or Ossius or Marcellus or Eustathius, Eusebius would surely have tried to clear himself of the charge of accepting a 'Sabellianizing' theology. His silence on this point suggests that in fact Constantine did not allow the 'hard-liners' at Nicaea to interpret the Creed in a way which was radically unacceptable to the Eastern conservatives; and this is perhaps confirmed by Eustathius' complaint that the 'ablest theologians'—himself and his friends, of course—were not allowed to express their views.[59]

Athanasius of course provides much more material for study; he uses the term *homoousios* perhaps 150 times in his genuine works; but many of these instances are mere reports of the opinions of others, and less than half of them really illuminate his own usage. When these are examined, one striking fact emerges; they are almost without exception closely geared to the actual clause of the Nicene Creed, that Son is *homoousios* with the Father. It is as if Athanasius had only learnt to use the term through his defence of Nicaea; and this seems to me to disfavour the view of its origin put forward by Lietzmann, (e) above. For if it had been current among monarchians in the East, it must have been used in other contexts; and one could hardly explain why Athanasius, in defending it, never reverted to such phraseology.

Thus Athanasius never says that the Father and Son are *homoousioi*; still less, of course, that the Father is *homoousios* with the Son. Nor does he ever connect the term with a noun referring to the Godhead as a whole; he does not speak of the 'consubstantial Trinity' (as he does of the 'indivisible Trinity'), nor of the 'consubstantial Godhead' (as he does of the 'one Godhead'). There is in fact a built-in asymmetry in his use of the term, which

[59] Theodoret, *HE* i. 8. 3; see my discussion cited above, p. 245.

suggests that he is moving only very cautiously away from the moderate Origenism of Alexander. And this conservative disposition is fortified by his constant insistence that the Father is the ultimate source, so that the Son is 'from the Father' (*Syn.* 50), or more precisely 'from the substance of the Father'; for these expressions suggest both the Son's essential unity with the Father and his distinct existence as derivative, not source. Again, although Athanasius of course accepts the doctrine of the Son's eternal generation, he avoids the symmetrical expressions of which Arius complained, 'the Father ever, the Son ever; the Father together, the Son together'; and in expounding the text 'I am in the Father and the Father in me' (John 14: 10, in *c. Ar.* iii. 1 ff., esp. 3) he by no means presses the suggestion of an exactly equal two-way relationship, but soon reverts to the traditional, and asymmetrical, images of the ray of light and the river springing from its source.

Once again, although Athanasius freely describes Christ as the Word and Wisdom of God, and uses these terms to demonstrate the intimate union within the Godhead, he does not develop Marcellus' argument that 'a man and his reason are one and the same thing' (fr. 61, in Eus. *c. Marc.* ii. 2. 31) still less bring *homoousios* into this context of argument.[60] One reason, I think, is that his use of theological terms is controlled by the long-standing Alexandrian principle that human analogies are imperfect and must be interpreted 'in an intellectual and spiritual sense'. Thus the second Person can be described, both as 'Son' or 'Offspring', and also as 'Word' or 'Wisdom'; and Alexandrian theologians feel no embarrassment in switching abruptly from one analogy to the other, using both 'intrapersonal' and 'multipersonal' terminology with great freedom. Thus there is felt to be nothing surprising in such phrases as 'He sits as *Word* at the Father's right hand' (*Decr.* 11, cf. *c. Ar.* i. 18), or 'the *Son* of God is . . . his thought and his living counsel' (*c. Ar.* iii. 65), where our first impulse might well be to exchange the titles 'Son' and 'Word'. Having made this point, one must surely add that the main weight of Athanasius' argument rests upon the Father–Son

---

[60] *Syn.* 51 *init.* provides a possible exception: the Son, being the Father's Wisdom and Word, is *homoousios* because he is 'the divinizing and illuminating (agency) of the Father', τὸ θεοποιὸν καὶ φωτιστικὸν τοῦ πατρός; see also what follows. But this passage still clearly emphasizes the distinction of function; the Son is the Father's executive, not vice versa.

analogy, though of course with the proviso that divine parenthood is exempt from human limitations, so that the divine Son is inseparable from his Father (*Decr.* 11; ibid. 20; *Syn.* 41) and the Trinity therefore indivisible (*ad Serap.* iv. 12). He does not therefore exploit the suggestion that God and his Word are (or are comprised in) a single personality; and if he does on occasion construe 'Father and Logos' with a singular verb (*de Inc.* 11. 7), he does not usually challenge the contention that Scripture uses the plural number in such cases;[61] even in *c. Ar.* iii. 11 *fin.*, where he comments on the singular verb in I Thess. 3: 11 ('Now may our God and Father himself, and our Lord Jesus, *direct* our way to you'), his comment is that there are not two givers of grace, but the Father gives grace through the Son; so that here too the distinction of persons is preserved.

To take a closer look, though in fairly brief compass, at Athanasius' use of the term *homoousios*, I think it may be instructive to consider the cases in which it is explained by analogies taken from the natural world and from human life; and I shall classify these analogies under four headings:

1). The analogy of human paternity, of father and son (*Decr.* 20, *ad Serap.* ii. 6, *Syn.* 41, etc.).
2). The analogy of continuous natural processes:
   (a) Fountain and stream (*Sent. Dion.* 24).
   (b) Source and ray of light (*Decr.* 23, 24, *ad Serap.* ii. 3, *Syn.* 51, etc.).
   (c) Vine and branches (*Sent. Dion.* 10).
3). The analogy of two men *simpliciter* (*ad Serap.* ii. 3, cf. *Syn.* 53, *Sent. Dion.* 10).
4). The analogy of mind and word (*Syn.* 51).

(I have given references to passages where *homoousios* is used; of course the analogies themselves occur very frequently in other contexts[62] which help to explain how Athanasius understood them.)

1). In expounding the analogy of father and son, Athanasius dwells on the fact of consanguinity. No doubt human fathers and sons are members of one and the same human species; but what is peculiar to their case is that the son actually derives his existence

---

[61] See e.g. Eusebius, *ET* iii. 5. 5.

[62] Cf. C. Hauret, *Comment le 'Défenseur de Nicée' a-t-il compris le dogme de Nicée?*, 36 ff.

from his father. However, the human father transmits to his son both his human form (not to mention particular inherited characteristics) and part of his own bodily matter. Which sort of transmission is it that Athanasius has in mind? His description of human generation in *Decr.* 11 suggests that he is thinking primarily of the material linkage. But of course the human analogy has to be modified in order to be appropriate to the divine life. Human generation is occasional, divine generation (for Athanasius) is eternal; human sons may become separated from their fathers, the divine Son is inseparable, he is 'in the bosom of the Father'. More important, the communication of physical life is only a crude representation of the communication of energy, love, and glory from the divine Father to his only-begotten Son.

Athanasius does *not* say, however, that the analogy needs qualification simply because it involves two persons; *homoousios* in this connection therefore does not imply 'one individual being' in the exact sense, namely that the personal distinction is to be cancelled. Nor does it express the fact that Father and Son (with the Spirit, understood) *together constitute* a single *ousia*. Athanasius does say something like this in *other* terms; they do constitute an indivisible Trinity, a single Godhead;[63] but the term *homoousios* is not used to convey this idea. What he intends by it has been well expressed in the phrase 'the full unbroken continuation of being';[64] the divine Father communicates to the Son, not just formal characteristics, not just a part of his divine life, but the fullness of his spiritual being, all that he has and is. Yet it should be noted that the relationship is an asymmetrical one; the Father initiates, the Son responds; Athanasius fully recognizes, not only a formal distinction of persons, but a distinction of function associated with them.

2). This last point is also clearly expressed in the group of three physical analogies, fountain and stream, source and ray of light, vine and branches. All three convey the notion of a common stuff (water, light, vine-tissue) emerging in markedly different forms. They also convey the notion of organic continuity, indeed of one-way communication: the stream comes *from* the fountain, the ray *from* the source, and not vice versa; and the vine

---

[63] *ad Serap.* i. 28.
[64] A. Robertson, *Athanasius* (*NPNF*), xxxii: 'The full unbroken continuation of the Being of the Father in the Son'.

analogy is probably to be understood in the same way, since the ancients knew that branches are nourished from their roots, but did not understand how the leaves themselves (by photosynthesis) help to maintain the whole plant.

Once again, it is clear that Athanasius does not mean (e.g.) that the ray is identical with its source in any exact sense, for an asymmetrical relationship obtains between them. Nor does 'one *ousia*' mean that they *together constitute* a single reality. This might perhaps be contested in the particular case of the source and ray, in view of the terms in which Athanasius speaks of them as one and indivisible (*Decr.* 23, 24; cf. *Syn.* 52, where they are not two lights, but one). But there is no word which could denote the complex entity consisting of the fountain and stream together; by speaking of *their* single *ousia*, St. Athanasius clearly refers to the water of which both are composed, and which flows from the former to the latter.

3). Rather different problems are raised by the much-discussed passages in which Athanasius compares the relationship of Father and Son to that of two men, or two members of some other species, without further qualification. Here we have a symmetrical relationship, which allows the thought of perfect likeness obtaining between the two Persons to be freely developed; on the other hand the suggestion of continuity, of organic interconnection, is much reduced. Of course Athanasius can call upon Platonic philosophy for the thought that there is a real identity of species; in every man the same universal Idea is present without modification. There is also the biblical doctrine that in some sense all men are one in Adam. But the force of these considerations is limited, since he has to admit that human beings are frequently divided by separations, conflicts, and moral disparities.[65]

It has been argued that Athanasius, influenced by a desire to reach agreement with the homoeousian party, finally came to accept this 'specific identity' as a definitive explanation of the term *homoousios*; in other words, he adopted a 'neo-Nicene' point of view. Although this is not the place for a full discussion, I must say that I do not consider this a balanced statement of the case. On the one hand, there is evidence that his thoughts were already turning in this direction when he wrote the *de Sententia Dionysii* in

[65] *Decr.* 20; *c. Ar.* iii. 18 ff.; *Decr.* 10.

the early 350s; for in Chapter 10 of this work he says that the Saviour is *homoousios* with us in respect of his manhood; which involves precisely the 'reduced' or 'generic' sense of the word that we are now considering. Yet in writing this work he was not influenced by the political necessity of combining against powerful adversaries, but by the theological motive of coming to terms with a powerful mind which moved in rather different channels from his own; for St. Dionysius, as we know, described the divine Persons as 'three hypostases', and strongly emphasized the functional distinction between them. On the other hand, there is no sign that in his later works St. Athanasius wished to withdraw the other analogies which more strongly express the organic continuity of Father and Son; since these are used to explain the *homoousion* in one of his latest writings, the letter *ad Afros* (c. 6). And as I have said, we entirely mistake the point of the Father–Son analogy if we treat it as equivalent to that of two men *simpliciter*.

4). I now come to what is perhaps the most interesting and delicate case. In his *de Synodis*, 51, St. Athanasius writes: 'Again, if the Son is not so by participation, but . . . is himself the Father's Wisdom and Word, in whom all things participate; it is clear that, being himself the divinizing and illuminating (agency) of the Father, in whom all things are divinized and vivified, he is not alien-in-substance with regard to the Father, but one-in-substance.' In this case Athanasius uses an 'intra-personal' analogy; he clearly means that in some sense the total reality of the Father, including his Wisdom or Word, is comparable to a single personality; moreover, to be illuminated (etc.) by the Father is *eo ipso* to be illuminated by the Son, and vice versa (much as with the sun and its rays) ; to this extent a real numerical identity is suggested. On the other hand, there is still a clearly marked asymmetry and distinctness of function; it is the Son who is the divinizing agency of the Father, and not vice versa; it is the Father, and the Father alone, who is the ultimate source of the divine light.

If my analysis of St. Athanasius is correct, it should help to eliminate two misreadings of his use of *homoousios*. There is a rationalistic misreading, which suggests that he came to use it simply to express the equal dignity of the Father and Son, relying on the analogy of two members of the same species. I have argued that this underrates the emphasis on shared or communicated life and light and being which is maintained in the later writings. And there is the romantic (or dogmatic?) misreading, which represents him as leading an advance towards an unrestricted view of the unity of the Persons, and as upholding their 'numerical identity of substance', using a phrase which I have criticized elsewhere. I have tried to show that although Athanasius undoubtedly does represent such an advance, as compared with Eusebius or Alexander, nevertheless there are conservative elements in his thought which should not be ignored. The Father communicates to the Son all that he has and is, the Son receives the fullness of divine being; yet the Father initiates, the Son responds, and not vice versa; the Father does not surrender, nor the Son usurp, his distinctive position; and it is only an oddity of our language if we represent this as some qualification of the divine generosity. How such teaching is to be summarized depends upon the care with which we choose our descriptive terms. I myself would say that, in view of the asymmetry and distinctness of function, we cannot claim that there is any consistent suggestion of numerical identity in the strict sense; whereas if we speak of 'numerical identity of substance', we are using a phrase which is too elastic to be useful for critical purposes.

X

CONCLUSION

IN the last two chapters I have dealt at some length with the doctrine of God as three Persons in one substance. The discussion may well have seemed over-technical to readers who are not professional theologians; but in any case, I would like to conclude with a brief review of the more general question of what is involved when we apply the term 'substance' to God. This will allow some earlier arguments to be summarized and connected, and a few new points to be added which the earlier treatment had to omit.

'Divine substance', so written in English, will probably suggest one or other of two notions; either a God conceived in metaphysical terms, as some kind of absolute or changeless being; or some kind of stuff, perhaps described as light, or mind, or spirit, out of which the divinity is said to be constituted. In modern usage 'substance' does not easily convey the idea of an individual or of a person, although for Aristotle human beings, and deities, were stock examples of substances. But the limits of our earlier discussion were set by the Greek word *ousia*, which covers a much wider range of meanings than the English 'substance'. We can therefore follow the scheme proposed in Chapter VI, and lead up to the more concrete questions by reviewing the statement that God exists.

What is the meaning of 'exists' in this context? We have already seen that the word has been very variously understood (above, pp. 7-11). In the logical empiricists' view it is not a predicative term; it does not refer to some activity or state of the subject, God. Rather, it forms part of a statement about the *word* 'God', to the effect that this word has a reference; put more informally, it indicates that God belongs with gold or lions or the sun rather than with phlogiston or mermaids or the phoenix. Of course, to explain the meaning of the statement 'God exists' is not to *state* that God exists; it merely defines the issue. Some philosophers construe the statement in this way, and regard it as true;

others, but as false; others have argued that the word 'God', as traditionally understood, gives such an imprecise specification that the statement 'God exists' fails to be significant; one has no sufficiently distinct idea of what its truth would involve. The believer in God, again, is not committed by his belief to accepting or rejecting this interpretation of existence; but if he does accept it, he will hold that the statement, even if not completely perspicuous, is both significant and true.

However, not all believers, and not all agnostic philosophers, do accept this treatment of 'existence'. It is possible to regard it as a very general descriptive term, comparable with 'life' or 'activity'; and on this interpretation there are at least two positions that the believer in God can take up. He may interpret it as referring to the basic and characteristic activity of every grade of being; and so will hold that God exists *par excellence*; his is the purest and most vital form of existence. This is the position adopted, for instance, by E. Gilson; and I have argued above that there is no sufficient reason to condemn this usage (which is usefully continuous with ancient thought), provided empiricist correctives are kept in mind. But from another side it is urged that existence implies some sort of effort or limitation; thus 'existing' is variously interpreted as 'cropping up as a phenomenon in the world' or 'taking a place as one being alongside others' or 'exerting human effort and decision'; and on this interpretation the believer has to reject, or at least qualify, the statement that God exists, on the score that God is the supreme reality above or beyond existence. This is a position which was at least suggested in antiquity by Plato, and rather more definitely by Basilides;[1] modern exponents of it include Kierkegaard, Heidegger, Brunner, Bultmann, Tillich, and Macquarrie.[2]

The two latter ways of interpreting 'existence' have some obvious attractions for theologians, and indeed for all believers. If it is possible to interpret the statement 'God exists' in a way

---

[1] Plato, *Rep.* 509 b; above, pp. 40, 161; Basilides in Hippolytus, *Ref.* vii. 20 ff.; his phrase ὁ οὐκ ὢν θεός is sometimes translated 'the non-existent God', which could mean 'unreal'; this is certainly what Hippolytus understands by it (whether in good faith or by polemical misrepresentation), but not what Basilides intends; he is thinking of a *source* of all being.

[2] See e.g. S. Kierkegaard, *Unsc. Post.*, 485; R. K. Bultmann, *Existence and Faith*, 61–3; P. Tillich, *Syst. Theol.* (London, 1953), i. 262–3; J. Macquarrie, *Principles of Christian Theology*, 108.

which responds to their conviction of the strangeness and majesty of divine being, they will be unwilling to lose this opportunity; to accept the logical-empiricist interpretation will seem to entail ranking God on a level with people and things. But, as I have argued above, the logical-empiricist view has an important service to perform in detecting sources of confusion. Nevertheless, once the dose has been accepted, it is possible to deal critically and fairly with writers who adopt one of the other conventions; and indeed, such flexibility is required in students of ancient thought. More tentatively I have suggested that the word 'exist' can be regarded as a limiting case of those verbs which predicate activities in increasingly broad and general terms, but also convey an increasingly strong presumption that actual cases and not fictions are being described. In this case, although its logical structure appears to be totally distinct, it really admits of parallels and approximations, just as a mathematical zero can be approached by numbers indicating magnitudes.

Our discussion of the term *ousia* went on to the purely problematical sense of the term, (B), corresponding to the English word 'nature' when one 'inquires into the nature of something'. In the light of categorial theories, to ascertain the *ousia* of a thing is to assign it to its appropriate category, whatever that may be. This usage involves a well-known difficulty; if the categories are supposed to be ultimate units of classification, how can one use a term such as *ousia* so as professedly to apply to all of them? For if one thus brings them into a more inclusive class, they cease to be ultimate. But this objection is not confined to the term *ousia*; it will apply to expressions like 'the forms of predication', or indeed the word 'category' itself; meanwhile we have noted (p. 137 above) that Aristotle himself applies the term *ousia* not only to one particular category (substance) but more generally in relation to others.

A rather similar objection has been made more recently in a form which recalls our discussion of existence. It has been argued that categorial statements cannot be descriptive; one cannot identify the bearer of a name unless one has already assigned it to the appropriate category; so a categorial statement cannot be made about the bearer of the name X; it can only be made about the name itself. The objector's point may perhaps be illustrated by recalling a ludicrous mistake I once made; if it were explained, 'Banking is an activity, not a province of China', one's informant would not be saying anything about banking; he would merely be indicating how the word 'banking' is used. On the same lines it has been argued that categorial questions and answers about God—say, 'How are we to think of God?'—'God is a substance'—do not really request and offer descriptions of God, not even minimal descriptions; such exchanges merely explore the use of the word 'God'.

Without staging a full discussion, I would suggest that a mistake has been made; one does not always have to assign a thing to the appropriate category in order to identify it; and certainly, if it has been identified, reassessments of its categorial status can be made without calling into question the various facts by which its identification was made. Thus I might ask whether a thunderstorm is a thing or an event (for we normally think of it as something that happens; but it can have a certain life and extent and a possibly changing location); or again, whether hearing is something one does, or something that happens to one. It might be objected that debates of this kind are unilluminating; but they would certainly be conducted with reference to recognized facts about hearing and thunderstorms. It would be totally implausible to say that such categorial questions have to be settled before we can understand what is meant by the words 'thunderstorm' and 'hearing'.

More generally, I would argue that the objection arises out of an unrealistic view of the role of ordinary language in relation to logic. The logician can determine certain functions for linguistic expressions which are sharply distinct, and he can suggest ways of expressing these distinctions by the careful use of ordinary language. But his influence on common usage is slow and uncertain. Suppose he says that some sentence of the form 'S is P' really defines the use of the *word* 'S', rather than describing S, which it stands for; he is thereby making use of a technical distinction between the linguistic mode of speech and straightforward description such as most users of the sentence have never considered. Now is he simply describing their normal use of it? In this case, although ordinary people have never thought of his distinction, he would be claiming that whenever they utter this sentence, they do always use it for the purpose which he isolates and prefers. But this is an unplausible claim;

for since ordinary usage is largely governed by analogy, and most sentences of the form '*S* is *P*' *are* straightforwardly descriptive, ordinary people would naturally presume that *this* '*S* is *P*' is descriptive; and, especially if the words employed are elastic (as 'God' and 'substance' certainly are) would tend to construe them so as to allow *this* sentence to make the same kind of sense as other sentences of similar form. Now in some such cases, admittedly, no good sense emerges. So the logician intervenes; though not by reporting, but by recommending. 'Never mind ordinary usage,' he will be saying; 'it will be clearer and better if you use and interpret ...' in this case 'if you use and interpret categorial statements solely as comments on the use of the subject-word.' Now this is a sensible sort of claim; and we have seen that there are circumstances in which this is the only admissible use (in the 'Banking' example). But it did not appear that these circumstances accompanied every utterance of the phrase (say) '*x* is a substance'; and if those observations were sound, it should be allowable to use 'God is a substance' as a straightforward, though very general, descriptive sentence. God is provisionally identified as the being whom we worship; it then occurs to us to wonder what comparisons will enable us to understand *what* we worship. God is love; but is this to be understood as a quality, or a relation, or a substance, a loving being? By saying that God is a substance, we may be claiming that God is a reality in his own right, and not just the creation of our fancy; he is not the projection of a mood, or a mythical focus of religious aspirations.

But this brings us to another problem. If we say 'God is (a) substance', are we not thereby assigning God to a class of beings, and so infringing his uniqueness? This indeed is the problem which gave rise to the schoolmen's Doctrine of Analogy: if any predicate applies only to God, we can never understand it; if it applies both to God and to creatures, he is no longer God.

One might reply by distinguishing between God's uniqueness *per se* and his uniqueness in all contexts of discourse. There is a distinction, partly seen by Aristotle, between a class and a genus. Aristotle states that there is no genus 'of' things that are (i.e. embracing all of them); but, what is less often remembered, he also claims that substance *is* a genus 'of' things that are (i.e. selected out of them), *de Anima*, ii. 1, 412 a 7. We should probably wish to reformulate this latter statement as a claim that though substances do not form a genus, they do form a class. And in theology, though we might naturally claim that God is *sui generis*, it is absurd to say that God cannot be included in any class; since if any true statement can be made about God, this assigns him to the class of beings to which a corresponding statement can be applied. Negative statements appear to provide a clear example; if we say, 'God is not a man', we thereby assign God to the class of non-men; and by similar reasoning, we would have to admit that God is *a* rational being, *a* moral being, etc., even though the suggestion of 'one among others' needs in its turn to be corrected. Classes can be purely artificial *ad hoc* assemblies, conveying no presumption of any further resemblance among their members. If God exists, it must be possible to construct a number of classes of which God is a member; and this may seem, or indeed be, irreverent; but it does not in fact impair the claim that God is unique.

The notion of a class naturally suggests that of a determinate number of members; but, it has been argued, substances cannot be enumerated; how could one count the number of substances in a room? Hence, it is argued, God cannot be *a* substance, or one substance.[3] Now the difficulty about enumeration, as the objector himself explains, is not peculiar to substance as such. If a jar breaks into pieces, it may well be impossible to count the pieces; conscientious *A* will include what impetuous *B* dismisses as negligible chips, and there is no telling which is right. But the point is surely that we cannot be sure of counting pieces. Pieces are not horses. Nevertheless, we know what it is like for a jar to break into just three pieces, and on occasion we are all prepared to say this and nothing else. Similarly, we know what it is like for a box to contain just three billiard-balls, and nothing else; and if it contains three billiard-balls, it contains three substances. (Or, of course, in another well-recognized sense of the term, one substance; it might be ivory.) More to the point, the whole process of enumerating gods and then eliminating all claimants but one belongs to a fairly primitive stage of theology; and once the notion of a unique divinity has been reached, the phrase 'one God' (indeed the name 'God' itself) has to be used with a different logic, though probably without completely sup-

[3] M. Durrant, *Theology and Intelligibility*, 85–6, 153 ff.

pressing the older usage. But such shifts of meaning are by no means peculiar to theology; there is a contrary shift, and a similar logical anomaly, in our modern habit of talking about 'other worlds' (other planets? other planetary systems?—one isn't always sure), while at the same time retaining 'the world' as a synonym for 'the universe', for all that, in space and time, exists.

What is the point of stating that God is an *ousia* in the categorial sense, a substance? The statement is general enough; it leaves a number of options open. Its principal function, as I see it, is to claim that God is not limited or prescribed by our experience of him, but exists in his own right; in this respect (if phenomenalism be rejected) he is analogous to an unknown physical object, say an undiscovered star. A star does not come into being by being discovered; and God is not brought into being by our human consciousness or metaphysical demands. Some modern theologians, impressed by the failure of confidence in classical metaphysics, have described God in terms which suggest that he is a mythical embodiment of that aspect of human experience which is taken to be most significant. 'We most naturally locate reality, not in another realm, but as the profoundest truth of this one' (J. A. T. Robinson, *The Human Face of God*, 22) is one of the more thoughtful expressions of such a view, and can perhaps be interpreted so as to uphold much of the traditional theology. But it requires some effort of mind to understand 'a truth', even 'the profoundest truth', as a *vera causa*, something that lives and acts. To characterize God as a substance is to stake a claim against reductionist theories which in effect represent God as dependent on the human experience which he is invoked to explain.

In claiming that God is a substance we do not, I think, prejudge the difficult and controversial question of his relation to time and change. There is of course some temptation to parade the purely specious difficulty which I have tried to resolve,[4] arising from the notion that in every being there must be an element which does not change, since it is that which persists through change, but also does change, since it is that to which changes occur. But apart from this, one may be tempted to suggest that if God is a substance he must be immune from change; or, alternatively, that he must be liable to change.

4 Above, pp. 21–2, cf. 98.

The first suggestion arises naturally from the notion that God is substance *par excellence*; just as qualities, relations, etc., inhere in and presuppose substances, so, it is suggested, all finite substances inhere in and presuppose God, as in some sense the ground of their being. Theologians like Macquarrie are following a very ancient tradition when they characterize God in terms of 'Being as such'; and granted the established connections of thought between being and permanence (above, p. 27), it is inevitable that 'Being as such' should suggest 'unchanging being'.

Two brief comments may be put forward. In the first place, any theology which suggests that God is the only ultimate reality, and accordingly that all persons and things are as it were adjectival to his being; such a theology has no doubt the peculiarity, and perhaps the merit, of exhibiting the uniqueness and the sovereignty of God in the most telling fashion; but it needs at the very least a qualification to allow for the wills and actions of finite beings, if God is not to be charged with sole responsibility for all that happens in the universe. Classical Christian theology, though often embarrassed in detail at this point, has at least attempted to uphold the conception of created but sometimes rebellious spirits acting under divine permission against the will of their creator, though prevented from finally frustrating it; God remains responsible for the grand design, but not solely responsible for failures and cruelties in detail; and in this respect his will is one will amongst others, since he has created other wills to stand beside his own.

But secondly, the notion that if God is a substance, he must be an unchanging substance, is I think a mere product of association. The classical conception of God presents him as a substance, and also as immutable; hence it is assumed that one conception necessarily involves the other, and criticisms are made of the 'static ontology' that is thus detected. But of course God can be, and has been, represented as a changing substance, and indeed as one that is ever-changing and infinitely adaptable; I have already noticed one or two ancient examples, at pp. 106, 171 above. In fact a recent writer has criticized the classical theology precisely on the ground that the concept of an immutable substance involves a contradiction. 'It is part of the very concept of substance that anything which falls under this category *should* admit of accidents . . . The idea of an unchangeable substance

... is a nonsensical one, hence to say that God is an unchangeable substance is itself nonsensical.'[5]

But this criticism in turn is misplaced; it relies on an overliteral reading of Aristotle's *Categories*. Aristotle does indeed say that a substance (say, a person or thing) admits of contrary determinations, as is shown by its changes; but his point is surely that, unlike other kinds of being, a substance can remain what it is *even though* it admits of contrary determinations. He does not state, even in this work, that change is a *sine qua non* of substance; and in other works, of course, the concept of unchanging substance is freely employed. It would obviously require much more than a paragraph either to attack or to defend this time-honoured conception; and ample space would also be needed to do justice to the large questions of God's relationship to time and change and human action. I only wish to submit that the description of God in terms of substance does not of itself prejudge the question whether God is, or is not, involved in change.

One could of course add that any attempt to make the *Categories* the sole definitive treatment of substance frustrates all theological exercise *ab initio*. As the Platonist commentators observed, Aristotle is there discussing examples of substance taken from common life; he deals with individuals, presuming them ranked in species and genera, and with these latter themselves, taking them to embrace numerous individuals. There is no room in such a construction for a being *sui generis*; nevertheless Aristotle soon comes to such a conception, and uses the term *ousia* to express it, as with the unchanging divinity of *Metaph.* xii. 6–9, 'a substance which is eternal and immovable and separate from sensible things'.

On the other hand, if our thesis is not that 'God is a substance' but, taking the anarthrous alternative that English usage permits, 'God is substance', it easily connects with the class of predicative statements reviewed above (on p. 167): God is Fire, Spirit, Light, Life, Mind, Love, etc. Some, though not all, of these predicates appear to be naming a substance in the more precise sense of a constitutive material or stuff; but allowance has to be made for some element of conscious metaphor, though no doubt at some times Fire, Spirit, and Light have been given a literal sense.

[5] M. Durrant, op. cit., 121–2.

How can such statements be construed? Clearly they do not simply offer alternative definitions. They are not convertible, as has often been observed; 'God is love' does not warrant its converse 'Love is God'. My impression is that, despite some attractive features which I mentioned above, such statements are felt to embody some element of paradox; and this arises, not simply from the physical imagery, which is most prominent in 'fire' and 'light', but from the fact that the predicates are what is commonly called 'mass terms'; that is, they refer to some type of reality however it is distributed and wherever it is found; they do not suggest any kind of over-all structure or organization. (It is true that the label 'mass term' may itself be misleading, like the corresponding Aristotelian phrase 'simple bodies'; if we speak of bread, this is not to imply that it exists as an undifferentiated mass; we simply omit to convey the fact that it is normally found in loaves; on the other hand if we speak of 'control', using what looks like a similar form, we may mean, not a general principle, but the particular controlling organization by which we ourselves are directed.) By the same token, 'love' can be no more than a collective term for all the various and separate acts and thoughts of love; and this suggestion comes to the fore if we proclaim that love is God. Again, to characterize God as 'mind' does not of itself dispel the notion of a number of unrelated mental acts; 'a mind' has the advantage of suggesting a unified consciousness and will; but at the same time it gives up the implication of uniqueness.

It can be noted at this point that Platonism offered certain built-in advantages for theological statements which are not provided by our modern logic of universal terms. We can take 'man' as a collective term, used to refer to the whole human population of the universe; or again as a specification which defines an indefinitely extensible class. Platonists saw men as constituted by their resemblance to, or participation in, an ideal standard form which could be called 'man' in the truest sense, ideal or absolute man; hence they had the opportunity of describing God as ideal or absolute life, mind, love, and so on. However, this was not an unmixed advantage; it is not at first sight easy to maintain that absolute mind is identical with absolute life, and so on, if only because they define different classes of particulars; and if so, then God can at best be identified with one absolute, say ideal goodness, which might be given a unique status along the lines suggested in *Republic* 509 b. Nevertheless some ancient Platonists argued that ideal goodness was identical with ideal unity and being; some again were prepared to characterize their first principle as mind; but another view was to describe God as 'beyond the Ideas', and so not identifiable with any of them.

The Platonic theory has often been regarded as a magnificent failure; and certainly since Aristotle's time it has been commonly thought to fail in at least one of its undertakings, namely in accounting for our use of universal terms. But this does not mean that it is empty of useful suggestions; and it would seem that the notion of an ideal standard, disengaged from confusing fellow-travellers, is still serviceable for theology. Indeed our interpretation of a text such as 'God is love' may well be coloured by Platonism; what can we mean, except that God is the purest and completest realization of this many-levelled activity? And at a homely level, the notion of a standard quantity or substance presents little difficulty, and even begins to elucidate a few problems. The standard yard is not a yard long by the same criterion as other objects (viz. by *agreement* with the standard yard); but undoubtedly it is a yard long, since it has length, and its length cannot be anything other than a yard. And there is no theoretical reason why the same object should not serve as a standard in more than one respect, defining not only a unit of length but (say) the purity of gold. From such modest beginnings one might go on to suggest, e.g., that God could be the source of morality without being either an arbitrary dictator or just another moral agent; or again, that apparently conflicting qualities like justice and mercy could be exhibited in a form which transcended the limitations of each of them.

The early Christian response to Platonism was of course different and much more various, since in late antiquity the theory of Ideas was presented in a number of different forms, and was regarded with varying degrees of favour or suspicion. Christian writers certainly came to characterize God by lists of predicates of the form 'absolute x, absolute y, absolute z';[6] but at a more reflective level, there are two lines of thought which call for attention. One was that God is the source of the Ideas. This did not

---

[6] So e.g. Eusebius, *ET* ii. 14. 6; similar lists are also applied to the Logos: ibid. i. 8. 4, Origen, *in Joh.* i. 9, Athanasius, *c. Gentes* 46, etc.

necessarily mean that they were regarded as created beings; they could be correlated with the divine Logos, and seen as means of God's self-expression; this doctrine is well developed in Philo and has some influence on Origen.[7] But later Christian thinkers became increasingly reluctant to acknowledge an element of plurality in the Son–Logos which they thought unworthy of the Father, or indeed any real division of functions between them; so the system of Ideas came to be seen as proceeding from the creative mind of the Godhead as such, and as finding expression in the created order. At best, therefore, it gave only a limited knowledge of the divine nature; and to that extent it became less attractive to characterize God in language reminiscent of the Platonic Ideas.

The other doctrine was a development of Stoic theology already discussed; although God as such was perfectly one and simple, he could be given a number of distinct titles (ἐπίνοιαι or προσηγορίαι) based on his different energies or operations in regard to the world and mankind. We have already noticed the theory that within the divine life itself all distinction of operations is transcended (above, pp. 187–9); the view we are now discussing accepts a real distinction of various operations or 'energies' of God towards the created world, which justify us in naming him by a number of distinct titles; but these intelligible 'energies' have then to be distinguished from the inexpressible divine essence from which they proceed. (It is sometimes suggested that this theory was developed by St. Basil and the other Cappadocians as a reply to the rationalistic theology of Eunomius; but in reality it appears to be older; it is clearly stated by Eusebius, *DE* iv. 15. 16; indeed Origen uses it to explain the different titles of the Son (*in Joh.* i. 112, 119–24) and could have applied it to the Father, in view of his discussion of the various views formulated 'in regard to God and his substance' (ibid. xiii. 123 ff.); although the technical terms ἐπίνοια and ἐνέργεια are not found in this passage, Origen explains that God is called Light because he enlightens the mind, Fire because he purges uncleanness, and Spirit because he gives the true life. Much the same teaching is found in Clement, *Strom.* v. 82; so in its essentials the theory is no doubt pre-Christian.)

This theology therefore uses the term 'energy' (as briefly noted

[7] See H. A. Wolfson, *Philosophy of the Church Fathers*, 270–80.

above, pp. 141–2) to stand for operations which are distinct from, and even contrasted with, the 'substance' or essential nature from which they proceed; and so necessarily conflicts with the Aristotelian formula taken over by many of the medievals, in which God's substance or essence is defined as his energy (Aristotle, *Metaph.* xii. 6, 1071 b 20, 1072 a 25; Plotinus, *Enn.* vi. 8. 12; Aquinas, *Summa Theologica* i. 25, etc.). But even where the contrast is accepted, the divine energies must be energies of a distinctive kind, when it is held that God is the sole sovereign and immutable being. There can of course be no question of regarding them as contingencies imposed by the actions of others (as with human beings, who can be 'energized', i.e. possessed, by demons, or transformed by the 'energy' of Christ, Irenaeus v. 13. 3, Hv. ii. 357). They cannot be 'accidents' of any kind. The term 'energy' can, however, be used of divine operations which are occasional, as well as for those which are eternally exercised. Thus Athanasius can use it for God's activity in creation (*c. Ar.* ii. 2), which he sees as extending over a limited period of time; but also for his eternal self-expression in the divine Son, who is his 'living will and essential energy' (ibid.), where the language approximates to Aristotle's identification of energy and substance. Origen, however, takes a converse position: the Holy Spirit is an 'energetic substance', i.e. an active being, not a mere energy or activity, *in Joh.*, fr. 37, p. 513; and similar pronouncements are made about the Son by Eusebius and by George of Laodicea.[8] Some writers see fit to describe the Incarnation itself as a divine 'energy' or activity (so Clement, *Strom.* v. 55. 3 and vii. 7. 7). Most commonly, however, the divine energies are regarded as eternal and invariant manifestations of God's power. One might perhaps regard them as divine attributes under a new description which brings out their dynamic and effective character. But sometimes at least, even if regarded as invariant, they are thought of as divine activities *ad extra*; so Basil can say that 'the energies are manifold ($\pi o \iota \kappa \acute{\iota} \lambda a \iota$) but the substance is simple ... and the energies reach down to ourselves, but his substance remains inaccessible' (*Ep.* 234. 1); and this distinction between the intelligible divine energies and the inexpressible substance from which they proceed became an authoritative position of later Eastern orthodoxy, which lies beyond the scope of this book.

---

[8] Eusebius, *DE* iv. 3. 4, *c. Marc.* ii. 4. 24, etc.; George *ap.* Epiphanius, *Haer.* 73. 12.

In thus distinguishing the inexpressible divine substance even from God's uncreated and eternal energies, the Eastern theologians are clearly using the term 'substance' in a more remote and specialized sense than any which we have yet encountered. Their usage would seem to raise the problems characteristic of negative theology in a specially acute form; but the negative impression is of course modified by the underlying assumption that the energies must after all correspond with the substance from which they proceed; and probably also by the older, Platonic, principle that every cause must be of greater value and power than some particular effect which derives from it. The sense of divine mystery can never dissolve the apprehension of divine goodness.

BIBLIOGRAPHY

An asterisk denotes introductory works

Reference works, History of Philosophy, Philology

*ARMSTRONG, A. H., *An Introduction to Ancient Philosophy*, London, 1947.
—— (ed.), *The Cambridge History of Later Greek and Early Medieval Philosophy*, Cambridge, 1967 (= *LGP*).
ARPE, C., 'Substantia', *Philologus* 94 (1940), 65–78.
BÄUMKER, C., *Das Problem der Materie in der griechischen Philosophie*, Münster, 1890.
COPLESTON, F., *A History of Philosophy*, i, *Greece and Rome*, London, 1946.
DE HOGOS-RUIZ, A., 'Estudio semantico del vocabulo οὐσία', *Anales de la Universidad Murcia* 10 (1951–2), 363–433.
DE VOGEL, C. J., *Greek Philosophy*, 3 vols., Leiden, 1949 (1969[4]); 1953; 1959.
DIELS, H., *Doxographi Graeci*, Berlin, 1879, 1965[4].
DÖRRIE, H., 'Hypostasis, Wort- und Bedeutungsgeschichte', *NAG*, ph.-h. kl., 1955, 55–93.
*EDWARDS, P., *The Encyclopedia of Philosophy*, New York and London, 1967.
GUTHRIE, W. K. C., *A History of Greek Philosophy*, 4 vols. published, Cambridge, 1962, 1965, 1969, 1975.
HADOT, P., and others, 'Existenz, existentia' in J. Ritter (below), vol. 2.
HIRZEL, R., *Οὐσία*, *Philologus* 72 (1913), 42–64.
KAHN, C. H., 'The Greek Verb "to be" and the Concept of Being', *Foundations of Language* 2 (1966), 245–65, repr. Indianapolis, n.d.
—— *The Verb 'Be' and its Synonyms* (Philosophical and Grammatical Studies ed. by J. W. M. Verhaar, 6), Dordrecht, 1973.
KITTEL, G., *Theologisches Wörterbuch zum Neuen Testament* (*TWNT*), 9 vols., 1933–73.
—— *Theological Dictionary of the New Testament* (E.T. of above by G. W. Bromiley), 9 vols., 1964–74.
KNEALE, W. and M., *The Development of Logic*, Oxford, 1962.
KÖSTER, H., 'Hypostasis', in Kittel, *TWNT* (above).
*PETERS, F. E., *Greek Philosophical Terms, A Historical Lexicon*, New York and London, 1967.
PRAECHTER, K., see UEBERWEG.
RITTER, J., *Historisches Wörterbuch der Philosophie* (in progress), Darmstadt, (i) 1971, (ii) 1972, (iii) (G–H), 1974.
STUDER, B., 'Hypostase', in J. Ritter, 1974 (above).
UEBERWEG, F., *Grundriss der Geschichte der Philosophie des Altertums*, 12th edition by K. Praechter, Berlin, 1926.
VERBEKE, G., *L'Évolution de la doctrine du pneuma du stoïcisme à St. Augustin*, Louvain, 1945.

WITT, R. E., 'Hypostasis', in H. G. Wood (ed.), *Amicitiae Corolla, Essays presented to J. Rendel Harris*, London, 1933, 319–43.

ZELLER, E., *Die Philosophie der Griechen in ihrer geschichtlichen Entwicklung*, II/i (Leipzig, 1889⁴); II/ii (Leipzig, 1879³); III/i (Leipzig, 1923⁵); III/ii (Leipzig, 1903⁴).

The philosophical theory of Substance and related topics

ANSCOMBE, G. E. M., 'The Principle of Individuation', *PAS*, suppl. vol. 27 (1953), 83–96.

—— and GEACH, P. T., *Three Philosophers*, Oxford, 1961.

BAMBROUGH, R., 'Universals and Family Resemblances', *PAS* 61 (1960–1), 207–22.

CARTWRIGHT, H., 'Heraclitus and the Bath Water', *PR* 74 (1965), 466–85.

—— 'Quantities', *PR* 79 (1970), 25–42.

CHAPPELL, V. C., 'Stuff and Things', *PAS* 92 (1970–1), 61–76.

DURRANT, M., *Theology and Intelligibility*, London, 1973.

EMMET, D. M., *The Nature of Metaphysical Thinking*, London, 1945.

—— 'The Ground of Being', *JTS*, N.S. 15 (1964), 280–92.

FARRER, A. M., *Finite and Infinite*, Westminster, 1943, 1959².

—— *Faith and Speculation*, London, 1967.

FEIGL, H., and SELLARS, W. (eds.), *Readings in Philosophical Analysis*, New York, 1949.

FLEW, A. G. N. (ed.), *Logic and Language*, Series 1, Oxford, 1951; Series 2, Oxford, 1953.

—— and MACINTYRE, A. (eds.), *New Essays in Philosophical Theology*, London, 1955.

FREGE, G., Philosophical Writings, E.T. by P. T. Geach and M. Black, Oxford, 1952.

GEACH, P. T., 'On What There Is', *PAS*, suppl. vol. 25 (1951), 125–36.

—— 'Form and Existence', *PAS* 55 (1954–5), 251–72. Revised version in *God and the Soul*.

—— *Reference and Generality*, Ithaca, N.Y., 1962, 1968².

—— 'What Actually Exists', *PAS*, suppl. vol. 42 (1968), 7–16, reprinted in *God and the Soul*.

—— *God and the Soul*, London, 1969.

GILSON, E., *Being and Some Philosophers*, Toronto, 1952.

HEIDEGGER, M., *Sein und Zeit*, 1927, Tübingen, 1953⁷.

—— *Existence and Being*, E.T. by W. Brock, London, 1949.

—— *Being and Time*, E.T. by J. Macquarrie and E. Robinson, London, 1962.

HUGHES, G. E., and LONDEY, D. G., *The Elements of Formal Logic*, London, 1965.

JONES, O. R., 'Identity and Countability', *Analysis* 24 (1963–4), 201–6.

KNEALE, W., 'Is Existence a Predicate?', *PAS*, suppl. vol. 15 (1936), 154–74; reprinted in Feigl and Sellars, 29–43.

—— 'The Notion of a Substance', *PAS* 40 (1939–40), 103–34.

KNEALE, W., and KNEALE, M., *The Development of Logic*, Oxford, 1962.

*LANGER, S. K., *An Introduction to Symbolic Logic*, London, 1937.

LAYCOCK, H., 'Some Questions of Ontology', *PR* 81 (1972), 3–42.

LOCKE, J., *An Essay Concerning Human Understanding*, London, 1690 (esp. ii. 23, 27).

LOUX, M. J., 'Recent Work on Ontology', *American Philosophical Quarterly* 9 (1972), 119–38.

MACQUARRIE, J., *Principles of Christian Theology*, London, 1966.

MARCEL, G., *The Mystery of Being*, London, 1951.

MASCALL, E. L., *Existence and Analogy*, London, 1949.

MEI, TSU-LIN, 'Chinese Grammar and the Linguistic Movement in Philosophy', *Review of Metaphysics* 14 (1961), 463–92.

MOORE, G. E., 'Is Existence a Predicate?', *PAS*, suppl. vol. 15 (1936), 175–88 (reprinted in Flew, *Logic and Language* 2, 82–94).

O'CONNOR, D. J., 'Substance and Attribute', in *The Encyclopedia of Philosophy*, ed. P. Edwards (above).

PARKINSON, G. H. R. (ed.), *The Theory of Meaning*, Oxford, 1968.

QUINE, W. V., 'On What There is', *Review of Metaphysics* 2 (1948), 21–38; repr. in *PAS*, suppl. vol. 25 (1951), 217 ff., and Quine, 1953, 1–19.

—— 'Identity, Ostension and Hypostasis', *Journal of Philosophy* 47 (1950), 621–33, repr. Quine, 1953, 65–79.

—— *From a Logical Point of View*, Cambridge, Mass., 1953, 1961[2].

—— *Word and Object*, Cambridge, Mass., 1960.

QUINTON, A. M., *The Nature of Things*, London, 1973.

RAEYMAEKER, L. DE, *Philosophie de l'Être*, Louvain, 1947[2].

—— *The Philosophy of Being* (E. T. by E. H. Ziegelmeyer), St. Louis, Mo., 1954.

RUSSELL, BERTRAND, 'On Denoting', *Mind* 14 (1905), 479–93; repr. in Feigl and Sellars, 103–15; also in *Logic and Knowledge* (below), 41–56.

—— *Mysticism and Logic*, London, 1918.

—— 'The Philosophy of Logical Atomism', *The Monist* 28 (1918), 495–527 and 29 (1919), 32–63, 190–222, 345–380; repr. in *Logic and Knowledge*, 177–281 (esp. Lecture V, 'General Propositions and Existence').

—— *The Analysis of Matter*, London, 1927.

—— *An Inquiry into Meaning and Truth*, London, 1940.

—— *Human Knowledge, its Scope and Limits*, London, 1948.

—— *Logic and Knowledge*, ed. R. C. Marsh, London, 1956.

RYLE, G., 'Categories', *PAS* 38 (1937–8), 189–206, repr. in Flew, 1953, 65–81.

—— *The Concept of Mind*, London, 1949.

—— (See also Wood, O. P.)

SEARLE, J., *Speech Acts*, Cambridge, 1969.

STRAWSON, P. F., 'On Referring', *Mind* 59 (1950), 320–44; repr. in Parkinson, 61–85.

—— *Introduction to Logical Theory*, London, 1952.

—— *Individuals*, London, 1959.

—— (ed.), *Philosophical Logic*, Oxford, 1967.

—— (ed.), *Studies in the Philosophy of Thought and Action*, Oxford, 1968.

STRAWSON, P. F., 'Categories', in *Ryle*, ed. Wood and Pitcher (below), 181–211.

THATCHER, A., 'Existence and Life in Tillich', *Scottish Journal of Theology* 27 (1974), 306–12.

TILLICH, P., *Systematic Theology*, 3 vols., London, 1953, 1957, 1964.

*WARNOCK, G. J., *English Philosophy since 1900*, London, 1958.

WITTGENSTEIN, L., *Tractatus Logico-Philosophicus*, London, 1922; new edition with new E.T., London, 1961.

—— *Philosophische Untersuchungen*, Oxford, 1953, 1958² (with E.T.); this also republished separately as *Philosophical Investigations*, Oxford, 1963.

WOOD, O. P., and PITCHER, G., *Ryle*, New York, 1970, and London, 1971.

Plato

ACKRILL, J. L., 'Plato and the Copula: *Sophist* 251–9', *JHS* 77 (1957), 1–7 (repr. in Allen, 1965, and Vlastos, 1971).

ALLEN, R. E., 'Participation and Predication in Plato's Middle Dialogues', *Philosophical Review* 69 (1960), 147–64, repr. in Allen, 1965, 43–60.

—— (ed.), *Studies in Plato's Metaphysics*, London, 1965.

AST, F., *Lexicon Platonicum*, Leipzig, 1835–8; repr. Darmstadt, 1956.

BAMBROUGH, R. (ed.), *New Essays on Plato and Aristotle*, London, 1965.

BERGER, H. H., *Ousia in de Dialogen van Plato*, Leiden, 1961.

BLUCK, R. S., *Plato's Phaedo*, London, 1955.

—— 'Logos and Forms in Plato: a Reply to Professor Cross', *Mind* 65 (1956), 522–9; repr. in Allen, 1965, 33–41.

BURNET, J., *Plato: Phaedo*, ed. with introdn. and notes, Oxford, 1911.

—— *Greek Philosophy* I; *Thales to Plato*, London, 1914.

CORNFORD, F. M., *Plato's Theory of Knowledge*, London, 1935.

—— *Plato's Cosmology*, London, 1937.

CROMBIE, I. M., *An Examination of Plato's Doctrines*, 2 vols., London, 1962–3.

CROSS, R. C., 'Logos and Forms in Plato', *Mind* 63 (1954), 433–50; repr. in Allen, 1965, 13–31.

—— and WOOZLEY, A. D., *Plato's Republic*, London, 1966.

DES PLACES, E., *Lexique de Platon* (*Œuvres Complètes*, ed. Budé, 14), Paris, 1964.

DE STRYCKER, E., review of F. Solmsen, in *L'Antiquité classique* 16 (1947), 148–50.

DE VOGEL, C. J., 'Platon a-t-il ou n'a-t-il pas introduit le mouvement dans son monde intelligible?', *Actes XI Congr. Phil.* [Bruxelles] 12, Amsterdam, 1953, 61–7; repr. in next work, 176–82.

—— *Philosophia* I, *Studies in Greek Philosophy*, Assen, 1970.

DÜRING, I., and OWEN, G. E. L., *Aristotle and Plato in the Mid-Fourth Century*, Göteborg, 1960.

FINDLAY, J. N., *Plato: The Written and the Unwritten Doctrines*, London, 1974.

FREDE, M., *Prädikation und Existenzaussage* (*Hypomnemata* 18), Göttingen, 1967.

GAISER, K., *Platons ungeschriebene Lehre*, Stuttgart, 1963, 1968².

GOSLING, J. C. B., *Plato* (*Arguments of the Philosophers*), London, 1973.

Hackforth, R., 'Plato's Theism', *CQ* 30 (1936), 4–9 (repr. in Allen, 1965, 439–47).

—— *Plato's Examination of Pleasure*, Cambridge, 1945 (repr. as *Plato's Philebus*, 1958).

—— *Plato's Phaedrus*, Cambridge, 1952.

—— *Plato's Phaedo*, Cambridge, 1955.

Hager, F. P., 'Die Materie und das Böse im antiken Platonismus', *Mus. Helv.* 19 (1962), 73–103.

—— *Die Vernunft und das Problem des Bösen in Rahmen der platonischen Ethik und Metaphysik*, Bern, 1963.

—— *Der Geist und Das Eine*, Bern and Stuttgart, 1970.

Ilting, K.-H., 'Platons "Ungeschriebene Lehren": der Vortrag "über das Gute" ', *Phronesis* 13 (1968), 1–31.

Krämer, H. J., *Arete bei Platon und Aristoteles. Zum Wesen und zur Geschichte der platonischen Ontologie*, Heidelberg, 1959, repr. Amsterdam, 1967.

—— *Der Ursprung der Geistmetaphysik. Untersuchungen zur Geschichte des Platonismus zwischen Platon und Plotin*, Amsterdam, 1964, 1967².

—— 'Retraktationen zum Problem des esoterischen Platon', *Mus. Helv.* 21 (1964), 137–67.

Loriaux, R., *L'Être et la Forme selon Platon*, Bruges, 1955.

Malcolm, J., 'Plato's Analysis of τὸ ὄν and τὸ μὴ ὄν in the Sophist', *Phronesis* 12 (1967), 130–46.

Marten, R., *ΟΥΣΙΑ im Denken Platons*, Meisenheim am Glan, 1962.

Mills, K. W., review of R. Loriaux (above), *Gnomon* 49 (1957), 325–9.

Moravcsik, J. M. E., 'Being and Meaning in the Sophist', *Acta Philosophica Fennica* 14 (1962), 23–78.

Oehler, K., 'Der entmythologisierte Platon. Zur Lage der Platonforschung', *Zeitschr. f. philos. Forschung* 19 (1965), 393–420 (repr. in Wippern, 1972, 95–129).

—— 'Neue Fragmente zum esoterische Platon', *Hermes* 93 (1965), 397–407.

Owen, G. E. L., [1971] 'Plato on Not-Being', in G. Vlastos, *Plato* (below), 223–67.

—— see also Düring, I., and next section.

Peipers, D., *Ontologia Platonica*, Leipzig, 1883.

*Raven, J. E., *Plato's Thought in the Making*, Cambridge, 1965.

Robin, L., *La Théorie platonicienne des Idées et des Nombres d'après Aristote*, Paris, 1908.

Robinson, R., *Plato's Earlier Dialectic*, Ithaca, N.Y., 1941, Oxford, 1953².

Ross, W. D., *Plato's Theory of Ideas*, Oxford, 1951, 1953² (= *PTI*).

Runciman, W. G., *Plato's Later Epistemology*, Cambridge, 1962.

Ryle, G., 'Dialectic in the Academy', in R. Bambrough (above), 39–68.

Saffrey, H. D., *Le Περὶ φιλοσοφίας d'Aristote et la théorie platonicienne des idées et des nombres*, Leiden, 1955, 1971².

Skemp, J. B., '῞Υλη and ὑποδοχή', in Düring and Owen (above), 201–12.

Solmsen, F., *Plato's Theology*, Ithaca, N.Y., 1942.

Stenzel, J., *Studien zur Entwicklung der platonischen Dialektik von Sokrates zu Aristoteles*, Breslau, 1917, Darmstadt, 1961³.

STENZEL, J., *Plato's Method of Dialectic* (E.T. by D. J. Allan), New York, 1940, repr. 1964.

—— *Zahl und Gestalt bei Platon und Aristoteles*, Leipzig and Berlin, 1924, Darmstadt, 1959³.

TARRANT, D., *The Hippias Major attributed to Plato*, Cambridge, 1928.

TAYLOR, A. E., *Plato. The Man and his Work*, London, 1926, 1937⁴.

—— *Plato. The Sophist and Statesman*, London, 1961.

THEILER, W., 'Einheit und unbegrenzte Zweiheit von Platon bis Plotin', in *Isonomia*, ed. J. Mau and E. G. Schmidt, Berlin, 1964, repr. in his *Untersuchungen zur antiken Literatur*, Berlin, 1970, 460–83.

THOMPSON, E. S., *Plato. The Meno*, London, 1901.

VLASTOS, G., 'Degrees of Reality in Plato', in R. Bambrough (above), 1–19.

—— (ed.), *Plato* I: *Metaphysics and Epistemology*, New York, 1971.

WIPPERN, J., *Das Problem der ungeschriebenen Lehre Platons* (*Wege der Forschung*, 186), Darmstadt, 1972.

Aristotle

ACKRILL, J. L., *Aristotle's Categories and De Interpretatione*, Oxford, 1963.

ALBRITTON, R., 'Forms of Particular Substances in Aristotle's *Metaphysics*' *Journal of Philosophy* 54 (1957), 699–708.

*ALLAN, D. J., *The Philosophy of Aristotle*, London, 1952.

ALLEN, R. E., 'Individual Properties in Aristotle's Categories', *Phronesis* 14 (1969), 31–9.

ANNAS, J., 'Individuals in Aristotle's "Categories" ', *Phronesis* 19 (1974), 146–52.

ANSCOMBE, G. E. M., and GEACH, P. T. *Three Philosophers*, Oxford, 1961.

ARPE, C., *Das τί ἦν εἶναι bei Aristoteles*, Hamburg, 1937.

AUBENQUE, P., *Le Problème de l'être chez Aristote*, Paris, 1962, 1972³.

BAMBROUGH, R. (ed.), *New Essays on Plato and Aristotle*, London, 1965.

BONITZ, H., *Index Aristotelicus* (in *Aristotelis Opera*, ed. Academia Regia Borussica, Vol. 5), Berlin, 1870, repr. Darmstadt, 1955.

BUCHANAN, E., *Aristotle's Theory of Being*, Cambridge, Mass., 1962.

CHERNISS, H. F., *Aristotle's Criticism of Plato and the Academy*, Baltimore, 1944, New York, 1962.

—— *The Riddle of the Early Academy*, Berkeley and Los Angeles, 1945, repr. New York, 1962.

CHROUST, A. H., 'The First Thirty Years of Modern Aristotelian Scholarship', *Classica et Mediaevalia* 24 (1963), 27–57; G.T. in Moraux, 1968.

COUSIN, D. R., 'Aristotle's Doctrine of Substance', *Mind* 42 (1933), 319–37.

DANCY, R., 'On Some of Aristotle's First Thoughts about Substance', *PR* 84 (1975), 338–73.

DENINGER, J. G., '*Wahres Sein' in der Philosophie des Aristoteles*, Meisenheim am Glan, 1961.

DE RIJK, L. M., *The Place of the Categories of Being in Aristotle's Philosophy*, Assen, 1952.

DE VOGEL, C. J., 'Did Aristotle ever accept Plato's theory of transcendent Ideas?', *Archiv für Geschichte der Philosophie* 47 (1965), 261–98; repr. in, —— *Philosophia*, I, Assen, 1970.

DIRLMEIER, F., 'Zum gegenwärtigen Stand der Aristoteles-Forschung', *Wiener Studien* 76 (1963), 52–67.

DÜRING, I., *Aristoteles: Darstellung und Interpretation seines Denkens*, Heidelberg, 1966.

—— and OWEN, G. E. L., *Aristotle and Plato in the Mid-Fourth Century*, Göteborg, 1960.

EDEL, A., 'Aristotle's Categories and the Nature of Categorial Theory', *Review of Metaphysics* 29 (1975), 45–65.

GEWIRTH, A., 'Aristotle's Doctrine of Being', *PR* 62 (1953), 577–89.

GUTHRIE, W. K. C., 'The Development of Aristotle's Theology', *CQ* 27 (1933), 162–71, and 28 (1934), 90–8. G.T. in Hager, 1969, 75–113.

HAGER, F. P. (ed.), *Metaphysik und Theologie des Aristoteles (Wege der Forschung*, 206), Darmstadt, 1969.

—— (ed.), *Logik und Erkenntnislehre des Aristoteles (Wege der Forschung*, 226), Darmstadt, 1972.

HAPP, H., 'Kosmologie und Metaphysik bei Aristoteles', in K. Flasch (ed.), *Parusia*, Frankfurt am Main, 1965.

—— *Hyle. Studien zum aristotelischen Materie-Begriff*, Berlin, 1971.

HARING, E. S., 'Substantial Form in Aristotle Metaphysics Z', *Review of Metaphysics* 10 (1956–7), 308–32, 482–501, 698–713.

HUNTER, E. D., 'Aristotle on Primary ΟΥΣΙΑ', *Archiv für Geschichte der Philosophie* 57 (1975), 1–20.

JAEGER, W., *Studien zur Entstehungsgeschichte der Metaphysik des Aristoteles*, Berlin, 1912.

—— *Aristoteles. Grundlegung einer Geschichte seiner Entwicklung*, Berlin, 1923 (E.T. as below).

—— *Aristotle* (E.T. by R. Robinson), Oxford, 1934, 1948[2].

JONES, B., 'Individuals in Aristotle's Categories', *Phronesis* 17 (1972), 107–23.

—— 'An Introduction to the First Five Chapters of Aristotle's *Categories*', *Phronesis* 20 (1975), 146–74.

KIRWAN, C., *Aristotle's Metaphysics, Books Γ, Δ, E*, Oxford, 1971.

KRÄMER, H. J., 'Grundfrage der aristotelischen Theologie', *Theologie und Philosophie* 44 (1969), 363–82, 481–505.

LACEY, A. R., 'Οὐσία and Form in Aristotle', *Phronesis* 10 (1965), 54–69.

LESHER, J. H., 'Aristotle on Form, Substance and Universals: A Dilemma', *Phronesis* 16 (1971), 169–78.

MACKINNON, D. M., 'Aristotle's Conception of Substance', in Bambrough, 1965, 97–119.

MANSION, A., 'La Genèse de l'œuvre d'Aristote d'après les travaux récents', *Revue néoscholastique de philosophie* 29 (1927), 307–41, 423–66. G.T. in Moraux, 1968, 1–66.

MANSION, S., 'La Première Doctrine de la substance', *Revue philosophique de Louvain* 44 (1946), 349–69. G.T. in Hager, 1969, 114–38.

—— *La Jugement d'existence chez Aristote*, Paris and Louvain, 1946.

—— 'La Doctrine aristotélicienne de la substance et le traité des Catégories',

Proc. 10th International Congress of Philosophy, Amsterdam, 1949, 1097
1100.

MANSION, S., 'Positions maîtresses d'Aristote', in Moraux, 1957, 43–91.

—— 'Notes sur la Doctrine des Categories dans les Topiques', in Owen,
1968 (below), 189–201.

MERLAN, P., 'Aristotle's Unmoved Movers', *Traditio* 4 (1946), 1–30.

MILLER, P., 'What Aristotle Should Have Said', *American Philosophical
Quarterly* 9 (1972), 207–12.

MORAUX, P., (*et al.*) *Aristote et St. Thomas d'Aquin*, Louvain, 1957.

—— 'L'Évolution d'Aristote', in the above, 9–41.

—— (ed.), *Aristoteles in der neueren Forschung* (*Wege der Forschung*, 61), Darmstadt, 1968.

MORAVCSIK, J. M. E. (ed.), *Aristotle* (*Modern Studies in Philosophy*), New
York, 1967, and London, 1968.

—— 'Aristotle's Theory of Categories', in the above, 125–45.

MOREAU, J., 'L'Être et l'essence dans la philosophie d'Aristote', in *Autour
d'Aristote: Receuil . . . offert à M. A. Mansion*, Louvain, 1955, 181–204;
G.T. in Hager, 1969, 222–50.

OWEN, G. E. L., 'A Proof in the *Peri Ideon*', *JHS* 77 (1957), 103–11, repr.
in Allen (Plato, 1965), 293–312.

—— 'Logic and Metaphysics in some Earlier Works of Aristotle', in Düring
and Owen (1960), 163–90.

—— 'Aristotle on the Snares of Ontology', in Bambrough (1965), 69–95.

—— 'Inherence', *Phronesis* 10 (1965), 97–105.

—— 'The Platonism of Aristotle', British Academy Lecture, 1965; repr.
in Strawson, 1968, 147–74.

—— (ed.), *Aristotle on Dialectic: the Topics* (Proceedings of the third Sym-
posium Aristotelicum), Oxford, 1968.

OWENS, J., 'The Reality of the Aristotelian Separate Movers', *Review of
Metaphysics* 3 (1950), 319–337.

—— *The Doctrine of Being in the Aristotelian Metaphysics*, Toronto, 1951,
1963².

—— 'Aristotle on Categories', *Review of Metaphysics* 14 (1961), 73–90.

—— 'Matter and Predication in Aristotle', in Moravcsik, *Aristotle*, 191–214.

PÖTSCHER, W., *Strukturprobleme der aristotelischen und theophrastischen Gottes-
vorstellung*, Leiden, 1970.

*Ross, W. D., *Aristotle*, London, 1923, 1956⁵.

—— *Aristotle's Metaphysics* (text, introduction, and commentary), 2 vols.,
Oxford, 1924.

—— *Aristotle's Physics* (text, introduction, and commentary), Oxford, 1936.

RYAN, E. E., 'Pure Form in Aristotle', *Phronesis* 18 (1973), 209–24.

SCHOFIELD, M., 'Metaphysics Z 3: Some Suggestions', *Phronesis* 17 (1972),
97–101.

SELLARS, W., 'Substance and Form in Aristotle', *Journal of Philosophy* 54
(1957), 688–99.

THEILER, W., 'Die Entstehung der Metaphysik des Aristoteles', *Mus. Helv.*
15 (1958), 85–105; repr. in Hager, 1969, 266–98, and in

—— *Untersuchungen zur antiken Literatur*, Berlin, 1970 (318–42).

THORP, J. W., 'Aristotle's Use of Categories', *Phronesis* 19 (1974), 238–56.

VERBEKE, G., 'La Doctrine de l'être dans la metaphysique d'Aristote', *Revue philosophique de Louvain* 50 (1952), 471–8.

VOLLRATH, E., *Studien zur Kategorienlehre des Aristoteles*, Ratingen, Düsseldorf, 1969.

WILPERT, P., *Zwei aristotelische Frühschrifte über die Ideenlehre*, Regensburg, 1949.

—— 'Zur Interpretation von Metaphysik Z 15', *Archiv für Geschichte der Philosophie* 42 (1960), 130–58; repr. in Hager, 1969, 367–98.

Post-Aristotelian Philosophy

ANDRESEN, C., 'Justin und der mittlere Platonismus', *ZNW* 44 (1952–3), 157–95.

—— *Logos und Nomos: Die Polemik des Kelsos wider das Christentum*, Berlin, 1955.

ARMSTRONG, A. H., 'The Background of the Doctrine "That the Intelligibles are not outside the Intellect" ', *EH* 5 (1960), 393–413.

—— (ed.), *The Cambridge History of Later Greek and Early Medieval Philosophy*, Cambridge, 1967 (= *LGP*).

ARNIM, H. VON, *Stoicorum Veterum Fragmenta*, 4 vols., Stuttgart, 1903–24, repr. 1964–8.

BICKEL, E., 'Seneca's Briefe 58 und 65', *Rheinisches Museum* 103 (1960), 1–20.

BRÉHIER, E., *Les Idées philosophiques et religieuses de Philon d'Alexandrie*, Paris, 1925.

BURKERT, W., *Weisheit und Wissenschaft*, Nuremberg, 1962.

DE LACY, P., 'The Stoic Categories as Methodological Principles', *Trans. and Proc. Am. Philol. Assoc.* 76 (1945), 246–63.

DES PLACES, E., *Numénius* (ed. Budé), Paris, 1973.

DE VOGEL, C. J., 'Problems concerning later Platonism', *Mnemosyne*, 4th series, 2 (1949), 197–216, 299–318; repr. with revisions in

—— *Philosophia* I, *Studies in Greek Philosophy*, Assen, 1970.

DIELS, H., *Doxographi Graeci*, Berlin, 1879, 1965[4].

DILLON, J. M., *Middle Platonism* (forthcoming).

DODDS, E. R., 'The Parmenides of Plato and the Origin of the neo-Platonic One', *CQ* 22 (1928), 129–42.

—— *Proclus, The Elements of Theology*, Oxford, 1933.

—— *The Greeks and the Irrational*, Berkeley, Cal., 1951.

—— 'Numenius and Ammonius', *EH* 5 (1960), 3–32.

—— *Pagan and Christian in an Age of Anxiety*, Cambridge, 1965.

DÖRRIE, H., 'Der Platoniker Eudorus von Alexandreia', *Hermes* 79 (1944), 25–35.

—— 'Zum Ursprung der neuplatonischen Hypostasenlehre', *Hermes* 82 (1954), 331–42.

—— 'Hypostasis, Wort- und Bedeutungsgeschichte', *NAG* 1955 (ph.-h. kl.), 55–93.

—— 'Die Frage nach dem Transzendenten im Mittelplatonismus', *EH* 5 (1960), 191–242.

DÖRRIE, H., 'Emanation. Ein unphilosophisches Wort im spätantiken Denken', in K. Flasch (ed.), *Parusia, Festschr. J. Hirschberger*, Frankfurt am Main, 1965, 119–41.

—— 'Die platonische Theologie des Kelsos', *NAG* 1967 (ph.-h. kl.), 23–55.

—— 'Der Platonismus der frühen Kaiserzeit', in H. Temporini and W. Haase (eds.), *Aufstieg und Niedergang der Römischen Welt, Teil* ii (*Principat*) (forthcoming).

EH = Entretiens sur l'antiquité classique, Fondation Hardt, Vandœuvres–Genève, esp.:

III (publ. 1958), *Recherches sur la tradition platonicienne*.

V (publ. 1960), *Les Sources de Plotin*.

XII (publ. 1966), *Porphyre*.

FESTUGIÈRE, A.-J., *L'Idéal religieux des grecs et l'Évangile*, Paris, 1932.

—— *RHT = La Révélation d'Hermes Trismégiste*:

1 *L'Astrologie et les sciences occultes*, Paris, 1944.

2 *Le Dieu cosmique*, Paris, 1949.

3 *Les Doctrines de l'âme*, Paris, 1953.

4 *Le Dieu inconnu et la gnose*, Paris, 1954.

GIGON, O., 'Die Erneuerung der Philosophie in der Zeit Ciceros', *EH* 3 (1958), 25–59.

GOLDSCHMIDT, V., *Le Système stoïcien et l'idée de temps*, Paris, 1953.

GOULD, J. B., *The Philosophy of Chrysippus*, Leiden, 1970.

HADOT, P., 'Être, vie, pensée chez Plotin et avant Plotin', *EH* 5, 107–41.

HARRIS, C. R. S., *The Heart and Vascular System in Ancient Greek Medicine from Alcmaeon to Galen*, Oxford, 1973.

HUBER, G., *Das Sein und das Absolute*, Basel, 1955.

KRÄMER, H. J., *Der Ursprung der Geistmetaphysik. Untersuchungen zur Geschichte des Platonismus zwischen Platon und Plotin*, Amsterdam, 1964, 1967².

—— *Platonismus und hellenistische Philosophie*, Berlin, 1971.

LAFFRANQUE, M., *Posidonius d'Apamée: Essai de mise au point*, Paris, 1964.

LANGERBECK, H., 'The Philosophy of Ammonius Saccas', *JHS* 77 (1957), 67–74.

LAPIDGE, M., 'A Problem in Stoic Cosmology', *Phronesis* 18 (1973), 240–78.

LEEMANS, E. A., *Studie over den Wijsgeer Numenius van Apamea met Uitgave der Fragmenten*, Brussels, 1937.

LONG, A. A. (ed.), *Problems in Stoicism*, London, 1971.

LUCK, G., *Der Akademiker Antiochus*, Bern and Stuttgart, 1953.

LÜDER, A., *Die philosophische Persönlichkeit des Antiochus von Askalon*, Diss. Göttingen, 1940.

MEIJERING, E. P., 'Zehn Jahre Forschung zum Thema Platonismus und Kirchenväter', *Theologische Rundschau*, N.F. 36 (1971), 303–20.

MERKI, H., 'ΟΜΟΙΩΣΙΣ ΘΕΩΙ. *Von der platonischen Angleich an Gott zur Gottähnlichkeit bei Gregor von Nyssa*, Freiburg in der Schweiz, 1952.

MERLAN, P., *From Platonism to Neoplatonism*, The Hague, 1953, 1960².

—— 'Greek Philosophy from Plato to Plotinus', in Armstrong, 1967, 11–132.

MORAUX, P., *D'Aristote à Bessarion*, Quebec, 1970.

—— *Der Aristotelismus bei den Griechen von Andronikos bis Alexander von Aphrodisias* (*Peripatoi*, 5), Berlin, 1973.

MORRISON, J. S., review of Burkert, *Gnomon* 37 (1965), 344–54.

NADEAU, R., 'Classical Systems of Stases in Greek: Hermagoras to Hermogenes', *Greek, Roman and Byzantine Studies* 2 (1959), 53–71.

NEBEL, G., *Plotins Kategorien der intelligiblen Welt*, Tübingen, 1929.

—— 'Terminologische Untersuchungen zu ΟΥΣΙΑ und ΟΝ bei Plotin', *Hermes* 65 (1930), 422–45.

NOCK, A. D., 'Posidonius', *Journal of Roman Studies* 49 (1959), 1–15.

—— 'The Exegesis of Timaeus 28 c', *VC* 16 (1962), 79–86.

NORDEN, E., *Agnostos Theos*, Leipzig, 1913, 1956⁴.

POHLENZ, M., 'Philo von Alexandreia', *NAG* 1942 (ph.-h. k.), 409–87.

—— *Die Stoa*, Göttingen, 1948–9, 1964³.

PRÄCHTER, K., 'Nikostratos der Platoniker', *Hermes* 57 (1922), 481–517.

—— See also section 1, s.v. Ueberweg.

PRANTL, C., *Geschichte der Logik im Abendlande*, i, Leipzig, 1927.

PUECH, H. C., 'Numénius d'Apamée et les théologies orientales au second siècle', *Annuaire de l'Institut de Philologie et d'Histoire Orientales* 2 (1934), 745–78.

REESOR, M., 'The Stoic Concept of Quality', *American Journal of Philology* 75 (1954), 40–58.

—— 'The Stoic Categories', ibid. 78 (1957), 63–82.

REINHARDT, K., *Poseidonios*, Munich, 1921.

—— *Kosmos und Sympathie*, Munich, 1926.

—— 'Poseidonios', in *Paulys Real-Encyclopädie der classischen Altertumswissenschaft*, 22. 1 (1953), 558–826.

RICH, A. N. M., 'The Platonic Ideas as Thoughts of God', *Mnemosyne*, 4th series, 7 (1954), 123–33.

RIST, J. M., *Eros and Psyche*, Toronto, 1964.

—— *Stoic Philosophy*, Cambridge, 1969.

SAMBURSKY, S., *Physics of the Stoics*, London, 1959.

—— *The Physical World of Late Antiquity*, London, 1962.

SCHMEKEL, A., *Die Philosophie der mittleren Stoa in ihrem geschichtlichen Zusammenhangen dargestellt*, Berlin, 1892.

SOLMSEN, F., 'Greek Philosophy and the Discovery of the Nerves', *Mus. Helv.* 18 (1961), 150–67, 169–97.

SPANNEUT, M., *Le Stoïcisme des Péres de l'Église de Clément de Rome à Clément d'Alexandrie*, Paris, 1957.

SZLEZÁK, T. A., *Pseudo-Archytas über die Kategorien*, Berlin, 1972.

THEILER, W., *Die Vorbereitung des Neuplatonismus*, Berlin, 1930, repr. 1964.

—— 'Gott und Seele in kaiserzeitlichem Denken', *EH* 3 (1958), 66–90.

—— 'Einheit und unbegrenzte Zweiheit von Plato bis Plotin', in *Isonomia*, ed. J. Mau and E. G. Schmidt, Berlin, 1964, repr. in W. T., *Untersuchungen zur antiken Literatur*, Berlin, 1970, 460–83.

—— 'Philo von Alexandreia und der Beginn des kaiserzeitlichen Platonismus', in K. Flasch (ed.), *Parusia, Festschr. J. Hirschberger*, 199–218; repr. in *Untersuchungen* (above), 484–501.

—— *Forschungen zum Neuplatonismus*, Berlin, 1966.

THESLEFF, H., *An Introduction to the Pythagorean Writings of the Hellenistic Period*, Åbo, 1961.

Tull, A. C., 'The Theology of Middle Platonism', New York, 1968 (typescript dissertation).

van Winden, J. C. M., *Calcidius on Matter, His Doctrine and Sources*, Leiden, 1959.

Verbeke, G., *L'Évolution de la doctrine du pneuma du stoïcisme à St. Augustin*, Louvain, 1945.

Wallis, R. T., *Neoplatonism*, London, 1972.

Walzer, R., *Galen on Jews and Christians*, Oxford, 1949.

—— *Galeni Compendium Timaei Platonis* (*Plato Arabus*, 1), London, 1951.

Waszink, J. H., *Tertullianus, De Anima*, Amsterdam, 1947.

—— 'Tertullian's Treatise adversus Hermogenem', *VC* 9 (1955), 129–47.

—— 'Der Platonismus und die altchristliche Gedankenwelt', *EH* 3 (1958), 137–79.

—— 'Bemerkungen zum Einfluss des Platonismus im frühen Christentum', *VC* 19 (1965), 129–62.

—— [Calcidius]: *Timaeus a Calcidio Translatus* (*Plato Latinus* 4), London and Leiden, 1972.

Whittaker, J., '*Ἐπέκεινα νοῦ καὶ οὐσίας*', *VC* 23 (1969), 91–104.

—— 'Ammonius and the Delphic E', *CQ*, n.s. 19 (1969), 185–92.

—— 'Neopythagoreanism and Negative Theology', *Symbolae Osloenses* 44 (1969), 109–25.

—— 'Neopythagoreanism and the Transcendent Absolute', *Symbolae Osloenses* 48 (1973), 77–86.

Wippern, J. (ed.), *Das Problem der ungeschriebenen Lehre Platons* (*Wege der Forschung*, 186), Darmstadt, 1972.

Witt, R. E., *Albinus and the History of Middle Platonism*, Cambridge, 1937, repr. Amsterdam, 1971.

Wolfson, H. A., *The Philosophy of the Church Fathers*, Cambridge, Mass., 1956.

Christian Theology

*Altaner, B., *Patrologie*, Freiburg im Breisgau, 1938, 7th edn. by A. Stuiber, 1966.

Andresen, C., 'Justin und der mittlere Platonismus', *ZNW* 44 (1952–3), 157–95.

—— *Logos und Nomos: Die Polemik des Kelsos wider das Christentum*, Berlin, 1955.

—— 'Zur Entstehung und Geschichte des trinitarischen Personbegriffes', *ZNW* 52 (1961), 1–39.

Bardy, G., *Recherches sur St. Lucien d'Antioch et son école*, Paris, 1936.

Baynes, N. H., *Constantine the Great and the Christian Church*, London, 1931, repr. with new preface, 1972.

Bethune-Baker, J. F., *The Meaning of Homoousios in the 'Constantinopolitan' Creed* (*Texts and Studies*, 7. 1), Cambridge, 1901.

Bianchi, U., *Le origini dello gnosticismo* (*Suppl. to Numen*, 12), Leiden, 1967.

Bigg, C., *The Christian Platonists of Alexandria*, Oxford, 1886, 1913².

BRAUN, R., *Deus Christianorum, Recherches sur le vocabulaire doctrinal de Tertullien*, Paris, 1962.

CADIOU, R., 'Dictionnaires antiques dans l'œuvre d'Origène', *REG* 45 (1932), 271–85.

—— *La Jeunesse d'Origène*, Paris, 1935.

—— *Origen, his Life at Alexandria*, E.T. by J. A. Southwell, St. Louis, 1944.

CHADWICK, H., 'Origen, Celsus and the Stoa', *JTS* 48 (1947), 34–49.

—— *Origen: Contra Celsum*, Cambridge, 1953, 1965².

—— *Early Christian Thought and the Classical Tradition*, Oxford, 1966.

CROSS, F. L., *The Study of St. Athanasius*, Oxford, 1945.

—— The Early Christian Fathers, London, 1960.

DANIÉLOU, J., *Théologie du judéo-christianisme*, Tournai, 1958.

—— *The Theology of Jewish Christianity* (E.T. by J. A. Baker), London, 1964.

—— *Message évangélique et culture hellénistique*, Tournai, 1961.

—— *Gospel Message and Hellenistic Culture* (E.T. by J. A. Baker), London, 1973.

DODD, C. H., *The Bible and the Greeks*, London, 1935.

—— *The Interpretation of the Fourth Gospel*, Cambridge, 1953.

DURRANT, M., *Theology and Intelligibility*, London, 1973.

ELZE, M., *Tatian und seine Theologie*, Göttingen, 1960.

EVANS, E., *Tertullian's Treatise against Praxeas*, London, 1948.

FARRER, A. M., *Finite and Infinite*, Westminster, 1943, 1959².

—— *Faith and Speculation*, London, 1967.

FESTUGIÈRE, A.-J., *L'Idéal religieux des grecs et l'Évangile*, Paris, 1932.

—— (and see previous section).

GEFFKEN, J., *Zwei griechische Apologeten*, Leipzig, 1907.

GRANT, R. M., 'Early Christianity and pre-Socratic Philosophy', *Harry Austryn Wolfson Jubilee Volume*, Jerusalem, 1965, i. 357–84.

GRILLMEIER, A., *Christ in Christian Tradition*, London, 1965, 1975².

GRUBER, G., *ZΩH, Wesen, Stufen und Mitteilung des wahren Lebens bei Origenes*, Munich, 1962.

GUMMERUS, J., *Die homöusianische Partei bis zum Tode des Konstantius*, Leipzig, 1900.

GWATKIN, H. M., *Studies of Arianism*, Cambridge, 1882, 1900².

HANSON, R. P. C., 'Did Origen apply the word Homoousios to the Son?', *Epektasis* (*Mélanges Daniélou*), 293–303.

HARNACK, A. VON, *Lehrbuch der Dogmengeschichte*, 3 vols., Freiburg, 1886–9.

—— *History of Dogma* (E.T.), 7 vols., London, 1894–9.

HATCH, E., *The Influence of Greek Ideas and Usages upon the Christian Church*, London, 1890.

HAURET, C., *Comment le 'Defenseur de Nicée' a-t-il compris le dogme de Nicée?*, Rome, 1936.

HYLDAHL, N., *Philosophie und Christentum*, Copenhagen, 1966.

IVANKA, E. VON, *Plato Christianus*, Einsiedeln, 1964.

JAEGER, W., *Early Christianity and Greek Paideia*, London, 1962.

KANNENGIESSER, C., 'Où et quand Arius composa-t-il la Thalia?', *Kyriakon* (*Festschr. J. Quasten*), 1. 346–51.

—— (ed.), *Politique et théologie chez Athanase d'Alexandrie*, Paris, 1974.

KELLY, J. N. D., *Early Christian Creeds*, London, 1950, 1972³.
—— *Early Christian Doctrines*, London, 1958, 1968⁴.
KETTLER, F. H., *Der ursprungliche Sinn der Dogmatik des Origenes (Beih. ZNW 31)*, Berlin, 1966.
KOCH, H., *Pronoia und Paideusis*, Berlin, 1932.
KRAFT, H., 'ΟΜΟΟΥΣΙΟΣ', *ZKG* 66 (1954), 1–24.
KRETSCHMAR, G., *Studien zur frühchristlicher Trinitätstheologie*, Tübingen, 1956.
LEBON, J., 'Le Sort du "consubstantiel" nicéen', *Revue d'histoire ecclésiastique* 47 (1952), 485–529; 48 (1953), 632–82.
LIETZMANN, H., *Geschichte der alten Kirche*, Berlin and Leipzig, 1936.
—— *A History of the Early Church* (E.T. by B. L. Woolf), London:
    1, *The Beginnings of the Christian Church*, 1937, revised, 1949.
    2, *The Founding of the Church Universal*, 1938, revised, 1950.
    3, *From Constantine to Julian*, 1950, revised, 1953.
    4, *The Era of the Church Fathers*, 1951, revised, 1953.
LILLA, S. R. C., *Clement of Alexandria, a Study in Christian Platonism and Gnosticism*, Oxford, 1971.
LOOFS, F., 'Das Nicänum', in O. Scheel (ed.), *Festgabe für K. Müller*, Tübingen, 1922, pp. 62–82.
MACQUARRIE, J., *Principles of Christian Theology*, London, 1966.
MEIJERING, E. P., *Orthodoxy and Platonism in Athanasius, Synthesis or Antithesis?*, Leiden, 1968.
—— *God Being History*, Amsterdam, 1975.
MERKI, H., 'ΟΜΟΙΩΣΙΣ ΘΕΩΙ. *Von der platonischen Angleich an Gott zur Gottähnlichkeit bei Gregor von Nyssa*, Freiburg in der Schweiz, 1952.
MESLIN, M., review of *Marius Victorinus . . . edd. P. Henry et P. Hadot (Sources chrétiennes 68–9)*, *RHR* 164 (1963), 96–100.
MOINGT, J., *Théologie trinitaire de Tertullien*, Paris, 1966.
NAUTIN, P., 'Candidus l'arien', *L'Homme devant Dieu (Mélanges Lubac 3)*, Lyons, 1963, 309–20.
OPITZ, H. G., 'Die Zeitfolge des arianischen Streites . . . bis 328', *ZNW* 33 (1934), 131–59.
—— (ed.), *Athanasius Werke*, Berlin and Leipzig, 1934–, esp.,
—— III. 1, *Urkunden zur Geschichte des arianischen Streites* (= *Urk.*).
ORBE, A., *Hacia la primera teología de la Procesión del Verbo (Estudios Valentinianos* I. 2), Rome, 1958.
ORTIZ DE URBINA, I., *El Símbolo Niceno*, Madrid, 1947.
—— *Nicée et Constantinople*, Paris, 1963.
OSBORN, E. F., *The Philosophy of Clement of Alexandria*, Cambridge, 1957.
—— *Justin Martyr (Beiträge zur historischen Theologie 47)*, Tübingen, 1973.
PANNENBERG, W., 'Die Aufnahme des philosophischen Gottesbegriffes als dogmatisches Problem der frühchristlichen Theologie', *ZKG* 70 (1959), 1–45; reprinted as,
—— *Grundfragen systematischer Theologie* (Göttingen, 1967), 296–346.
—— *Basic Questions in Theology* (E.T. by G. H. Kehm, London, 1971), vol. 2, 119–83.

PRESTIGE, G. L., *God in Patristic Thought*, London, 1936, 1952² (= *GPT*).

QUASTEN, J., *Patrology*, 3 vols., Utrecht and Westminster, Maryland; 1950, 1953, 1960.

RICKEN, F., 'Nikaia als Krisis des altchristlichen Platonismus', *Theologie und Philosophie* 44 (1969), 321–41.

RITTER, A. M., *Das Konzil von Konstantinopel und sein Symbol*, Göttingen, 1965.

ROBERTSON, A., *Athanasius: Select Works and Letters*, Library of Nicene and Post-Nicene Fathers, Vol. 5, London, 1891.

SAGNARD, F. M. M., *La Gnose valentinienne et le témoignage de Saint Irénée*, Paris, 1947.

—— (ed.), *Extraits de Théodote* (*Sources Chrétiennes* 23), Paris, 1948.

SCHNEEMELCHER, W., 'Zur Chronologie des arianischen Streites', *TLZ* 79 (1954), 393–9.

SCHWARTZ, E., *Zur Geschichte des Athanasius* (*Gesammelte Schriften* 3), Berlin 1959.

—— *Kaiser Constantin und die christliche Kirche*, Berlin, 1913.

SIMONETTI, M., 'Nota sull'ariano Candido', *Orpheus* 10 (Catania, 1963), 151–7.

—— *Studi sull'arianesimo*, Rome, 1965.

—— *La letteratura cristiana antica greca e latina*, Florence and Milan, 1969.

—— 'Le origini dell' arianesimo', *Rivista di storia e letteratura religiosa* 7 (1971), 317–30.

—— *La crisi ariana nel iv secolo*, Rome, 1975.

SPANNEUT, M., *Le Stoïcisme des Pères de l'Église de Clément de Rome à Clément d'Alexandrie*, Paris, 1957.

STEAD, G. C., 'The Significance of the *Homoousios*', *Studia Patristica* 3 (*Texte und Untersuchungen* 78), Berlin, 1961, 397–412.

—— 'Divine Substance in Tertullian', *JTS*, n.s. 14 (1963), 46–66.

—— 'The Platonism of Arius', ibid. 15 (1964), 16–31.

—— 'The Valentinian Myth of Sophia', ibid. 20 (1969), 75–104.

—— ' "Eusebius" and the Council of Nicaea', ibid. 24 (1973), 85–100.

—— ' "Homoousios" dans la pensée de Saint Athanase', in C. Kannengiesser (ed.), *Politique et théologie chez Athanase d'Alexandrie*, Paris, 1974, 231–53.

—— 'The Concept of Divine Substance', *VC* 29 (1975), 1–14.

—— 'Ontology and Terminology in Gregory of Nyssa', in H. Dörrie *et al.* (eds.), *Gregor von Nyssa und die Philosophie*, Leiden, 1976.

—— 'Rhetorical Method in Athanasius', *VC* 30 (1976), 121–37.

*STEVENSON, J., (ed.) *A New Eusebius* (*Documents Illustrative of the History of the Church to A.D. 337*), London, 1957.

*—— *Creeds, Councils and Controversies* (*Documents Illustrative of the History of the Church, A.D. 337–461*), London, 1966.

STRONG, T. B., 'The History of the Theological Term Substance', *JTS* 2 (1900–1), 224–35; 3 (1901–2), 22–40; 4 (1902–3), 28–45.

TELFER, W., 'When did the Arian controversy begin?', *JTS* 47 (1946), 129–42.

TILLICH, P., *Systematic Theology*, 3 vols., London, 1953, 1957, 1964.

WASZINK, J. H., *Tertullianus, De Anima*, Amsterdam, 1947 (and see previous section).

WEBB, C. C. J., *God and Personality*, London, 1918.

WOLFSON, H. A., *The Philosophy of the Church Fathers*, Cambridge, Mass., 1956.

ZAHN, T., *Marcellus von Ancyra*, Gotha, 1867.

ZIEGENAUS, A., *Die trinitarische Ausprägung der göttlichen Seinsfülle nach Marius Victorinus*, Bamberg, 1972.

INDEX OF BIBLICAL REFERENCES

INDEX OF ANCIENT AUTHORS

INDEX OF MODERN AUTHORS

The sign '&' indicates a reference both to text and footnote: e.g. '223 & n. 2'

INDEX OF SUBJECTS